Moses's Principia

221 np
B53 a.t.
y

MOSES's
PRINCIPIA.

PART II.

Of the Circulation of the Heavens.

Of the Cause of the Motion and Course of the Earth, Moon, &c.

Of the Religion, Philosophy, and Emblems of the Heathens before *Moses* writ,

And of the *Jews* after.

In Confirmation of the Natural History of the Bible.

With NOTES.

VOL II.

By *J. H.*

The THIRD EDITION.

LONDON:

Printed for J. HODGES, at the *Looking-Glass* over-against *St. Magnus's Church, London-Bridge.*

M.DCC.XLVIII.

Abbreviat. Explicat.

A.   *Joh. Avenarii, Lib. Rad. seu Lex. Ebraic.* Witteberg. 1589.

B. C.   *Joh. Buxtorfii, Lex. Chald. Talm. & Rab.* Basil. 1639.

C.   *Edm. Castelli, Lex. Heptaglotton,* Lond. 1669.

Coc.   *Joh. Coccei, Lex. & Com. Hebr. & Chald.* Francof. 1589.

M.   *F. Marii de Calasio Concord. S. B. Hebr. & Lat. cum conven. al. Ling.* Rom. 1621.

R.   *Gul. Robertson Concordantiale, Lex. Hebr.* Lond. 1680.

S.   *Valent. Schindleri, Lex. Pentaglot.* Hanov. 1612.

T.   *Thomassini Gloss. Hebraic.* Paris, 1597.

INTRODUCTION.

I Have in the firſt Part traced *Moſes* through his Deſcription of the Creation, of the firſt Motion, the Formation of Light, and their Conſequences, an Expanſion and its Effects in forming the firſt Shell, or Shell of the firſt Earth, carrying down the Waters, forming the Surface, &c. and through the Diſſolution of that Earth, and a Repetition of thoſe Acts, or Reformation at the Flood; and by indiſputable Regiſters, I have convicted ſeveral Kidnappers, and reſtor'd the Children to their proper Fathers: Tho' I have walked with the Inſpir'd Light in my Hand, yet we are to remember, that ſo far it was chiefly intended to ſhew the manner of Forms which exiſt not now, and of Actions which are ceas'd, or tranſacted otherwiſe; and ſo are the Objects of our Conception or Understanding by Faith and not by Sense; and those Parts which admit of Observations and Experiments, are some slightly touch'd, because the manner of the Reformation, or making of those Forms which exist, and are brought to the Test of Sense by a large Appendix, which has been shew'd and is ready to prove its Truth by vast Numbers of Observations, cannot take effect, till that Part of the Revelation, which shews the Formation and Manner of the Operation of the settled Agent which formed them; and will likewise come under the Cognizance of Sense and Reason, be explain'd. This might have appeared in publick sooner, had not the Adversaries suggested, that *Moses* had his Philosophy from the *Egyptians*; and so made it necessary for me, first, to shew that his chief Business was to determine Natural Philosophy, which I hope they will acquiesce in; and lest that should not satisfy some who have given Occasion to enter into such Enquiries, I shall in their proper Places give them some Evidence out of their own Scriptures: But though it plainly appears, that this Part of the *Revelation* was writ to cure the Madness of the Naturalists and Star-gazers; yet still they

from

from time to time have brought in many ſtrange Whims, and at laſt for them rejected this Scripture; ſo I muſt reject all their Dreams, and take the Scripture as at firſt. As there is no real material Cauſe offer'd to begin or carry on any Motion or Action in any Article, of any Natural Philoſophy now exiſting, that I have ſo much as heard of; nor any thing but Names, and unintelligible, and incomprehenſible Words, intended to repreſent Ideas of incommunicable Powers, which amount to no more than: " So ſome Things come together by Sympathy, I call Sympathy a mutual Conſent or Attraction of Things without any apparent Cauſe; as Antipathy a Sluggiſhneſs, or *Vis Inertiæ*. Theſe Properties run through Animals, Plants, Stones, &c. (a)".—As St. *Paul* ſaid to the *Athenians*, The God that they ignorantly worſhip'd, he ſhew'd unto them; ſo I may ſay of *Moſes*, The Cauſes of the Operations which ye ignorantly attribute to imaginary Names or Powers, them ſheweth he unto you: Such a Philoſophy as every reaſonable Man has either underſtood or ſearched for. " Such a Motion as this is the proper Subject of

(a) Cardani de Subtilitate, Lib. 18. p. 638.

iv INTRODUCTION.

Enquiry, which without a new Generation shall contain in itself the Cause of its own Continuance (*b*)." As I am for reviving this Material Philosophy in Motion, &c. and am by and by to bring in the Addition of Sense so far as that can go, and of comparing Revelation with the things seen, and of drawing Deductions from either or both; and as none of the present Philosophers were so much as the Inventors of the Words, they use for their imaginary Powers; and as they may still have the Lone or Liberty of using the old Tables to estimate the comparative Velocity of each Globe, &c. to find out an Eclipse, or &c. or of telling us they improve them; I can have no great Difference with any of them who are in Being at present; nor can I fall under the Displeasure of the Divines, since those modern Authors who have meddled most, and as some tell me most learnedly with a few general Names of the Gods of the ancient Heathens and their Worship, and the Worship of God under the *Mosaick* Law, have made the Men stupid, their Objects first living, and then dead Kings, those dead Kings Devils, whether real or

---

(*b*) Cardani de Subtilitate, Lib. 17. p. 625.

imaginary

INTRODUCTION. v

imaginary they tell us not, and the Stars named after them; all their Images, Spheres and Reprefentations for magical Ufes or jugling Tricks: The Beafts facred, becaufe thefe Devils, as they thought, appear'd in their Shapes; and have alfo made *Mofes* pick up all thefe Reprefentations of Devils and magical Practices, to form a Place of Worfhip, and introduce almoft all their Practices for a Form of Worfhip to the Being we take for our God: I cannot put Things in a worfe Light, and fhall, I hope, put them all in a natural and more honourable State, fhew the ancient Heathens to have been great Philofophers, their Service to the Powers which formed, fupported and fubfifted them without Revelation, natural, that properly paid to God as Author of thofe Powers, and that thefe Men and their Evidence, the latter Heathens were Fools, and Worfhipers of Devils or nothing; nor can I have any Difputes with them with refpect to the prefent Tranflations, becaufe in the Manner of doing it, I only attempt to explain a few Words, which I take to be expreffive of the natural Powers, and which they have not thought fit to tranflate, and the Senfe of a few Phrafes, which as they fay were fpoken, *ad captum humanum,*

vi INTRODUCTION.

humanum, and so not capable of being brought to the Test of Truth by Observations and ocular Demonstrations, which I also take to be spoken philosophically, with which in either Sense they pretend not to have any Business. I shall pass over the History of the Formation of Vegetables in this; because at last they have for the present yielded their spontaneous Productions, and agree that each has its Seed in its self; and because nothing can be said clearly about it, till the Operations mention'd be further explain'd, and because such Weeds as they have planted, can never be destroy'd till their Roots be pluck'd up; I mean till they be dispossessed of their imaginary Cause of the Motion of the Globes, and because no useful Herb will thrive among Weeds.

As my Intent is no other but to make the Scripture intelligible, which has no Difficulties in these Points, but what has been made by Philosophers, who have always adapted the Meaning of some of the Words about the Heavens, and from them the Translators, to the Notions and Philosophies of the Times and Places: For 'tis but lately that they were so silly as to pretend to give any Accounts about the Formation of the Earth; and it has been often predicted,

predicted, that medling with it would be their Ruin, except where the Tranflators, by unneceffary Jealoufy, have made God's Agents himfelf, their Actions his perfonal Actions, and the Defcriptions of their Subftances the Defcription of his Effence: In order to fet thefe right, I muft obferve what Things were made at the Beginning by God, what Names he gave them, what has been made by Imaginers fince, and what Names they have given thofe imaginary Things or Actions; what Errors are inferted into the Tranflations, &c. and take the Liberty not only to throw off all the Opinions of the Philofophers, but their very Names of material Things or Actions, in the Tranflations or Paraphrafes in all Languages; and begin with them alfo, as if the Scripture were newly writ, or at leaft as the *Jews* left it; and take the Names and Relations as they ftand in Scripture; and where any Difpute arifes between the Original and the Tranflation, whether the Thing, Action, or &c. be the fame as it is tranflated; I fhall be determin'd by the Comparifon, Defcription, Situation, Action, or Ufe of the Thing or Word in other Places of the Scriptures, without any other Allowance than to vary the Senfe of a Word; for Example, of

Action according to the Effect it will have upon the Thing it is joined with, or where such Action has Effects in Succession, and the Interpreters have not put the first or that which is proper; I mean only of the Word in each Citation, upon which the Stress turns; for to correct each Word would take up too much Room, and make Confusion; and as I am sufficiently convinced that there was no other Difference between the Language of the *Chaldeans* and that of the *Jews*, who staid longer with them than those of other Countries, tho' there is little preserv'd of that, or any other Language, but what was writ long after the Books of *Moses*, nor by the Natives of *Chaldea*, but by the *Jews*, long after the Captivity; nor any Difference between either of theirs, and those of other Countries, than what had been produced by Time, their different Notions in Philosophy, and so in Worship, in their Employments or Manner of Living; so where a Word occurs not in Cases enow to explain it sufficiently, we must get what Helps we can from the Languages nearest in Place or Time: If a Word happens to be but once or twice us'd in the Bible, and no sufficient Explanation, and we find the same Word

or

INTRODUCTION.

or Branches of that Root in *Chaldee* or any other Language, they have concluded it of that Language, tho' perhaps 'tis only from Occasion of using the Word, from the Accident of Books being preserv'd, of their coming to the Hands of those who have writ *Lexicons, &c.* Where any Word in Scripture is taken from something in Use in the Place where the Scene of Action treated of was, or in some other Nation, or Allusion made to Things which were the fittest to compare with, or illustrate by, which were not in Use among the *Jews*, and for which perhaps they had no expressive Words; or if God was pleas'd to condescend so far as to use Words which other Nations us'd for the celestial Agents which they worship'd as Gods, and the *Jews* understood: In order to set them right, as those Words in some Cases may not, and in some cannot, each have a Root or Affinity to other Words in their Language, tho' there be some Difference in spelling and forming the Words of the first Languages in the Countries whither the People were dispers'd, and by degrees Names, different from those us'd for Things before the Dispersion were given, and Names for Things which had no Existence before they parted, nor among the
Jews.

Jews. Though at firſt the Law prohibited the *Jews* from ſo much as naming the Objects of the Worſhip of the Heathens by their Names; and tho' lower down we find a Decree among the *Jews* to excommunicate ſuch as ſhould ſtudy the Philoſophy of the *Gentiles*; and tho' no doubt the *Gentiles* had Laws to prohibit the Study of the *Jewiſh* Books; and tho' the Heathen had us'd Characters which had Reference to the Parts of their Worſhip, and ſo could not uſe the Characters of the *Jews*, but made their own Characters, Letters each in their own Language, which beſides their Uſe as Letters or Repreſentatives of Sounds retain'd their myſtick Meanings, and were alſo Repreſentatives of the Things or Actions they had ſignified in the Attributes of their Gods, or the Rites of their Religion: There may be ſome good Reaſons to allow Explanations, from what we can know of ſuch Words in Books of thoſe Languages writ afterwards.

As we have no other Books preſerv'd which were writ by thoſe who perfectly underſtood the Language of the firſt Books of the Bible; each of the Authors of the Paraphraſes, or Tranſlations preſerved, ſave what they had by Tradition, had but the

ſame

INTRODUCTION. xi

same Rules as we have, that is, to compare the several Passages where each Word was us'd in the Sacred Books; and those who followed successively after, to compare them also with the Thoughts of the Authors who, as aforesaid, in the Declension of that Language, had paraphrased upon these Books, or of their Cotemporaries in neighbouring Languages, or of those who had used the same Words in human Writings. If it happen'd that the first Paraphraser or Translator by Mistake or any Opinion of his own, or otherwise, happen'd to fix a wrong Translation upon any Word, or a wrong Sense upon any Sentence, or, but one, where the Word has several coherent Senses, which the Word or Sentence could tolerably bear; they or the next would be inclin'd to apply the same Signification, as near as possible, where the same Word or Words occurr'd; and I am afraid there might be other Reasons than Ignorance, or Mistake, for Defects, particularly concerning the Words I am endeavouring to set right: If the *Jews* who return'd from the *Chaldean* Captivity, or those of their Posterity who writ the *Targums, &c.* understood the Meaning of the Jewish Worship, that it was directed to keep them out of the
Crimes

xii *INTRODUCTION.*

Crimes they suffer'd for; 'tis no wonder that they evaded explaining the Meaning of the Particulars, and the Meaning of the Objects, and Forms in their false Worship, to hide as far as they could the Baseness of those of their Fore-fathers who had offended. 'Tis as improper to consult with any one of that Race, about the natural Powers, which the Heathens and some of their Fathers took for God, about the Idolatry, Forms and Manners of the Worship of that false God, or of the Signification or Intent of their Law which was adapted, or of the Scripture which was most of it writ to cure them of those Crimes; as 'tis to consult with the Persons in any of the Cases stated by the Author of *Ecclesiasticus*, xxxvii. 11. *& seq.* And while they were under the Dominion of the *Chaldean* Governors, or afraid of their Power, if they had been inclin'd to give an Account of their Gods, besides that it was exposing those of their Fathers, who had been guilty, they durst not insert any thing which expresly ridicul'd that false Worship; and if any such Books were writ before or then, no doubt but the *Chaldeans* would do what they could to destroy them; and the Case would be the same, when they were under

INTRODUCTION. xiii

der the *Grecians* and the *Romans*: Nay, if the Bible had been writ, or the LXX. had explain'd it openly with respect to their particular Gods, they without a continu'd Interposition of supernatural Power must have been destroy'd; so to explain them now, we must, together with *Moses*'s Relation, first consider the Names and Attributes which the Natives of *Canaan*, &c. gave to their God, which are recorded in Scripture, left standing, *Hebrew*, or as they pleas'd to point and pronounce them in our Translations; and which the *Lexicons* from the *Jewish Rabbies* have made this, or that, or any thing; and try to explain them by the Usage of those Words in Scripture, and by the Claims which Gods made of those Names and Attributes, first to himself, and secondarily to the Agents, which he claims by Creation and Formation; because it will appear, that a great part of their Religion and their Philosophy was the same; and that though their Religion was false and disapprov'd, their Philosophy was true, and approv'd by God, and so will discover an unknown Treasure; and though it be not the Business of this Part to meddle with those Points of Worship; and though I shall chiefly pursue the Title; yet as they and it are thus coupled together; I shall be forced to enter

ter a little into them, becaufe together, by degrees, they will fhew us, that there had been a Revelation of the Powers and Motions in this Syftem from the Beginning, or before *Mofes*, without writing: That acknowledging, that God created and form'd the Parts of the Heavens into a Machine, fo as of its felf to continue Motion, and each of its Powers; and fo as to move fome Things, produce other Things, &c. and that it acts as fuch without any other, or incommunicable Power, and is ftill fubject to God, inwardly in the Heart, and outwardly by proper Emblems, Actions, or Words, was the firft and natural Service, or Religion, prior, and of a Nature infinitely fuperior to the moral Law: And amongft thofe where the Knowledge was retain'd, and the Revelation loft, or rejected, acknowledging in the Manner aforefaid, that this Machine acted as independent of God, or that it had fome incommunicable Powers in its felf, would be Religion without a God, and in that Senfe Natural Religion; and was the Religion of the ancient Gentiles or Heathens; and that the ceremonial Law or Religion of the *Jews* was to inculcate the firft natural Service, and to oblige them to perform the Acknowledgments

to

INTRODUCTION.

to God, in behalf of his Machine, firſt in the Mind, as appears Job xxxvi. 24. *Remember that thou magnify his Work* [in creating and forming this Machine] *which Men behold.*—Pſ. xxviii. 5. *They regard not the Works of Jehovah, nor the Operation of his Hands.* Ibid. lxxiii. 28. *That I may declare all* [מלאכותיך] *thy Works,* the Word uſed *Gen.* ii. 2. for the Mechanical Powers of the Machine then completed.—And *Jer.* vii. 18. for the Operations of the Heavens—*Pſ.* cxliii. 5. *I remember the Days of old, I meditate on all thy Works, I muſe on the Work of thy Hands.* Iſa. v. 12. *They regard not the Work of Jehovah, neither conſider the Operation of his Hands.* Secondly, outwardly by proper Emblems, Actions, or Words, as (though in ſome Things oppoſite) thoſe without God perform'd them to each Branch of Power in the Machine; and that this Service of the Mind in every Branch, is prior to Chriſtianity, and ſo to be confeſs'd before a Man can be of the firſt natural Religion, or a *Jew*, Deiſt, or Chriſtian; and that the Bible needed no Paraphraſe in the Time of the firſt *Jews*, their Emblems, Services, *&c.* explain'd it: That when they were carried into Captivity and loſt their Emblems, and durſt not perform the Services,

vices, as *Psal.* cxxxvii. 2. *We hang'd our Harps upon the Willows in the midst thereof,* (of the Rivers of *Babylon.*) Ver. 3. *For there they that carried us away captive, requir'd of us a Song,* (Heb. *the Words of a Song*) *and they that wasted us,* (Heb. *laid us on Heaps*) *requir'd of us Mirth, saying, Sing us one of the Songs of Sion.* Ver. 4. *How shall we sing the Lord's Song in a strange Land?* (Heb. *a Land of Strangers.*) They lost the Knowledge of the Service of their Religion, and so in a great Measure of their Philosophy; that the *Jews* after their Return from their Captivity had imperfect Emblems, and perform'd not proper Services; that when Christ came, his Disciples preached to the Heathens, who understood these Powers in general, to leave them and render their Service to the living God. That this will explain the Scriptures; and all the Actions in this Machine, and the Origin, and lead us to the Descents and Names of the Gods of the latter Heathens in other Languages, and of the Creatures and Things which were sacred, or Representatives or Idols to each of them; and of all those which we have call'd the Games of the Heathens; which were both philosophical, and in their Way religious. Hence we shall be

able

able to shew to the Heathens, and the *Turks* by Revelation and Demonstration, that every Power they worship is material and mechanical, and so by its self unalterable; hence all the Positions of Properties in Matter will drop, and their Worshippers with them: And if there remain any thing about the latter Heathens of other Languages which those do not perfectly clear, we must be forc'd to take the Accounts of those who wrote in those Countries, where they had those Objects for their Gods, and such Accounts as they were in no Danger of being punish'd for; and next these, the Accounts of those who had been Heathens, and were converted to the Christian Religion, who were the most able and the most likely to give true Accounts of what it was then; tho' indeed it was varied from what it was at first, and darken'd with additional Fooleries; and lastly, their Figures of their Symbols, Inscriptions, &c. which have been preserved.

In Things relating to Scripture, or Things contain'd in Scripture, the private Opinion of this, or that Man, or Self is nothing, except it be shew'd that there are latent Meanings of the Words, which have always been allow'd, though

INTRODUCTION.

not us'd in the Places, which will make the Defcriptions Senfe and Truth; I bring not in any one's Opinion to confirm the Scripture, nor do I value any one's Opinion which oppofes it; 'tis below me to make any fuch Comparifon: I had made a vaft Collection concerning Things of this Nature from human Writings, and thought I fhould have had great Service from them, but am pleafingly difappointed in finding that the Scripture will explain the antient human Writings, but needs not them to explain it. I mention a few of them who confirm it, to fhew that many antiently, as they call it, either underftood the Scripture, or underftood the Things by Tradition; and a few of the latter, who oppofe it, to fhew that thefe Meanings of the Scripture, by being mention'd, demolifh thofe who have fet up other Schemes; tho' the Signification of a Word in the Tranflation of the Scripture be not to be chang'd for making it Senfe without the Authority of Ufage; yet the true Senfe of the Words in the Tranflation about thefe material Things, when changed by the Authority of Ufage, muft alfo appear, by the Defcriptions agreeing with the Things defcrib'd, and by the Connection of the Hiftory: For befides

INTRODUCTION. xix

sides Verbs of Action already mention'd, the Name of an Agent may have several Significations arising from the several sorts of Actions it performs, or the several Manners of performing them, or where it is ministerial of its several Offices or Operations, upon several sorts of Beings, or several sorts of Matter, or by the Effects or Consequences of its several Actions, or Ministries to its self, to other Beings, or to Matter; so the same Agent, for the Reasons aforesaid, may have a different Name for each or several of those Actions or Offices, and the same Word has different Senses, as 'tis join'd; for Example: A Word of Action, when 'tis join'd with God, with an Angel, with the Soul of Man, with the Body of Man, with a Beast, with the Heavens or Agents in Nature, it must have comparative Significations; when Words are us'd in the Sense of the Heathens about their Religion, tho' what they took for a God, or an Attribute be expressively nam'd; yet the Images, Figures, Beasts, Birds, Trees, Flowers, Stones, or &c. which they made Representatives of it, and the Service or Form of Worship, are each call'd by the same Name, and so one; for Example: A Beast which is made Representative of several Powers has, besides its descriptive Name, several of those representative Names, and several of the chief Attributes are claim'd, and us'd for God, and the Representatives are sometimes call'd by those new Names in the *Mosaick* Law. Nay, the same Word for an Agent from different Mouths, signifies different Things; nay, sometimes directly opposite: As for Example, the proper Word or Name for God in the Mouth of a *Jew*, was God, and in the Mouth of a Heathen was the Heavens: If a very few of the Governours or principal Agents be misnam'd in our Translations, and the principal Actions be not understood, but they attribute that to one thing, which belongs to another; it will not only make Nonsense of each Relation where such Mistake happens, but by misconstruing the Words apply'd to it, those Words, where join'd to other Names, are liable by such Example to be misconstru'd, and so make Nonsense of those other Passages, where those Words are us'd; and by the same Means it will confound the Rules of Grammar; it will make strange Confusion in the whole, or at least in very many Parts; and as every Word always conforms to the Perception every Person has of the Thing, or Action,

if

if his Perception be true, the Idea the Word raises of the Thing or Action is true; if strong, strong; if weak, weak; if false, false; and if there be any such Mistakes which are antient, our Grammars, Lexicons, Concordances, &c. will all be accommodated to such Mistakes, either with Variations in the Words, or with Figures, or different Senses, or different Pointings: And if by such Mistakes the Action of one Agent be attributed to another, that will introduce the Necessity of attributing Impossibilities, such as acting where 'tis not present, contracting and extending the Dimensions of its Parts, and all the Contradictions and Nonsense necessary to support Error or Lies; and what is still worse, none of the Comparisons between those Things, and those they should illustrate, will hold: If there be any Words or Names which have been antiently neglected, and they should now appear to be Words of Consequence; we shall find little Notice taken of them, and little collected from the same, or Words nearly related to them, in that, or other Languages. If the Meaning of the Words in the Descriptions of these natural Things, can be so far understood, that it will suit their Actions, and make their Manner of acting intelligible, and without any other Allowance than in the Sense aforesaid, in respect to what those Words are coupled with, or the Intent of the Speaker, one Sense of each Word will run through the whole, and the Science of Nature and Theology would strengthen each other reciprocally.

There are no Words for uncreated or spiritual Things, their Conditions or Actions, but what are us'd for, and take their Significations from created material Things, their Conditions or Actions, because our Ideas or Conceptions come in by our Senses; so our Capacities and Situation make it necessary, that Revelation of Things, or Actions, we cannot come at, should be convey'd to us by Comparisons, by using Names or Descriptions of Things, which have been revealed, or which we can see, or which are nearer us, or which are better understood. We take our Ideas from material Things, and their Conditions and Actions, and the Scripture takes them from the greatest, first, that is the Root, and so down to the smallest; the greatest bears the Name for the Idea alone; the lesser, which perhaps have not the full Idea that was in the greatest, with Words of Distinction; and even the Divine Writers

are

INTRODUCTION. xxiii

are forc'd to employ those Ideas, to convey Ideas of Spirits, Spiritual Things, and Actions, and one *Hebrew* Word used for a material Thing, was apply'd upwards or downward; and though the Moderns, in each Language, have coin'd several distinct Words, for each one *Hebrew* Word, as one when apply'd to Matter, another when apply'd to the Mind, &c. they have very little regard in the Translations, but often for the sake of the Beauty of a Figure, an Excuse for Nonsense, a Lie, or both, they have apply'd, for Example, Pride to inanimate Things, and Height to the Mind; and though those are small Faults in Things understood, yet in great or abstruse Matters they make strange Work; and those Comparisons are not only made of Things which are or might be better understood, but always of Things which are indisputably true, and have the nearest Resemblance; and by this Method we are not only helped to Ideas of the Things reveal'd, but to Attributes and Descriptions of the material Powers, which are often more strongly represented in such Comparisons, than they could be in simple Descriptions: But as there is nothing we know, that is sufficient, by Comparison,

rison, to raise sufficient Ideas of the Things we are about to treat of; he has also compared them to Things we most admire: God has done (if one may be allowed to use such an Expression) all that we can see possible, to explain these Things and Actions, both by Things below, and Things above. As there is nothing in this World which can raise any perfect Idea of that in another, He who was admitted to a View of that State, could not convey any Idea thereof to others: But as the Agent in that Condition and Action they call the Light, which I suppose to be Atoms of the Heavens, melted out of small Grains successively at the Sun, and press'd outward, is the most powerful and glorious of all the inanimate System, which comes within our Knowledge; the Persons who made no Mistakes, have represented some of the Attributes of God, some of the Glories of a future State by it; and as the Contrivance, Operation, Power and Oeconomy in that, appears more evidently than that in the spiritual Empire, the Words which are used for that, are used for this; and they are treated as if they were the same, because they were directed, performed and supported by the same Attribute call'd Wisdom, and because

cause they are the most noble Comparisons; and as Men had suppos'd, that these Powers rival'd his Authority, shewing how he form'd, and order'd the Matter with those Powers in this Heaven, and that they, as it is express'd, did his Will, or obeyed him, answered the End of his Revelation more than if he could have shewed them, that the Ministers or Angels of that Heaven obey'd him; and from this, when the Scriptures are speaking of the great Actions they perform, 'tis common to mistake them, and also the Writings of the Heathens, and take their Names or Descriptions of the material Powers in this System, which God made his Governours or Deputies, and which the Heathens took for Gods, for God himself, or for his Angels. Though when the Prophets consider them, as set in Opposition to God, they make them Vanity and nothing. As the antient Fathers, when treating of Religions, historically tell you, that the Figures, &c. which the Heathens accounted sacred, and which had most of them been taken into the Temple of God, were Emblems of Mysteries in Philosophy, Representations of Powers in Nature; but when preaching to the Heathens against those Powers,

Powers, as keeping Men from, or set in Opposition to Christ, Devils, and the Emblems, Instruments of Magick, Trumpery, or &c. Indeed there was always among Men of each Religion, some, who gave themselves up to the Devil, and he had great Power among the later Heathens: But the Religion of the antient Heathens had nothing to do with the Devil, except as it was a Sin, nor with Magick, any other than natural Magick, fore-telling the Courses of the Orbs, and pretending to foretell the Events of Things by the Clouds, Stars, &c. Notwithstanding our learnedly wicked Men, as this Dirt serves their Turn, endeavour to put it upon us with the Authority of the Fathers literally; and though there cannot be any Bodies here of Sizes at Distances so situated, or of such Operations, either in Degree, or in all Circumstances; yet the Globes, the Agents, and the Actions are express'd by Words, which are also us'd for Things here, or Things here are compared with them; and there are some smaller Actions, which, by the Assistance of those Powers, in some sort resemble them; so that Things in another State, and Actions to us invisible, are compared to, and explained by Things and
Actions

INTRODUCTION. xxvii

Actions in these Heavens, as Things and Actions in these Heavens are explained by Things on the Earth; Things or Actions at greater Distance, less familiar, or less understood, by those which are nearer, with which we are more familiar, and which, if we apply to, we may understand. And 'tis a Rule not only in divine Writings, and amongst antient human Writings, but still in those of intelligent Men, to compare Things they would illustrate, to Things which not only resemble them in some considerable Points, but to such as certainly exist, and are or may be clearly understood. Every Idea we have of God, and every Name or Word we use for one of those Ideas, are taken comparatively, either positively or negatively from the Things or Actions of the Things he has created; and they cannot otherwise be express'd or comprehended by us. This is not a Diminution of God, but the Measure of our Capacity; the Word for the material Heaven is us'd for the immaterial Heaven; the Word for the corruptible Spirit is us'd for the incorruptible Spirit; the Word for the material Light is us'd for the ineffable Light; the future State is represented by this System as God emitting Light, and that reflecting

flecting from the Angels, the Bodies of the Saints; their Difference as the Difference among the Stars, the Agility of glorified Bodies, to that of Fire, Light, &c. Nay, though the Actions of the Mind of Man be known to himself, yet the Ideas of them cannot be convey'd to the Knowledge of another, but by comparing them with the Actions of these Agents, of or in the Heavens: And as *Isaiah*, to set the *Jews* right in some Things, says, *Chap.* xl. 18. *To whom then will ye liken God?* &c. So I may say of the Celestial Fluids, Powers and Bodies, whereunto shall even the inspired Writers of the Scripture compare them? For though the infinite God be compar'd to these Things without any Likeness, but in the Shew of his Power, except that he has contriv'd them, so as to supply and support themselves with what seems to us, and will be till he vary them, a perpetual Power of Motion and Action, for the Ends he design'd them, without any other Law than that of Mechanism; and as it is made a Minister to support his Creatures, and diffuse Good to them; and being worshipp'd for that, and Attributes given to it, most of them are claim'd by, or ascrib'd to God, and in that Sense made his Attributes; or as

in

in its three Conditions and Offices it raises the strongest Idea we can have of the Trinity: And though the Illustration of the Personality, of the Attributes, of the Actions of God above or below are taken from these, and his Justice and Order from that in this, the Distributions of his Favours from those in these; yet the Operation about a Spark of Fire represents the whole justly, and so in real Likeness we may compare these Things as they are, properly, with lesser Degrees of the same Operation.

In short, the *Hebrew* Language was form'd by God, and was adapted to express material Things by Words, which described the Things by the Condition each of them were in, without Paraphrase or Enlargement, and so conveyed perfect Ideas of the Things by the Words; and those Words in Scripture which described the Condition of each material Thing, and their Actions, are infallibly chosen and employed for the Mind, its Actions, Spiritual Things and their Actions; and thereby from Things which we could understand, convey'd to us the most perfect Ideas we could have of Things and Actions we could not otherwise understand. Tho' in truth where a *Hebrew* Word

Word is apply'd to, or us'd for a Person, or Thing, or &c. the first in Dignity or Consequence which is vested with all the Perfections any inferior Persons or Things, or &c. of the same Sort in any Degree is possess'd of, 'tis as we may say then an original Word; and in how many Senses soever the Word is found in sacred Writ, those Attributes, or &c. will all be found in the Original. These are the Roots and Stems in the *Hebrew* Tongue, and the Branches will ascend or grow from the Thing, not from the Word; so when we find an Attribute apply'd to the Godhead, whether personal or borrow'd, suppose of Power, apply'd to the Author of Power, all Powers are in him, in others only derivatively, and in Branches, and these Branches still in smaller Degrees. צדק or שלם שלה, &c. is an Attribute of Christ, each of them signifies several seemingly different Things, all in Christ; but when one of these Words is apply'd or us'd for one of the Things, which is but a Derivative, that has one, or perhaps more, but not all the Branches in it. When a Word for Power is applied to the Heavens, they have all material Force or Power in them, and all the material Force or Power, in other Things, is

derivative

INTRODUCTION. xxxi

derivative from them; and when the same Word is applied to a material Being or Thing, possess'd of a Degree or Branch of that Power or Force, it expresses only that Degree or Branch. We have retained the Use of Letters to form Sounds, but the Words of the modern Languages, which are either arbitrary, and not adapted to express the Condition of material Things, and thereby to convey to us Ideas of immaterial Things, convey the Conjectures of that Race of Men, who have set up Descriptions of the Conditions of Things, which they are not in, and attributed to them Powers they are not possess'd of, and so convey either no Ideas at all, or false ones; so we have lost the proper Use of Words for material Things, and the Benefit which arises from the Comparisons between them and immaterial Things, by using Sounds without proper Significations, and hence arises the Confusion in modern Languages, and such Difficulty of understanding them, or conveying true Ideas of Things by Words used in them.

Tho' the Scriptures were writ to be understood, and for the Benefit of all, none can receive that but such as have Capacities to understand them, or such as are

willing

willing to be inform'd by those who understand them; and Things which are only demonstrable by Evidence, deduced from other Things, cannot be demonstrated to those, who do not examine the Evidence in those other Things, because without that they can form no Deduction. If there be any Points in the System of Religion, which are not evident to the Sense or Reason of Men, illiterate, of weak Capacity, and small Application, such Men may be directed in them by what Men call Reason or Conscience; and such Points may be term'd common Cases, or Cases generally known in common Law. If there be other Points which will be evident to Men of human Learning, considerable Capacity, and of great Application, such may be term'd Cases in common Law; and yet Conscience or Reason can know nothing of them, without Reading and Application to understand the State of the Case, and Reason of the Evidence which determines those Points. But if there be Points in Religion, which were necessary to be reveal'd, and that there is visible Evidence to support the Truth of some of those Points in Religion, which has also been necessary to be revealed, and other Evidence which arises by Search in natural Things; I doubt Reason or Conscience has but a small Share till the Person who is to judge understands those Writings, which may be term'd Statute Law, till he sees the Reasons upon which those Laws were made, and till he also sees and understands the Evidence, which is to support those Points: And how willing soever the Laity may be to excuse the Clergy, and at the same Time to believe the base Conjectures of Libertines, I doubt it lies upon the Clergy to explain those Points to Demonstration; and how near soever this may approach to the Manner of Decision of such Points in the *Roman* Church, I doubt People who cannot understand, must have their Conscience or Reason directed by such whose Business it is to inform themselves and others; because they have no other Means to direct them in such Cases. And any Order of Men, except that Order dignified by, and entrusted in the Affairs of State, or any one of the rest, except such a one as has employ'd his Time in illustrating some of the Points, next in Consequence to that of proving there has been Revelation or Communication between God and Man; who take a Volume in their Hands and affirm, that an invisible, omnipotent, and omniscient Being has revealed it, and that every Sentence in it is true and sacred; or that there is any Man, or Order of Men, who have an infallible Power of explaining it; and that the first Part contains an Account of his Creation, and Operations in the several Parts of Matter; and that each Description is intended for Evidence of the rest; and that he has, in Condescention to our Capacities, given us comparative Descriptions to raise Ideas of his Power and other Attributes, by those Operations in Matter; and cannot shew there are any such Things, Situations, or Actions, and at the same Time pretend to understand the invisible Actions, describ'd by Comparisons of them, will always, notwithstanding other Qualifications or Conditions, except those from the Civil Power, or &c. be contemptible; and more so if they, instead of labouring by all Sorts of proper Methods to explain them, teach Schemes set up by *Lucretius*, *Aristotle*, and such who denied any such Being; or which, upon this Account is the same Thing, denied the Truth of any such Revelation; and in the highest Degree so, if they continue to initiate Youth, successively to spend their Time in studying Books, which, as they are taken,

tend

tend to the same End; which, if properly explain'd, would all tend to illustrate that Knowledge of natural Things in those sacred Books, they are ignorant of; and those Books or Men to whom they pay this Deference will be followed: And though the Freethinkers make a continual cry against the Prejudice of Education, I think that is very unjust; for as Education is managed, the Advantage is on their Side. The only Plea which I have heard offer'd for introducing *Aristotle* is, that the *Arabs* when they broke into *Europe*, having been long possess'd of his Books, and made Comments upon them, were too expert in that Way of arguing for the Christians (who had not seen those Books) till they had read them, and were by that Means able to pay the *Arabs* in their own Coin; tho' it was not to make that a Science, but to evade their Pretensions to Science; not to be mix'd with Christianity, and preach'd in Christian Pulpits, but to be studied by some who should make it their Business to detect those who made any such Attempts: Because greater disgrace cannot be done to any Body of Men, than by those who act, under pretence of being Members, directly contrary to the End of their Institution. And a few aspiring Clergy, who would not be content

tent to be Ministers to God or Christ, but Makers of Gods, or Chrifts, lifting themfelves as Andrews to, and fo ftriking in with the adverfe Party, make it pafs Current, that they know that *Mofes* knew nothing of the Matter, and that the whole is a Cheat. If it appears, when the Notions of the Authors now follow'd, are compar'd with Scripture, that any of them, or any of their Creatures who propagate them, who have had Education, and fpent their whole Time, as they pretend, in ftudying Nature, have fhew'd that they are capable of forming one juft Thought, or difcovering one valuable Truth, fo that they are fit in any Inftance, or in any Meafure, to direct the Minds of Mankind, I'll give up and fuffer them to lead me.

The Method directed perhaps to Man at firft, however prefcribed to the *Jews*, was to meditate upon the Works of God in the Creation and Formation; this was the Work for which their Sabbath was fet apart, while they preferv'd the Knowledge of thefe Works, and fo obferv'd the Sabbath, that proved the Being, and preferv'd the Senfe of the Obligations they were under to God, and them in their Duty. When they neglected that, and loft that Knowledge, fo often complain'd of under the Term of the Breach of the Sabbath, they

INTRODUCTION. xxxvii

they fell away from God. If the antient Heathens had worshiped God through the Powers that they saw existed in his created System, as those who pretend they would give a good Turn to it assert, there would have been little or no Occasion for those Exclamations against them in Scripture: But alas! tho' we should be so charitable to hope or allow that some few of the wisest of them did, that Suggestion in gross has no Foundation. And the antient Heathens all worship'd the Powers of the Heavens instead of God; and they maintain'd that false Religion, even against the Power of Miracles, by being able to shew the People that their Accounts of the natural Things were consistent with the Things which were Evident. When the latter Heathens attributed Powers which appear'd to be inconsistent with the Attributes of this material Machine, they begun to divide and dwindle: Whenever the Clergy of the true or the false Religion (for there never was more than two; where God was not serv'd, these Powers, his Deputies, must be serv'd) were Philosophers, and maintained, that the Knowledge of natural Things was consonant to the Revelation they had, or the Tradition, or Founda-

xxxviii INTRODUCTION.

tion of the Religion they profess'd, the Body of the People follow'd them: But whenever any Set of Divines of either Religion cannot make Philosophy, or the Account of natural Things consonant to what they teach for Scripture, or sacred Truths; or whenever any other Set of Men have been able to shew really or to Appearance, that such Knowledge was inconsistent with their Religion, or have prov'd, or been suffer'd to contradict, or pretend to prove their Scripture, or Tradition, false in those Points, so that the Clergy could not disprove, gainsay, or hinder them; those Clergy have been in danger of falling into Contempt, their Scripture or Tradition has not been believ'd; the Opponents have carried away the Body of the People into such Notions, even in Religion, as they thought fit to propagate.

Christ before he bestow'd the Spirit and Power upon his Disciples, order'd them to search the Jewish Scriptures for Evidence of God of himself, &c. but at the same Time, Christ shew'd them in several Instances, that the *Jews* had destroy'd the Intent of the Scriptures, by their Interpretations or Traditions; so I have good Authority for the Method I take: He
does

does not refer them to the LXX, Translations, Targums or Traditions, much less has he referr'd us to them, or Traditions since writ, nor to Rules of Grammar, or Pointings, whereby they have endeavoured to justify the wilful Errors or Mistakes those before them had made; and tho' every one knows, the *Jews* have not only grown more ignorant in these Matters, but worse and worse ever since; I cannot expect to escape falling under the Displeasure of those who have spent most of their Time in studying, and making themselves Masters of all their allegorical, or other ways of Evasion, nor their Charge against me, for disparaging them; particularly our primitive—will rave to see his *Sam. Pent.* demolish'd. Let the Scripture be true, though all Men should be made Lyars. How I shall stand with those who thought that Words were arbitrarily fram'd, and that there was a Set of them selected for Divine Things, and Actions, without any Relation to Matter, and so could never come at any Knowledge of their Significations, but as others or they were pleas'd to give them, must depend upon their respective Degrees of Value for the Truth. After the Disciples of Christ had the Power of Miracles, and while

while that lafted, they had no need of the *Jewish* Scriptures, they had Nature at a Beck to give their Hearers ocular Evidence; after that Power ceas'd, the Difciples, who fucceeded that Power, were again left to the Evidence of Facts in that Scripture, to prove God the Creator and Contriver of the natural Powers: There was no Occafion to prove that again in the New Teftament. The Primitive Fathers did not join with the Adverfaries, who under the cover of Mathematicks, brought in Whims oppofite to Scripture or Religion, nor tamely gave up the Points, but boldly confuted them: And to mention one Inftance treated upon in my firft Part of this, at *p.* 57. *& feq.* the greateft of them thought it not below them to rummage the hard Rocks in the higheft Mountains, and in the deepeft Works, and moft difficult of accefs, to convince thofe who doubted of the Truth of the Hiftory of the Diffolution of the Earth, at the Flood, by ocular Demonftration, from the Bodies lodged in the Stone there. Do not all Men, who are appointed, or intend to bring about any thing, choofe and purfue the moft proper Means? If they fee that People will be kept, or gain'd by nothing but Demonftration,

that

INTRODUCTION.

that the Scripture was writ by those who understood Nature, should not some of them pursue That? But on the Contrary, 'tis now so far below the Dignity of our Clergy, who have manag'd the Scripture, so that they cannot produce it, and expect their Words should be taken, to examine, whether the Scripture be rightly translated, to look into Nature themselves, that they will not so much as look into the Books of those who have done it for them; so that they have suffered one for thirty Years to keep Possession of what the Primitive Fathers had demonstrated; and the Arguments, which another about thirty Years before him had publish'd upon those Bodies of Stone, as his own Discoveries and Deductions, and under the Credit of that evident Truth, to vent and support a thousand Contradictions to Scripture and common Sense; and I doubt not to give several such Instances of others. As the Chiefs of the Church of *Rome* stand charg'd with pretending to a directive Power over the Minds of their Followers, though perhaps 'tis only over their Pens and Tongues, there seems some Excuse for their Clergy, to neglect the Demonstration of the Accordance between the Revelation of the Formation and Action

of

of natural Things, and the Facts. But the Clergy of this Church, who pretend to no Authority over the Minds of their Followers, but what they demonstrate from the Scriptures, have no Manner of Excuse for neglecting to labour continually, till they can explain that Evidence. Talking of the Authority of the Church will not do now, that of Scripture must do. Understanding and using the Branches of Learning, Grammar, Rhetorick, Logick, &c. will not do; they must shew that the Scripture is true, and writ by infallible Men, and in a Manner not to be mistaken; and till that be done, those who fall or are drawn by the Diligence of the Adversaries into other Sentiments, for want of such Evidence, I am afraid will be able to charge a Neglect upon those who should have been their Leaders.

I have endeavoured to move some great Genius's, to set these Matters in a clear Light; and since they have not attempted to explain them, though I should not have been very desirous of understanding any Language, already translated into my own, no otherwise than those who translated it understood it, much less by those Rules of Grammar, Pointing, &c. which

I can see in many Cases are false, or by following the Authority of those Persons, who I see were either oblig'd by Fear, or design'd to mislead us in the Intentions and principal Points, convey'd in the Writings of that Language; yet I am ready to take any Pains, and shall be content to bear the Blame of breaking (if there were Occasion) through all those Rules, to come at the Design of Writings of so great Consequence; because that once known, will not only make those Books be read and studied in another Manner, but will find itself Rules, if not immediately, at least in a short Time. Tho' the first Inducement to every well meaning Man should be to inform himself, If he attains any Knowledge which is wanted in so important a Case, nothing should deter him from publishing it.

It will, at some Time, be shew'd, that the Heathens took their natural Religion and Philosophy from the Worshipers of the true God, and apply'd it to his Legates; and I intend to shew that God took natural Religion, and Philosophy, with many additional Symbols, back from the Heathens for the *Jews*; and as the Christians were *Jews* or *Gentiles* converted, and each of their Religions had consisted

xliv INTRODUCTION.

fifted chiefly in afcribing to, and thanking their God for the great Motions and Operations in Matter; it wou'd feem very ftrange, when Chrift had declared, that the Ceremonial Law was holy, and juft, and good, and that he came to make it perfect, and to be a Pattern to others; if we did not daily fee that almoft every one who renounces Communion with a Church, or Body of the fame Religion, goes into contrary Extremes; that they are for leaving it by Wholefale, good as well as bad; that there is not in the antient Liturgies any Foot-fteps of the Particulars of this Service. Indeed tho' fome of the *Jews* who oppos'd Chriftianity, would have it believ'd, that their Religion had fomething in the Ceremonies beyond natural Religion, or Philofophy, and the Types of Chrift: And others infifted, that even their Ceremonies ought to be obferved to preferve Philofophy, or the Knoledge of the Motions and Actions of Matter, till Idolatry fhould ceafe, or till the End of this World: And fome of the Heathens, who came in, were for bringing in fome of their Philofophical Gods, as Co-adjutors with God; fo that they forced the Chriftian Church to caft out their Philofophy with their Gods; and

INTRODUCTION.

and as Philosophy began their Religion, it, where Christianity prevail'd, ended with it. And tho' the *Jews*, Heathens, and Christians, neglected the atheistical and poetical Books, as not worthy their Notice, so let the Atheists keep them; they destroyed the Books of the Heathen Religion and Philosophy, that not one, as we know of, remains: If they had but preserved one of them, or the primitive Churches had expressed a few of the Works of those Agents, and attributed them to the true God, we should have few Atheists now. The Demonstration of God's Power, in creating and forming the Powers in this Machine, to answer so many Ends, is not diminished, nor they debased, because that wise Men took them for Gods, but vastly magnified, and our Service of Praise to him, for framing of them, is thereby made much more necessary. If our pious Reformers had understood *Hebrew* or Philosophy, as well as they did *Greek* or Divinity, and in Imitation of the Royal Prophet had but put in a few Lines of Praise to God for forming this Machine, to perform what it does, and so expressed the Acts of God's ordinary Providence, it had not been left to Chance or Properties, and had prevented all the Trumpery we have had of late, the Difficulty of re-
trieving

INTRODUCTION.

trieving what is once lost, and of dispossessing People of received Notions, tho' ever so false and inconsistent.

I have, in the former Part, consider'd *Moses*'s Relation of the Heavens, their Changes of Names, Conditions, and Operations, so far as in general concerned the Earth: I have got over the great Difficulty, the Situation of Things, which obstructed the Reduction of the History of those Things to Sense. I hope I shall find the rest less difficult, and that I shall want no Succedaneums. I am now to reconsider his Relation of the Heavens from the Beginning, as it concerns them more immediately, in the several Views every the most minute Thing can be consider'd in; and afterwards proceed with them in the same Condition as they were in when they form'd the Earth, till they have form'd the Celestial Bodies; and after that as a Machine fram'd, so as to produce and carry on a perpetual Motion of every Part of themselves, and of every thing within between the Sun and the fixed Stars, and to carry on all temporal Motions and Powers. As these Powers were each a God to the Heathens, I intend not to enter into the Branches of the Attribute they comprehend in one Word, but only shew each in gross; because as those Powers

ers are only now Philosophical, those Branches will shew themselves, when these Powers come to be consider'd more distinctly, and in their Operations upon smaller Parcels of Matter, and illustrated by Observations and Experiments. I shall be forced in my Progress to speak of Things as they are in this Machine, or mention Things before in Course I come at them, that I may be understood, and explain the Thing I am then upon; or all along shew one Part of the Machine by the rest, and prove each of the Parts I mention beforehand in its Course.

I am aware I shall be censur'd for proceeding in the Manner I shall take, of mixing the Significations of the Words in the Discourse, and so breaking the Thread of it; perhaps they will say, I had better have explain'd all the Words apart, and then us'd their Significations only in the Discourse. But as I am forced to make my Ground good as I go, and cannot possibly explain a Sentence, till I have explain'd the Words of chief Use in it, I choose to let it go so, because it may shew to others the Method and Steps I have taken, to attain the End; not for an Example of regular Writing, but of tracing out other Truths, because the first is a Science, the latter seldom attempted. We

INTRODUCTION.

We cannot expect exact Translations of the Heathen Words, for the different Conditions and Actions of the Air, except the Translators had underſtood its, or their, different Attributes, Conditions, Actions and Effects, ſo as to have been able to make proper Diſtinctions; nor are we to expect proper Diſtinctions of the Situations or Courſes of the Motions of the Parts of it, in the ſeveral Conditions; becauſe ſome have made the Circumference or Verge, ſome the Orb of the Sun the higheſt; ſome make the Centre of the Univerſe in the Sun, ſome in the Earth. If I can ſet the whole right, I ſhall ſet them right.

Where the Tranſlations of the Bible come near the Senſe, I ſhall cite them without any Obſervations; becauſe if the chief Points be ſet Right, they may hereafter be eaſily ſet Right.

I ſhall meddle as little as poſſible with the *Greek* Language, but take the Tranſlations, not only of the Divine, but Human Writings (tho' many of them are imperfect) as they ſtand, becauſe the Words in their Philoſophy, and Theology, are us'd in the New Teſtament; and tho' they are of great Importance to the Underſtanding of it, they cannot be underſtood, or ſafely meddled with, till this be explain'd, and they by it.

MOSES's Principia.

PART II.

GEN. CHAP. II.

SINCE I writ the firſt Part, I have ſhewed that this Hiſtory was not writ to ſatisfy Men's Curioſity, but to root out the Imaginations Men had got into their Heads, and to renew proper Ideas of God's Wiſdom, Power, &c. And ſo indeed is every Part of the Scripture, and each Part againſt the Imaginations which prevailed, when it was writ; and in this Senſe every Word in Scripture is to be taken, in the ſtrongeſt and fulleſt Signification, not only in the preſent, but in the Conſequent; even a ⊃ *ſicut*, the moſt like that any thing can be.

Ver. 1. *In the Beginning God created the Heaven and the Earth.*

Several of our moſt notorious Men have very lately made a Jeſt of the Beginning of this Syſtem, at the Time *Moſes* mentions, and others of the Creation, for which they can have no Authority; nor can Men have any more from God, than an *ipſe ſcripſit*, who ſhew'd that all Nature was at his Maſter's Command before he writ it, with the Confirmation of the other Prophets, and of Chriſt. And theſe Men alſo make ſeveral Objections againſt the Conciſeneſs, and the Manner of their writing of this Hiſtory, as though it were only a ſhort Tradition, and not to be underſtood: If they had Capacities to underſtand it, every Criminal is at Liberty to find, or pretend to find Faults in the wording of his Indictment.

Some have made Doubts, whether the Word ברא here ſignifies to produce the Subſtance, or to form it. M. *Heb.* ברא *Create:* "It is ſaid of any Thing that from Non-exiſtence proceeds to Exiſtence, *ib. Chald. & Syr.* ברא, where God created any Thing from nothing, or produced something New and Remarkable from another. *C. Isad,* A Foundation. *Chald.* An Element, or first Principle. Every Element returns to its own Element. R. D. *Sam.*— 1. q. *Ar. Atzul,* Roots, Origins, *Lit. Dam.*' The Heathens were for making the Power of bringing forth the Atoms, and forming them, which they called Creation, an Attribute of what they took for a God: And the Divines have been puzzled to ascertain the Meaning of the Word, because 'tis afterwards used for Whales, and every living Creature, formed out of Matter in the Water, and Man; where 'tis as necessary as the Word is for Heaven and Earth, because the Atoms of the Matter, which Creatures are made of, are neither Atoms of the Heavens, nor of the Earth, nor of the Water. 'Tis *Gen.* ii. 7. עפר מן האדמה which *Glassius in Philol. Sacr.* p. 858. would spoil with a Figure, and there could not be any Description of that Matter while in Atoms dispersed through the Water and Earth, till God made some of them be collected and formed. And if there had been twenty Species of Atoms differing as widely as those do, he would have gone with the Word ברא through them all, or have sufficiently implied it; as the

Atoms

Atoms which conſtitute Man are created, the Atoms of Beaſts which form the Body of Man ; of Fruits which form the Body of Man and Beaſt ; and of Plants, which form the Bodies of Beaſts, are ſufficiently included. Indeed the Food of Fiſh is not ſo viſible to Man; *Chaldee Paraphraſe* on *Pſal.* cxxxix. 16. " Thine Eyes ſaw my Body, and in the Book of thy Memorial were all my Days written on the Day the World was created, all Creatures were created at the firſt, nor is one like another among them :" In *Heb.* v. 15, 16. *My Subſtance was not hid from thee, when it was formed in Secret, it was ſpun beneath in the Earth* *. This ſet right, there are alſo Diſtinctions between creating and forming, *Gen.* ii. 3. — The whole of מלאכתו his material Legate which God created to act. *Theſe are the Generations of the Heavens and of the Earth, for which they were created, when Jehovah the Perſons in Covenant had formed the Earth*

---

* God knows every Atom which compoſes each Man's Body from its firſt Accretion in the Earth, and ſees it through all its Stages till it becomes Part of the human Body: The Atoms which compoſe our Bodies are brought together, ſpun, net, or accreted within the Surface of the Earth, thence raiſed into Fruits, &c. ſo into our Bodies.

and

and the Heavens. 2 *Mac.* vii. 28. *Vulgate.* " I beseech thee, Son, look up to the Heaven, and to the Earth, and all that in them is, and understand that God made them of nothing, and all the Race of Men; so it shall be, that thou shall not fear — *Lat.* — — Beholding, that thou mayest understand that God made them when they were not, and the Race of Man was made in the same Manner. Fear not — *Syr.* — and consider and behold that God made these things of what did not exist before: Also in the same Manner the Human Race had its Existence: Be not therefore afraid of this cursed Fellow.— *Isa.* xliii. 7. I have created him, *(viz.* Man) יצרתיו I have formed him, I have also made him, *Maim. Mor. Nev. Part* 2d. c. 30. For the Foundation of our Law is that God created this World of nothing." With respect to the constituent Parts of Solids, saying, that he created them in loose Atoms, sets aside all Cavils, for nothing can be said of forming an Atom, but giving it Solidity, Size and Figure, and that is what is expressed by creating it. The Word ברא is never used but for simple Creation or Production of the Matter in Atoms from nothing; but there is one Exception, it appears, that Part of the Atoms of the Heavens were created, and in the same Act concreted into small Grains which is called Spirit, so that Part of God's Action is represented by a Participle of this Verb, not as continually, but as in a few other Cases referring to the Time, where the Action of Creation was joined with that Action; which served to the same End, and is now an Action of the Heavens, which continually and successively concrete a Proportion of its constituent Atoms into Darkness, or Grains, or Spirit to be the Instruments of Motion; the Matter to keep the Fire in Action, and supply it with Atoms to be divided or separated by that Action, and sent out in Light, and for all the intermediate Uses they are employed in for supporting this Machine, those material Legates, or Ministers, and this whole System, as *Isa.* xlv. 7. *Forming Light, and* בורא *concreting Darkness*; ver. 18. *Jehovah who concreted the Heavens; he the Persons in Covenant who formed the Earth and made it: He who framed it. Was it not created in loose Atoms? He formed it to be inhabited.* Ibid. xlii. 5. *God the Jehovah who concreted the Heavens, and stretched them out, who spread forth the Earth and its Products.* Amos iv. 13. *He that formed the Mountains and*

concreted

concreted the Spirit. Though these be Actions of, or Accidents to the Atoms of Matter, which are so small, and contrived on purpose, so that none of our Senses can directly, or immediately take Cognizance of them; yet all material Operations depend upon, and are produced, and govern'd by them, and they have been taken, by the greatest Part of Mankind, for a God, and their Actions for the immediate Acts of a God: So God has been pleased to record these Matters in the strongest Light; nay the forming one of these Grains, as the highest Demonstration of the Perfection of his Wisdom.

There are some who do not speak out plainly, that they think Matter is eternal, who would gladly set up something eternal, and they reason thus; They cannot conceive, but there must have been Space before Matter, because Matter exists in Space: There are some who pretend to know, that the Part we call Heaven, is most of it empty Space, and pretend to prove it by shewing, that they have said, that the Comets and Planets move by Projection, (of which hereafter) and have lost very little of the Velocity of the Motion, which was communicated to each of them at their Out-settings in their present Journeys; which must have been more abated, if there had been much Matter to obstruct them; and that Light moves freely where it pleases, which it could not do, nor does where there is any Thing in its Way; and because they have said, that some Power of Gravitation (of which also hereafter) acts not according to the Quantity of the Surfaces of the Particles upon which it acts, (as mechanical Causes use to do) but according to the Quantity of solid Matter; and that there are some sorts of Solids, nay even of Fluids, which no Force can compress into less Extent, which weigh not, for Example, $\frac{1}{10}$ so much as others do, and so the rest of the nine Parts must be empty Space; and that some sort of Matter can, when confined, be compress'd, for Example, into $\frac{1}{10}$ Part of the Compass it takes when at Liberty, and even then will weigh little or nothing; and that any given Quantity of solid Matter, by being capable of being infinitely divided, (of which also hereafter) is capable of being infinitely extended, in despight of that common Maxim, that the Parts are equal (in Extent) to the Whole; and that Matter cannot move, without Space to move in. Others indeed tell us, that their God

is

is an infinite Substance, and so constitutes Space and Infinity, and so infinite Space; so on purpose to make infinite Space, they have made such a God; and tho' it is contrary to an express Precept to attempt, by any Thing in the Heavens above (if Space be any Thing, or be there) to give us any Similitude to raise any Idea of God; that will not do their Business. I always took Space, in my Sense, to be a Word for the Dimension of any Atom, or Body, or Fluid, and so constitute by creating Matter in Atoms, either fluid or adhering; and in their Sense to be an imaginary Word, supposing the Matter can be removed, and the Void or Dimension exist, " Space is an imaginary Local (*a*), " and such a Void with Substance in it, is a Contradiction in Terms; because a solid Substance, or a Substance of Solids exists, and we know nothing of any other manner of Existence, therefore they conclude every other Existence must be a Substance. Whether Extension, which is an Attribute of Beings, which God has created to form, supply, and support our Bodies, have any Relation to the Substance of God, I

(*a*) Alstedi Encyclopædiæ Index, p. 606.

leave

leave the World to judge, seeing the Author of this Account allows, that created Bodies possess each their respective Space, without Interruption from the Substance of God. If the Substance of God exists in Matter, or in a solid Atom, then that Existence does not constitute Space, or at least does not want such a Space as they aim at to exist in; for if it exists within the Substance of solid, created Atoms, as well as where there is none (if any such Place there be) the Presence of his Substance neither wants, nor constitutes Space nor Fulness; and if all what they call infinite Space were full of Solids, his Substance would nevertheless exist. If the Substance of God was once infinite, and does not exist in created solid Substances, then that Substance is diminished by Creation, and not infinite. If a spiritual Essence, or Person exists in Space, or wants something, which he terms Space, to exist in, and that one Essence or Person fills all, or that infinite Space, there can be no more spiritual Essences or Persons but that one exist. Besides it seems a pretty strange Deduction, that the Substance of that Being, which created all Things, which we have any Knowledge of, and has not the Properties of other Substances, but suffers them to possess

possess all the Space we know of, and consequently wants no Space that we know of, should, by, or for, its own Existence, constitute infinite Space. If the Substance of God constitutes infinite Space, it must be such a Space as contains that Substance, and consequently no Void nor Space to admit Bodies, nor for them to move infinitely in; and if no Void, the Juggles, the Quibbles of joining a Particle of Space, and always together, and a Moment of Time, and every where together, till its Existence, or perhaps more properly, till such a Non-entity, for which the Word is constituted, and of which I can frame no Idea, be proved, will not impose it upon us. They also say, certainly the Framer and Lord of the Universe is never no where; put it the reverse, and it is (if it be spoke with Regard to himself only) the Framer and Lord of the Universe is ever present, where he is present, (if with Regard to his Dominion) is ever potentially present, where he rules; (if with Regard to himself and the Universe), he is in some Manner present in every Part of the Universe: But if the Universe be created and not eternal, and finite and not infinite, all these Words determine not that the Substance of God, either before the

Crea-

Creation or now, is infinitely extended, nor even that his Power of Framing and Dominion is at prefent, infinitely extended; and though he has ftill, and always will have, a Power of extending them, I cannot conceive how at any Period of Time it can be truly faid to be infinitely extended. The folid Bodies God has created, are each in its Place fubftantially prefent, and he by them has conftituted Space (if they will have it called fo) where each of them fubfifts; but call it what they pleafe, it is their folid Subftances; and there is no Occafion for conftituting Space for folid Subftances beforehand, Creation does it. Whatever is co-eval with God, is God, and whatever is co-eval with created folid Matter, is the Subftance of that Matter, and whatever Words they ufe, when a few Deceptions of our Senfes are obviated, and Matters fairly ftated, even the Ideas of each, and what they call Space, cannot be parted. When he fays, God by exifting conftitutes Infinity, he has not told us of any Thing, but only of Space; I hope he does not mean Infinity of Matter, if he does, he will lofe his infinite Space, and if Matter be finite, what is infinite Space for? it can have no Relation to created Matter: I know not

what

what he means by a Particle of infinite Space, if instead of that he had said, the Space of a Particle, I could have understood what he meant, as the Antients meant. B. C. "*Melusa*, Space, a void Place: *Latitude, Area*, He who selleth a Court, sells nothing but the *Melusa*, the Space of the Court. *Tal. Bara Bathra*, fol. 67. 1. In the *Misna*, the same Place, the Space in which Air is, is called *Auira*, Air." He also tells us, that God by existing, constitutes Duration and Eternity, and proves this the same Way; every Moment of Duration is every where, tho' Matter be composed of Particles, and Time of Moments; how Particles will make up Infinity, or Moments Eternity, I cannot conceive; Infinite, either Way, apply'd to God, expresses, that his Essence had no Commencement, nor will have any Determination, or Cessation; but that Epithet is no more applicable to Extension, than it is to any other uncertain, or false Attribute of God. Whatever Comparison we make between God and other Things, to explain our Idea, of the Manner of his Existence, they not only come short, but differ vastly; suppose of some Beings which have Duration and Power of Action, and that it seems to us, that a Substance is necessary to every Being while it exists, and Space necessary to every Substance, and that Time, or Duration, seems to be necessary to every Being while it endures, and that Power is necessary to every Agent while it continues an Agent; be it some sort of Matter, which we suppose has mechanical Powers, be it some living Creature which has bodily Powers, or some Prince which has political Powers; and suppose it seems, that God exists in Substance, in Space, in Duration, in Power, tho' indeed after what Manner only he knows, 'tis as wide to compare the Substance of inanimate Matter, or the Body of a Creature, or the Person of a Prince, (the Image of God in him excepted) to the Substance of God; or the Space they exist in, to the Manner of the Existence of his Essence, as 'tis to compare the Manner of their Duration, or the Manner of enjoying, or exercising their Power, to the Manner of his Duration, or the Manner of enjoying or exercising his Power (tho' Time or Duration is certainly enjoyed in common among all Beings or Substances while they endure; much more certainly than that all Beings are Substances) because in created Beings they are all derivative, and temporary, and finite:

nite: Time was when those Things which are now his Creatures, had neither Substance, Space, Duration, nor Power, and may be when some of them, in all these Respects, may cease; but God's Duration and Power is in his Essence, and his Essence in his Duration and Power; they must necessarily be inseperable, or as they put it of Space, his Being constitutes Space only for his own Being, not for his Creatures, other than so much, and of such a Sort, as he is pleased at Creation or Formation to communicate to them; not for Comets and Planets to have Duration to all Eternity; not for Matter to enjoy its Powers, either such as they imagine it has, or such as really has, to all Eternity. As every Thing which can be said of God is comparative, and taken from created Things, or what relates to them, so is his Time, we can but say before any Time; his Duration has nothing to do with Creatures, nor they with Duration, but the Time they endure; nor has his Space any Thing to do with Creatures, or they with Space, but the Dimension of their Bodies. If we were to take the Comparison thro', as we have no other Idea of Substance but Space, one might have expected it should have constituted Impenetrability; but the Idea

he

he gives of this Substance is, that it hinders nothing from passing in it, either shifts and gives Way, or lets other Substances possess its Space. They may say truly he constitutes Power, but yet he could, and as I shall shew, has created Matter with Space, Duration, &c. without any Power of Action. But lest their reasoning in these Points should not be sufficient, they have cited a Heathen Author, and several Texts of Scripture, with a Complement of, *So the Antients thought*, to prove that all Things are contained in the Substance of God, and that his Substance constitutes infinite Space; but they do not at all speak to the Point, or determine any thing about the Substance of God, much less that it constitutes infinite Space: Those Texts were to set the People right, and free them from some mistaken Notions about the Power, and other Attributes of God, but not to describe his Substance, and make it constitute infinite Space; and there are other Texts which determine the Points quite contrary. I have shewed already, and shall add Proofs below, that most of the Scripture was writ to determine the Contest, whether the Creator and Former of all Things and Powers was God; or the Heavens and their Powers was God; and
how

how what was a God, ought to be represented and worshiped: So whatever the Heathens, or Unbelievers, attributed to the Heavens; by way of Claim, God, the Prophets, Christ, and his Apostles, attributed to God the Father, to Christ, and to the Holy Ghost: (this settled) When St. *Paul* was at *Athens*, among People who knew nothing of the true God, and mocked at Immortality; he takes Advantage of the Attributes of their God, in their Writings, by intermixing them with the Attributes of, and applying them to the true God; he begins with an Inscription, *To the unknown God*, which they took to be an invisible Power, innate in the Heavens, their God; under the Cover of this Word, he tells them, that *God made the World —— was Lord of Heaven.* ——The first was new to them, and destructive of their God, if *made* be to be taken for Creation; but if it be taken for Formation, the Heavens made this Orb, &c. as the Scriptures and their Writings agree; but the latter was the antient Title of their God, sometimes Lady of Heaven — *He giveth to all Life and Breath and all Things.*——These were antient Attributes of their God, *Vossius de Philos. Christ. &c.* " It is fit to honour the Cæleſtial Gods with theſe Things, by which we ourſelves are nouriſhed, ſupported and live, and which they have vouchſafed from the Benignity of their Deity to give us for Suſtenance." In the Scriptures moſt fully in *Iſaiah*, *Jeremiah*, and *Hoſea*,—*That they might ſeek the Lord if haply they might feel after and find him, tho' he be not far from every one of us.*——This is dexterouſly inſinuating, that the Object of their Worſhip, which was always viſible, and ſolidly preſent, was not the God, but that he was inviſible, unfound, and unknown to them.—*For in him we live, and move, and have our Being ; as certain alſo of your own Poets have ſaid, for we are alſo his Offſpring.* Here he again cites the moſt evident Attributes of their God, the Heavens, the Air: In it, (but if a God) in him we live, move, and have our Being materially, and alſo by its, or in its Operations and Powers ; this he applies to the true God, *Glaſſ. Philog. p.* 1478. "There remain ſome Citations from profane Writings, three of which are in the Apoſtle *Paul.* Acts i. 17, 28. *For in him* (the Lord God) *we live, move, and have our Being as certain of your Poets have ſaid,* &c.——This Hemiſtich *Clemens Alexandrinus* atteſts to be taken from *Aratus* in his

his *Phænomena*, Strom. v. fol. 123. and he produces the entire Passage of *Aratus* consisting of a few Verses. In *Aratus* this Hemistich is attributed to *Jupiter*, which *Paul* taking Notice to be perversly and altogether unjustly made an Attribute of *Jove*, he most justly restores it to *Jehovah*. *Clem. Alex.* v. *Strom.* p. 435. And *Aratus* in his *Phænomena* saith,

From Jove we spring, shall Jove be then unsung,
Jove who to sing enables ev'ry Tongue!
Where'er we Mortals go, where'er we move,
Our Forums, Cities, Streets, are full of Jove;
He flows the swelling, ebbs the falling Tide,
With him in Harbour safe the Vessels ride,
We seek him, taste him, breath him every where,
And all in common his kind Influence share.
  And then infers:
For we his Offspring are.

" And indeed all this both in Prose and Verse, that is sung of *Jupiter*, refers the Mind to God; for that I may at once speak it, it, *Democritus* writes that there are few Men under the Light, who stretch out their Hand hither, which we *Greeks* call now the Air.

Ibid. 415. *Sphinx* is not the Intelligence of the Universe, and according to the Poet *Aratus*'s Opinion, the conversive Force of the mundane System: But it may be perhaps the Tenour and Stress of the Spirit pervading and by its Compressure bounding the System: Yet it is better to suppose it the Æther (*or Mixture of Light and Spirit*) that bounds and binds all things, according as *Empedocles* faith."

> *The Sun's great Principle, shall first be sung,*
> *And whence the visible Creation sprung;*
> *The Earth, the flowing Sea, the humid Air,*
> *Titan, or Æther's all encircling Sphere,*
> *That binds the whole and confines.*

Vossius de Orig. & Prog. &c. — " All Things are full of *Jove*.—*Maro* as *Servius* notes, uses *Aratus*'s Expression." " *Macrobius Saturn. &c.* called the Sun *Phaneta* from the *Greek Phaos* and *Phaneros*, *i. e.* Light and Illumination, because it is seen by all, and beholds all. It is called *Dionysos*, as the Poet says, from *Greek* too, *Dineisthai* and *Peripheresthai*, that is, because it is carried round in a Circle, whence *Cleanthes* writes it is so termed from *tou Dionysai*, because by a daily Impetus from East to West, making Day and Night, it compleats its celestial Race. Naturalists call it *Dionysos*, *Jupiter*'s Mind, because they make the Sun the Mind of the World. The World also is called Heaven, which they term *Jupiter*. Whence *Aratus* in his Phænomena. From *Jupiter* we have our Being."

I need only insert the next three Texts, to shew that they are nothing to the Purpose. *Deut.* iv. 39. *That the* Lord *he is God in Heaven above, and upon the Earth beneath:* There is *none else.* Ibid. x. 14. *Behold, the Heaven, and the Heaven of Heavens is the* Lord's *thy God, the Earth also and all that therein is.* Psal. cxiii. 4, 5. *Who is like* Jehovah *our Aleim, who exalteth himself to dwell, and humbleth him to look down in the Heavens and in the Earth.* The next, as far as an Allusion can carry the thing, is expressly against the Purpose for which it is cited. 1 Kings viii. 27. *But will God indeed dwell on the Earth? Behold the Heaven, and the Heaven of Heavens cannot contain thee, how much less this Houſe that I have builded?* — Ver. 30. *And hear thou in Heaven thy dwelling Place.* It alludes to the Palace or Court of a Prince; and though a Prince cannot be ſaid to be confined to his Palace, yet it may be ſaid to be his dwelling Place; and here he ſays, is the Earth a fit Place for God, (as the *Chald. Par.* renders it) for his Majeſty, or can the Heaven, or Heaven of Heavens ſuſtain his Glory, or be fit for his Reſidence, much leſs this Houſe? and after this, no leſs than eight times in this Chapter *Solomon* prays, that God would hear them in Heaven, his dwelling Place. The next is as oppoſite as Words can make it, nay, carries it too far. Job xxii. 12, 13, 14. *Is not God in the Height of Heaven? and behold the Height* (Heb. *Head) of the Stars, how high they are. And thou ſayeſt, How doth God know? can he judge through the dark Cloud? Thick Clouds* are *a Covering to him, that he ſeeth not, and he walketh in the Circuit of Heaven.* *Eliphaz* ſtates this Syſtem, or the Circumference of the Heavens, as it really is environed with *Caligo* and thick Clouds; and there the Heavens make their Circuit, as will be ſhewed below, and he places God's Reſidence above theſe; and then ſuppo-

supposing *Job* a Man ignorant of the Power of God, as the Heathens pretended to be, makes him say, How doth God know? can he judge through the dark Cloud? thick Clouds are a Covering to him, that he seeth not, &c. And the next and last is, *Jer.* xxiii. 23, 24. Upon a Notion, that God was departed from the Earth, had ceased to interpose in the Manner he did formerly in their Deliverances, could not see their Actions at that Distance, and that *Baal* (of whom hereafter) was present every where, saw and did every thing; upon these Dreams they thought to divert the People from God to *Baal:* As Ezek. ix. 9. — *For they say, the* Lord *hath forsaken the Earth, and the* Lord *seeth not.* So *Jer.* is directed to say, — *Am I a God at hand, and not a God afar off? can any hide himself in secret Places, that I shall not see him? saith the* Lord. *Do not I fill Heaven and Earth? saith the* Lord. The first Expression of this Kind is, Gen. xiv. 19. — *The most high God, Possessor of Heaven and Earth.* What is Heaven and Earth? Space, or Matter created? Are they not some Things which God created, solid Atoms of Matter; those of Earth adhering in Bodies or dense Fluids; those of the Heaven in Orbs, Darkness, Fire,

Light, Clouds? &c. Exod. xxiv. 10. *And* עצם *the Substance of the Heavens for Clearness.* Thus he filled, and by filling formed this Dimension, and this includes what the Heathens took for their God: But this is not all, as the Heavens or Light was, and is an Agent, and pervaded the Pores of all Things, and so filled the Intervals between the Atoms, even of the Earth, and was God's Vice-Roy or Deputy, he claims it as one of his Attributes. God is called Fire, the Father of Light, Christ the Light, and the Holy Ghost the Spirit; not only as these Things are used for Representations of them, but as they are his Agents; so their Substances, their Actions, their Glory His, though created and material; they are also spoken of by way of Claim, in as strong Terms as if they were himself, or Attributes of his, which is the same. And so even of what they render Clouds; his Strength is in the Clouds, so the Earth is full of the Knowledge, Goodness, &c. of the Lord. Not content with the Evidence in God's Word, that he exists, and is possessed of his Attributes, as *David* says, *Psa.* xciii. 5. *vulg.* 112. *He dwelleth in the Height, and respects the humble Things in Heaven and Earth,* they attempt to give us an Idea,

by

by Philosophy, of something that is not Space, but constitutes Space (I suppose he means by possessing it) in him (I suppose he means in this Substance) are contained and moved all Things; but without mutual Passion, God suffers nothing from the Motions of Bodies, nor do they suffer any Resistance from the Omnipresence (I suppose he means from the Substance) of God; one might make strange Deductions from these and some others of his Positions. Every Atom is a solid Substance, and of some sorts of them are Compounds or Solids of Substances; of other Sorts, gross Fluids of Substances; and of another sort in Grains, Spirit of Substances; and of the same sort loose, the subtlest fluid Fire, and Light of Substances; of the last sort there is a created fluid Substance in, and by which the Orbs move, which the first Heathens knew to be a Machine composed of three Parts, yet took it for their God; and to which, the later Heathens, from whom we have our Language, gave the Attributes of te rnal, Infinite, all Eye, all Hand, &c. In Scripture God claims the Machine, and all the Attributes the Heathens then gave to it, to himself, and we borrow those Words to convey Ideas of the Personality:

Whe-

Whether he took some of these Words from Scripture, or from the later Heathens, tho' they in some respects, express the Manner of the Existence of the God of the Heathens, as *Clem. Alex.* &c. "But let me not pass by the *Stoicks*, who say that God pervades all Matter, be it never so vile and abject; who openly disgrace their own Philosophy. *P.* 43. But they indeed say, that God pervades the Essence of all Things; but we say, that he is only the Maker, and this by his Word." That does not make it follow, that these Attributes express the Manner of the Existence of God, any more than they express him to be a framed Machine, nor do they any Way favour this Notion of Space; Indeed there were some Atheists among the later Heathens, from whom these Notions of Space and Powers in Bodies to move in it were taken, but they are not well cited; and I am afraid this infinite Space will prove a Child of *Satan*, and only father'd upon God; and if they had not produced this, we had had no Philosophy, nor no Philosophers. I see not that God intended to give us any Idea of his Substance, Dimension, or Figure; but when they rival'd him with his Creatures, upon account of their Presence, and his Distance, he says,

shall

shall not I who have produced from nothing Substances contiguous, and so continuous, which by their Solidity fill, and so constitute Heaven and Earth; and who have given Dominion to the Heavens, be able to keep my Sovereignty over them? or in such like Comparisons, shall not I who made the Eye, see, &c. As Motion has some Relation to Substances, and as 'tis the chief, if not the only Business of Philosophers to consider, I expected this Substance should have constituted Motion; but they have so contrived Matters, that it cannot move; so that Affair is left to Chance and occult Qualities; palliating infinite Motion with a timeless Projection, which I am afraid were taken from Men of less Knowledge and more Wickedness, than the Heathens had: And tho' he says these Thoughts of his were the Thoughts of the Antients, these Texts produced were not upon the Point in Issue; when the inspired Men addressed themselves to God, as cited above and repeated, 1 *Kings* viii. 39, 49. *Then hear thou in Heaven thy dwelling Place.* 2 Chron. vi. 21. *Hear thou from thy dwelling Place, from Heaven.* And as the Heathen made their God a Power in the Heavens or Air, to distinguish his Residence from the material Heaven,

Heaven, they frequently use proper Words. *Deut.* xxvi. 15. *Look down from thy holy Habitation from Heaven.* 2 Chron. xxx. 27. *And their Voice was heard, and their Prayer came up to his holy dwelling Place,* (Heb. *the Habitation of his Holiness*) *even unto Heaven.* Pſal. xx. 6.— *He will hear him from his holy Heaven,* (Heb. *from the Heaven of his Holiness.*) Iſa. lxiii. 15. *Look down from Heaven, and behold from the Habitation of thy Holiness, and of thy Glory.* Zech. ii. 13. *For he is raiſed up out of his holy Habitation* (Heb. *the Habitation of his Holiness.*) To this the Holy of Holies was an Alluſion. Pſal. cxxxii. 5. *Until I find out a Place for the Lord, an Habitation for the mighty God of Jacob.* And moſt expreſsly Pſal lxviii. 5. *Exalt him that rideth* [the Charioteer, Driver, Governor, Preſider] בערבית *upon the Heavens* [in the Mixture] ביה *in the Eſſence his Name,* or, of his Place or Subſtance. Eſd. viii. 20. *O LORD, thou that dwelleth in Everlaſtingneſs.* And ſince, *Our Father which art in Heaven;* and when ſpeaking of his Power, *Micah* i. 3. *For behold Jehovah cometh forth from his Place.* Tho' it appears by the Scripture, as it is underſtood, that this Attempt to found a Deſcription

scription of the Manner of the Existence of God, and of infinite Space, is without any Foundation; when 'tis shewed which are the proper Attributes of God, and which those claimed for his Agents. there will be no Pretence left. But having no Business with, nor no Occasion either for infinite or finite Space, as I said, the solid Atoms of Matter being all contiguous, and so continuous, and the smallest Order less than our Conception can reach, we shall proceed upon the created Matter call'd Heavens, and shew that the Scripture is very express, that this System is full of created solid Matter, *M.* תבל *Tebel,* 'The World,' *C.* 'the habitable World, *Syr.* the Universe.' As the Word בל or בול is a conditional Name of all, or Part of the Heavens, and signifies the Mixer, or Mixture which flows, or descends to the Centre, and is us'd in the Religion of the Heathens for a God, and has several other Significations as Attributes, and is found with single Letters prefixed, as ת. ב. י. *&c.* which no Rules of Grammar will support, and if they should, they would not alter the general Sense of the Word (and also has other Words prefixed and joined to it, of which hereafter) by which it appears they, as
many

many of the Words the Heathens us'd in their philosophical Religion, are compounded Words, and where the last Letter of the first, and the first of the second Word are the same, but one is writ, as תבל from תבה a Vessel or Ark, a Place for all Creatures, except Fishes to live in, and בל or בלל; and תבל is us'd, *Lev.* xxi. 20. for the transparent Sphere of the Eye, with opake Spots in it; and נבל of נבב a concave Thing, a Sphere, and בל; and יבל of יבב to cry out, howl, and בל, &c. *Job* xxxiv. 13. *who set in Order the Earth for him, who gave him Power over the Earth, and who formed the whole Globe.* Psal. xc. 2. *And thou formed the Earth and the Globe, or Sphere.* Job xxxvii. 12. *On the Surface of the Sphere of the Earth.* Psal. l. 12. *The Sphere is mine, and its Fulness.* Ibid. lxxxix. 12. *Thine are the Heavens, and thine is the Earth; the Sphere and its Fulness; thou didst form them.* Here Fulness is expressive of the Solidity of the Atoms, or Parts of a Fluid; and founded is lying or pouring them one upon another; this shews how God has fill'd the Heavens, by the Face of this being joined to the Face of the Earth: And because Men live upon

upon the Earth, tho' in this, some have taken it, or it has been sometimes used for the Earth; but here it is put in Distinction, and all the rest accord, and all Nature will shew it is true; most particularly the Actions of the Firmament.

No Comparison can be made between created Matter and God; Number, Extension, Duration, Mechanism, Impulse, Motion, &c. have Relation to him, as depending on him, but none to raise any Idea of the Manner of his Existence or Action, otherwise than as they shew his Wisdom, Power, and Goodness to his intelligent Creatures: The only natural Means we have of coming at any Image of him is in ourselves, that Spark which diminutively exists like him in each of us, and has a Power of imitating him in some of his Actions or Attributes, which Matter has not. God order'd his Prophets to make Similitudes, *Hos.* xii. 11. *And I spake by the Prophets, and I multiplied Visions, and by the Hands of the Prophets* אדמה, *I gave Similitudes:* But so far from allowing others to give us Definitions of him, he has forbid the making or using of Similitudes, and shewed it impossible to make any, *Isa.* xl. 18.

To

To what will ye liken God! or what Likeness will ye equal unto him? Ibid. lxvi. 5. *To what will ye liken me, and make me equal? and compare me I that we may be like.* The Heathens never pretended to give any Definition, or to raise any Idea of God, as many of them own, collected in *Girald. de Deis Gent. &c.* " Among others *Plato*, as *Apuleius* interprets God is Incorporeal, Ineffable, Indiscribable.—For *Plato* saith in *Parmenides*, that no Name can be given God, that he cannot be defined, he cannot be comprehended, that he does not fall under the Cognizance of our Senses, nor can any Idea be formed of him; wherefore he is indiscribable, ineffable, incomprehensible, and uncognizable by any Being." 'Tis no Wonder that those who have mistaken *Aratus*'s *Jove* (the Air) for God, and that that *Jove* constituted an infinite Vacuum, should find no Room for a Christ.

Since the Words import, that God gave these things an Essence or Existence; as there may be several Sorts of Essences, Existences, or Manners of Being, we are next to consider the Manner of their Existence, " M. את *At*, denoting the very Substance of a Thing, B. C.—Particle that
is

is not divisible, an *Atom. More Par.* I. *cap.* 73. *Voss. Ibid. &c.* Democritus he thought, that Atoms were the Principles of all Things, by whose mutual Contact and interweaving, during their Motion, every thing was generated. *Ibid. &c.*—An Element is that of which any thing is first compounded, so that itself be in it, and specifically be indivisible into any other Species.—They call the Elements of Bodies, those Particles that are the last into which the Bodies are divided, the Bodies no longer differing in Kind;—*Galen* and others,— Naturally the first and most simple Parts, and which cannot be resolved into any other. B. C. *Ibid.* יסוד—Hence with the Naturalists, an Element is the first Principle of all natural Things;" lately called the Impenetrability of Bodies. This in general was never disputed, and for any thing I know, it agrees with the latest Definition, that—Matter is a Heap of Substances—extended—its Parts distinct Substances, ununited and independent on each other. They pretend to say, they know not what is the Substance of any thing whatever — and that they know not by any Sense or reflex Act, the inward Substances; and I cannot inform them any farther, than that God made each of these Atoms or Substances exist in manner of a Solid, terminating at its Surface; and though they say they know not what any one of them is, that is only to blind you when they tell you they know not the Substance of God; they and we know these Substances here are impenetrable and possess Space, and so are; but neither they, nor we know any thing of the Substance of God, or how he bees. If they had aimed at Truth, and laid this down, as I think they intend it should be taken, they would have said, we know as much, or we know no more of the Substance, or Manner of the Existence of the Substance of this Matter, than we know of the Substance of God, or the Manner of the Existence of the Substance of God; and then something might have been offered to determine the Assertion. I think they say, that the Essence or Substance of all Matter is the same, and I see not how there can be any Degrees of Solidity; if there be not, there can be no other Difference among those Atoms or Substances, but in Figure and Size; and a Difference there must be, because they, when loose or unformed, had different Names. The Atoms of the Heavens are not Atoms of the Earth, nor the Atoms of the Earth, Atoms of the Heavens, nor the Atoms of Creatures,

called

called עפר מן האדמה Atoms of Man, for whose Body those of all the other Creatures were created, Atoms of either Heavens or Earth; and these three Names appear to be only a Distinction of Genus, for each of them must have a Distinction of Species, as in those of Earth, Stone, Metals, Water, &c. The *Rabbies*, and I think almost all Writers, in Effect allowed, that Atoms, however disguised by dissolving a Body of them, putting them into new Combinations by Fire, or, &c. always retained their Figures and Sizes, and were capable of being reformed into their first Order. This in many Cases admits of Demonstration. " *C.* יסד First Principles, Elements—*Chald.* Every Element returns to its proper Element." God by his Power supports or continues the Existence of every Atom which exists; and if the Motions, or Actions, or Effects of Matter, or what we call Nature be mechanical, and arose from the Disposition of those Atoms, and from their being once put into Motion, and be maintained by the Numbers, Sizes and Figures of those Atoms; supporting their Substances, and Figures, supports their Power of acting naturally or mechanically. Indeed the Rubbish Writings of the latest Heathens shew us, that they were

mad

mad with Notions of Tranfmigration and Tranfmutation, and metamorphofing of Souls, Bodies, and inanimate Matter (whether effentially or apparently I am uncertain) into I cannot tell what, no more than I can tell how nor why; and it appears that fome of them had Accefs to the divine Writings, and other Antient Books; and it appears that in many Points they underftood them, and that the wifeft of them laid down Pofitions, that the Atoms of each Sort differed in Figure and Size, nay even pretended to give us the different Figures, and comparative Sizes of thofe Atoms; which fhews it impoffible, without altering their Figures or Sizes, to change any Clafs of them, from one into another kind of Matter, fuch as another Clafs of Atoms were framed to conftitute: Yet whether they were afraid of the People, or whether they feared the People would deftroy their Works if they did not allow them their Whims, I know not; but we find that they, even in Contradiction to themfelves, without giving us any Account how any fuch Change could be made, fometimes threw in a Dafh of that Leaven; an evil Opinion once produced, is fcarce ever deftroyed: But this has but barely fubfifted among a few *Roficrucians*;

yet

MOSES's *Principia.*

yet as far as I can judge there has been a Defign, by Neceffity, to make fome of their Schemes lefs inconfiftent, of reftoring it; I hope the Defigner will become the firft Example.

Some pretend that thefe Atoms of Matter are infinitely divifible; if any Agent in Nature performed that, it would put an end to all Oeconomy in this Syftem immediately: But this is only to raife a Duft to cover fome Defects in their blind Syftem, that fmall Orbs can give immenfe Quantities of Light continually without Supply, or any confiderable Diminution; and fo thefe Atoms are only divifible in their Heads: I dare fay they will never offer to give us any intelligible Account of this, or ever fhew us any Evidence.

They alfo tell us a dark Story, that there is fome Thing or Caufe, whether material or immaterial they fay not, lodges within the Surfaces of thefe folid Atoms, fo that each requires all other Atoms to come to it; and as they happen to join in Alliances, and fo be ftrongeft in Quantity or Numbers, Diftances confidered, though ever fo immenfe, others obey; or that each of thofe folid impenetrable Atoms continually fends out fmaller Bodies or Spirits, to fetch in all other Atoms to it; and that they

prevail,

prevail, or are prevailed upon in some such Proportion, or that each has an Inclination to meet or follow all others; and that this Inclination, at the most immense Distances, is more exactly determined, than any Mathematician can by Numbers or Measure; or any Judge can determine a Cause, by such Proportions. Upon another Occasion these Substances cannot think, or are not capable of being made to think; but this sort of Work is surely more difficult than thinking; these are Powers, which were never by any Man supposed to be communicable to either Man or Angel. The Devils became what they are by some such Imagination, and they seduced Man by such a Suggestion; and they have since supported their Dominion, by suggesting and making Men believe for many Ages, that there were such Powers in the Fluids of Airs or Heavens; and now by suggesting, as it was foretold they would, when they were cast out of the Air, that there are such in the Atoms of the Earth, and other Solids. The Heathens took that in which many Powers did exist, and in which they imagined some such Powers to exist, to be their God. Our Philosophers, for so they call themselves, when they come to speak of their God, make him a Substance,

stance, and so are forced to make it infinite; because they say upon that Occasion, Power without Substance cannot subsist: Did they discover by this sort of natural Philosophy, to wit, Attraction or Gravity, that the Substance of God must be infinite, because his Virtue and Power cannot subsist, where his Substance does not subsist? On which side is the Compliment? If these Powers be ascribed to the Substance of each Atom of solid Matter, is it not more than they allow to the Substance of God? Is there any thing but infinite Power, which shews the God? Is not even infinite Wisdom a Power of viewing, considering, judging, and acting justly or perfectly? If these Words, *Power without Substance cannot subsist*, were applied to an Atom, or an Orb of Atoms, how would it be understood? Would it mean, that they had no Power of Action beyond their respective Surfaces? nor could emit either Bodies, or Spirits, or Virtues, which could move or influence other Atoms, or Bodies at Distance, either in Fluids, or what they call Space, to come to them? And if an Atom cannot think, nor is acted upon by other Matter mechanically, how can it either move itself, or know the Proportions there is in other Parcels of Matter, at immense Distances, and the Proportions of the Distances to steer always a proper Course?

They also tell us, that one solid Substance, or Mass of Substances, being by Chance, or any way, for they tell us not how, moving, is by pushing another capable of communicating, and that pushed is capable of accepting, and having a Power of moving eternally in a right Line impressed upon it, and with the first given Velocity, till something interrupt or abate it. They have not proved that there ever was, or is any such Space, or ever was, or is any way of proving either, except they prove that it is impossible to imagine.

They say a very small Proportion of that immense Quantity of solid Bodies, which remain fluid, are sometimes obedient to these Laws; but that the immense Remainder [Light] acts in Opposition to all their Laws; no body knows whence it comes; I think they say the Matter of the Comets is the Fuel of some of it; 'tis always rambling about what they call their infinite Space, and no body knows what becomes of it.

They tell us of one other Power to move, or rather return Motion, which may be ty'd up in some Sorts of dense Solids, some

Sorts of Fluids, and some Demi-solids, which not only move themselves, but other Bodies or Fluids by way of Projection; when you have bent some Sorts of Solids, they, 'tis evident from some occult Cause, attempt continually, and when freed, with great Velocity regain their pristine Position. The second is a very unaccountable Story, though by their way of seeing, it appears to be true, that every one of a Genus of Atoms, or a Species, I know not which, but surely different from all the rest, and so not mutable, may be rolled up like a Watch-spring, and will whisk out again, which if true, quite spoils my Notion of solid Substance or Solidity: If it bends 'tis not solid, and if it has, as it must have a thousand Joints in it to be rolled up, I cannot conceive how it can spring of itself. The third which is only composed of a Mixture of some sorts of Fluids and Solids, from being warm extends itself leisurely; and a Mixture of other sorts of soft Powder, Salts and Fluids, without having an Atom ever bent that they know of, will, from the Approach of a Spark of Fire, with immense Velocity exert inconceivable Force, always contrary to their Law,

There are many of the moſt conſiderable Actions, as I ſaid of the Motion of the Fluid of Light, which they acknowledge are tranſacted in Oppoſition to all their Laws, and are Actions each directly oppoſite to other, which they refer by wholeſale to a moſt ſubtle Spirit, penetrating groſs Bodies, and lying hid in them, by whoſe Force and Action the Particles of Bodies attract one another mutually at the leaſt Diſtance, and cohere upon Contact; and electrical Bodies act at greater Diſtances as well by repelling as attracting neighbouring Bodies; and Light is emitted, reflected, and refracted, and inflected; and Bodies heated, and all Senſation is excited, emitted; and the Members of Animals are moved according to the Will, to wit, by the Vibration of this Spirit, propagated along the ſolid Capillaments of the Nerves, from the external Organs of Senſe to the Brain, and from the Brain to the Muſcles. They pretend not to have fully demonſtrated the Laws of the Actions of this Spirit, but laid down theſe Poſitions for the Philoſophers of the next Age to find them out. I dread to think what ſuch an arbitrary Spirit as this, if it ſhould fall into ill Hands, and they give Laws to it, might do; which by penetrating groſs Bodies,

and

and lying hid in them, can attract the Atoms of Bodies, and make them as close and as hard as a Diamond; that at Distances can both attract and expel; that can by other Words extract and emit Light out of the Atoms of solid Bodies, and at any Distance make it play more Tricks than a dancing Bear; that by another Word called warming solid Bodies, can remove their Atoms from each other; that by another Word called Vibration, can propagate itself, and do almost every thing relating to Sensation and Motion in Animals. They say, they judge by the Appearances of several things, but cannot reach the Agent; and they have been pleased to tell us, that a most subtle Spirit does several great Actions, but do not say they judge of it or its Actions by Appearances, nor tell us how; indeed their Agents, which they suppose do their Work, do none of them appear, nor is there any Appearance that there are any such Agents; nay the Agent which really does them does not appear, *Ecclef.* xvi. 21. *It is a Tempest which no Man can see, for the most part of his Works are hid.* I do not pretend to say, that this Extract is what they have said upon every Point, nor the different Opinions upon each Point; nor shall I attempt it more exactly;

actly; because no one can extract, no more than he can translate a Relation of Agents which never existed, and of their Actions which never were, nor could be performed, and so cannot be understood. If I were to offer any thing of my own I should be afraid to say these Things were once believed, because hereafter it may derogate from the Veracity of any Author; but as 'tis to be founded upon Scripture, my Reputation will not be of Benefit nor Damage to the Design. Destroying any one of these Positions, destroys all the rest; and will prove, that when they had once imagined one thing, they have been only forced to make another Supposition to answer that, and so on: Indeed the best way will be by proving there are real Powers, which need no such Suppositions; neither Space to move in, nor occult Properties to move them, nor any other of these mentioned, but such as come within the Cognizance of our Senses or Intellects. This created Matter is said to be of an orbicular Figure, a Sphere, and so must have a Center and Circumference, as *Job* xxii. 14. *And he walks upon* חוג (*V*. round the Poles; *S*. the Circuit. *Zant. Pag*. the Line which goes round the Heavens,) *the Circulation*, and so circular Surface or *Circumference*

cumference of the Heavens. The Word הוג is also used upon the Occasion of appointing Statutes, for something to act upon the Surface of the Sphere of Waters, before the Earth was formed, Job xxvi. 10. *He has described a Circle upon the Surface of the Waters.* And upon Occasion of forming the loose Atoms, of which the Earth was made into a Circle or Sphere, which loose Matter the Translators have mistaken for the Deep, Prov. viii. 27. *When he described a Circle upon the Surface of* תהום *the Chaos* † (loose Atoms;) and 'tis also used for the Surface of the Shell, or Sphere of this Globe, the Earth. Isa. xl. 22.—*Upon the Circle of the Earth,*—but as you will see, 'tis for the Sphere, in which it makes its annual Course. And also the Word תבל which has been cited to shew that all Matter is contiguous, has always been taken to signify a round Figure or Sphere, Job xxxiv. 13. *Who gave him Power over the Earth, and who formed* תבל כלה *the whole Sphere?* Jer. x. 12. *Who made the Earth by his Power:* מכין *framing* (preparing, disposing, and so making a Machine of) תבל *the Sphere*

† *i. e.* formed the Chaos into a Sphere, or spherical Shape.

by

by his Wisdom, and by his Understanding stretching out the Heavens.

Though the Matter of the Heavens be immeasurable, by any Means in our Power, as Prov. xxv. 3. *Of the Airs for Height, and of the Earth for Depth, and of the Heart of Kings* (i. e. *The Eternal Three*) *there is no searching out.* Job xxiii. 11. *Does not his Height terrify you? — Has not God made high the Heavens? And behold the Heads of the Stars, how high they are.* — xxxv. 5. *Look to the Heavens, and see; and behold* שחקים (the Airs in Conflict) *the Æthers, they are too high for thee.* Jer. xxxi. 37. *If the Heavens can be measured.* 2 Esdr. vi. 6. *Before the Heights of the Airs were lifted up.* Yet that Fluid Matter is finite, as well as the solid Matter of the Earth, and has circumferential Limits or Extremities. Besides what has been said of the Contiguity of the Atoms of this Matter, and the Rotundity of the whole, *David* speaking of the *Shemosh*, which is press'd to, melted at, and flows from the Sun, and which they have translated Sun (of which in its Place) Psal. xix. 4. *Their Line is gone out through all the Earth, and their Words to the Extremity of the Sphere :*—v. 7. *Its going out is from one Extreme of the Heavens, and its Revo-*

Revolution upon (or at) their other Extreme, and there is nothing hid from the Heat thereof. Here the Sides of the Matter of the Heavens, next the Sides of the Orb of the Sun, are put in Opposition, and so that Matter made a Sphere; and as this reaches all the Universe, we are sure the fixed Stars are not Suns; and though the Matter of the Heavens be mixed between the Atoms of all other things, yet they are said properly to have Extremities from the Sides of the Orb of the Sun in the Center, or from the Sides of this Globe of the Earth. As we are placed between the Heavens and the Earth, in the Heavens tho' upon the Earth, this Face of the Heavens is called an Extremity or Side, and that Part at the end of each Hemisphere or Horizon, or that Part on the opposite Side of this Globe, is called the other Side or Extremity of the Heavens; as it is said of the Extremies or Ends of the Earth; which has made People imagine the Prophets had described the Earth as a Flat. Isa. xiii. 5. *From the Extremity of the Heaven, or Air.* Neh. i. 9. *Cast out to the Extremity of Heaven.* Deut. iv. 32. *From one Extremity of the Heaven, to the other Extremity of Heaven.* Jer. xlix. 36. *The four Extremities of Heaven.* The Situation of the Heavens being in this
Figure,

Figure, this Orb included in them, and ſo they next above us; and though finite, ſo extenſive, that we cannot ſee through them, nor have any Idea of what is beyond them, are for that Reaſon, and no other, according to the modern way of reaſoning, infinite. Indeed the antient Heathens meant nothing elſe by infinite but a Circle, or the circular Motion of the Matter of the Heavens, which they repreſented by a Serpent turning its Tail into its Mouth: The later Heathens had other Pretences, becauſe they ſaw them poſſeſſed of Powers next to infinite, and knew not when, nor how they came by them. I ſay, though we are in one Extremity of them, or in one Face of them, as Face ſignifies *the fore Part of any Thing*, and moſt properly ſo of a Fluid; yet we are forced to ſpeak as if we were out of them; for when we ſay to, or towards, or into the Heavens, we only mean further up or into it, as Exod. ix. 8. *Sprinkle it towards the Heaven*; or when we ſay out of it, Exod. xvi. 4. *Bread from Heaven.* Joſ. x. 11. *Great Stones from Heaven.* 2 Kings i. 10. *Let Fire come down from Heaven.* Iſa. lv, 10. *Rain and Snow from Heaven*; only mean to this Extremity or Face, or to the Face of

the

the Earth; and becaufe of the uncertainty of the Diftance fuch things are faid to come, it raifes fuch an Idea as *M.* gives of the Adverb רחוק *a remote Place far off or at a long Diftance.* Thus the Prophets and we fpeak of Matter; but when the Prophets fpoke of Angels, Beings of another Nature, or of God, they can fay nothing that we can comprehend of that, but that he is the moft High, his Dwelling is above the Heavens, or in a Heaven with fome Characteriftick, which diftinguifhes it from thofe created. And I muft for the prefent hint, that tho' neither Antients, nor Moderns were able to make any tolerable Computations of Diftances of Bodies in them; yet, though thofe Diftances be immeafurable, we may make Eftimates vaftly beyond their Extents, even as well as we may of that of the Earth, or any of the other Orbs; and I may fome time be able to fhew, that the Moderns have fwell'd the Dimenfions vaftly beyond thofe of the Antients, without any further Light, but only to make their Notions of Attraction or Gravity lefs inconfiftent, made the Diftance to the Orbs of the Stars vaftly longer, and fo the Circle, in which thofe Orbs are, vaftly greater, for fear they, the Orbs of the Stars, fhould attract or gravitate to each other, *&c.*

but they never tell you their Motives, but yet tell you truly, that they cannot underſtand why the material Heavens ſhould be ſo high, either as they have made them, or as the Antients made them for the Service of this Orb, or laſtly of Man; becauſe they have no Notion of the Mechaniſm of them, nor what Diſtance from the Center to the Circumference is neceſſary for changing the Condition alternately, and thereby producing the Circulation of that which circulates all other Things; nor of what Uſe the Orbs of the Stars, either viſible or inviſible, may be in that, beſides others. And for want of this Knowledge, or becauſe they are ignorant of any Service they can be in this Syſtem, as they had contrived it, they will make new Species of Creatures, new Suns, new Spaces, and new Worlds for them; and they have the Front to tell you, this is for the Glory of God; 'tis true if they mean their own God; nay they will ſay any Thing at preſent, of the true God, if you will but allow the Scripture either imperfect by being unintelligible, or by being too ſhort, or to be falſe in ſaying Things were made at the Time when, or for the Uſes which they were not made, or in any other Point; and that for the future you are to be governed

verned by them. And many who might know, and pretend to believe the Scriptures, which are sufficient for Philosophy as well as for Salvation, are caught in this Snare.

While they dream'd of Waters above the Heavens, they made שמים a compound Word of שם *there*, and מים *Waters*. This Mistake is set right, and 'tis shew'd that those Waters were only above the Airs in the Abyss, when the Shell of the Earth was in forming, and שמים *Abr. Ezra* says, "is a Dual of שם, *i.e.* two Places; whereby the Heavens are taken for the two Poles." This is also explain'd in my first Part. It was at first in two Places within the Sphere of the Earth, and without; or, perhaps after the Air in the Abyss was brought up, it may be plural from the two opposite Conditions, one Part still ascending, and one descending; one acceding, and one receding, exclusive of the third Part in the Condition and Action of Fire; (of which hereafter) and שמים to speak generally, are the Atoms of every Thing in this material System, except Atoms of the Earth, Water, Vegetables, and imbodied Animals, and those Vapours Parts of them, which swim in the Heavens, and make Part of the Atmosphere of the Earth. To speak particularly, that dry Fluid which

extends

extends from the Earth, or more properly now from the Sun, to its Extremities beyond the fixed Stars, which then contain'd in it the Atoms, which conftitute the Orbs of the Sun, Planets, Moons, and Stars, 'tis likely difpers'd thofe for each in Spheres at proper Diftances, as thofe of the Earth and Water were; and fince the Earth, and thofe celeftial Bodies were form'd, fill'd all between the Bodies, and all the Pores of all Bodies and Fluids included in it.

By the Power of God, the Matter of the Heavens and the Earth was created and exifts; and by what I can gather from Scripture and Obfervations, in an immenfe, tho' determinate Number of Units, and that each of them exifts after a Manner we call Solidity, whereby each Unit is poffefs'd of its Part of Quantity or Space defcribed by its Figure, and limited by its Dimenfion or Extent, and thereby is impervious and inflexible; has no other Qualities, Virtues, nor Powers, nor no Inclinations, neither external nor internal, appurtenant, infus'd, or annex'd to it, nor iffuing out of it, but is wholly paffive, and liable to external Accidents, fuch as refting upon one another, being moved by one another, and being refifted by one another, and being rubb'd againft one another

ther in passing by one another, adhering to one another, and being dissolved or divided from one another, and changing Places with one another.

Those Units adhering in certain large Masses, in certain Forms, are call'd Solids, by certain Names, as the Earth, the Moon, &c. and the Parts of the Earth, as Stone, Gold, Silver, &c. those which do not adhere, or but seldom, save only in very small Masses or Grains, are call'd Fluids, and are of several distinct Species, as Water, Air, &c. and Units dispers'd in them, which when collected form Vegetables and Animals; every Mass when form'd, and every Mass now, has a certain Number of those Units or Parts in it, and the several Parts of each Species of Fluids have the rest; each Species hath its determinate Number, and there is the same Number in all now, as was created.

Tho' the *Genus* of Atoms constitutes the Heavens a Fluid, or so that they are kept fluid, the Word does not express their being a Fluid, but implies it; as they are passive, the Place, the Substance; and as they are active, the Name, the Agent of the Heavens, or Fire, or of the Heavens in the Action of Fire. *M.* שׁם with a Point on the left Hand, signifies, Position,

שׂום and שָׂם to set, to set to, to dispose, to constitute. *Hiphil* הֵשִׂים *the same*, to set, to set to, repose, impose, dispose, place, *Hophal*, to be set, &c.—שׂוּמָה something set or placed, or hidden, or set by, a Treasure. תְּשׂוּמָה a Position, Society, Communication, *ibid. Chald.* and *Syr. &c.* so שָׂמִים the Places, the Placers, the Shifters, the Disposers. The Heavens were at first the Scene, the Place of Atoms for Things, and for them to act upon those Atoms to form those Things; soon after they were, and are now the Theatre for the Sun, and the *Shemosh*, the other Celestial Bodies, and their Stars; the Earth, all Creatures, (Fish excepted) and all for Man; and as Agents, the Formers, the Disposers, the Placers, the Shifters of all; the Producers, Augmenters, &c. of some. The Mistake of their Derivation, introduced the Distinction by Pointing, and the שֶׁמֶשׁ another Name for this Matter, which will be consider'd in Course, is singular; a compound Word of שָׁם and מֻשׁ the Heaven receding, issuing outward from the Sun: They translate this the Sun, the Name of a Star, but we have lost the Signification of the Word Star, as well that as all the rest; for Star is neither the Orb, nor the Matter acting in it, or upon it, but a Flux of the Atoms of

the

the Heavens from the Orb in ſtreight Lines, till it be reflected or reverted; and by this Motion becomes an Agent, and is by God appointed a Ruler, a Governor, a Diſpoſer of the Inſtrument of Motion, and of the Things moved, of which in their Courſe; and in the *Chaldee*, and other Languages, is us'd for a cheif Servant, a Miniſter, ſo for Miniſtring. In the *Arabian* Tongue שמש has all the ſame Significations of the Flux of Light iſſuing from the Sun, of Miniſter, &c. "and *M.* ſays by a *Metaphor, Chald.* to ſtand, to inhabit, to cohabit, to lye with, to have an Affair with, to make uſe of. But it needs no Metaphor. In my Eſſay to a natural Hiſtory of the Bible, I have ſhewed, that the Tower of *Babel* was for an Altar to the Heavens; and tho' I have taken the Word שם as it ſtands for Name in the Tranſlation, by the Parity of Uſage, which will hereafter appear between the Thing repreſented, and Repreſentative, it may be an Image of the Heavens; and I have ſhew'd, that Religion was the Cauſe of the Diſperſion. You have heard of the Wickedneſs of the Natives of *Canaan*, and ſeveral Hints about it, that is, about their falſe Religion, I muſt ſhew you their Gods, and the Articles of their Creed, each in its Place; becauſe they not only explain moſt of the Expreſſions,

ons, which seem difficult in the Bible, but also the Philosophy of that People, and of those Times. They had a Temple to the Heavens, mentioned *Numb.* xxxiii. 49. *Jos.* xii. 3. בית הישמת. *Jos.* xiii. 20. בית חישמות. These Words are terminated as the Natives express'd them, and not terminated as the *Hebrew*, but like other of their Words, as *Jos.* xix. 8. and 44. בעלת and *Jos.* xv. 24. בעלות which the *Hebrews* write בעלים, or as the same Word when us'd for Names, *Gen.* ii. 20. שמות. The Rabbies have left us generally every Interpretation, but the chief or true one, בית הישמות *Beth-Jesimoth*, or *Bethsimuth*, the House of Desolations, from *Beth*, and *Shemim*, or the House of Repositaries from *Beth* and *Shem*, or the House of Names from *Beth* and *Shem*. Whether the Servants of God gave the Epithet of שם the Name, without any Addition, to express the Excellency of the material Machine of the Heavens, which was to be Supreme, and govern all other created Matter; or the Heathens gave it that Epithet when they had taken it for a God; 'tis plain upon that Abuse, God not only reclaims, or claims all the other Attributes of Power in the Heavens given by him, and abus'd by them to himself, as his, but

also

also that Epithet; so that it is often us'd, joined with his, or my, and frequently with יהוה and with Christ; and this is a general Name, whether it be taken as expressive of the Substance which is subdivided into three Parts, or descriptive Names, which each express its Condition, as Fire, Light, and Spirit; or of their Office, as Placers or Disposers of other Things; or they are the Root of Names of other Matter, by Reason of the Dignity of their Office in Matter; or as the Heathens took them for a God, or Gods; or it be expressive of the Names, which are also Generals, as *Moloch*, *Malcom*, &c. or of the Names of *Gad*, the Troop or the Hosts, the particular Powers or Effects of their Operations as a Machine, and were each taken for an Attribute or distinct Deity, will be shew'd in their respective Places, makes no Difference.

Though I shall need no Evidence to support or explain the Scripture, as they have introduced a God from a Heathen to make Space, we must shew what this *Jupiter* was from the Heathens, and that will at the same Time shew, that this Worship of the Heavens was almost universal.

Kirch. ob. Pamph. &c. " Therefore the
Egyptians

Egyptians signifying the immense Obscurity of the Divine Nature, said that Darkness which is placed beyond all Knowledge, was the first Principle of all Things. Thence that they might honour it in proper Places, they performed their sacred Rites and Ceremonies in subterraneous Cells, which they called sacred Cisterns, and thrice invoked unknown Darkness, that is the Triform God infolded within three separate Cells, which *Damascius* a *Platonic* amongst others, particularly takes Notice of.—They reckon Darkness the first Principle, which was placed beyond all Knowledge; they thrice invoke Incomprehensible Darkness."

Gyrald. &c. " We read of Night being worshipped, whom *Aratus* the Poet calls *Archaian Nucta*, that is ancient Night) (or as I would render it Night, the Principal, Chief, or Capital) as his Interpreter saith: She had sacred Rites paid her according to *Hesiod*'s Opinion, because she was the antientest of the Gods. And to omit for the present what *Orpheus* and *Hesiod* deliver, one of whom asserts Night to be the Daughter of *Chaos*, and the Mother of Light and Day: The other sings a Hymn made to her, with Incense, and calls her the Mother of Gods and Men, and the Genesis or Origin of all Things."

Ibid.

Ibid. "The *Atlantides*, a People of *Africa*, &c. say, that first of all the God *Ouranos*, that is, Heaven, reigned among them; that he married many Wives, by whom he had forty-five Children, particularly by *Titea* seventeen, who were called after their Mother *Titans*."

Bar. Herbert de Relig. Gent. p. 15. *Sanchoniathon*. His Words are these: "*Cælus* (i. e. the Heaven, or Air) when he received his paternal Kingdom, took the *Earth* for his Wife, and begot upon her four Sons, *Ilus*, who was called *Saturn*, *Betylus*, and *Dagon*.—"

Gyrald. p. 169. "The Souls and Heavenly Minds that preside over the Spheres of this Heaven, or Air, were called by the *Gentiles*, *Uraniæ*; that is, celestial Nymphs, whom they also term'd *Muses* and *Sirens*, as *Plato*, *Macrobius*, and others have said, and *Proclus* especially."

Voss. p. 256. "You have in an antient Inscription at *Rome* dug up from the Mount *Cælius*, these Words, COELUS, (i. e. the Heaven, or Air) THE GREAT, THE GOOD, THE ETERNAL BEING. In *Aldus* in *Grut*'s *Orthography and Inscriptions*, and which is cited by Lord *Herbert*, *Eng.* p. 88.

Spencer de Leg. Heb. p. 60. "All the *Sabaists*

Sabaists believed the World to be eternal, because according to them the Heaven is God, *Maim. Mor. Nev. p.* 422. *Ibid. Plin. Hist. lib.* 2. *c.* 1. Heaven, the eternal immense Being, &c."

Pauli Merulæ Cosm. p. 9. "*Anaximenes* was his [*Anaximander*'s] Disciple and Successor, who attributed the whole Cause of Things to the Air, which was infinite in its Nature: He neither denied the Being of the Gods, nor omitted the Mention of them, but believed the Gods to have sprung from the Air, and not the Air to have sprung from the Gods."

Gyrald. p. 9. "*Anaximenes*, the Son of *Euristatus*, and himself a *Milesian*, said, the Air was infinite, and attributed all Causes to it: According to *Augustin*, he said, the Gods were of Air; but *Cicero* writes, that he made the Air itself God, as others did the Æther."

Vossius, p. 219. "HERE, (Ηρη) *Juno*, with the *Greeks* is the Element of Air, and corresponds with *Dis*, that is, *Jove*, or the Æther."

Gyrald. ib. p. 110. "*Sanchoniathon* in the *Phœnician* Theology reckons *Belus* among the Sons of *Saturn*, and asserts him to be *Jupiter*; the same as *Eusebius* doth.'

Voss. l. 2. *p.* 194. "*Belus* was *Cælus* (*i. e.* the Air) or *Jupiter*." Bibl.

Bibl. Max. Patr. Tom. 4. *p.* 46. "The *Persians* and all the *Magi* that inhabit the Borders of the *Persian* Kingdom, hold Fire in cheif, and think that it ought to be preferred before all the Elements: They therefore divide *Jupiter* into two Powers, transferring his Nature to both Sexes, and representing the Substance of Fire by the Image of a Man, and a Woman. They make the Woman with three Faces, interlacing her with monstrous Serpents.—Worshipping a Man the Driver of Oxen, they transfer his *Sacra* (Religious Solemnities) to the Power of Fire, as his Poet has delivered down to us.—Him they call *Mithras.*"

Gyrald. Ib. p. 9. "*Heraclitus,* the *Ephesian,* believed the Gods to be of Fire, as *Varro* and *Augustin* report. *Origen* said, that Fire was intelligent. *Simplicius* relates *Hippasus* the *Metapontine* to have the same Sentiments."

Vossius: "*Jupiter* was not *Cælus,* (*i. e.* the Airs) or *Uranus*; but the Sun together with *Cælus,* (or the Air.)"

Just. Lipf. v. 4. p. 184. "*Lipsius* himself and the Stoicks make him the Great God, the Prince of the rest.—Hear *Firmicus,* one of the Sect, "Oh! Sun thou best and greatest Being, who possessest the middle of Heaven, the Mind and Temperament of the World, the Cheif and Prince of all Things."

Kircher, p. 220. "*George Cedren* in his Book of the Origin of *Constantinople*, *Jupiter* was not only taken for the Creator, Virtue, and Mind of all Things, but sometimes for the Heaven or Air."

Kircher, p. 404. "That is to say, the Efficient Mind, together with the Word (the *Logos*) containing Circle within Circle, and whirling round with great Rapidity, turns back the Machine to itself: It commanded it to revolve from Beginning without a Beginning, to End without End: For it begins its Revolution always where it ended.

Ibid. Mercury, after he had shewn, in the first Chapter the Generation of the Word in part, in the 3d Chap. of *Pimander*, hath these Words: "The Holy Light is sent out, and the Elements are concreted from under the Sand by an humid Essence—And a little after: And the Heaven appeared in seven Circles, and the Gods appearing in the Figures of Stars, together with all the Forms of them, and the Deities which are in them, are intermingled with them, and the circular Conversion is bounded, the Air being put in Motion

tion by the Divine Spirit in a circular Courſe; for every Deity by a peculiar Virtue brought forth what he was commanded in his Commiſſion to do."

Gyrald. Ibid. p. 192. " But *Heraclides* of *Pontus*, affirms, the famous Oracle of *Serapis* to have been *Pluto*'s, which upon a certain *Ægyptian* King conſulting it, to know who was happier than himſelf, is reported to have returned this Anſwer:

In Chief is God, the Spirit, and the Word
Are one with him, theſe three in one Accord.

Cæl.Cal.Cag. p. 238. "Which Account tho' it be fabulous, yet doth it lead to a natural Truth: Since the *Ægyptians* call *Jupiter* a Spirit, to which the lucid and igneous Nature is an Enemy, which is not indeed the Sun itſelf, but hath ſome Affinity with the Sun. But Moiſture kills the dry and ſapleſs Faculty, and increaſes and ſtrengthens Exhalation: And from Exhalation, Wind or Spirit is concreted and blows."

Voſſius, Lib. 2. p. 347. " Where (namely in *Ethiopia*) *Jupiter* was the Ether, or the Air and Ether.—*Plutarch*—The *Ægyptians* call *Jupiter* a Spirit, to which a dry and igneous Nature is oppoſite, and an Enemy:
This

This igneous Nature is not the Sun, but hath some Affinity with the Sun; the Moisture extinguishing the excessive Dryness, encreaseth and corroborates Exhalations, by which the Spirit or Wind is fed or nourished."

Gyrald. Ibid. p. 74. " It is better to set down some Verses of *Orpheus*, which are taken from *Apuleius*.

Jove is the Spirit of all Nature's Frame,
Blows in the Wind, and blazes in the Flame;
The Deep beneath, the radiant Sun above,
The Moon's reflected Light are Parts of
Jove.

Voss. Lib. 2. p. 230. *Xenocrates* the *Chalcedonian*, and *Almeon, Stoicks*, say, " A Star is a Divine Substance composed of Æther.— *Augustine* in his 4th Book of the City of God, c. 11. The *Stoicks* say that all the Stars are Parts of *Jupiter*, that they all live and have rational Souls, and therefore without Dispute are Gods."

Selden. de Diis Syris, p.227. " The *Jews* worshipped the Heavens as the Primary Deity according to Relation. The praised Verse of *Petronius* follows:

Let him address Heaven's Ears supreme:
In-

And *Juvenal*, in his fourteenth Satyr, says of the *Jews*:

They nothing but the Clouds and Heaven adore as Deities.

So *Strabo* in his sixteenth Book teacheth from *Moses*, but falsely.

Gyraldus and *Alcmæon* of *Crotona* attributed a Divinity to the Sun, Moon, and the rest of the Stars, and also to the Soul.

Bibl. Max. Patr. Julius Firmicus of the Error of prophane Religions, *Tom.* 9. of the Creation of the World against the Philosophers. " The *Assyrians* and Part of the *Africans* will have Air to have the Pre-eminence of the Elements, and they worship it under a Figure of their own fashioning."

Gyraldus: *Diogenes Apolloniates*, another Hearer of *Anaximenes*, said, that the Air indeed was the Matter of which Things were made; but that the Air itself was indued with divine Reason, without which nothing could be made out of it. So *Augustine*, and *Simplicius* have more to the same Purpose."

Ibid. " *Uranus* [*i. e.* the Heaven, or Air] was worshipped in many Places, and that with human Sacrifices, chiefly in all *Africa* and *Lybia.*"

Vol. II.   I   *Ibid.*

Ibid. "The *Africans* worshipped *Cælestus*, who by *Lactantius* is called *Uranus.*"

Gyraldus. "The *Persians* and *Massagetes* called the Air, [Heaven] *Jupiter:* But the Sun was their greatest Deity, to whom they sacrificed Horses, *&c.*—They held Fire in chief Esteem."

Ibid. "The *Persians*, as *Strabo* reports, thought Heaven, or Air, *Jupiter*, which as *Herodotus*, and *Origen* attest, they called the Circle [Circulation] or Circuit [Rotundity] of the Air."

Ibid. "*Jupiter* was also called by the Antients *Physicus*, that is, Physical, Natural, as *Theon* testifies, and then they interpreted him the Air."

Ibid. "We will now produce the Opinion the *Persians* had of the Gods. The *Persians* erected neither Statues nor Altars: They thought, as *Strabo* writes, the Heavens the Deity, which they took for *Jupiter*. They worshipped the Sun, whom they called *Mithras*, *&c.*

Lord *Herbert*: *Philo Byblius* from *Sanchoniathon* in *Eusebius.* "They thought this God to be the sole Governor of Heaven, Air, calling him *Baalsamen*, which in the *Phœnician* Dialect is *Lord of Heaven*, with the *Greeks* is *Jupiter.*"

Gyraldus.

Gyraldus. " The *Brachmans*, wife Men of *India*, faid, that God was Light, not fuch as the Sun, or Fire, but that Reafon by which the occult Myfteries are made manifeft to the wife, as *Origen* faith."

Vetuft. Tabulæ Ægypt. " Hence prevailed the Opinion among the *Egyptians*, that the Sun and Moon were the Eyes of *Orus*, quite oppofite to the Sacred Hiftory, in which we read, that God conftituted them the two great Luminaries in the World. As to *Jupiter*, he was no other than the World [Univerfe] or Part of the World; fo that it would be difagreeable to recount here the Teftimonies of *Orpheus*, *Empedocles*, *Arnobius*, and others. Hence Antiquity called the Sun, *Jupiter*'s Eye, and the Mind of *Jupiter*, of the Heaven, of the World.*"

Lord *Herbert.* " What the *Latins* call *Cœlum*, Heaven, the *Greeks* call Æther: The Verfe of *Ennius* fo often repeated in *Cicero* refpects this: — Behold this bright Sublime [of Heaven] which all call *Jove*."

Gyraldus. " *Cleanthes* of *Affus*, a *Stoic*, made *Æther*, the fupreme God."

* Apud Apuleium de mund. apud Plutarch. de Placit. Philof. lib. III. adverf. Gent. Macrob. lib. I. Sat. c. 21. & 19. Plutarchus, lib. III. adv. Hær.

Macrobius.

Macrobius. " But those who have more diligently searched out the Truth, say, that the *Penates* (Houshold Gods of the Heathen) are those by which we (*penitus*) inwardly breathe, by which we have our Bodies, by which we possess our Reason. They tell us, that the middle Æther is *Jupiter*; the lowermost with the Earth is *Juno*; and that the Summit, or topmost Part of the Æther is *Minerva*."

Gyraldus. " Those are called the *Cælites*, or superior Gods, which reach downward from the higher Æther to the Sun, and order the Springs [Secrets, Mysteries] of hidden Causes, and are represented without Passions. The secondary Gods are those from the Sun to the Moon, &c."

Ibid. — " For the Motion of the Air, that is, *Juno*, creates Winds.—Some have made the Winds themselves Gods, as principally *Orpheus*, who offers Hymns to them, with Frankincense, &c." with vast Numbers of Accounts from other Authors.

Lord *Herbert.* " Æther, *Jupiter*, Air, *Juno*, &c. *Sigonius*, &c. St. *Augustine* reads to *Baal* and *Astartes*; and explains it by *Jupiter* and *Juno*."

Gyraldus. " *Philo Byblius*, not the *Jew*, and *Eusebius* write, that *Jupiter* was called by the *Phenicians*, *Beelsamen*, which

Name

Name in our Tongue signifies, *The Lord of Heaven.*"

Kercher, &c. " For as *Baal* is *Jupiter*, so *Baalis*, or *Belthis*, is *Juno*, or *Venus*, to whom *Adonis* or *Thamuz*, and *Venus* or *Asteroth* are correspondent; (of which, the one is the *Beel* of the *Assyrians*, the other is their *Beltis*) to whom answer *Osiris* and *Isis*, the *Jupiter* and *Juno*, or *Venus*, of the *Egyptians*. Again, as *Baal-Samin* is *Jupiter Olympius*, so *Baalet-Samin* is *Juno Olympia*, &c."

B. C. *Sammael*. " Rabbi *Eliezer* says, *Sammael* is the chief Prince in the Heavens; and likewise the same in the Book *Zohar*, f. 28. 2."

Cælius Calig. " There is, besides, extant a certain very old Oracle of *Serapis*, of which, when *Nicocreon* King of the *Cyprians*, enquired, Which of the Gods he was, and what was his Form? he received this Answer:"

Such is my God-head, as I tell to thee:
Heav'n's starry Vault my Head, my Womb
  the Sea;
Earth is my Footstool, Æther is my Ear:
My far-enlightning Eye the Sun's bright
  Sphere.

I 3 *Gyraldus.*

Gyraldus. "*Mela Pomponius, Apis*—divinely and by heavenly Fire conceived."

Gyraldus. "*Nephelegeretes Zeus:* That is *Jupiter*, the Driver together or Collector of Clouds, from *Ageiro* and *Nephele*, because he compels the Clouds, and as some have translated it Cloud-compelling; There is frequent Mention of this in *Homer*, *Hesiod*, and the rest of the Poets: *Phurnutus* expounds it in the same Manner. There are some who will not have it derived from *Ageiro*, but rather from *Egeiro*, that is from his exciting or raising Clouds. *Lucian* makes Mention of it in *Timon?*"

Ibib. "The Stoicks for the most Part, defined God to be a divine Substance, intelligible, and igneous without Form, but who can be turned into and made like to any Form he pleases."

Ibid. "But while I am mentioning the Gods of the *Gentiles*, let me give you *Pliny's* almost ridiculous Opinion of the Gods. He in his 2d Book writes in this Manner: To seek after their Form or Figure, I look upon as a Weakness of human Nature. Whoever is God, if he is indeed any other than the Sun, and wherever he is, he is all Sense, all Eye, all Ear, all Mind, all Soul, all in himself."

Vossius.

Voſſius. " The great *Pythagoras* led the Way to *Plato* in this. For *Cælus* or *Ether* with him was God; and the Stars he judged to be the Eyes of his Deity. *Epiphanius* againſt Hereſies writes thus of this Affair.—*Pythagoras* makes God corporeal, namely the Heavens: He gives him the Sun, Moon, and the other Stars, and celeſtial Elements for Eyes, and other Members, ſuch as Man is compoſed of."

Voſſius. " *Poſidonius* in *Stobæus* — God is an intelligent and fiery Spirit, having no Form, but turning himſelf into all Forms, and aſſimulating all Things to himſelf. And before him *Zeno* in *Laertius*, God is a Spirit pervading the whole World—Spirit is a kind of Body, whence *Laertius* in *Zeno*—The Soul is a Spirit, and therefore a Body, namely a more rarified Body, and of finer Parts."

Voſſius. " For *Ariſtotle* ſaith, that the Heavens are alive. But whoever ſaid a Wheel lived becauſe it was turned round by the Wheel-wright?— He has alſo given us a ſhort Account of the Faculties he attributes to the celeſtial Soul in his Book of the Nature of the Heavens, *Sect.* 5. *Chap.* 8. We have aſſigned the Soul eſſentially to be a Soul informing the Heavens, that it is indued with an intellective Faculty, becauſe

because it ought to have Knowledge of Intelligence; it should be indued with a a Motive Faculty, because it ought to move the Orbs, and with an appetitive Faculty, because it should desire Intelligence; nor can there be Motion without Appetition or Will."

Ibid. "He leads into the Sect of the *Peripatetics* by the Arguments, that the Heaven is moved thro' its own Means, and therefore hath an internal Principle of Life and Motion."

Vossius. "*Lactantius* in his 7th Book, Chap. 2. Sometimes they so confound Things that God is the Mind of the World, and the World is the Body of God.

All art but Parts of one stupendous Whole,
Whose Body Nature is, and God the Soul.

So *Manilius*——
The World has Life and Reason steers its
  Course,
Since thro' its several Parts there moves one
  Soul,
That fashions, breathes, and animates the
  Whole.

Ibid. "*Seneca*——This Whole in which we are contained, is one, and is God, and we are his Copartners and Members.

Ibid.

Ibid. "The Opinion of *Cleanthes* pleased *Pliny, viz.* That the Sun was the Soul of the whole World, or rather the Mind; then we ought to believe him the Principal, Governor, and Deity of Nature, admiring his Works."

Ibid. "*Asconius* upon *Tully*'s 2d Oration against *Verres.* They thought that no Temples should be built to the Gods, especially since the whole World was scarce sufficient for the Sun alone, which they worshipped."

Vossius. "What the *Latins* call *Cælum* (Heaven) the *Hebrews* call *Shemim*, the *Greeks Æther*, whether it be from απ Θεειν, that is, as *Apuleius* interprets it, from its rapid Rotation, which was the Opinion of *Aristotle* in his said Book of the Heavens, and also of the Writer of the Book *of the World*, and *Apuleius* his Paraphraser: Or, as *Anaxagoras* thought, from τυ αισθεσθαι, that is, Burning, because it is kindled and ignited Matter.—Whence *Ennius* in *Thyestes*:

Behold the ignited Ether *fiery bright,*
Which to call Jupiter *all Men delight;*
Behold this great Sublime, that glows above,
Which all conspire to name, Celestial Jove.

Ibid.

Ibid. But the *Greeks* and *Romans* more usually meant Heaven by *Jupiter*; which was in Imitation of the East, and among these the *Persians*; of whom *Herodotus* thus writes in his first Book.—They call the whole Circumference of Heaven *Jupiter*.

Ibid.
Oh thou who by the Air's conversive Force,
Drives in its constant circulating Course;
Thou shining Vortex of the Heaven's vast Sphere,
Jove Dionysius, mighty Father, hear.
Of Earth and Sea thou radiating Flame,
That's chang'd through all, and yet in all the same,
All generative Sun.

Ibid. Plato in *Phædrus.* ——— *Jupiter* therefore, the great Leader or Charioteer in the Heavens, driving his rapid Chariot, proceeds first, setting and keeping all Things in Order. Him follow the Host or Assembly of Gods and Demons, marshalled into eleven Parts, [Divisions, or Columns:] *Vesta* (the Solar Fire) remains alone (or fixed) in the House of the Gods.

Ibid. &c. For, as with the *Egyptians*, so with the *Stoicks*, *Jupiter*, who physically is the Spirit, or Air, pervading all Things,

Things, is the Origin or Genesis of Souls.

Voss. &c.—Nor do these belong so much to the Parts of the World, as to its Spirit or Soul, which mingles itself throughout the whole Body of the World, and has various Names of Gods and Goddesses, according to its various Effects, &c.

Ibid. &c. Eustathius.—For, because *Jupiter* is the Etherial Air. *Aer*, and *Aetos*, as the *Greeks* call the Eagle, seem to be derived from the same Verb *Ao*, which is *to blow, breathe*, &c."

These few Hints out of vast Numbers of Volumes, which might be brought, are enow to shew, that the God of the Heathens made no Vacuum, but fills all they call Space, and the Intervals between the Atoms of other Matter, moves and produces all things; and I shall shew that God gave it those Powers for those Ends. Tho' I intend not now to explain the Names, and assign each its Office; I must Hint, that for want of settling Terms, not only the Philosophers, but the Divines, and the Atheists cite Evidence about God frequently, not to their respective Purposes. The latter Heathens attributed Life, Motion, *Mens*, *Anima*, &c. to the Part of the Heavens, in that Condition we
call

call Fire, and placed it in the Center, or in the Orb of the Sun; and Life, Motion, Power of Pervasion, Eyes, Wisdom, Intelligence, Influence, &c. to the Light, שמש, Sol, that Part of the Heavens in Motion or Circulation, from the Center to the Circumference, which not only pervades the other Parts of the Heavens, and other Fluids, but the Intervals in all Solids; which since Men judged by Appearances, has been mistaken for the Orb or Fire of the Sun; I suppose because they saw nothing shine like that: And Life, Motion, Strength, Power of moving and forming other Things, to the Spirit, Æther, &c. issuing from the utmost Circumference to the Sun, pervading or passing between the Parts of Light, and acting upon other Fluids and Solids; And all Power, &c. to *Jupiter* or the Heavens, in this Circulation. And as the Heathens call the distinct Powers, produced by this Circulation or their Effects upon Matter, Sons or Daughters of *Jupiter*, of *Uranius*, the Heavens, the Airs; and Demons, or the Princes of the Air; which the Scriptures call Angels, Ministers, Hosts of the Heavens; and as God claims them, of God, Words cited from Heathens do not always, in these Points,

ex-

express or discover the Intent of a Philosopher; and the Constructions which have been made of them, either by modern Divines, or Atheists, do not clear them sufficiently, or give them Authority enough to be taken for *Data* to build a Foundation to support a Philosophy, or Laws to govern the Universe. Nor will the Manner of reclaiming God's Sovereignty over these Powers in Scripture, give any such Idea of his Essence, as would destroy the Powers, nay Being of these material Agents, and leave room for Philosophers by their Imaginations to constitute infinite Space, and other Powers in their steads.

The Moderns finding Descriptions of this Power in the Writings of the antient *Jewish* Rabbies, think when they writ שמים they meant God, and when cited and translated, have interposed God, as "All Things are in the Power of Heaven (*i. e.* God) except the Fear of Heaven (God) *M.* says, by Synecdoche *Shemim*, Heaven, is God himself dwelling in Heaven." Indeed the *Chaldeans* called the שמים or the Power of its Operations, the *Egyptians* שמש, and the *Arabians* שמס, and almost all the World except the *Jews*, one of their Gods, as I have already shewed, and will more fully explain

plain; and the Rabbies us'd שמים for יהוה, I suppose by mistaking the meaning in God's Speech by *Daniel* to *Nebuchadnezzar*, who was doomed to live in the Fields, under the open Heaven, like a Beast, have the Heart of a Beast, eat Grass, experience the various Effects of the Operations of the Heavens, Light, Heat, Darkness, Cold, Wet, Dry, &c. for seven Seasons or Years, *Dan.* iv. 26. *from which Time thou shalt know* די שלטן שמיא *that the Heavens do rule.*" This indeed, as translated, seems giving up the Point, and yielding that the Heavens were Master, or at least, that their Name and God's was confounded: But 'tis very properly expressed, the Heavens had a limited Dominion given them only over Matter, *Gen.* i. 16. But God had reserved the Rule in the Kingdoms of Men, and in despight of the Heavens would make him sensible of it: And the Word די if it be *Hebrew*, " Signifies *Satis, enough, sufficient* — if it be *Chaldee*, is used for the *Hebrew* Word שאר *quantum, how much; quemadmodum, how or in what Manner.*" And the Word שלטן is generally put for the Power of a Viceroy or Deputy, or as derivative or limited, except in this Chapter, where it is put comparatively; and

when

when the King came to himself, he says, — *I blessed the Most High — whose Dominion is an everlasting Dominion — and he doth according to his Will, in the Army of Heaven. — I — praise, and extol, and honour the King of Heaven;* — or else they only consider the Word, as signifying Names. It seems hard to reduce this Word שם, which in many Places signifies Name, which is a Sound, or Characters of Distinction for a Thing, and so a Substitute for the Thing, to be the same as Place; but if there be no other Place in this System, but what is Things, then Place and Things are the same; and tho' שם be a general Name for Place, and Heaven be the Matter or Place which includes all; when we come to particular Things, each Atom or compound Thing possesses, each cannot be deprived of, its Space, however environed by this general Place, or however the Figure of the Compound be altered, whithersoever it be shifted; nay, as to Substance, whithersoever its Parts be dispersed. The Rabbies also confounded this Word thus used, with Words substituted by God for himself, but without any Authority or Example in Scripture: For the Name which God has so substituted, is himself, as *R. David* in *B. C. Isa.*

Isa. xvi. 21. "*And they shall know that my Name is Jehovah*—writes—It is the same as, because *I am Jehovah*, for himself is his Name, and his Name is himself." But as each of the Names God has been pleased to distinguish himself by, in Opposition, is not arbitrary, as most other Names are,-but has Reference to the Case where 'tis used; tho' we translate them God, Lord, &c. and tho' each of them by some Attribute implies that he is God, none of them can express the Manner of Being, as אדם expresses a Composition of a Sort of solid Atoms, or &c. and as most of his Names or Attributes, are Names or Attributes given by the Heathens to the Heavens, and only claimed, not for his Essence, but from them, as their Substance, Form, Motions, Actions, &c. are his. If the Heathens intended to express the Host, the Power under the Word Name, then this is a claimed Attribute, and if their Hearts who used it were right, it is right; so late, *Is it from Heaven*, (the Name) *or of Men?*

As we hinted in the first Part, besides the incomprehensible Power of God in creating this immense, tho' determinate Number of Atoms, which are capable of possessing no other Powers but Mechanism,

nism, his infinite Fore-knowledge and Wisdom will some time be seen in designing, contriving, and forming them; and there are several general Words in Scripture which have relation to the Atoms of the World, and particularly to the Atoms of the Heavens, as well before as after they were created, in contriving before, as after in establishing the Parts; as in summing up these Actions, of contriving, creating, and forming, the Adverb כן *recte*, mechanically is employed; and in other Places, such as כון מכין *M.* to make ready, prepare, settle, establish, confirm. The Heathens made a God under this Name, or כיון *Amos* v. 25. C. "כיון— *Amos* v. 25. the Name of an Idol. *Saturn.* See *De Dieu* upon the Place. *Seld.* &c. 348. *Kirch. Oed.* 1. 386.— *Rab. Macin,* the Temple built by *Solomon*—Astrology"; and one of the Columns which was set up to support the Representations of the Spheres mentioned, 1 *Kings* vii. 21. was called יכין C. *Heb.* & *Chald.* "to prepare, compare, direct, constitute, establish. *Chald.* to intend, be intent, to do any thing industriously, studiously, and with Design.—The Science of the Disposition, namely, the Celestial, that is, Astronomy: Also Affection, Quality, Constitution, *More.*

Vol. II. K *Syr.*

Syr. To put on the Nature, natural Condition of a thing, Physical Dispositions or Qualities. C. *Æthiop.* כין an Artificer, a Workman, Creator." Pf. xciii. 1. xcvi. 10. *Yea,* תבל *the Sphere* תכון *is framed, it cannot fail.* Jer. x. 12. מכין *framing the Sphere by his Wisdom,* ibid. li. 15. (V. *hath prepared.*) Pf. lxxxix. 3. *In the Heavens* תכן *hast thou established thy Truth.* ver. 6. *The Heavens shall confess* פלאך *thy surprising Work,* O Jehovah. Prov. xiii. 19. *He has framed* (S. *prepared*) *the Heavens with Understanding.* Ibid. viii. 27. *When* הכין *he framed the Heavens, I was there.* Pf. civ. 5. *He has founded the Earth upon* מכיניה *its Bases, (Supporters.* V. S. *its own Stability.) Ibid.* cxix. 90. כוננת *Thou hast framed* (established) *the Earth, and it shall abide.* Ibid. ver. 73. *Thy Hands made me, and* יכוננוני *framed me.* Among Men doing what the Word properly signifies, would be designing by Plan and Model, procuring or providing fit Sorts and Quantities of Matter, binging them near to the Place of Use, and fitting each for its proper Use, and putting them together, each in its proper Place, and in proper Order, as the Tabernacle by *Moses*, and the Temple abovementioned by *Solomon*; which were made by Models shewed, and were to imitate the Heavens as far as poffible in Miniature, and were to be fet up without any Alteration of the Materials upon the Spot, and without Stroke or Noife of Ax or Hammer there. And as thefe Heavens are fuppofed to be a Reprefentation of the Refidence of God, for which the fame Word מכון is ufed, 1 *Kings* viii. 39, 40, &c.

As the Parts of the Tabernacle, and afterwards thofe of the Temple were to reprefent the Part of, and Powers in this Machine of the Heavens, and could not do it by Motions, or real Operations in Miniature, there was no other Way but to do it emblematically; and if fo, we muft fhew what thefe Emblems were, what they reprefented, and what the End or Defign of thofe Reprefentations were: We have fome general Hints of this, that there was fomething hid; I fhall give you a few of them, and afterwards, in Courfe, fhew you what thofe hidden Things, that occult Philofophy in each Branch was.

Spencer de Leg. Hebr. cites *Clemens Alexandrinus, Strom. Lib.* V. *p. m.* 556. *al.* 405: ——" But all who have treated of Divine Matters, the Barbarous Nations, as well as the *Greeks*, have hid the Principles of Things, and delivered down the Truth enigmatically, by Signs and Symbols, and Allegories, and Metaphors, and such like Ways and Means."

Ibid. 787. *Philo*, in his Life of *Moses*. (*Spencer.*) " Among the Arts and Mysteries, which he says *Moses* learnt from his Masters the *Egyptians*, he reckons—Philosophy by Symbols, Hieroglyphicks, and Marks of Animals."

Vossius, Lib. III. p. 634. " This was all the Difference: The Signs of the *Greeks* and *Romans* were artificial; the *Egyptian* were natural Signs, and living Images of the Gods, as *Clemens Romanus* saith."

Spencer, p. 183. " The Hieroglyphical Way of writing, which the *Egyptian* Priests had in their holy Affairs, contained a Wisdom, or Knowledge, in some Respect similar to that which was retained in the Worship of the true God. For in the Temple of God there was great Use of Fire and Water; because, as I think, these hieroglyphically denoted Purity."

Heb. viii. 5. *The Tabernacle, the Shadow and Exemplar of heavenly Things.*

Spencer de Leg. Heb. p. 774. " *Thou shalt not make to* thyself *any graven Image.* —As much as to say, I reserve to myself, who am the Lord of my own Laws, the sole

sole and entire Power of appointing any Image or Symbol in my Worship, &c."

Ibid. p. 188. "It is very likely, that within the Veil of the *Mosaick* Law, lay hid certain Secrets of Philosophy.—*Philo*, in his Book entituled, *Who is the Heir of Divine Things*—says, That the sacred Candlestick, with the seven Lamps and Branches was a Representation of the Course of the seven Planets."

Ibid. p. 189. *Grotius*'s Notes on *Wisd. Solom.* ch. vii. ver. 9. "The seven Stars, called Planets, were signified by the seven Lamps of the Temple—by the other Parts of the Candlestick.

Kirch. Obelisc. Pamphil. Lib. II. *c.* 7. *De Dieu*, upon *ch.* ii. *v.* 8. of the Epistle to the *Colossians*.—" The *Hebrew* Doctors made the whole Tabernacle or Temple, and its Ceremonial Services refer to Philosophy."

Ibid. p. 561. *Josephus*'s *Jewish* Antiquities.—" The threefold Division of the Tabernacle was in Imitation of the Nature of the Heavens."—*De Dieu*, on *Acts* vii. " *viz.* That Nature and Power, which gives all Things their Existence, Fitness, and Disposition."

Clem. Alex. Strom. Lib. V. p. 409. " This Enigmatic Covering of Things is

plainly

plainly shewn from the Account given us by the *Hebrews* of the seven Inclosures of the old Temple; which had a reference to something; and also the Apparatus of the Ephod, which by various Symbols, relative to the visible Creation, enigmatically represented the Mechanism that reaches from the Heaven to the Earth, &c." and in several Pages following.

Ibid. Spencer, p. 739. *Zepper. Leg. Mosaic. Explan. Lib.* IV. *c.* 9.—" The New-moons were instituted as a Memorial of the Light first formed by the true God, the Creator of the Heaven, Sun, Moon and Stars, and who is also the Governor of the Motions and Revolutions of the heavenly Bodies, and their Operations and Influences upon these Elementary Bodies, and the Change of Seasons: And to this Creator and Governor did they return Thanks for the Benefit of created Light, in their New-moons, and acknowledged themselves his Subjects, &c."

Kircher Oedip. Ægypt. T. 2. P. 2. p. 87. " There scarcely occurs any Hieroglyphick, where there is not something Spherical or Circular."

Spencer, de Leg. Hebr. p. 754. Speaking of the Arks of the Heathens, *Clem. Alex. Protrept.* p. 12. " In which was only

only repofited the Privy-member of *Bacchus.*—*p.* 14. In it were laid up *Indian* Wheat, Pyramids, Pieces of dreffed Wool, Cakes or Wafers, made of Oil and Honey, full of Studs or Boffes like Navels, [ufed in Sacrifice,] fome Corns of Salt, a Serpent, *Perfian* Apples, a Rod, *(Spencer* adds) And many other Things, which I have neither Leifure nor Inclination to enumerate at prefent."

Ibid. p. 647. *More Nev.* P. 3. c. 32. " He fays, they were to facrifice, until the Memory of Idolatry was abolifhed out of the World."

Adrian Cocq. Ethnica facra, p. 8. "The *Hebrew* Doctors referred the whole Tabernacle or Temple, with all its appendant Ceremonies, to Philofophy, as *De Dieu,* upon *Acts* vii. 43. and therefore they contended, that the *Mofaick* Ritual fhould alfo continue as long as the World, that the Knowledge of Nature, which was couched under it, might there be learned."

As Man had forfeited by fuppofing incommunicable Powers in Matter, indeed one Intent of the Symbols and Ceremonies in the Tabernacle and Temple, was to keep that Race of Men from falling in that Point; but there was another more noble,

noble, and more extenſive, couched under ſome of them, repreſenting or prefiguring the perfect Obedience, and great Sacrifice; which was to reſtore to all Mankind what had been forfeited, which belongs not to this Part.

But doing what this Word כון implies by God, was creating each Atom of Size and Figure, fit for its reſpective Uſe, and in ſuch proper Places, and ſuch proper Numbers of each Sort, which were of ſuch different Sizes and Figures, as amounted to the Quantities of each Globe in Solids and groſs Fluids, and as they are termed Diſtances in the thinneſt Fluid between; ſo that after he, by his immediate Power, had put the Atoms of that dry Fluid into ſuch Motion, and Condition, in reſpect of Adheſion, Diſſolution, &c. that the Power ſhould be ſucceſſively renewed, each Atom ſhould make each other find its proper Place, and for all Ages keep each in its Station or Courſe, ſome in that of active, ſome in that of paſſive; in which Reſpect the Word שׁמים is frequently uſed to expreſs, as the Matter of the Heavens were at firſt, Deſolation, and when ſet to work, are ſaid to be Aſtoniſhment, Admiration, &c. deſigned by a Fore-knowledge beyond the Conception

ception of Man: First, with respect to the Figures of the Atoms, those which were to adhere, for such Degrees of Adhesion as were necessary among those of each Sort: Those which were to continue Fluid, for that small Degree of Adhesion, which is necessary in each Sort of Fluids; among some Sorts, to make them cleave, or become humid, and especially those of the Fluid of the Heavens (which are the only Sort in the Heavens, we can come at, and make Experiments upon, and in that manner consider, because those of the Orbs of the Globes are inaccessible) to be dry, and so only proper for that Motion among themselves, and between the Atoms of all other Fluids and Solids, they were designed for, without any considerable Degree of Adhesion to any of them; and only capable of being formed in the slowest Degree of that Motion into small Masses or Grains. Secondly, with respect to their Sizes, that there might be such a Degree in Difference in the Size of each Order, that whether in Atoms, or Grains of Solids, or Fluids, or in Atoms, or Grains, of that particular Fluid of the Heavens, that they each might be so differently taken hold of, and operated upon, that

at

at the Formation, each Sort by Degrees of Precedence, and Recedence, might be separated; that Atoms of the Solids should, each Class by taking Place of, and giving Place to others, be separated, and form'd; that the Atoms of the Fluids loose or in Grains, should, each Class, by taking Place of, and giving Place to others, be separated into Classes; that the Grains of the smallest Order of Atoms, or those of the Heavens, should *vice versa*, in Fluxes take Precedence of the Atoms of that Class, and each larger Grain of the smaller; and that the Atoms and smaller Masses of that Class should recede in the contrary Order, the Atoms first, the smallest Grains ext, &c. That in Consequence of the Difference of the Sizes of the Atoms of each Order, with some Allowance for their Figures, whether contiguous or adhering, they all, except those of the smallest Order should form Interstices, or Pores of such different Sizes and Figures, so proportioned, that in an infinite Compressure the Atoms of the grosser Fluids, and small Masses of the thinnest Fluid, should pervade some, and act upon the Atoms; and that the Atoms of the thinnest Fluid, when loose or melted, as the Scriptures and the Writings of every Sect of the Heathens inform

inform us, and as we can in sufficient Degree demonstrate to the Senses, should pervade, fill, and occasionally pass through the Pores between the Atoms of all other Classes, whether loose or adhering; between some, for a short Distance, near directly; between others more obliquely; so that not only in the first Formation, but in the Series of dissolving and reforming Things, the Fluid of the Heavens, in a Mixture of Masses and Atoms, should be capable of pressing, or compressing the Surfaces of each Atom, loose or adhering; and the Surface of each Solid or Fluid, of all other Sorts in Proportion to its Size, and thereby separate each Sort into Classes, for their respective Uses, as well in the Globes above, as in this; and fix those Atoms for Solids, in Proportion to the Fitness of their Figures and Sizes, with proper Degrees of Solidity, those for Fluids in proper Degrees of Fluidity; and should also be capable for the future, by pervading the Intervals or Pores of all other sorts of Atoms, whether adhering or fluid, to give each Atom that respective Degree of Tendency they call Gravity, towards the Part where the opposite Pressure is most obstructed by Fluids, or Solids; and that those Atoms or Masses of Atoms of the smallest Order or thinnest

nest Fluid, may pass and repass freely among themselves. But as every Atom of each Order must be larger than one of the Intervals form'd between the Atoms of the same Order, that the Atoms of this smallest Order cannot pass between those of the same Order, when adhering in a Mass, nor dissolve them, till they come into that violent Action, we call Fire, or other violent Collision; so that by Mixture of these Atoms and Masses without, and Atoms within the Pores they should be able to press, and compress, and by taking greater Hold of one Sort of Atoms, than of another Sort, in Proportion to their respective Sizes, whether in Atoms, or Masses of Fluids, or in large Solids, they might in all Ages give Precedence in Motion; and by having greater Hold of the Masses composed of the smallest Order in a Proportion to their Sizes, than of those Atoms loose, to those Masses such Precedence. And Thirdly, as the Atoms differ in Size and Figure, only with Respect to the Number, and so Quantity of each Sort, that there should be as many Orbs as are necessary, that each Orb might be of proper Size, and of a proper Sort of Atoms, and where there is Occasion, proportional Quantities of each Sort necessary; that the Atoms of the Airs should

should not only be each of such Figure and Size, but in such Numbers, and so placed in Intervals between the Matter of the Orbs, and beyond them, that they should constitute proper Distances between the Orbs, whether fix'd or moving, to answer their Ends; constitute such a Quantity, and so Distance on each Side, from the Center of that Fluid, and such an Increase of Dimension between the next adjoining Rays, issuing from the Center, that those Atoms melted at the Center, having no other Way of moving those before in Lines before them, nor of being moved by those in Lines behind them, but by Contact and Impulse of the Masses driven in by the Compressure towards the Center, in the reverse Order, may have such a Distance to move in, and have each Ray so far spread, that they might slacken their Motion, till they by the Compressure, should be reform'd into Masses, and so be made liable to be returned; so that whether by some of these Atoms of the Heavens, being at first put into small Masses, and some loose, mixed in each Place, by a greater Proportion of Atoms, or small Masses being in some Places, and a greater Proportion of larger Masses, being in other Places; or by the Interposition of the Matter

ter of the Globes, or particularly of the Atoms of that Globe, which were contrived for that Fluid, to act the Part of Fire in, or after what Manner, whether perform'd in any mechanical Way, or that Manner which he by his supreme Power acts, and which he can only understand, he put it into that Motion of Fire, or Light, so as by Degrees from the Center, or instantaneously from the Center, to the Circumference, to raise an Expansion, or Stress upon each other, and upon each Atom of all other Things; that, that Compressure should at, or near their Circumference make those Atoms adhere in Grains so close that other Atoms could not pass between them there, but act upon them by that Compressure, as if each of them were a Solid Unit of that Size, and each when press'd by larger on one Side than on the other, to be driven to the Place of the Action of the Fire, and be remelted, and by being so driven, force those melted to recede in like Manner, and on every Side in all Directions, till they in their Turns should reform into Grains, and return on every Side, and in every Line to the Fire at the Center, proportion'd of proper Sizes, and proper Numbers, to support and supply the Fire constantly,

stantly, to issue a due Proportion of Light, and so by a Capacity of being alternately divided, and re-adhering by Motion once set forward, to continue that Motion, and successively place the Atoms on one Side of the moving Globes, and Masses on the other Side, to incline them towards the Centre in Circles, by pressing the Masses behind each into the hindmost Edge of Atoms or Light, to give them Progression and some Rotation; and to move all Solids and Fluids, so as Vegetables once form'd, might be reform'd, with such Parts and Tubes, as it should act in; and Animals, with such Parts, Vessels and Organs of Sense, that it might enable them to move, operate upon their Senses, raise Ideas, Perceptions, &c. and all the intermediate Actions and Motions. So that the least Error in any of these and many other Points, too numerous to be mentioned in this Place, would spoil the Motion or Use of this Machine, which I am attempting to explain: As any Error would in the Atoms, which constitute the Parts, or in the Disposition of the Parts of the Machines which act in this, and by this for Man, nay, even in the Machine or Microcosm Man. And as this Word has passed through most Languages to us, and

its

its Meaning is well underſtood, and that the Word Mechanick is a Deſigner or Engineer, one who contrives as well as works; and the Word Machinator (tho' it has been miſapplied) is a cunning Deviſer or ſubtle Contriver; and though our Imaginer's Motion, &c. cannot be carry'd on by Mechaniſm, without their imaginary Powers, which might be true for any Thing they know, I ſhall proceed upon the Authority before me.

When God had put all this Syſtem in Order, *Moſes* ſays, *Gen.* ii. 1. *Thus the Heavens and the Earth* יכלו *were finiſhed, and all* צבאם (*Daniel* uſes the Word חיל) *the Hoſt of them.* Ver. 2. *And the Perſons in Covenant* כל *perfected on the ſeventh Day* מלאכתו *his material Legate, which he had made: And reſted on the ſeventh Day from the Whole of his* מלאכת *material Legate which he had made: And the* Aleim *bleſſed the ſeventh Day, and ſanctified it; becauſe that on it he* שבת *reſted from the whole of his material Legate, which the* Aleim *created to act.* Theſe Words have further Significations than the Tranſlation gives them. M. כלי a Veſſel, an Inſtrument, Houſhold-ſtuff, Arms, Embelliſhments, an Utenſil, an Apparatus, a Furniture of any kind, *Exod.* xl. 33. *And Moſes*

Moses יכל *finished* המלאכה *the Work.* 2 Chr. viii. 16. *Now all* מלאכת *the Work of* Solomon *was* תכן *prepared unto the Day of the Foundation of the House of* Jehovah, *and until* כלתו *it was finished: So the House of* Jehovah *was perfected.* The Parts, the Works, such Symbols or Representatives of those Powers in the Heavens, as the Heathens worshiped them by, which were imitated in the Tabernacle and Temple, are called by the same Names as the Powers were called, not only generally, as מלאכת and צבא, but each by their peculiar Names, of which in their Places. 1 *Chron.* xii. 37. *With all* כלי צבא *Instruments of War for the Battle.* Ver. 33. *Instruments of War,* Deut. i. 41. Jer. li. 20. &c. Thus every Composition of Atoms, or Parts of Matter, which is made a Machine, an Instrument capable of performing what it was designed for, is perfect. C. צבא To war, minister, assemble, or meet together in a regular Manner, and at a stated Time, *Pec.* to holy Offices, *Exod.* xxxviii. 8. 1 *Sam.* ii. 22. The Word implies a Troop of Powers, which are employed in any Service. Here 'tis not in the the Service of the Tabernacle, or Temple, as above, though each of those was a Representation of this; nor in the Service of

War, as it is generally translated; nor in another System, as it is sometimes represented; but in the Administration of this material System, and every thing in it. Though in my *Essay to the Natural History of the Bible*, I took the Translation as it stood, by which it was impossible to retrieve the Signification of the Names of their Gods, or to prove the Relation to, or the Share each had in this Operation, much less to shew what they were by the Sirnames the People gave each of them from the Places, &c. in later Times; and did not think proper to shew how their Gods were distinguished; but only in gross, that they worshipped the Powers of the Heavens. As each of the several Parties, which went off from *Babel*, differ'd in their Sentiments, each called themselves their Countries, Cities, and Temples, by some chief Name of Condition, or Branch of Power in the Operation; so the *Jewish* Writers called the Heathens in gross *Zabii*, from their worshipping these Hosts; and tho' the....*Spenter* could not find what the Word meant, and so wisely made Devils of what they worshipped; and tho' no Mortal that I know of, ever offered to shew what it meant, except that because the People, some Time after, call'd a Star after

ter the Name of several of them, some have taken them for Stars; as for Example, the Star or Planet we call *Mercury*, was only called after *Mercury*; and so the Star of *Mercury*, the Power, or God; but *Mercury* the God was not the Star: I must in Course shew them distinctly and authentickly. And tho' I have in the said Essay, *inter al.* cited these Texts, I cannot omit them here, *Deut.* xvii. 3. *And hath gone and served other Gods, and worshipped them, the Sun, the Moon, or any of the Host of Heaven.* 2 Kings xvii. 16. *And worshipped all the Host of Heaven.* Ibid. xxi. 3. *And worshipped all the Host of Heaven, and served them.* ver. 5. *And he built Altars for all the Host of Heaven.* Ibid. xxiii. *To Baal, to the Sun, and to the Moon, to the Planets, and to all the Host of Heaven.* 2 Chron. xxxiii. 3. *And worshipped all the Host of Heaven, and served them.* Zeph. i. *And those that worshipped the Host of Heaven upon the House-top.* And God frequently claims these Powers of the Heavens as his, by designing, contriving, creating, and making them; and declares them to be at his Command, and his Servants, as *Isa.* xlv. 12. *My Hands stretched out the Heavens, and all their Host I commanded* Syr. *And to all their Host I*

gave Commandments.—Arab. *I commanded all the Stars into Being.* Deut. iv. 19. *And left thou lift up thine Eyes unto Heaven, and when thou seest the Sun, and the Moon, and the Stars,* even *all the Host of Heaven, shouldest be driven to worship them, and serve them, which the Lord thy God hath divided* (imparted) *unto all Nations under the whole Heaven.* 1 Kings xviii. 15. As *the Lord of Hosts liveth.* Ibid. xxii. 12. and Chron. xviii. 18. *I saw the Lord sitting on his Throne,* and *all the Host of Heaven standing* (supported) *by him on his Right Hand, and on his Left.* Neh. ix. 6. *Thou,* even thou art *Lord* alone; *thou hast made Heaven, the Heaven of Heavens with all their Host—and thou preservest them all, and the Host of Heaven worshipeth thee.* Psal. cxlviii. 2. *Praise him all his Hosts.* Isa. xxxiv. 4. *And the Host of Heaven shall be dissolved,* &c. Jer. viii. 2. *And they shall spread them before the Sun, and the Moon, and all the Host of Heaven, whom they have loved, and whom they have served, and after whom they have walked, and whom they have sought, and whom they have worshipped.* Ibid. xix. 13. *Upon whose Roofs they have burnt Incense unto all the Host of Heaven.* And *Ezekiel*'s Vision
was

was shew'd, and is writ to shew God Master of those Powers. And here we may see that the Troops, the Forces are of one sort, and the Stars of another, *Dan.* viii. 10. *And it waxed great against the Host of Heaven, and it cast down some of the Host, and of the Stars to the Ground, and stamped upon them, yea magnified himself even to the Host.* As I have hinted, the three Names of Condition were *Chamah*, the Part of the Heavens in the Action of Fire at the Sun; and *Ashteroth* the Streams of Light from the Sun, Moon, and Stars; tho' I think *Ashteroth* is a compound Word of עש or עשת, of which in its Place, and תור a Star, a Stream of Light, &c. as they terminated תורת, as they are all from one, all the Streams of Light, and so-included the first two; and *Baalim*, the Grains of the Air returning from the Circumference of the Heavens to the Sun, and צבא the Hosts, which either by their Example or in Ridicule, *Isa.* lxv. 11. calls גד a Troop of Deities, are the several Manners in which the Motion of the Light, and the Grains called *Baal* or the Spirit, exert their Strength, Power, &c. or have their particular Effects and Operation upon Matter, and were then each worshipped at its respective Temple under an expressive Name, as the Psalmator, Supporter, Projector, &c. And, perhaps, hence the Heavens were called by the Word used for Names, or the Word used for Names was taken from them; and perhaps, שם which the Translators have rendered Name, *Gen.* xi. 4. might be an Image, or Representation of the Heavens, or of some Branch of Condition or Power in them.

After he in ver. 2. has repeated the Word יכל and mentioned the Time, the seventh Day, lest the Word for Powers or Forces should not be sufficiently expressive, that they were subject to God; he expresses these Things by another Word, rendered *his Work*, with the Addition of, *which he had made*, viz. מלאכתו which is a Word of Office, of ministerial Service. *M.* לאך. " *Lac*, signifies a Mission, לאך whence is formed מלאך *Melac*, one sent, a Legate, a Nuntio or Messenger, and thence an Angel." In the *Hebrew* a מ prefixed to a Substantive of Action, expresses an Agent, or Instrument to perform that Action. In general every Thing in this System, or in the Superior, that is not God, is of his creating, and forming, or making, and so is his Work; and as he made every active Being and Thing to serve him, this Word is used for every Being employ'd by him,

him, whether those of a superior Order, or Men, or such of his inanimate Works as he has given mechanical Motion to, and constituted Governors, and are employ'd, and continually in Motion in his Service; these are Legates as well, and much more so, than the spiritual Angels; and if those Above have Names given from these Below, Names express'd by Things we know, or may know, that confounds not the Things and the Angels, they have each different Employments. When the Prophet speaks God's Words, the inanimate are distinguish'd by being Feminine; when the Words of the Heathen, they may be of either Sex, as they made these Powers. And tho' the *Jews* out of Zeal called them evil Angels, I shall shew that they are obedient Angels, and act for the Service of Man, as Psal. civ. 4. *who hath made the Winds his Agents, and his Ministers the Flaming Fire.* And so when set forward, their ministerial Works were stiled God's Works; but the Heathen and perverted *Jews* called the Result of God's Contrivance, Creation, and Workmanship, the Effects of this Machine, the Work of the Heavens, and attributed every thing to them, and served them; sometimes as a Power or Goddess, and sometimes as a God under this Name; the Works, or the Ministers, or Things em-

employed by the Heavens, and thereby robbed God of his Dominion; as *Jer.* vii. 11. xliv. 17, 18, 19. למלכת השמים rendered *Work, Queen, Army, Workmanship of Heaven, of the Heavens:* By the LXX, *Jer.* vii. 18. ςρατία, Exercitus, *Army*, the same as צבא, Syr. Jer. vii. 18. *Celestial Militia:* xliv. 18. *Heavenly Army*; Chald. *Celestial Star*, in other Nations variously pronounced, מלכום, מלכן, מילך, מלך, מולך, &c. At the End of *Vossius* R. M. *Maim. of Idolatry,* "This was their Error: Since, say they, God created the Stars and these Spheres to rule the World, and hath placed them on high, and made them Partakers of Honour, and makes use of them as his Ministers; we do indeed well to praise them, and extol them, and pay them Honour. And this is the Will of the Blessed God himself, That we should magnify and reverence whomsoever he hath raised up to, and dignified with Honours: As a King wills that his Ministers should be honoured, which is doing Honour to the King himself."

Spencer de Leg. Heb. p. 898. *Origen contra Celf. Lib.* V. *and Grotius Annot. ad Mat.* i. 10. "The *Jews* call those Spirits, which are placed between God the Creator of all Things, and Men, sometimes *Aleim,* sometimes *Melacim*; the first of which
signifies

signifies, in *Greek*, *Theous*, *Gods*; the other, *Angelous*, *Angels*. And *Pythagoras* took these Appellations, &c."

Gyraldus de Diis Gent. p. 419. " The Name of *Angels* is common to both the *Greeks* and the *Latins*, who in the *Hebrew* are called *Malacim*. *Phila* thought the *Angels* of the *Jews* were what the Gentiles termed *Demons*." When the late *Jews*, in their Translations, invoke God to deliver them from the Worshipers of those Powers, they speak plain, as B. C. רום *Psal.* lvii. 6. *Be exalted above the Angels* (Agents) *of the Heaven, O God,* &c. Sometimes with Adjuncts, which denote the particular Action, as אדרמלך, אנמלך, and God claims these Powers by Name, *Zeph.* i. 5. *And them that worship, and swear by the Lord, and that swear by* מלכם *Malcham. Jer.* xlvi. 18. *As I live, faith* מלך *the King, whose Name is the Lord of Hosts.* The Prophet *Isaiah* turns these Words upon the perverted *Jews*, chap. viii. 21. *Therefore* (בה *on it,* or *for that Reason*) *shall the Snare* (Error) *and* (spiritual) *Hunger overflow: And it shall come to pass, when they are hungry they shall be angry with themselves, and curse* מלכו *their King, and* אלהיו *their Gods, and look upward.* The Difference in the Meaning of this
Word

Word was in the different Sentiments of the People. He who has the Command of the Troops, or Strength, or Force, is King; the Heavens exercised or executed the Strength or Force of these Troops: To those who thought they were employed by, and obeyed God, they were Angels, and delegated Governors, or Viceroys, and God was King; to those who thought they were not at his Command, they were King. The Heathens used this Word for these material Powers, C. Ar.—" The Angel of the Dew drove the Flame of Fire from the three Children. *Ab. Phar.* II. *Dynast.* 75.—The *Arabians* attribute to every Element, to the Planets, the Signs of the Zodiack, and the Mansions of the Moon, to each their respective Angels." *Kirch. Oed. Ægypt.* F. II. P. I. 384. And in our Translations we have made some of the Names of some of these Powers, Angels, as שרפים כרובים, &c. because our Translators thought Hearkening and Praising (of which hereafter) fitter for intellectual Angels, than for mechanical Angels; tho' I think 'tis more to the Point in hand, and more advantageous to Man to be convinc'd, that the greatest Powers he can see, obey, and so hearken to and praise God, than to be told that Powers which he cannot see,

praise

praise him; and therefore I must bring these Orders of Angels into our Sight by the Authority of *David*, in the very Words above. *Psal.* ciii. 20. *Bless* Jehovah, *ye his* מלאכיו *Agents, that excel in Power, that perform his Word, that obey the Voice of his Word: Bless* Jehovah, *all his Hosts, his Ministers that do his Pleasure. Bless* Jehovah, *all his* מעשיו *Workers, in all Places of his Dominion.*

When he, *ver.* 3. had told you, that God blessed the seventh Day, and hallowed it, he tells you the Reason, because he then שבת rested, presided without Action. This has reference to what went before, implies that he had worked the six Days, that is, applied his innate immaterial Strength and Power to set forward, first one Part, then another, or Part after Part of the Matter of which these Agents were formed, and keep them going till they were all formed and made a perfect Machine; and then he ceased to apply, withdrew his immediate Power from his Instruments, Operators, material Legates and Ministers, (made a Cession to them, or, as before expressed, made them Governors, Rulers and Hosts) which God had created לעשות *to make;* Why not, that *They* might work or make? why did he create?

Only

Only that he might make them? Surely for some further End: When he rested, were Things to stand still? What was to work? Were not his Ministers to work? Yes surely, and this is a very extensive Word, applied in Scripture to all Sorts of Work, all Sorts of Making, and they, except in some Miracles, have done all the Work, and made every thing that has been made since. But if this Word for his material Legate be singular, then the Noun to this Verb must either be *Heavens*, or *Armies*, which is only the Things, or the particular Powers in them.

There are also general Words which express, that the Heavens govern themselves, and the Earth by his Contrivance, and so by his Appointment, and Laws, *Job* xxxviii. 33. *Knowest thou the Ordinances of Heaven* (the Airs?) *Didst thou appoint their Dominion over the Earth?* Jer. xxxiii. 25. If I *have not appointed the Ordinances of Heaven and Earth!*

Tho' the true Signification of the Word שמים Heavens has been laid down, yet we are to consider the Manner of the Speeches in Scripture, concerning them, and some general Names for their Powers. In the History of the Formation, when they were made Agents, the Actions they perform-ed ed one by one, are attributed to them, or the Powers in them, and then positively to God; after they were possessed of these mechanical Powers, and were mistaken for a God, and the Operations or Effects of these Powers attributed to them; except in a few physical Descriptions, we are to consider the chief Intent of the Scripture was to assert the Superiority of God, and his Dominion over the Powers the Heathens attributed under various Names, of Conditions, Effects, or Operations, and by Figures of them, to the Heavens; and tho' God no way divested the Heavens of their mechanical Powers they had upon their Formation, nor intermedled, except in Miracles, he not only claims them in general to be his, as Deut. x. 14. *Behold the Heaven of Heavens is the* LORD's *thy God.* 1 Chron. xxix. 11. *For all that is in the Heaven and in the Earth is* thine, Job xli. 11. *Whatever is under the whole Heaven is thine.* Psal. viii. 4. lxxxix. 11. *The Heavens are thine*, and the Effects of their Powers and Actions to be the Effects of his Powers and Actions, Psalm lxxiv. 16. *The Day* is *thine, the Night also* is *thine; thou hast prepared the Light and the* שמש *Sun* (Shemosh) ver. 17. *Thou hast set all the Borders of the Earth: Thou hast made*

Summer

Summer and Winter. Pſal. lxxxix. 30. *The Days of the Heavens;* but even expreſſes them as if (tho' only in the Senſe aforeſaid) each Power or Act of theirs, were a perſonal Power or Act of his; and the Voice of the Heavens, which was the God of the Heathens, and to whom they attributed that Voice, by way of Claim, as moſt of his other Attributes are, is called the Voice of the Lord; their Light, the Light of the Lord, Job xxxvii. 2. *Hear attentively the Noiſe of his Voice, and the Sound that goeth out of his Mouth.* Ver. 3. *He directeth it under the whole Heaven, and his Lightning* (Light) *unto the Ends,* (Wings) *of the Earth.* Ibid. Pſal. xviii. 13. The Breath of the Heavens is called the Breath of the Lord. Job xxxvii. 10. *By the the Breath of God, Froſt is given:* The Strength of thoſe Parts of the Heavens which communicates it to the reſt, is called God's Strength, as Pſal. lxviii. 35. *Aſcribe Strength to the* Aleim, *his Excellency is over* Iſrael: *And it is his Strength which is in the Æthers.* The Power of the Firmament of Heaven is called the Power of God. Pſal. cl. 1. *Praiſe him for the Expanſion his Strength.* The Power of the Firmament of Heaven is called the Power of God. The Compreſſure of the Heavens,

vens, as *Job* says, xxxvii. 18. *Which is strong, and as a molten Looking-glass.* xxxviii. 14. *It is turned as Clay to the Seal, and they stand as a Garment:* As well in the first Acts which were attributed then to the Firmament as now, is called the Hand of God. Psal. xcv. 5. *And his Hands formed the dry Land.* Ibid. cii. 25. *Of old hast thou laid the Foundation of the Earth: And the Heavens are the Works of thy Hands.* Isa. xl. 12. *And plan'd the Heavens by Measure.* Job x. 8. *Thine Hands have made and fashioned me together round about*; Psal. cxix. 73. *Thy Hands have made me and fashioned me.* Ibid. cxxxix. 5. *Thou hast beset me behind and before, and laid thine Hand upon me.* If the *Hebrew* Words were not construed as arbitrary Words, but as I have hinted of Condition or Office, and suppose it taken from that Root, and so to the Hand of Man, and that the Heavens be consider'd as the Instrument which is obedient to his Being, and with which he handles and operates upon Matter, then the Word which is also used for the Heavens in that Action, is properly applied to the Parts of any other Creature, as of an Ape or Spider, with which it can, and when with them it lays hold of and operates upon other Things:
And

And when this Word is borrowed or applied to God, as all Words of him are, it helps us to a borrow'd Idea: And in Truth and good Sense, these Agents which obey him and operate upon other Things are his Hands, so of Eyes, Wings, &c. The Motions of the Heavens and their Powers of moving other Things, are called the Motions of the Lord. Under whatever Name or Attribute the Heavens in any Part or in any Condition relating to these Powers or Motion, were properly called, or whatever Figures they were represented by, and however those Representations were called, as Wings of Eagles or Hawks, Head of Ox, Eagle, or Hawk, Serpent, Lion, &c. or other of their Parts; or however those Parts which represented those Powers were mixed in a Figure, whether a Serpent that represented Fire, or such a Figure as they called a *Seraph*, or such as they call the *Cherubims*, flying with a Chariot, and in it the Representation of the Agent that rules them, the Representation of the Powers which move the Orbs, and operates by Pulsion or Pressure upon Matter, which were used, as we shall see in the Scriptures, and still more evidently in those of the Heathen Countries, from whence they had their Rise, God condescends

MOSES's *Principia.*

descends to put in his Claim in the plainest, tho' low Comparisons; he makes himself not only the Presider, but the Steerer of the Ship, and the Driver, as a Charioteer was of the Horses which drew the Chariot of War, or &c. of the Matter and Powers which rule and move the Heavens, and every thing in them, which he had constituted in that Office. But before I can go further, I must beg leave to observe, that there is a general Error in the Translation, where they use one Word for two Things, which differ as much as any two Things can differ; Things in which there is no Mystery, and which surely the Capacity of Man might understand, and have distinct Ideas of; I mean here the Word רכב: they make מרכב signify a four wheel'd Chariot, and רכב when they please some Sort of a Chariot, I suppose a two wheel'd one; and when they please a Rider on Horseback, or one carried in a Chariot, or a Charioteer, or Driver of some sort of a Chariot, I suppose they mean of a four wheel'd one; but I suppose there was a sort of Men, פרשים which we may call *Equites*, who rode on Horses, and רכבי who were Riders upon any Beast, as Horses, Asses, or Camels, when express'd; when not, *Armigeri*, or what you please, who

who rode in Chariots, and drove, carried Darts or Inſtruments of War, and fought in the Chariots. Where רכב is tranſlated a Chariot, it ought always to be as above, ſave that it is Singular and Plural, and מרכב a Machine to be drawn or driven, a Cart, a Chariot to carry, without regard to Number of Wheels or Perſons; for as it is, they have left us no Word or Name at all for theſe *Armigeri*, and have applied Attributes to a Chariot, which belong to a Man; and thereby they have not only made Nonſenſe of the Words, or Sentence where the Word רכב is miſconſtrued, but by miſapplying Words apply'd to it in that Senſe, thoſe Words joined to other Names are liable, by their Example, to be miſconſtrued, and to make Nonſenſe of thoſe other Paſſages where they are uſed; for Example, *Exod*. xv. 21. סום *The Horſe and* רכבו *his Rider*. Iſa. xxi. 7. *And he ſaw* רכב *a Chariot* (S. *Riders*) *with* צמד *a couple of* (*joined to*) פרשים *Horſemen*; *and* רכב *a Chariot of Aſſes, and* רכב *a Chariot* (V. S. Aſcenſores, *Riders*) *of Camels*. Hag. ii. 22. *I will overturn* מרכבה *the Chariots and thoſe that* רכביה *ride in them; and the Horſes and* רכביהם *their Riders ſhall come down*. 1 Kings xxii. 34, and 2 Par. xviii. 33. *Therefore he ſaid to* רכבו

רכבו *to the Driver of his Chariot, turn thine Hand.* 2 Sam. viii. 4. *and* 1 Par. xviii. 4. *And* David יעקר *houghed all* הרכב. 1 Kings xx. 21. *and* י־ך *He smote the Horses and* הרכב *the Charioteers.* 2 Kings ii. 11. *And behold* רכב *of Fire, and* סוסי *of Fire—My Father, my Father! the* רכב *of* Israel, *and* פרשיו *his Horsemen.* Psal. lxxvi. 6. *both* רכב *the Charioteer, and* סום *the Horse* נדרם *are cast into a dead Sleep.* Jer. xlvi. 9. *And* התהוללו *rage* הרכב *ye Charioteers.* And so when these Words are applied to the material Parts, Agents, or Powers, which move the Heavens, and move, or drive, or carry the Orbs and other Things in them, they are to be used as aforesaid, as performing there, what such Agents or Machines do in Things we understand here; and when God, by way of Claim, says he does these Things, he is not speaking of himself, 'tis, as always he does them, by the Parts of this Machine which he fram'd, in Opposition to any Thing misattributed to it; as Psal. civ. 3. *making* עבים *the Grains of Air* רכובו *his Drivers,* by the Firmament, which is the Wings of the Spirit, the Agent in Motion, and the *Shemosh* which was constituted a Ruler; and his Course is as Psal. xix. 7. *His going forth is from*

M 2 *the*

the End of the Heavens, and his Return is from the End of them. Nay the Driver, as it has feem'd in a more lofty Stile of intellectual Powers; but indeed only of the Figures, the Reprefentations of thefe Powers of Motion, which carry other Things, as the Heathens called them Cherubims. I muft beg Leave to obferve, that the Sitting or Driving here mentioned, is neither Refidence nor Acting, but as Lord, Prefiding, Governing, Ruling, taken *verbatim* from the Defcriptions of the State, and the Manner of Government of an Earthly Prince, over his Subjects and Forces; as Jer. xvii. 25. and xxii. 4. *Kings and Princes* ישבים *fitting upon the Throne of* David, רכבים *commanding,* ברכב *of Riders and Horfe*; fo prefiding over the Heavens, Cherubims, and all the particular Hofts.

Pfal. ii. 4. *Dwelling in the Heavens.* Ibid. *Sitting on.* 1 Sam. iv. 4. *Jehovah of Hofts who dwells in the Cherubim.* 2 Kings xix. 15. 1 Par. xiii. 6. Ifa. xxxvii. 6. and Pfal. lxxx. 2. *Thou that dwelleth in the Cherubim* הופיעה *fhine forth,* irradiate.

This expreffes what the Cherubims are, and what they do, 'tis applied to עפל Grains of Air, or the Spirit, as after explained.

MOSES's *Principia.* 117

Pſal. xcix. 1. *He ſitteth on the Cherubim*; let the Earth חנוט *decline.* What Motion this was will appear in its Place. Deut. xxxii. 26. *There is none like unto the God of* ישרון, *who rides upon the Heavens to thy Help; and his Excellency* שחקים *the Æthers. Vulg.* "There is no God like the God of the Upright: The Rider of the Heavens thy Helper: By his great Power the Clouds, the Æthers, run to and fro." Pſal. lxviii. 34. *Sing to the Lord, Selah; who rides upon the Heaven of Heavens,* which קדם were of old (to the East.) Ver. 5. *Exalt him who rules in* ערבות *the Mixture.* Dan. viii. 8. Zach. ii. 6. *Four Winds of Heaven.* Pſal. civ. 3. *Walking upon the Wings* רוח *of the Spirit.—Was ſeen upon—did fly upon the Wings of the Spirit.* Pſal. xviii. 11. and 2 Sam. xxii. 11. *He rode upon a Cherub and did fly.** Job xxxvii. 3. *Light upon the Wings of the Earth.* Ezek. x. 5. *The Sound of the Wings of the Cherubim.*

All theſe are to be taken in the Senſe abovementioned, as having created and contrived theſe Powers to move or carry

* This is juſt ſuch Picture as the Olympick *Jupiter* made, a Man riding upon an Eagle with its Wings expanded, and a Thunderbolt in the Hand of the Man.

the Globes, &c. making them fly by the Wings of the Spirit, or more immediately in the Miracles, when he shew'd that he rul'd over those Powers, and made them act by new Rules, and so shew him or his Power. If they were taken otherwise, they would give Men Ideas highly derogatory of the Being of God; so that allowing the Sovereignty of God over these Powers, which was what the Scripture was chiefly design'd for, these Assertions of these Actions or Motions, are to be taken in a physical Sense, as much as those at first are, where 'tis said, that each Branch or Power, in the Operations of the Heavens, first did this, or that, and then that God did the Thing mention'd; and each Branch of Power, in the Operations of the Heavens, does each act proper for that Power to do as it did then; and the several Powers conjointly carry on the Operations of this System, as they did at first when God rested from his Work.

Many things are said in Scripture of this Matter שמים *Heavens*, under that general Name; some without Distinction, perhaps, in the State they were created; some distinguished to be as it was, after some small Proportion of Atoms in them
were

were form'd into Solids, or denſe Orbs; and as thoſe Solids have one general Name, as the vaſt Remainder of Atoms form a Fluid, as Parts of the Claſs of Atoms remaining fluid in different Situations, or Conditions, or Actions, have different Names, and have had different Repreſentations, I ſhall conſider each Part under its Name, and its Repreſentations afterwards; and becauſe I cannot give Evidence of the Manner of God's firſt Actions, before the Heavens were a Machine, I muſt conſider Things and Actions ſince the Heavens were perfect, and God reſted from his Work, with things ſpoken of before.

Ver. 2. And ‏חשך‎ Darkneſs was upon the Face *(Faces)* of ‏תהום‎ the Deep; (The looſe Parts which now conſtitute this Globe, which is call'd the Earth.)

The Word ‏תהום‎, as it appears by Uſage, expreſſes the Condition of Matter being in Atoms or ſmall Grains, looſe and apparently fluid, and is apply'd to the Parts of this Globe, Earth, Water, &c. was here to the Whole; but ſince the Atoms of the Earth were form'd into a spherical Shell of Stone, &c. 'tis apply'd to the Sphere of Fluids which remain within, and those at the Apertures, with proper Words annexed to distinguish which. The Word חשך *Darkness*, which is also a Name of Condition with the Words adjoyning of Situation, apply'd here to the Matter of the Heavens, expresses the State those within the Sphere, and those without the Sphere were created in. This Matter was created at Rest, not then moved by the joint Action which produces Light; since that Action commenc'd it signifies the State of any Part of them, which is behind any thing which obstructs the Motion of the Parts of Light, or of any Part which is out of the reach of the Motion of the Parts of Light, or some Parts of the Atoms coagulated into Grains, so large, in such Quantity, and so near each other, that they obstruct the Motion or Pervasion of the Parts of Light among themselves, and among those behind them; and tho' any one of these Conditions or Situations is enough to prevent, not only that Effect it has upon the Eyes, which of late has been accounted the Chief, or only Use of Light, tho' there were no Eyes then; but besides that it was inactive,

as

as to all its other Uses or Effects, and only enjoy'd its Solidity, and so its Resistance or Capacity of possessing what they call so much Space, or, in plain *English*, of possessing its self in the relative Places where it was as it was, tho' any Part in a Capacity to be moved, when mov'd to possess the same Quantity in any other Place, or as soon as some of them were in Grains or Masses, those in Grains or Masses in a Capacity to be divided, when divided to possess the same Quantity in any other Places; for as before laid down, no Atom, which is as determinately as I can express it, a solid Unite, can ever augment or diminish, much less be dispossest of its Space or Extension; and tho' I cannot perceive that Atoms could by any natural Means then adhere in Masses or Grains, yet it appears soon after, some did by immediate Power, as *Amos* iv. 13. *and concreting the Spirit*, which is the Name of these Masses in the Condition of Motion, or of moving; the Things spoke of, in the next Words were concreted, and by God's supernatural Power the Atoms of each were kept together till he gave his *Fiat*, and endur'd Friction till they were dissolved and produced Light; yet since there has been, and is both Motion

tion and Compreffion, thefe Atoms can mechanically, and to our Conception intelligibly, be form'd by Adhefion of the Atoms of the Air, or Parts of Light which are the fame, into Maffes, Grains, *Nebulæ*, which tho' in that Motion, in which they return thro' the Light to the Fire in the Action of making and fending out Light, keep the Light in a due Degree of Clearnefs; yet when interrupted fo as to be in too great Proportion, tho' the Flux of Light have free Paffage to one Side of the Confines of them, can interrupt it and fo diminifh its Paffage to, and Effect upon thofe Things on the oppofite Side; as this, and thofe next following, are only Names of Condition, and the Matter changeable in Condition, and does not ftay, or is not ftored in, and fo as from a Stock fupply'd from any Place or from any Body, as they fuppofe Light to be, but is either out of the reach of, or periodically hid from, or continually mixt among thofe of Light; *Job* fays xxxviii. 19. *And Darknefs, where is the Place of it?* V. 3. *has fet Bounds to the Darknefs.* Pf. cxxxv. 7. *bringing the Spirit out of* מאוצרותיו *his Treafures.* Which is a continu'd Act, firft from his Treafure of Atoms of which it is form'd, and fo from the Mint, the Place where it it is form'd; and secondly, from the Places where it is in greater Proportion than 'tis in others, to those Places where the Fluid is thinner, or to those where the Resistance is by the Interposition of a Solid or Fluid, diminish'd on one Side. The two Opposites, the Center and the Circumference, are the Sources where this Matter is amassed and divided. There are several Words which express that these Grains are form'd, the Agent that forms them, the Manner of forming them, the Matter they are form'd of, *viz.* the loose Atoms of the Heavens, which have been melted from Masses for Light; that these Masses when form'd, constitute Darkness, of which next, and are employ'd to other Purposes, and many Things are said of their Actions, of which hereafter.

Joel iii. 4. שמש *The Light of the Sun* (as you will see hereafter it is) *shall be turned into* חשך *Darkness* (or, to storken'd condensed Air.)

M. צלם " Image, Similitude—it's a
" Shadow which is the Image of a Body.
" צלמות, The Image of Death, Dark-
" ness, compounded of צל Image and
" מות Death: *If.* xvi. 3. Make thy Sha-
" dow like Night."

Job

Job xii. 22. *And bring forth the Shadow of Death to the Light, (or cause it to come into, or, become Light)* Am. v. 8. *Changes into Morning the Shadow of Death.* As Light is Life, and Shadow, if continu'd, would be Death; here the Shadow of the Earth in Night, is call'd the Shadow of Death.

Ver. 2. ------and רוח the Spirit of God ------

What this is, when *Moses* writ, was well understood by every one: But as this is a Name of Office, and this Knowledge has been neglected, and all the rest of the Scripture has been writ to set us right; so before I can come to that, I must prove by latter Scripture its Existence, shew whether it be Atoms or Substances compounded of Atoms; If Substances, tho' I cannot shew the Manner of God's acting by his supernatural Power, if they are successively dissolved and reform'd, I must shew the Manner and Place in which they are form'd by this Machine, after it began to operate, what course they take, how dissolved, &c.

M. אפן

M. קפא *Kpa.* Its Signification is Coagulation, to be coagulated, congealed, condensed, to grow together, to come to a Consistency.

קופא *Kupa.* Consistent, growing together, coagulating, condensing.

קפאון *Kpaun.* Any thing coagulated, as Cream, Cheese, Concretion, Coagulation, the Consistence of any liquid Substance, as Milk and Water, Congelation, or Freezing, Snow congealed; any Thing coagulated, dark, or dense. *Zech.* xiv. 6. *There shall be no Light,* יקרות the Atoms of Light shall יקפאון be congealed (darkened.)

B. C. גלידא גליד *Gelid, Gelida.* Frost, Dew, Ice. *Zech.* xiv. 6. אלהן ערי וגליד but Privation and Congelation, or Concretion, namely of Light.

B. C. קפא to be joined together, to cohere, to coalesce, to congeal, to concrete, to be condensed, to be coagulated.

B. C. קרש *Keres.* To coagulate, to condense, to be congealed. *Job* xxxviii. 30. *The Waters are condensed as a Stone,* namely, by Cold, that is, congealed.

M. עבה *Obe.* Its Signification is Density. 2 *Sam.* xxiii. 4. *Like the Morning Light shall he arise, like the Light of the Sun in a Morning without* (Densities fities.) *Exod.* xix. 9. *In the Denfity of* הֶעָנָן *the Cloud.* 2 *Sam.* xxii. 12. עָבֵי *Denfities* (or denfe Grains) שְׁחָקִים *of the Æthers.* 1 *Kings* xviii. 45. *And the Heavens were black with Denfities.*

1 *Kings* vii. 46. " In the מַעֲבֵה Denfity of the הָאֲדָמָה Earth tranflated in our Bibles the Clay Ground. 2 *Chron.* " In the עֲבִי Denfity of the הָאֲדָמָה Earth."

Job xxxvii. 16. *Doft thou underftand* מִפְלְשֵׂי *the forming the denfe Grains, the wondrous Works of him who is perfect in Knowledge.* I muft explain the Word מִפְלָשׂ, becaufe tho' a Grain of Air is prefs'd, and fo has Weight, this has no Relation to its Weight, but to the Manner of its being form'd.

M. פָּלַשׁ *Peleſs.* " Its Signification is a Covering in Duft, and Afhes. פָּלַשׁ *Kithpbhel* הִתְפַּלֵּשׁ to roll in or be covered with Duft, or Afhes." And the Meaning is, doft thou know the Agent which carries on the rolling in, and covering with the Afhes, or Duft, or Atoms of the Heavens, and fo growing of a denfe Grain of Air.

If there were any Part of, or as they call it, Place full of this Fluid compreffed by the reft, and through which the Units of this Fluid in Motion from the Light, did

not

not pass and keep the Parts divided, I think I can convince any Man, that has as much Reason as to believe the Scripture, nay one that has common Sense, and were but (if that be possible) indifferent, and believed neither Side, that it would not only, as *Moses* says of that in *Egypt*, where that Motion was in some Degree suspended, be felt; but that it would approach much nearer the Degree of Density which they call Solidity, such as that of Water, where there is not a sufficient Quantity of those Atoms of the Heavens, to pervade or pass between them; and when so, to obstruct the Passage of Light much more than those of Water in form of Ice, nay almost totally: And I think by many Texts of Scripture, it appears they are in this Condition at the uttermost Extremities of the Heavens, as Job xx. 6. *His Head reach to to the Density.* xxii. 14. *And thou saidst how can God know? Can he judge through the thick Darkness? The Density is a Covering to him that he sees not.* Isa. xiv. 14. *Above the Height of the Density;* and the antient *Jews* understood them so, and the Heathens thought so; sometimes Things are best shewed by Contraries, though to shew them, be not in Course; yet as *Job* xxxvii. 11. *Yea* ברי

the

the Clearness יטריח *wearieth the Density.* What *Clearness* the opposite Condition of Part of this Matter is, you may see, *Cant.* vi. 9. *Clear as* חמה *the solar Fire.* That חמה is Part of this Matter of the Heavens in the Condition of Fire in the Orb of the Sun, will appear afterwards, and טרח is with great Labour to support an Incumbrance; in plain *English* that Part of the Matter of the Heavens in that Condition it is in the Orb of the Sun, with great Labour dissolves the Masses of coagulated Air pressed into it.

M. עלט " Its Signification is Darkness, Cloudiness. עלט from whence is עלטה Darkness, Cloudiness, the Evening Twilight.

Ezek. xii. 6. *Carry it forth by Dark.*

B. C. קבל *Kebel;* Darkness, Obscurity, Mistiness, used *Gen.* xv. 12.

Joel ii. 2. Zeph. i. 15. " A Day of ענן and ערפל Darkness.

M. ערף " The Neck, Subversion, Distillation. To distill, flow, to fall down, drop by drop. — It is an Epithet of the Heavens or Stars, so called because they distil and drop down Rain and Dew upon these lower Parts. *Chald.* to distil, drop down.

Deut.

Deut. xxxii. 2. *Shall drop as Dew.* xxxiii. 28. *His Heavens shall drop down Dew.* If. v. 30. M. *Behold Darkness,* צר *with Grains of Air, for the Light is storken'd in its Defluctions.* Ibid. *Zant. Pagn.* C. " By this the Marrow concocted from the Brain distills and moistens the Bones, as the Dew from Heaven does these lower Parts," bending the Neck, and so bowing the Head forward, is an Abridgment of casting the Head to the Ground, a Sign of Worship or Subjection, and breaking off or cutting off the Neck, is letting the Head fall, or casting it to the Ground; so this Word, as a Verb, is well rendered *drop down* for Doctrine, and for Dew; and as a Subst. for these *Nebulæ* which are continually cast down from the Circumference of the Heavens to the Orb of the Sun, and in their Way upon the dark Side of the Earth, *Defluctiones, Stillationes.*

M. קדר *Kdr,* Obscurity, Blackness. 1 Kings xviii. 45. *And the Heavens were dark with Densities and with Spirit.* Ezek. xxxii. 7. *And make their Stars dark.* Joel ii. 10. שמש וירח (which are as you will see the Light flowing from the Sun, and the Light flowing from the Moon) *shall*

130   MOSES's *Principia.*

be dark. Mich. iii. 6. *The Day shall be dark over them.*

M. קרר signifies *Cold;* another conditional Name: The Effect of the Presence of those Grains, of the Matter of the Heavens, of their Incapacity of pervading the Pores of, and thinning mix'd Fluids, and moving them, of their Capacity of compressing and fixing them.

Gen. viii. 22. *Cold and Heat.* Psal. cxlvii. 17. *who can abide his Cold.* Job xxxvii. 9. *and Cold from* מזרים. Here is a Description of the Places from whence these Grains which produce Cold come, and though out of course, I must take it in.

M. מזר *Mazar.* Its Signification, is something Foreign, Alien — the Planets — the celestial Signs — ממזרים that is, the North Winds which disperse the Clouds. *Jerom.* from *Arcturus:* See זרה but first זור I. What it signifies is Compression, Breaking. Whence the Verb זור and זר that is to shake, dissipate, stamp to Pieces, to press, compress, squeeze out by Compressure. Thence מזור Compression, a Squeezing out.

IV. It signifies Alienation זור and זר to alienate, *&c.*

Also

MOSES's *Principia.* 131

Also זרה and זרא, ה and א changed one for the other, Diſperſion, Alienation, Abalienation, &c. &c. מזור the ſame. *Chald.* זר and זאר to decline, to recede, to divert or turn aſide. *C. Ibid. Arab.* — to diverge unequally, the one going outward the other inward. *M.* זרח It's Expoſition is, to be ſcatter'd, diſperſed, Diſperſion, Contrition, or Breaking into Pieces — a Circle, a Crown, a Circuit, Circuiting and whatever is thence derived. — A Periphery, Circumference, a Crown, a Circle—Ventilators, &c. This Word is a Name of Situation, Condition, &c. and anſwers all the general Deſcriptions or Uſages of the Word, tho' ſeemingly different, but cannot anſwer the ſingle Gueſſes, for which there is no Uſage—Theſe Grains come from the moſt diſtant Places and ſo Strangers: They are driven to the Center, and by the Compreſſion of thoſe ſucceſſively following, broken and diſſolved in the Action of Fire at the Center, expreſs'd and diſperſed alternately to the Circumference, coagulated there, and ſo they are from the Places, whither the Light of which they are form'd is continually diſpers'd in the moſt extenſive Senſe every Way, and to the furtheſt Diſtances, and the wideſt Spreadings, and ſo from the Diſper-

N 2 ſions,

sions, and they are from the Periphery, Circumference or Circle, and they are from the Places of Circulations, Revolutions, or Returnings, and so to the most minute Circumstance. And this will make the other Place, in which it is us'd, intelligible.

Job xxxviii. 32. *Can'st thou cause* מזרות *the Grains to go forth in their Season?* in proper Time, Quantity, of proper Sizes, &c. to answer their Ends.

M. אפל *Apl.* It's Signification is Slowness. This is but one single Guess and false. It's Exposition is Darkness — it is more than חשך, it is used to express Grains of Air, or any other Matter concreted very strongly or closely, and so implies hard.

Jer. ii. 31. *Have I been a Wilderness to* Israel! *or Jah, hard* (barren) *Ground?* Job xxx. 26. *I looked for Light, and there came Darkness.* Prov. vii. 9. *in the black and dark Night.* Job xxviii. 3. אבן *Concrete of* אפל *Darkness, and the Shadow of Death.* To explain this אבן must be explain'd.

M. אבן *Lapis,* &c. 'Tis a Name of Condition for a Heap of any Species of Atoms, or small Grains of them, which by Compressure are made to concrete, and adhere strongly; and because Atoms or

Grains

Grains of Stone, (for moſt Sorts were firſt form'd into Grains or Sands) are moſt generally in that Condition, and they moſt common, 'tis applied ſingly to a Piece of any of the common Sorts of Stone; when to any particular Sort, with the Addition of the Name of the Species or of the Uſe or Value; and likewiſe to any Concrete, as of Metal, Water, Air, or Fire, with the Addition of the Name of the Species of Atoms ſo concreted. The *Vulg. Tranſl.* has one Word, *Zach.* v. 8. Maſſam, *viz. Maſſam plumbeam,* which if it be taken for a Heap of Atoms cohering, a Lump, 'tis the proper Signification, and the Heathens us'd ſuch Words to the Point in Hand.

Deut. viii. 9. *Its Concretes Iron.* Joſ. x. 11. *great Concretes from Heaven,* &c.—*More which died with the Concretes of Hail.* 1 Sam. xxv. 37. *His Heart died within him, and he became a Stone* (Concrete), *Job* xxviii. 2. *Braſs is a Concrete* פיצ *melted,* (adhering by Compreſſion, as you ſee the Word ſignifies) xli. 15. *His Heart* פיצ *hard as a Stone.* xxxviii. 30. *Like a Stone, the Waters are hid.* Iſa. xxvii. 9. *All the Stones of the Altar as Chalk-Stones.* xxx. 30. *And Hail-Stones.* Ezek. xxviii. 14. *In the Midſt of the Stones of Fire.* Zach. iv. 10. *Stone of Tin.* Exod. i. 16.

i. 16. *When you see them upon* האבנים *the Masses* (they sat upon.) Jer. xviii. 3. *He wrought a Work upon the Masses* (they work'd upon, *Anvil.*)

So אפל is a Word of Condition general for any Sort of Atoms, so form'd into hard Grains. *Exod.* ix. 32. *The Wheat, and the Rye were not smitten; for they were* אפילת *in hard Grains.* (The Wheat and the Rye were not liable to be hurt by the Hail, because they were formed into hard Grains.) *Exod.* x. 22. *And there was thick Darkness,* (of concreted Grains of the Atoms of Light.) *Jer.* xxiii. 12. *Their Way shall be unto them* כחלקלקות *as slippery Ways* (of small smooth Grains of Stones, such as are worn round in the Torrents) *by* אפלה *shall they be driven, and fall by it.* Isa. viii. 22. *And dense Grains that* מנדח *are impelled.* This Word דחח expresses, that these Grains of Air were driven in by Force, not one Word of the Language of Gravity nor Attraction.

M. צור *Jur,* " Of natural Things — To press, compress, fix — *Subst.* a Rock, Stone, *&c. Chald.* and *Arabic,* to fix by Pressure, or Compressure." This is also a Word which expressed the Thing by Condition, and in general signifies to environ,

environ, and bind any Parcel of Things by Implication, *close, by Compressure,* and the Substantive any Thing which is so bound *by Compressure.*

M. צרור *Jrr, Jrur,* Is a Stone, a Pebble, a Stone used as a Weight, a little Gravel, or Flint-Stone. Whence a Scruple or small Weight, a Binder, &c.

Verb. צור To bind, bind together, bind up, sew together, strain, constrain, press, compress, to be in Straights and Afflictions; but these Significations you have in the Root צור.

M. יצר *Jjr.* Its Signification is Formation — To form, make, operate, fashion, of Mud, Clay, or Wax, for Instance; or to give a new and express Form to any Matter—To press, compress.

מצר *Mjr,* Straits. It may be derived from צור or צרר, as likewise the Verb when it signifies, to straiten.

Zeph. i. 15. *A Day* צרה *of Things bound, and* מצוקה, (of which next.)

Isa. v. 30. *Behold Darkness* צור (Bindings of Air) *for the Light is darkened in its Defluctions.*

Isa. xxx. 6. *The Land* צרה (of bound Parts of the Earth, Stone, Rock) and צוקה.

Psal. cxvi. 3. מצרי (Instruments of Binding) *The Chains of the Grave.*

Pfal. xcv. 5. *His Hands* יצרו *bound faſt the dry Land.*

Iſa. xliv. 10. *Before me was no God* נוצר *formed.*

Job xxvi. 8. צרר *binding the Waters in his denſe Grains.*

Prov. xxx. 4. *Who bound the Waters in a Garment.* I muſt bring in a Paſſage which explains theſe, though it be in other Words out of that noble Deſcription in *Job*, of the ſecond Formation of the Earth and Sea after the Flood, which has puzzled Friends, and made an Objection for Adverſaries, by miſtaking it for the firſt; when the Stars were reſtored to their Offices, and there were Sons of God to ſhout for Joy.

Job xxxviii. 9. *And ſhut up the Sea within Doors, when it broke forth, it iſſued from a Womb; when I made* עבן *the Cloud its Garment: And* ערפל *Darkneſs* (Defluctions of Grains) *its ſwaddling Band,* what they now call the Atmoſphere, in which theſe denſe Maſſes are included, whether dark or light, by which all Things are bound. The Word צרר or צרור ſeems to be a Diminutive of צור.

Prov. xxvi. 8. *As he that* צרור *binds a Stone in a Threſhing Engine.*

Amos

MOSES's *Principia.* 137

Amos ix. 9. *And not* צרור *a Grain,* (the Matter of what they speak of, Corn bound and so hard) *shall fall upon the Ground.*

2 Sam. xvii. 13. *Until there be not one* צרור *small Stone* ; (any Matter which was bound, and so form'd a hard Body used in building a City.)

M. צוק *Juk in Kal,* To adhere, cleave to, *Hiphil* הציק to make, adhere—To press, to bind fast, to constrain, to restrain—Pressure, Coarctation." This is a Word which implies the comparative Situation of any Thing, it must environ some other Thing or Things, but expresses Action, and the Manner of Action, pressing the Thing inward on every Side, or compressing it; and the Effect straitening or forcing the Things, or Parts of the Things into the least Compass, or closest to one another, thence to Actions upon the Mind, &c. and it has no other Signification. Indeed this and other Actions, are but the Effects of the Motions of the Heavens, and this of רקיע Expansion. I have shewed, under the last Word, other Texts which express what is implied in this encompassing or binding up Things with the Atmosphere: This Word expresses what is implied in the last Word, and is added in some of the Texts,

to

to express the Manner how they were bound, *viz.* by Compression, as

Zeph. i. 15. *A Day of* צרה *Bindings,* (or Environings) *and* מצוקה *of Compression.*

Isa. viii. 22. מועף *And Motion of Compressure,* and אפלה *by Grains of Air impulse.* This Motion by Compression, which implies that the Things are more pressed on one Side than on the other, as all Things near the Earth are; and Things being impell'd by Grains of Air, will not be consistent with our present Manner of speaking of the Language of our Philosophers; but if all inanimate Things be moved by Compressure, and impelled by Grains of Air, then we shall trust what *Isaiah, &c.* say in other Matters, and trust Philosophers no more.

M. יצק *Jink,* "His Exposition is Effusion, pouring out—יצוק *Pabul,* founded poured out—מוצק and מצק Participle passive, *Niphil*, something poured out, or in a Condition to be poured out, fusible, strong, robust, firm, hard. These Differences, nay direct Oppositions, according to our modern Philosophy, cannot be reconciled; but if what they render pouring out of Fluids, which are kept so by the common Agency of the Light, or melted

by

by Fire, or letting them fall, and fixing the Parts of such as will fix in Grains or dense Bodies, which we call Solids, be performed by the same Action of the same Agent; and that Action has only different Effects, upon different sorts of Atoms, or on each same sort in different Conditions; and is performed by the Action of Pressure or Compressure, according to the general Signification of this Word; then the Word does but signify one sort of Action, and if Scripture be true, this determines the grand Question; and carrying down Oil, till something stopt it, was the same Action, and perform'd by the same Agent as carries down melted Brass, till something stop it, and makes the Parts adhere and become strong, hard, &c. and if into a Mould or &c. figured it; and the same as fixes the Parts of Stone together, or carries the Part of a Stone so fixed downwards, till something stop it.

Gen. xxviii. 18. *And* יצק *poured the Oil upon his Head.*

Exod. xxxvi. 36. *And cast for them four Sockets of Silver.*

Job xli. 14. *The Flakes of his Flesh adhere* יצקו *compressed*——ver. 15. *His Heart* יצוק *firm as a Stone, yea firm as the nether Mill-Stone;* and though they have

given

given the Word צוק seemingly other Significations, *Station, placing,* &c. it has but that one Signification before mentioned.

Jos. vii. 23. *Laid them out before Jehovah.* They let the Things be pressed down, or fall, or laid them before the Lord.

1 Sam. xiv. 4. *And between the Passages, by which* Jonathan *thought to go over unto the* Philistines *Garrison,* מצב *there was a sharp Rock on the one Side, and a sharp Rock on the other Side. And the Name of the One was* Bozez, *and the Name of the other* Seneh. *The fore Front of the One was situate* מצוק, (in the same Sense, or the Instrument of straitening them) *Northward.* 2 Sam. xv. 24. *And* יצקו *they set down* (they let fall, or settle, or be pressed down and so stand) *the Ark of the* Aleim. Job xxix. 6. and צור *the* Press יצוק *poured me out Rivers of Oil.* xxxvii. 18. *Hast thou with him* (viz. with Grains) תרקיע *expanded* לשחקים *the Æthers,* (of which in its Place) *which are strong as* ראי, a Mixture of Metals and Minerals, as Brass, which could not be a Glass for looking thro', because it could not be transparent, nor for a burning Glass. Indeed the *Jews,* after the first Temple was destroy'd, used to collect Fire by burning Glasses from

the

the Heavens for their Sacrifices; and so the Heathens for their sacred Fire.

Vossius de Orig. & Progr. Idol. p. 328.—
" And if the sacred Fire was extinguished it was not lawful to light it by any common Fire, but (to use *Festus*'s Words concerning the Fire of *Vesta*) it was the Custom of the *Romans* to bore a Plank of unctious Timber till it caught Fire, and a vestal Vingin carried it upon a Brazen Sieve, into the Temple. But the *Grecians* used to kindle Fire by placing Combustibles in a concave Vessel and receiving the Rays of the Sun in its Center, according to *Plutarch* in *Numa*:" Which shews the Strength of this Conflict, (as the Word שחק signifies) by instantly dissolving the hardest Bodies: But the Words will not bend to this: These ראי or מראה were for Telescopes to observe the Change of the Moon, the Eclipses and Stars, which *Moses* took from the People, and made a Vessel of for the Tabernacle, as you may see *Exod.* xxxviii. 8. and so no more Mention of their Use: And they must be Concave or Reflex, and so exceeding close or dense as מוצק expresses, poured down and compress'd, strong from Compressure or an Instrument of Strength, so no room for Elasticity. *Job* xxxviii. 8. *Who can number the others in Wis-*

dom, and נבלי *the Defluxions of the Heavens who can cause to lie down in Compressing the Duft* למוצק *to Concretes that* רגבים *Grains adhere?* 1 Sam. ii. 8. *The* מצקי (Inftruments of Compreffion, the Compreffors or *Compreffions:* And if they will have it confequently, as they will fee by a greater Degree of Compreffure, in one Line than in another, *the Motion*, and fo Places, or Courfes, or *Stations*) *of the Earth are Jehovah's.* The fame Agent which God faid bound the Water, Abyfs, and Seas, is here faid with the fame Inftruments, and in the fame Manner, to bind, comprefs, and make adhere, not only Grains of Air, or folid Parts of, but the whole Earth. Thus the Atoms of Stone, and thofe of Metals in the Water, after the Diffolution of the Flood, were by Compreffion driven to each other, and fo form'd into Grains before they fettled: Thus the Atoms of Metal, after Diffolution in Spirits, are form'd into Grains: Thus the Atoms of Salt in Water are form'd into Grains: Thus the Atoms of Spirits are form'd into Grains: Thus the Atoms of Air form into Grains, and at fuch Sizes refpectively as the Compreffure of this Fluid gets comparatively fufficient Hold of them, each is prefs'd down, or

moved

moved by the continual Contact, and material Impulse, during its whole Course, according to the Rules aforesaid, with the Matter and Impulse remaining upon it when stop'd. You will see hereafter these Grains of Air are form'd near the Circumference of the Heavens; and each is, when form'd of sufficient Size, press'd down in a streight Line to the Center of the Sun, and some of them in that Course to the Earth, &c. they are call'd נבלי *Nebulæ*, and the Word is well explain'd, *Isa.* xxxiv. 4. *And all the Host of Heaven shall be dissolved, and the Heavens shall be rolled together as a Scroll, and all the Host of them* יבול *shall fall down as a Leaf* נבל *falls from the Vine, and as* גבלת *a falling Fig from the Fig-tree.*

That it may not be objected that these Words, which have been construed Grains of Air, Defluxions, &c. are any way confounded or us'd promiscuously by the sacred Writers, with Words us'd for the Clouds and Vapours in our Atmosphere, such Clouds as are composed of a Mixture, Part of such Grains, but mostly of Vapours from Atoms of Water, Vegetables, &c. approaching near each other, and in some small Degree adhering, so as to obstruct Part of the Light in its

Pas-

Paſſage: I muſt ſhew the Words uſed for them.

Gen. ix. 13. *I have ſet my Bow in* עָנָן *the Cloud.* Exod. xix. 9. *I come unto thee in* עָב *the Denſity* עָנָן *of the Cloud* Deut. iv. 11. *With* חֹשֶׁךְ *Darkneſs,* עָנָן *Clouds, and* עֲרָפֶל *Grains.* Job xxvi. 8. *And the* עָנָן *Cloud is not rent under them.* Pſ. xcvii. 1. עָנָן *Clouds and* עֲרָפֶל *Grains round about him.* Ezek. viii. 11. עָנָן *a Cloud of Incenſe went up.* xxxviii. 9. 16. *Like* עָנָן *to cover the Earth.*

The Vapours which conſtitute Part of theſe Clouds, have their proper Names directly oppoſite to Defluxions. The Word נשא ſignifies to lift up, and carry, from that Condition they take their Name נְשִׂאִים which we render Vapours, and the Word קטר Smoak Incenſe. But they are chiefly uſed for the light Vapour, and Smoak carry'd up by the latter immediately from the Fire; and the Sacrifices, becauſe they were ſo divided by Force into Vapour, and ſo lifted up, are ſo call'd; and to this Operation, at the Orb of the Sun, the burnt Offerings of the Heathens were made.

Pſal. cxxxv. 7. *He cauſeth* נְשִׂאִים *the Vapours to aſcend.*

Prov. xxv. 14. *Vapours and Wind without Rain.* Jer. x. 12. and li. 16. *Hath stretched out the Heavens by his Discretion; when he utters his Voice, there is a Multitude of Water in the Heavens, and he causes Vapours to ascend from the Ends of the Earth.* Psal. cxlviii. 8. *Fire, and Hail, and Snow and* קיטור *Vapour*. And these Vapours falling down, are called by other proper Names as מטר *Rain*, ברד *Hail*, שלג *Snow*, &c.

As Part of the Matter of the Heavens has been expressed by the Condition of been concreted into Grains, by their Office of impelling Things, and of their Course by that of נבל Defluxions; and as the Heathens worshipped something, in some Places, by the Name of בל, or בול in others of בעל, we shall shew that they are all the same. No doubt the Heathens gave additional Titles of King, Lord, Antient, &c. to what they served as God; but those general Titles determine nothing. The Word בעל is used among Men for one who had the Power to make another move or act, as Lord, Husband, an Officer among Men, who rode and fought in Chariots, &c. in animate Things 'tis the Agent which moves and acts upon other

Things, and by its Force makes them move or act, which is one of the three Names of the Parts of the Heavens in that Condition, or with that Power. The first is expressed by the Word חמה, the second by שמש & *al.* and the third by בעל, as 'tis expressed 2 *Kings* iv. 24. with an Epithet שלשה, the third *Idol*, (or as I should construe it, the RULER in THREE) and so construed the third Power by the Cabalists in *Hortum nucis*, Fol. 51. 1. *C. Syr.* "ביל *Bil*, *Jupiter*, Ibid. and *B. C.* בעל *Baal*, contracted בל. The Name of an Idol, which the *Assyrians*, *Persians*, and *Babylonians* worshipped. Hence *Jupiter* is called *Belus*. *Pliny* l. 6. c. 26. *Syr. Jupiter* the Lord of Heaven, 2 *Mac.* vi. 2. *M.* הבל. It is also by a *Metonymy* put for the Air, an Exhalation, Wind, Breath, and Vapour, which soon vanishes; or an Idol which is nothing. *Chal.*—Calefaction, an Heating. *C. Chald.* Smoke, Vapour, Exhalation, an Halitus, or warm Stream. *C. Syr.* יבל, Spirit, Wind." But to come close. *C.* בלל, " To mix together, to mix with, to besprinkle, to mingle, *Subst.* Mixture:" When an Agent, as a false God is always taken to be, 'tis the Mixer, which is the most expressive Word for these Grains, which

where

where all is full, cannot move without mixing with one or both of the other two Parts, and as you will see, always moves into the thinner or smaller Parts, and disperses them; and that we might not be mislead in such Cases, and where the Word is not *Hebrew*, the sacred Writers have given us explanatory *Hebrew* Words as in this Case of בעל *Jos.* xv. 59. קרית בעל בעלה איה. *Ibid.* xv. 9. היא קרית יערים קרית יערים. They construe this the City of Woods; whatever their Images were of, their Gods were not Wood. He is speaking here of a City dedicated to a Gods or at least what they took for a God, as 2 *Kings* x. 25. עיר בית הבעל. *The City of the Temple of* Baal; and there were Temples, and Altars, and Sacrifices, and Feasts to him almost every where; his imagined, in one Sense, real Dominion, was not confined to Woods; the sacred Writer intends to shew us what this God was; the Ark was left, 1 *Sam.* vii. 1. at *Kirjath-jearim*, when it was fetch'd thence 2 *Sam.* vi. 1. this City was call'd בעלי יהודה and *Jos.* xviii. 14. *Kirath Baal*, which is *Kirjath Jearim, a City of the Children of Judah.* The Jod in ערים is the same as in בעלי, and עדה is a Word of Condition, of the Part of the Heavens they call בל,

O 2 the

בעל, which is to pour out or down; and to prove this the Jod is left out, *Efdr.* ii. 25. קרית ערים: and as the Word expresses the pouring down of the Grains or Spirit of the Heavens, which is one of the three chief Agents, and that Action one of the three chief Actions in this Machine; 'tis applied to the Spirit of God in the same Sense, Isa. xxxii. 15. *Till the Spirit* יערה *be poured upon you from on high.* Psal. xxxiii. 6. *And by the Spirit of his Mouth all the Host of them.* 'Tis likely to this Power were the Pourings out or down, or as they called them, the Drink-Offerings of the Heathens, after claimed by God. This Matter in this Motion had several additional Attributes, and they made this Word, and one of the highest Attributes, synonymous, as *Jud.* ix. 4. בית אל ברית v. 46. בית בעל ברית.

As I have begun to shew the Philosophy of the Heathens, and thereby the natural Powers, though it be not my Business, I must hint what their Magic so much talked was. The Word *M.* ענן, *Clouds,* "Also to divine or augur from the Aspect of the Heavens or Clouds. *B.C.* ענן An *Augur,* Sooth-sayer, Cloud-monger, one who foretels future good or bad Fortune by the Clouds. As these People

had

had neglected revealed Knowledge, and so taken the Heavens for a God; and as Men have always made diligent Search for the Knowledge of the Will of what they took for their God, both here and with respect to Futurity; and as these had no other Way, except when it thunder'd, but by observing the Differences in the Appearances of their God, which was in Fire, or Lights, and Clouds; and as the Lights were generally uniform or periodical, they had the most Opportunity to make Observations upon the Clouds. This was their own Imagination, or a Consequence of imagining that it was a God; their Philosophy was what they had retain'd of the Traditions of Revelation, but their Divinity was their own, false in the Root and in every Branch, and when they were once fallen into this Delusion, no doubt it run very high, and these Observers and Discoverers of the Will of their God were in high Esteem. It required as much Power to bring these Grains to the Place, or to make them concrete there, as to dissolve them there, and to send forth Fire and Light; and this Cloud expressed by this Word, was a joint Attendant with the Light in all the Manifestations, and is predicted to be one in the last,

Dan.

Dan. vii. 13. *With the Clouds of Heaven.* Against this Vice was the long Attendance of the Cloud in the Wilderness, to shew God the Master of what they took for Director or Declarer of the Events of Actions or Presages of Things. Hence the severe Laws against עננים *Augurs,* &c. Hence Clouds of Vapours from the burning of Incense: Hence all the Expressions of Claim: Whether the Result of the Augurs Observations, and his Answer was the Rise of Oracles, and what Relation the Attributes worshipped at the Temples, mentioned *Jos.* xv. 59. בית ענות and *Jos.* xix. 38. and *Jud.* 33. בית ענת may be considered some other Time.

Ver. 2. --- רוח the Spirit of God מרחפת moved upon פני the Face *(Faces)* of the Waters.

M. רוח *Ruah*—Dilation—Space, Interstice; רוח is the Spirit, Wind, a Blast. Plural רוחות is spoke of various Things which are moved, and are not seen. *S.* Particularly and properly of the Air, Elementary Wind, a Gale of Air, a Whirlwind, and Storm. *K.* רוח is to Respire, or Dilate. *Pag,* or to be dilated and relaxed;

relaxed: As רוח the Wind comes from hence, it is not improperly expounded, to blow, blow out, which is, to respire or breath; but it is taken impersonally, it is relaxed, refreshed, refrigerated. It includes Motion and Agitation.

C. Chald.—רוחגיות Men who imagine they can deduce Virtues from the Celestial Bodies. *Cosri. Buxt.* 178, 195, 232.

We shall find that רוח is a Name of Office, and as it was the first material Agent that acted, it could not be made a Name of Condition, nor could a Verb of the same Letters express the Agent and the Action, as in other Cases, because it acts in different Manners, upon different Subjects; so where acting upon inanimate Things, 'tis generally attended with a Verb to distinguish; we find that it was concreted, *Amos* iv. 13. *And concreteti the Spirit.* That it is Part of the Matter of the Heavens, *Dan.* viii. 8. and xi. 4. *Zech.* ii. 6. and vi. 15. *The four Spirits of the Heavens.* And this is what our Philosophers call Space, which puts itself successively into the Place of any Thing in Motion, or which it moves, as *Gen.* xxxii. 16. *and put* רוח *Spirit betwixt Drove and Drove.* Exod. viii. 15. *that there was* הרוחה *Respite,* (Spirit instead of Frogs) though the proper Word for Space, or Dimenſion of Matter, is רחב: that the Grains called the Spirit, in ſeveral Caſes have the ſame Attributes, under other conditional Names; that each of the Parts which compoſe this Agent, are concreted Grains of Air, ſuch as obſtruct Light. 1 *Kiugs* xviii. 45, *The Heavens darkned themſelves with* עבים *Denſities and* רוח *Spirit,* (Grains in Motion.) Theſe that were to move upon the Faces of the Waters, when there, though at reſt, yet compreſſed, and are the ſame, as *Job* xxvi. 8. *Binding the Waters* עביו *in his Denſities.* Vid. Prov. xxx. 4. And the ſecond Time, or at the Reformation, *Job* xxxviii. 9. *When I made* ענן *the Cloud its Garment, and* ערפל *Defluxions of Grains its ſwadling Band.* This is the ſame as thoſe ſaid to be impelled *Iſa.* viii. 22. It is contrived and framed for the chief Inſtrument in the Machine, and ſo for Operation, Prov. xxx. 4. *Who hath gathered the Spirits in his Fiſts?* Who hath gathered and bound the Atoms, which compoſe each Grain of the Spirit in the Firmament of the Heavens, which is all along called his Hands? *Iſa.* xl. 13. *Who* תכן *the Spirit of Jehovah?* I take the Word תכן to be a Compound of תכה to conjoin, and כון proportionably to its Office, or fitly.

M.

MOSES's *Principia.*

M. תכן "Signifies Number and Sum, to weigh, to number, to dispose by Numbers, to direct, fit up, farbricate— *Jerom.* תכנית, their equal Libration or poising.

B. C. Ibid. and תוכן, a Numberer, Auditor, Arithmetician, and Astronomer, numbering the Stars, and laying out the Heaven or Air." So previously who has given the Spirit Proportion in Number, Size, Weight, *&c.* And here consequently, as speaking of an Agent, given it the Power of Pressure, and thereby of weighing, prefering, separating, sorting, and disposing the several Classes of Things; and further with respect to Size, who made the Atoms of such proper Figure and Size, that when they concreted to proper Sizes, till the Compression should take hold of, and return them, that then they should not be driven into, or through the Pores of other Things, but be able to press and drive them. This is expressed, *Job* xli. 7. *One is so close to another, that* רוח *the Spirit* (these Grains in Motion) *cannot come between them.* Job xxvi. 13. *By his Spirit he garnished the Heavens.* We have Descriptions of its Formation, Place where formed, Change of its Course, Descent, Impulse, binding by the Sizes of its Parts, supplying and exciting the Fire, and being melted, ed, As this Spirit, these Grains are said to be his Drivers, so they are said to be made his Angels, his Legates, *Pf,* civ. 21 *Making the* עמים *Densities* רכבו *his Drivers: walking* (they, not he) *upon the Wings of the Spirit: making the Spirits his Agents.* It is said to be invested with that superior Power, or comparatively, that greater Degree of Pressure than the smaller Parts, and so with Precedence, which moves Bodies in this Fluid. *Job.* xxviii. 25. *To make* לרוח *the Spirit* משקל *the Instrument of Weight.* Chald. *Making Weight by the Spirit or Air.* Pſal. lv. 9. *From the Spirit raised by a Tempeſt.* cxlviii. 8. *The Spirit of the Tempeſt fulfilling his Word.* Ibid. cxlvii. 18. ישב *he causes the Spirit to blow, the Waters flow.* Job xxxvii. 9. *The Breath of Jehovah maketh Ice:* (or perhaps, from the Breath Strength is given to the Ice.) Eccl. i. 6.—*goes round in a Circle: the Spirit coming on; and in its Rounds the Spirit returns.* And Job xxxvii. 1. *Yea, that which is clear tears to pieces* עב *the Denſity. The Cloud ſcatters his Light, and it is turned round about by his Counſel; that they may do whatſoever he commanded them upon the Face of the World on the Earth.* But I muſt refer theſe two laſt to their Place. It is deſcribed to have Wings, Inſtruments

struments of Strength for Motion of itself, and for carrying other Things, which are by the greater Hold, the Compression has upon the Grains, its Parts, than it has upon the Atoms or Parts of Light; so that one Part successively impels another, and that the whole is both Agent and Patient. 2 *Sam.* xxii. 11. *Psal.* xviii. 11. *Upon the Wings of the Spirit.* Job xxxviii. 13. *Didst thou make the Dawn know its rising? That it might take hold of the Wings of the Earth.* And that it compresses on every Side, as well as by pressing more on one Side than on the other, or indeed often by being less resisted on one Side, than on the other, drives. *Hosea* iv. 19. *The Spirit bound her with its Wings.* This Power among the Heathens was represented by Wings of Birds, or Imitations of them upon Images. In Allusion to its acting upon Fire, *Isa.* xxxiii. 11. רוחכם אש תאכלכם *Zant. Pag. Your Spirit shall be a Fire which shall consume you.* Ezek. iii. 13. *The Noise of the Wings of the living Creatures that touched one another, and the Noise of the Wheels overagainst them: and the Noise of a great rushing. So the Spirit lifted me up, and took me away, and I went in Bitterness* בחמת רוחי *in the Heat of my Spirit.*

Though

Though the Spirit is one of the three Parts, in respect of Condition and Action, into which the Heavens are divided, and sometimes by the Heathens included in the Word *Darkness* sometimes in *Heaven*, as the several Writers or Translators fram'd different Ideas of it, 'tis sometimes express'd by the Word *Air*, frequently by that of *Æthers*; and 'tis also frequently expressed by *Spirit*, which as I have shew'd, is the same as *Bell*, *Jupiter*, &c. And they have also given Attributes to it, according to their Ideas of it.

Justi Lipsi, Vol IV. p. 587. " Air includes Fire, and is a *Greek* Word, but received, saith *Cicero*, into Use among the *Romans*, and latinized: with them it is the Spirit or Soul, according to *Cicero*: Sometimes Heaven, and a Void or Vacuum."

— *Stobæus* in his physical Eclogues — " and both add — This is an Etherial Body, the Seed of Procreation of the Universe, and the Measure of a certain Period."

Polyglot. — " *Ægypt* was formerly called *Aeria*, *Airy*, from the Air, as *Eusebius* remarks in his Chronicles."

The whole Nation of *Æthiopia* was first called *Ætheria*, *Ætherial*, as *Pliny* in his

his natural History of the World, Book VI. Chap. 30."

Voſſius, &c. *Vitruvius Lib.* 9. c. 4. "This seems to be the Cause that some Stars are temperate, some hot, and some cold, namely, all Fire sending up a Flame toward the Places above it. Therefore the Sun scorching with his Rays the Æther above it, makes it glowing hot, in which Places the Star of *Mars* performs its periodical Revolution, and therefore its made hot by the Heat of the Sun. But *Saturn* which is next to the Extremities of the Mundane System, and touches the congealed Regions of Heaven, is very cold; and thence *Jupiter* who performs his Revolution between both the others, must have the most agreeable and moderate Effects between the extreme Heat of the one, and Cold of the other. So *Pliny* the younger—Book II. Chap. 8. The Star of *Saturn* is of a cold and freezing Nature."

Voſſius, Ibid. p. 259. *Stobæus* in his physical Eclogues, and Chapter of the Nature of the Heavens, p. 52, 53.—"*Empedocles* said the Heavens were solid, concreted in the Manner of Ice by Fire, and Air; and that they contained in each Hemisphere the Nature of both Fire and Air. *Stobæus* adds, that *Anaximander* thought

thought the Heaven or Air to be a Mixture of Hot and Cold. And as you may see in *Achilles Tatius*'s Phænomena, p. 85. *Florentine* Edition, he made the Heaven or Air rapid or circulating, partaking of Fire. *Parmenides, Heraclius, Strato,* and *Zeno,* made it only igneous, as *Stobæus* reports in the same Place. But what Need is there to produce many Authors, when *Aristotle* himself acknowledges that all before him assigned the Heavens some an aerial some an igneous Nature; for so he writes in his second Book of the Heavens, Chap. 9. — If the Bodies of these Stars be carried, whether it be by the Plenum of the Air, diffused throughout the whole, or of the Fire, as *All* say —"

Voss. de Phys. &c. — *Gen.* Chap. 1. " *Moses* here makes Mention of a double Efficient, the *Spirit* whence Motion, and the *Light* whence Heat — And I am much inclined to think, that by the *Spirit of God moving upon the Waters, Moses* does not mean the third Person of the Holy Trinity, but the Spirit created the first Day by the Trinity, and afterwards put into Fossils and other Things that are called inanimate, to be the Vehicle of the motive Faculty, and with Light the Vehicle

cle of Heat, to be the Cause of the Preservation of the several Species of Things, and of the Generation of new Individuals."

Vossius de Orig. &c. — *Diodorus* of *Osiris* and *Isis*—" The Nature of these two Deities contributes much to the Generation of all Things, the one being igneous and spirituous, the other moist and dry, but both having in common the Property of the Air: And by these are all Things generated and nourished."

Ibid. &c. " Of the Heathen Philosophers *Democritus* did not acknowledge any Spirits; nor did *Aristotle* any other than such as moved the celestial Orbs. Some construed him otherwise."

Vossius de Physi. Christ. &c. —" *Apuleius* says the true Name of the Goddess, is *Isis*, to whom at almost the End of the Book he addresses his Prayers in these Words:

" Thee, the Powers above worship, the infernal reverence. Thou circulates the Earth, illuminates the Sun, governs the World, treads under Foot *Tartarus*. To thee the Stars answer, the Deities rejoice, the Elements serve thee, at thy Word the Winds blow, the Clouds are collected, the Seeds sprout, the Sprouts grow."

Kircher

160 MOSES's *Principia.*

Kircher Obelisc. Pamp. p. 342.—*Virgil. Æneid.* 6.

"The Spirit internally nourishes, and a Mind infused thro' each Part, agitates the whole Mass, and mixes with the great Body, *viz.* of Nature."

Ibid. *Kircher, &c.*—"*Horus* in Book I. Ch. 64. shews in express Words, that the Spirit of God pervading all Things was signified by a Serpent—They signify the Governor of all Things by the Perfection of the same Animal, painting again an entire Snake. So it is with them the Spirit which pervades the whole Universe. How aptly they expressed the vivifying Spirit of the World by the Wings of an Hawk, *Mercury* seems to touch in these Words, The Efficient Mind with the Word or Logos, containing Circles, and whirling them round with great Impetus, hath given Rotation to his Machine, and continued that Rotation, from Beginning without Beginning, and to End without End, for it always begins where it ends."

Kircher, &c. 399. "They signified by Wings the Motive Power in God, or a certain Form penetrating all Things, which *Iamblicus* calls the Spirit of the World.— *Plotinus* the third Mind, *p.* 402.—*Abenephus*, the *Arabian*. And by the Figure of

MOSES's *Principia.* 161

a Circle supported with the two Wings of an Hawk, they denoted the Spirit of the World, p. 403. A Fragment of *Sanchoniathon*, wrote in the *Old Chaldee* or *Phenician* Tongue.—" Zus hu Asphira A'cra-
" nitha, meni Arits Chuia; Asphira hu
" Chiyl d'Alha dilh la Strura ula Shulma
" acrahn mdyh; vchnia hu rucha d'Alha
" dmchina cul ylma. *Jupiter* is a feigned Sphere, from it is produced a Serpent; the Sphere shews the Divine Nature to be without Beginning or End; the Serpent, his Word, which animates the World, and makes it prolific. His Wing, the Spirit of God, that by its Motion gives Life to the whole Mundane System."

Clem. Alex. Strom. Lib. V. p. 431. The *Stoics* say, that God is a Body or Substance, and a Spirit as to his Essence, as he is certainly a Soul.

Kircher ob. Pamph. p. 419. *Porphyry* says, that an Hawk was dedicated to the Sun, because it is the Symbol of Light and Spirit; of the one, upon Account of the Swiftness of his Motion, of the other, for his soaring on high, the higher Regions being fuller of Light than the lower. *Ibid.* In the Exposition of the Fable of *Isis.*

Vol. II.   P   *Vossius*

Voffius de Orig. & progr. Idol. Lib. II. p. 193. Demoft.—*Harpocration* upon the Word λικνϕορος, the Van, or winnowing Inftrument, is neceffary in all Initiations and Sacrifices.—An old Poet in *Plutarch*, and *Clem. Alexander*'s Admonition to the Gentiles.——*Worfhipping with confecrated Vans.* There was a triple Purgation of the Soul in the Heathen Rites; one by Air, another by Water, and a third by Fire. The winnowing Inftrument, or Van of *Bacchus*, belongs to the Air, as likewife the Ofcilla, or little Images, hung upon Ropes, and fwung in the Air in the Service of *Bacchus*.

Clem. Alexand. Strom. Lib. V. p. 443. *Orpheus*—fpeaking of God, that he doth not fall under our Sight, faith, that he was known only to one Perfon, a *Chaldean*, whether he means *Abraham*, or his Son, by thefe Words. "None but a certain Firftborn, of great Antiquity, a Branch of the *Chaldean* Stock; he was a Proficient in the Knowledge of the ftarry Vortex, and Motion of the Sphere; how it compleats its Courfe round the Earth, moving round in a Circle equally upon its own Axis: And how the Spirit rules in the Air, and in the Waters.

Ibid.

Ibid. Strom. vi. p. 471. And again, by the Study of Astronomy being lifted up above the Earth, he will ascend with his Mind to the Heavens, and be carried round with their Circumgyration: always contemplating Divine Things, and their Relations and Harmony, one with the other, raised by whose Impulse, *Abraham* gradually ascended to the Knowledge of the Creator.

Kircher Oedip. v. 1. p. 253. says, the Tradition of *Abraham*'s Discourse with *Nimrod* was mention'd by *Hieron.* l. 9. in *Gen.* and divers others, and this by *Raffi R. Chaia*. And when *Nembrod* set Fire before him, and commanded him to worship it, *Abraham* retorted, Rather worship Water, that extinguishes Fire. *Nembrod* said to him, then worship Water. If so, worship the Clouds that drop down the Water. *Nembrod* answer'd, then worship the Clouds. To this *Abraham*, If so, the Wind is rather to be worshipped, that drives and dispels the Clouds. *Nembrod* again, worship the Wind. If so, saith *Abraham*, Man ought much more to be worshipped, who understands the Wind. You trifle, said *Nembrod*, at length growing in a Passion, I worship Fire alone, and therefore cast thee headlong into the Midst thereof; let the God come whom thou worshippest, and let his right Hand deliver thee, &c.

M. רחף *Rhp*, its Expofition is to be moved, Motion.———*Gen.* i. מרחפת moved itfelf. *M. Blew.* The Word רחף fignifies Motion, or as a Verb, to move or be mov'd; but with a מ, it, after the *Hebrew* Manner, fignifies for Motion, or an Inftrument of Motion, as רכב and מרכב; &c. And this compound Word could but be ufed upon this Occafion, becaufe there is no other Inftrument or Means of Motions in this Syftem; fo the Senfe is, the Spirit was made the Inftrument of Motion, with an Expreffion of Claim, (of God;) becaufe you, by the Citations above, and more fully hereafter, may fee the Heathens attributed an invifible Strength or Power, without any Inftitution, or at leaft, without any Controul from God, to the Matter of the Heavens, which operated upon Things materially. Indeed, the two other Places, where this fimple Verb is ufed, exprefs the Manner of this Motion to be forward, and backward, or every way, as fluttering or trembling; and it could not be otherwife here, where all is full, as the larger Grains preceded, the fmaller muft recede.

By

By a מ being prefixed, the Word רוח is in a few Instances made an Agent of Compressure and Motion.

S. מרח *Mrah,* hath three Significations: First, to bind round, רדידה to roll in fwadling Cloaths, to fwaddle, to plaifter over, put upon. *Noun.* מרוח bound, compreffed. 2. *Syr.* מרח *Chaldee. Hiphil.* אמרח to become bold, rafh,—*Chaldee.* מריח bold, rafh, מרחות Boldnefs, *Rabb.* מרח To ventilate. מריחה Ventilation, winnowing, or cleaning of Corn; and all from רוח the Spirit, Wind. 3. *Arabick* מרח *Mrah,* ח *Cheth* pointed above, anoint with, *&c.*

C. *Ethiopic.* To draw, lead, led forth, a Leader, General.—

M. פנה *Pnah.* Its Expofition is Afpect, to turn the Face, to turn, to turn forwards from one to another, to turn back, to turn to any Thing, to fee any Thing by turning to it. It fignifies *that* which is turned towards us, פנים *Pnim,* or *Panim,* the Face, the Fore-part of any Thing. This may be taken in a general Senfe. If this Motion was only to comprefs, and was to every Part of the Surface (as the Waters were in a hollow Sphere) within and without; for the Spirit within expands or ftrives to move outward, and that without inward, so forms an Atmosphere, binds both from without, and from within; all the Force is in this, it binds all Solids, and compresses all Fluids, even in Motion, as well as at Rest; because the Atoms in large Quantities of grosser Fluids, or large Concretes, obstruct some considerable Part of the Pressure of the opposite Spirit, or that which presses on the opposite Side, and so each Spirit on each Side drives any other small Quantity of Fluid, or Concrete, which is near the Surface of such great Quantity of Fluids or Concretes, to it; and also wherever any Part of this Fluid is thinned by the Action of Fire, or by Light, issued from that in Fire, or the Spirit, or gross Grains, are separated from the small ones by any Means, the next Spirit, as the Word sounds, rusheth thither, and pushes every Thing in its Way with Force, proportionable to the Thinness and Extent of the Part so thinn'd; when exceedingly and suddenly thinn'd with a Force next to infinite, and drives out the thinned Parts with equal Velocity, and with a Force of another Nature; because it consists of small Parts, they enter the Pores of any Thing in their Way, to pervade or dissolve, rather than impel, as Lightning, &c. except

they

they be directed by the solid Sides of the Tubes they pass in, and can detach some larger Atoms to act with.

But to keep close to the infallible Method the divine Writers have used to distinguish the same Thing by its different Situations, Conditions, or Offices, as these Grains are called ערפל when falling down upon, עבן when binding the fluid Mixture, or Body, without Power of moving it, &c. and רוח when they were made an Instrument to move it, supposing God acted then, as the Matter does now, by Compressure, no Blast could begin unless the Sphere moved, or the Fluid were made thinner on one Part of the Surface than on the other, nor could continue unless the Sphere continued to proceed, or that, or another Part were successively made thinner. If the Sphere had been set a going, and the Compressure, and so Impulse had been continued, it would have moved the Sphere streight to the Confines of the Heavens. If one Part of the Fluid were made thinner, and the Spirit rush'd in there, and moved the Sphere, and all that which push'd in successively had been made so, the Case would have been the same, except the Fluid were made thin in another Part, and the Spirit should rush in there, and incline the Sphere's Course from a right Line, and at the same Time turn the Sphere or Orb upon its Center or Axis. If the Fluid, upon the next adjoining Part of the Surface of the Sphere, were thin'd or small, and so the thin Part were issued thither, the Spirit would successively have a new Face opposite to its Push, or a new Part turned to it, or face it, and in one Rotation of the Sphere it would turn all its Faces, even without considering its Declination; so in progressive Motion the thin Parts of the Fluid, whether they, or it, be light or dark, which in this Case is only consider'd as its Parts are smaller, and less Hold is taken on each of them by the Compressure, than upon the Grains, and so lighter than the Grains, and are only driven upward or outward by those Grains, or this Spirit, beautifully express'd by the Verb, M. שאף *Sap, Its Signification is the drawing in of the Spirit or gross Air, Attraction*; but signifies only a Condition, whereby 'tis liable to admit the Spirit, by receding and giving Room or Place to it, as *Eccl.* i. 5. *Anhelus oriens ipse ibi*, admitting the Spirit, and receding from its Place; so the said thin Parts rule and direct this Force of the Spirit, as you will

will find soon after they were appointed to do; but as there was no Light then, nor no natural Means to make any to direct this Force, no more than there was any natural Cause of Compressure to move, we must believe that God used his supernatural Power; and we may suppose that he begun in the same Manner as they proceed: And if we take it in the obvious Meaning of the Word, that is, of the Parts turn'd to, and so successively facing the Face or Course of the Spirit, so that the Sphere turned and gave a new Part successively to the Push of this Agent, or to that Part where the Spirit had the greatest Power, and so the Power of Motion, as the Word פנה is used of other Things quite through the Scripture, as xxxii. 15. *And he turned.* Lev. xxvi. 9. *For I will turn to you.* Numb. xiv. 25. *Turn you.* Jer. ii. 27. *They have turned unto me their Back, and not their Face.* Ezek. x. 11. *To the Place whither the Head turned,* and many more; and is used to the very Point in Hand, Psal. xc. 9. *All our Days* פנו *are turned about in thy Wrath.* Jer. vi. 4. *Wo unto us for the Day is turned about; for the Shadows of the Evening extend themselves;* and other Verbs which express the Earth's Motion

by

by the Action of this Agent; as *M.* נשׁח
To blow, to breathe. Cant. ii. 7. *Till it
blows Spirit in the Day;* then the Sphere
of Water, &c. would not only turn round,
but also have local or progressive Motion,
as the same Matter soon after form'd into
an Orb had, and has by the Spirit successively driving into the Light, flowing to one
Side of this said Globe from the Sun, soon
after also form'd; and this Part, or the Edge
of Light where the Spirit exerts its Force,
is called by the same Name, as you may
see in C. where the *Syr. Æthiop.* &c. use
it for this Part, or what we call the Evening; and it is called, *Gen.* iii. 8. *At the
Spirit of* (when it blowed Spirit in) *the
Day.* The Verb is used for this Operation of the Spirit, (*M.* נשׁב), it signifies
impelling or *blowing*, as Exod. xv. 10.
Thou didst blow with thy Spirit) is used
for the Twy-light of the Evening, when
this Force which impels the Earth is exerted, as Prov. vii. 9. *In the Twilight, in*
ערב יום *the Evening of the Day*, (another
conditional Term) *in the Mixture*, where
the Spirit pushes into the Light, &c. or the
Part where the Force is exerted, tho' im-
perceptible in the Length of one of our
Bodies, because all being full, 'tis performed by Precedence and Recedence, and
by

by the Progression of the Earth, &c. At this Time and Place the Motion and turning of this Orb began; and thus (as 'tis taken) before Light the Evening was, and after the forming of Light, the Morning was the first Day.

But this is not only one Part of the Motion of this Fluid, but indeed, tho' by supernatural Power the first Part, yet now the last Part, or an Effect of its natural or mechanical Motion; and as it happened among the Heathens to be the chief Attribute of the moving Powers of the Heavens, perhaps God, in his Prescience, thought fit to begin here, to shew that he could make it perform the very Effect, without the mechanical Cause; though we have Account here that the Spirit was made the Instrument of Motion, not this, nor perhaps the next, is the Account where the Machine was founded, but that it was step by step establish'd; and there are the Places to shew what the Motion of this Agent mechanically does in all its several Parts; and in the whole, that the Motion of the Parts of this Fluid, in the three different Manners, in different Conditions, with different Accidents, and so called by three different Names, not only

ly attempts, as I have shew'd in the first Part, to expand itself, as the Word is taken to signify, but that by Consequence these Motions and their Effect, Compression and their Effect, or Consequence upon themselves, alternate Division, and Re-adhesion of the Atoms of this Fluid, as they are now established in a Course, are the Causes of all Motion, Formation, Accretion, Productions, and of the Divisions or Dissolutions of such Substances, whose Conditions are assigned to be mutable. *Moses* tells us this Power of Motion first begun upon, or against the Faces of the Waters; and tho' he tells us that this Motion soon after reach'd to the Extremities of the Heavens, because its Effect, Expansion, reach'd thither, yet we hear little more of this Agent, by this Name, in this Part of its Action, till *Solomon* gives us a perfect Account of the Manner of its Operation in moving this Orb, in *Eccl.* i. because it always, in the natural Course of Things, after the Machine was establish'd, attends Light, is the Counterpart, or indeed the first Part of that Motion, by moving into the Center of it, supplying Matter for it, and making it move outward, or the contrary Way; and as one may, say, they when establish'd, reciprocally

MOSES's *Principia.* 173

ly affist in forming one another, and then speaking of the one is implying the other, and speaking of either implies the Condition and Motion Part of the Fluid is in, which we call Fire: As Things were soon after establish'd, the first or chief End of the Spirit was to supply the Fire with Matter, or with itself to be melted at the Orb of the Sun, express'd by other Verbs, as *M.* נפח to blow, to breath, to cherish, Job. xx. 26. *A Fire not blown shall destroy him.* Isa. liv. 16. *That bloweth the Coals in the Fire.* Ezek xxii. 20. *To blow the Fire upon it,* which will come under that Head; tho' the next conditional Name of Part of this Fluid, which we render Light, is now put into that Condition by Fire, another conditional Name of Part of the same Fluid; yet perhaps that Light was made supernaturally, or by other Means, or in another Manner, without Fire, because it was afterwards worshipped.

The Natives of *Canaan* had a Temple to their God, the Heavens under this Attribute, *Jos.* xv. 53. בית־תפוח which expresses all the Action of the Spirit, not only in moving the Earth and other Orbs, but in supplying the Fire, dividing and forcing out the Light, and so partly belongs

longs to Fire. And I find *C. Chald.* נחשא the Name of a Bird. נפח *Ethiopic*, "To blow an Horn, Trumpet, to command the Trumpet to be sounded," which makes me suppose that this Attribute was worshipped with Wind Musick, and if נפי be related, perhaps with Vocal: And *Ar.* ארן "To diffuse Odours, to yield a Fragancy as Spices, Incense, or such like Things," which makes me suppose, that this Attribute was also worshipped with burning Perfumes, whence those Services were required by God of the *Jews*.

The Motion of the Spirit horizontally, whether such as the Regular or Trade Winds near the Equator, or those here seemingly irregular, of whatever Uses they are, whether for Refreshment, purging the Air, or other natural Uses, or whatever artificial Uses we make of them; tho' they are not under Consideration here, as being the smallest Actions of this Agent, and so not worth naming; yet they are all governed by the same Law, when any Part of the Air upon the Surface of this Globe, is made grosser than another, either by Vapours from below, or Clouds from above; the grosser Parts are pushed forward into the next which are thinner, and what we call a Storm or Wind, is

made

made thereby; and when the Defluxions from the Surface, or Extremities of the Heavens, moving in ſtreight Lines towards the Orb of the Sun, happen near the Line of the Horizon, of any Part of the Surface of this Globe, they are then perceptible and cold, eſpecially when the horizontal Motion is the ſame Way; but the Grains from the Extremities deſcend gradually, and they, as Spirit, take Place of the Light in the Evening gradually and regularly; ſo that there can never be any room to make any Motion downward, or with that little Degree of Declination like Wind, becauſe they are ſucceſſively every Moment fill'd with the Spirit.

Ver. 3. And God אמר ſaid יהי אור ויהי אור let there be Light, and there was Light.

M. אמר. To ſay, command, decree, conſtitute. *Acad. Orat.* 1695. p. 29. who who made the Machine of the World, not with an Hammer, but a Word, who pinned together the ſeveral Parts of the Elements, not with Iron, but a Command.

The Word יהי is render'd *Interlineary* and *Chaldee*, Sit, *Let there be*. *Vulg. Septua-*
gint

gint, *Syriac, Samaritan,* Fiat, *let there be made.* *Arabic,* Effet, *that there should be.* *Persian,* Esto, *Be there.* This cannot refer to the Act of Creation, for all the Atoms of Matter were created at first. The Word expresses Existence, and the Substantive, or other Verbs used with it, must express the Manner. This must be a Change in some Accident or Condition, which something already created was liable to, and which God, or something which he had created, and obey'd him, was capable of putting it into, and must be in some of these Manners, let there be form'd, or let there be made, or let there be such Motions as will produce such Accidents, so that the Matter may be in such Condition, in such Motion, and with such Effects: Let the Atoms, if loose, adhere in Grains or Forms; if adhering in Grains or Forms, let them be dissolved to Atoms; if they be in Motion or moved, let them rest; if at Rest, let them be moved in this, or that Manner, so as they may be in a Condition to perform all the Actions Light is intended or commanded to execute. This Existence has not Relation to Being, but to Form; for though the Matter exists in Atoms, till some of them are put together, they are not a Grain; so though the A-

toms

toms exist in Grains, till they are divided, and in Motion, they are not Light; as *Isa.* xlv. 7. *Forming Light, and concreting Darkness.*

M. אוּר, Light, Splendor, Illumination, Morning Light, the Morning, Day-break. *Plur.* אוּרִים Lights, Luminaries. מָאוֹר, a Luminary, a lucid Body, a Body full of Light. *Plur.* מְאוֹרֹת and מְאוֹרִים. Where the Sun is mentioned, it is the Moon; when joined with the Moon, it is the Sun, the Fountain of Light; whence *Apollo* is called *Orus*, or *Horos.*

אוּר Fire kindled and burning, a Flame; the Focus or Place where Fire is in Action. *Verb Kal* אוּר and אָר, to shine, shine upon, be shining, lucid.— *Niphal* נָאוֹר, to become or be made lucid, to be illustrated, illuminated. *Hiphil* הֵאִיר, to illuminate, send out Light, to illustrate, make lucid or shining; to inflame, kindle. אוּר some render it the Sun, or Light; some Lightning, a Flash of Light, &c.

M. אֵשׁ, according to the *Targumists*, is an hot and burning Wind.—

C. אוּר *Heb.* the same.

Chald. אֲוִיר, Ἀήρ, Air, — also Space, a Void, or Vacuum, a Place where there is nothing but Air. *Chol. f.* 24. 2. *Pl. Ba. Bas. f.* 163. 1. *Ibid. B. C.*

Syr. ——— Hierusalem.

Vol. II.   Q   —The

178　MOSES's *Principia*.

——— The Heat of Fire, or of the Sun.
B.C. אור to ſhine, ſhine upon, to be ſhining, or be made to ſhine, to be illuminated, *Heb.*

אורייתא ſee in its Place in ירה *Heb.* to caſt, project, deject, caſt headlong, to dart, dart out, be darted out.

אורה אורתא Light, Luminous.

מאור Light, a Luminary, that which gives Light.

אויר Aer, *αηρ*, Gen. i. 20. על אויר רמיע שטיא in the Air of the Expanſe of the Heavens.

איירין ſee below in its Order. אלי־ אלופילס, Ἡλιωπολις, *Heliopolis*, the City of the Sun.

Theſe are Tranſlations, but not Explanations. I ſhall inſert one Obſervation, how it has been conſider'd in Condition; the *Hebrew* יקר ſmall Light, ſo Clear, Bright, and ſo Precious, Honourable, Glorious, &c. *Chald. B. C.* קפא "Any light thing, which by its Lightneſs ſwims upon the Top, vile, of ſmall Price or Worth:" I ſhall inſert the Paſſage, to ſhew how vile their Explanation is. In *Gemara*: what is that which is ſaid אור יקרות קפאון. *Zech.* xiv. 9.— זה אור שקיר בעולם הזה וקפוי לעולם הבא It is Light that is precious in this World, but vile in the other. *Peſachim Fol.* 50. *Col.* 1. At the End of the Chapter, a
Gloſs

Gloss קוץ that is קל light, and every light thing is called קפרי, because what is light swims upon Water, and the *Hebrew* Word צוף in the *Targum* is rendered קפא. But we must defer considering the natural Meaning of the Word, till we have consider'd the Condition it might be in, before the Engine was put together.

Perhaps God, for the Reasons hinted above, did not take the same Steps, in putting this Machine to work, as it must have taken, if there had been any Tendency in the Atoms, to have set it forward themselves; and therefore, Light, whose Condition or Form is naturally produced by Fire, which naturally exists and acts in the Pores or Intervals, or between the Atoms of other fit Concretes or Fluids, (as *Zech.* xii. 6. בכיור אש בעצים, *like an Hearth of Fire among Wood*) was formed before there was any concreted Matter, or fit Fluid, except Spirit, for Fire to act in: Indeed, the Grains composed of the Atoms of the Heavens might be divided in any Part, by a great Degree of Friction in Motion; or that which is intermixed may be separated by receding, and so become Fire, and act the Part of Fire, as *M.* רצץ, it signifies, *to break, wear to pieces. Nahum.* ii. 5. *They shall run like Lightnings*, or act the

Part of Light, as *Pſal.* lxxvii. 19. *The Lightnings lightened the World:* But naturally that cannot ſubſiſt above a Moment in the open Air, becauſe the Spirit preſſes in, and diſperſes them, as we ſee plainly in the Night; but here he did, as he ſhew'd them in the Wilderneſs he could do; he made the Action of Fire ſubſiſt in the open Air, for then there was no Concrete nor Matter for Solids together, except the looſe Atoms of the Water and Earth in a Sphere; and form'd the Spirit, and made it ſupply the Fire, and ſend forth the Light without diſſipating the Parts in the Action of Fire; ſo as Light in the ſettled Courſe of Things is formed or produced by that Action we call Fire, which is naturally tranſacted in the Pores between the Atoms of other Matter; his forming here is uſed for the Action of Fire, which expreſſes one of the three Conditions of the Parts of the Heavens: Firſt, in Grains, as it was made at firſt, and as it is ſucceſſively reformed, and preſſed toward the Part where the Action of Fire is. Second, the Part in Action of Fire, the Machine or Manner in which the Darkneſs or Grains, preſſed in, are divided and formed into ſmall Parts or Atoms. Third, thoſe ſmall Grains, or Atoms of the Heavens, iſſued in Fluxes or Streams, which

MOSES's *Principia.* 181

which are called Light, till their Motion fail, and they be reformed to Darkness or Grains, and returned; indeed they never appear as Darkness between the Extremities of their Ascent, and the Orb of the Sun, because they return thro' the Light, except where that Light is interrupted; and Light in this Sphere, is but a Mixture of the Atoms of Air, issuing from the Fire, and the Grains of Air going towards the Fire; except where the Grains of Air are in some Measure obstructed, in their Return on one Side, and the Light on the opposite Side; for if they were all small, or all Grains, and in the same Degree of Motion, and the Interruption of either were to continue a little longer in the same Part, neither would answer their Ends, but destroy us; but the Grains which the Light finds on one Side in their Retreat to the Sun, and the Light, which the Grains find on the other Side in its Retreat, towards the Circumference, or in their small Motions horizontally abate the Action of each other, while the Rotation is making an Exchange: And though God does not tell us how he at first made this Light, yet the Word אור must express, or imply all the three Parts of the Operation, Spirit, Fire, Light, or some Manner of Action, which did the same Thing as Fire does; and as

there

there can be no Words for his Actions, but borrow'd ones, when, as aforesaid, he did the same Thing in the Wilderness, to shew them that Matter in this Operation, was not a God, but how these Things were set forward; and if they had had any such Whims, as to have imagined, that there were Properties in Solids, to create and send forth Light, or that the Light was Part of the Fuel, or that Matter was infinitely divisible, and infinitely extendible, to have cured them; for over the Wilderness where this was supported, there was nothing but Air in its three several Conditions. He form'd it into Grains in the Day, when all about was Light, and melted the Grains, and form'd them into Light, in the Night, when all about was Dark, and supply'd the People with Light, and the Fire with new Grains. Thence the Machinating of this Operation, which produced at first a Flux of Light without the natural Cause, tho' how, we cannot say, is attributed to God, as an Act precedent, preparatory, the Manner how he infused these Powers into the establish'd Machine. *Pfal.* lxxiv. 16. אתה הכינות מאור ושמש. *Thou preparedst the Instrument of Light, and the Stream of Light from the Sun.* And he, in effect, said to the *Israelites*, that Appearance of Cloud, and

and Fire, and Light, which you saw, and out of which I spoke, was neither like Sun, nor Moon, nor any other Body or Being: It is a Representation of the Manner of my Action, and of the Agent, by which I set all Things forward, and have made them do all Things here below in Matter, but not to be imitated, or resembled, or represented by any Thing: And tho' *Moses*, in describing the Formation of Things, uses not the Word which they used for Fire; and tho' that Action in the Wilderness was perform'd by God's immediate Power, and not by natural Means; he uses the Word אש, which they used for natural Fire, part of the Object of their Worship, and attributes the giving of Light to it in that Action. But as our Translators have not done Justice to a Word, which occurs in these Texts, I must endeavour to do it.

M. עמד signifies a Station or Standing, as it is understood; and a Pillar or Column which is derived from its Standing.——to stand, stand under, subsist, consist, persist, to remain, endure, stay, persevere, to be silent, to hold one's Tongue: To be stabile, firm, fixed; to rest, stand still, cease. *Hiphil* העמיד to make to stand, to fix, constitute, confirm,

firm, make strong, establish, place. *Hophal* העמד to be made to stand, be established, placed. על עמדי upon his standing, that is, in the Place where he used to stand.

מעמיד supporting himself, strengthning himself, 1 *Chron.* xviii. מעמד placed, constituted, made firm, strong, to stand.

מעמד, a Standing, a Station, Constitution, a Ministry, Order, Office, Magistracy.

עמדה, the same; also a sustaining, a staying up, a Stay, a Defence.

עמוד and עמד, a Statue, or standing Representation, a Column, or Pillar, so called from its supporting an House, and standing under it, and from its Form: The Cloud, Pillar of Cloud and Fire, the Pillar of Fire. *Plur.* עמודים and עמדים Columns or Pillars.

עמדי, the same as עמי, with me, with myself, or before me, or in my Presence. *Psal.* xxii. 4. *Thou art* עמדי, *with me*, as if he had said, *in the Place where* I *stand:* It is not found, save only with the Pronoun of the first Person.

R. עמד is to stand. *Pag.* to support one's self; to consist or stand fast, to subsist: it is the Opposite to the Verb מעד, the Letters being transposed, which signifies,

fies, to stagger, reel, waggle, be weak, loose, or unsteady.

And as many Mistakes have been made and contended for, about the Signification of this Word, which is also a Word of Condition, by applying more Conditions than one to it, and using it for Conditions, which may be joined with the Condition it expresses, though not in one *Hebrew* Word, but are distinct Conditions; and though sometimes they are together in the Thing, and sometimes asunder, yet they are to be separated in Idea, and therefore have separate Words: And I find the same Practice has been used with the *Latin* Words, and there is nothing to set them right; we must not take Constructions by Similitudes, or where the Ideas meet; I must endeavour to find one Sense which will suit each: The Word has no Relation to being continued or fixed in a Place, nor to Time, so as to express the Duration or Existence of the Atoms, which compose the Subject, for that cannot be separated while they or this material System exists, but expresses a Power within or without, to continue the Subject in the same Condition; it signifies to subsist, or be subsisted, to sustain, or be sustained, to support, or be supported, or to support,
and

and so sustain, or make subsist, whether spoken of Persons, of Powers, of Force, of Law, of Charge, of Office, of Service, of Actions, of Pressures, of Motions, of Forms, of Strength, of Hardness, or &c. For though, in the Cases aforesaid, that which is subsisted, or sustained, or supported, may stand still, yet it may be subsisted, sustained, or supported, and not stand still; that which sustains, or supports other Things, and so makes them subsist, may stand still, or stand fixed, as Columns which support the Form of a Building, and so Supporters are supposed to do; or may be as Solid, or in such a Figure as a Column is, but it does not follow, that every Supporter should stand still; for we see and feel the Water supports that which swims in, or upon it, and the Air supports Fowls which fly in it; and the Scriptures say, the Air supports all Things. But, to proceed: In Comparisons where this Word is used, *Pf.* cii. 25. *Thy Years are throughout all Generations; before thou foundedst the Earth, and the Heavens the Work of thy Hands. They shall* ואברו *perish, but thou* תעמר *shalt endure.* This takes in God in all his Powers or Attributes, and the Heavens with all their Powers, real or imaginary,
which

which the Heathens set up for their God; these imaginary Powers were to perish soon after, those real Powers at the End of this World; God was to support his Deity, theirs was to be destroy'd. Of a King supporting a People, 2 *Chron.* ix. 8. *Because thy* Aleim *loved* Israel, להעמידו *to establish them for ever, therefore made He thee King over them, to do Justice and Judgment.* This was not to nail them down like Statues, nor was it only to keep them in Being, but by his Administration to support them in their Privileges and Possessions, *Dan.* xi. 8. *He shall stand Years against the King of the North.* 2 Kings x. 4. *Behold, two Kings stood not before him; and how shall we stand?* Judg. ii. 14. *Could not stand before their Enemies.* 2 Chron. xxvi. 18. *They stood against Uzziah the King.* 1 Kings xx. 4. *There stood War at* Gezer. Here *Support* is applied to the Power, Strength, Motion, Action of Men, Horses, &c. in War. *Dan.* xi. 11, 13. *And shall set up a great Multitude.* Here 'tis applied to the Power and Actions of levying an Army implied, and of supporting an Army expressed. *Exod.* xviii. 23. *Then thou shalt be able to endure, and this People shall also go to their Place in Peace.* Here 'tis applied to Office, thou shalt

shalt support thyself in executing the Office of governing, or judging this People in their March. 2 Chron. xix. 5. *And appointed Judges in the Land.* He by his Authority and Power supported them in executing Jugment. Numb. i. 5. *that shall stand with you,* (who shall support with you (as we say) help to bear the Burden in executing the Thing given in Charge. Ibid. iii. 6. *And present them before* Aaron *the Priest, that they may minister unto him.* Here they were not to support equally or jointly with him, but to support under his View, as Persons under an Overseer, with Charge that they were to minister or be obedient to him. 1 Kings xii. 6. *And King* Rehoboam *consulted with the Men* עמדים *that stood before* Solomon; here 'tis apply'd to those who supported *Solomon* with their Council. 'Tis to support a Person in any Employment or Condition, nay even in the common Functions of Life, as well as extraordinary Cases.

Psal. xxiii. 4. *Though I walk through the Valley of the Shadow of Death, I will fear no Evil; for thou* עמדי *dost support me.* So far from signifying to stand, that when that was required, Ezek. ii. 1. *Support thyself upon thy Feet,* when the Manner

ner is not mentioned; 1 Sam. xiv. 9. *If they say thus unto us:* ערמו *be still till we come to you, then will* עמדנו *we stand still in our Place.* Dan. x. 11. *stand upright, —I stood trembling.* So of the Arm which was not made for standing upon, but an Instrument to support the Hand, Dan. xi. 15. *The Arms of the South shall not stand.* Of inanimate Forms. Isa. xlvi. 7. *Set him in his Place, and he standeth; from his Place shall he not remove.* His Form was supported, but he could not support the Power of Motion. Of Heavens, and Earth, and People, Isa. xlvi. 22. *As the new Heavens, and new Earth, which I shall make, shall remain before me, saith Jehovah, so shall your Seed and your Name remain.* Here is something promised to his People and their Seed, more than simple Duration; such a Support to them as he gave to the Heavens and Earth, and as was necessary to them in Life, Generation and Production, Food and Conveniencies; so that they might answer his Designs in the several Offices of Life, not to stand fixed no more than the Heavens and Earth stand fix'd; but as sure as I support the Heavens and the Earth, in their Conditions, Motions, &c. so shall your Seed be supported in all the Functions

ons and Enjoyments neceffary; but that is not all he fays, as the new or prefent Heavens or Earth are fupported in his Service, fo fhould they and their Seed be fupported in his Service, the fame Thing as we pray for, *Thy Will be done on Earth, as it is in Heaven,* Pfal. xxxiii. 8, 9. *Let all the Earth fear Jehovah; let all the Inhabitants of the World ftand in Awe of him; for he fpake and it was; he commanded and it ftood.* The Act of Creation gave the Matter Exiftence in Atoms, it is true, that was not a World, *ipfe dixit* gave the Parts Formation, and what was neceffary to make it a World; after that we find he gave Precepts to fome Parts to fupport thefe Conditions and Motions, and govern the reft; if any one can fhew that the Part which the Conteft has been about, was commanded to remain fix'd, doubtlefs it has been obey'd. *Pfal.* cxlviii. after the Author has included almoft every Thing in the Creation in general Words, and particularly enumerated almoft all that have Motion or are moved, he fays, ver. 5. *Let them praife the Name* Jehovah; *for he commanded, and they were created. He has alfo eftablifhed them for ever and ever: He has made a Decree which fhall not be broken.* He fupports every Part in its pro-

per

MOSES's *Principia.* 191

per Condition, Motion, &c. none vary from his Precepts. cxix. 90. Thou haſt כוננת machined (or contrived as Part of the Machine) *the Earth and it abideth.* It ſhall be ſupported, as it was deſigned to be, in its Conditions, Motions, or &c. Hab. iii. 11. *The Sun and the Moon ſtood ſtill in their Habitation; at the Light of thine Arrows they went, at the ſhining of thy glittering Sphere.* They make שמש the Sun; ſo if this Word ſignifies to ſtand fix'd, then they make the Scripture affirm that both Sun and Earth ſtand ſtill or fixed; and they make ירח the Moon, ſure none ever imagined that it ſtood, but theſe as you will ſee are Fluxes of Light; and the Word expreſſes that they were ſupported in their Courſes, till the Light of his Arrows, and the Lightning of his Darts diverted them. Eccleſ. i. 4. *And the Earth abideth for ever.* I muſt defer this till I have explained ſome Words which are joined with it, and ſhew what it does; but for the preſent that this Word ſignified to ſtand ſtill, or fix'd upon a Foundation or Columns, could never have entered into any indifferent Head, much leſs have admitted of a Diſpute, if the Philoſophers of the Time, had not firſt run wrong themſelves, and then drawn in the Tranſla-
2 tors,

tors, and they had not implicitly followed one another, and afterwards the Church had not contended for their Authority, or Infallibity in tranflating it. What this Bafis to the Earth is, the fame Prophet by way of Claim, has exprefs'd. Pfal. lxxv. 4. *The Earth and all the Inhabitants of it are diffolved :* I תכנת *proportioned* (the Force of) *its Supporters. Selah.* Job ix. 6. *Who fhaketh the Earth from its Place ; and the Supporters of it tremble.* xxvi. 11. *The Supporters of Air.* 1 Sam. ii. 8. *Becaufe* מצקי *The Compreffures of the Earth are* Jehovah's, *and he has placed the World upon them.* If the Preffure of the Air, which they divided into Columns, as we do the Surface by Lines, were taken off, all dry Bodies would turn to Duft; and that Duft, or thofe Atoms mix'd among thofe of the groffer Fluids, would be as they were created, and when they were diffolv'd, fluid; and this Word is not ufed for fuch Pillars as are only Standers fet up for Memorials or Statues, but מצבה *Exod.* xxiv. 4. *And builded an Altar under the Hill, and twelve Pillars. Deut.* vii. 5. *And break down their Images* (Statues or Pillars) or fuch as was to be fet up befide the Altar to the Lord in *Egypt*, mention'd *Ifa.* xix. 19. Not fuch as were fet up; *Judg.* ix. 46.

at

at *Beth-el-berith*, call'd, *Judg.* ix. 4. *Baal Berith*, call'd צריח, which fignifies *Exaltation*; and fo in building a high Tower, and in Temples to the Heavens, a Place for making Obfervations, and perhaps for Sacrifice. And מעמד, 1 *Kings* x. 12. *Pillars for the Houfe of Jehovah*; *and for the King's Houfe*; but 'tis ufed for fmall Poles of Wood which fupported the Tent, or itinerant Tabernacle when it ftood, and for Pillars which fupported the Temple. In thefe Places 'tis ufed in Ridicule of the Heathens, who reprefented this Power, which fupports the Earth, &c. by Columns or Supporters in their Temples. *Judg.* xvi. 26. *Suffer me that I may feel the Pillars, whereupon the Houfe ftandeth.* ver. 29. *And* Sampfon *took hold of the two middle Pillars, upon which the Houfe ftood.*——And *Efther* i. 6. Where were *white, green, and blue* Hangings, *faftened with Cords of fine Linen and Purple, in Silver Rings*, and *Pillars of Marble*. And thefe conftant, tho' marching Miracles, in fupporting the Cloud and the Fire, was to fhew that he was Mafter of thofe Actions or Powers; and tho' the Tranflators have fuppofed, that this Cloud and this Fire was, each of them, in the Figure of a Column, which if they had been, that might have been expressed with an Addition of some Word which signifies *like*; but as it is, what Authority have they, that each was like a Column? The antient human Writers thought the Cloud cover'd them from the excessive Heat of the Sun by Day, as *Wisd.* xix. 7. as namely, *A Cloud shadowing the Camp*; and perhaps the Fire kept them from the Cold of the Night, included under the Expression of giving them Light. Indeed, the Word is used, *Judg.* xx. 40. *When the Flame began to arise up out of the City with* עמוד עשן *a Pillar of Smoak*. But this will not clear the Point, for it may be read as the rest, without *as*, or, *like*, a Support of Smoak. *Exod.* xxxiii. 9. *The cloudy Pillar descended, and stood at the Door of the Tabernacle. Nehemiah* shews what this Standing was, ix. 19. את עמוד הענן לא סר, *the Pillar of the Cloud departed not from them.*—The Support of the Clouds did not let the common Actions of Wind, or &c. dissipate or drive the Parts of the Cloud from over them. This Word is used to the most violent Motion or Succession of the Grains or Atoms of the Air, *Ps.* cvii. 25. *Sustains the stormy Wind*. But when he would express its standing still, or ceasing, *ver.* 29. יקם *He makes the Storm a Calm.* So of Fire,

Fire, *Neh.* ix. 19. *the Pillar of Fire by Night, to give them Light.* Pſal. lxxviii. 14. באור אש *in the Light of Fire.* cv. 39. *And Fire to enlighten the Night.* So when it is carried to ſpiritual Actions, which go on in a Series of Succeſſion, *Pſal.* cxi. 3. cxii. 3, 9. *And his Righteouſneſs endures for ever.* 1 Chron. xvi. 17. Pſal. cv. 10. *And* עמידה *hath confirmed it to* Jacob *for a Law.* xxxiii. 11. *The Counſel of* Jehovah *ſtandeth for ever.* xix. 10. *The Fear of* Jehovah *is clean, enduring for ever.* Whether this Cloud, and this Fire, which were ſupported of, in, and by the Air; the Cloud by its preſſing ſome of its Parts into Grains, and preſſing the Grains together; and the Fire by preſſing in a ſufficient Quantity of Grains, melting them, and preſſing them out in Light, and ſo ſupporting the Action of Fire, by ſupplying and diſcharging the Matter, whereby God ſhew'd himſelf Maſter of theſe Actions, were alſo in Figures like the Columns which the Heathens made Supporters of to their Temples, and thereby repreſented the Columns of Light and Darkneſs which ſupport the Earth; and if they were like Columns, whether they were in Imitation of thoſe of the Heathens with their Tops inverted, or they were with Bases much wider, like a Pyramid, resembling them as they really are; or that of Light was like a Column from the Orb of the Sun to the Earth, or &c. and were also to shew, that he had likewise the Command of those Columns with the Powers of supporting the Earth, which the Heathens attributed to the Air; tho' they, for whose immediate Service these were produced, saw and so knew, is not now easily determined. I have shew'd that *Baal* signifies the Grains of Air, flowing from the Circumference to the Sun, to supply the Fire; but as those Grains are employ'd to many other Uses, among others, to support the Earth, &c. in their Motions, the *Canaanites* had a City dedicated to the Heavens, under that double or joint Attribute of *Judg.* xx. 23. תמר בעל and *Deut.* xxxiv. 3. The City התמרים; and I think 2 *Par.* xxviii. 15. ירחו. The Word תמר is render'd, *Cant.* iii. 6. *Joel* ii. 30. in the *Heb.* iii. 3. תמורות עשן *Pillars of Smoke*, of the Heavens in that Condition, and 'tis like, as they express'd it, *the Lord the Supporter*; and as the Thing represented, and the Representation had always the same Name, תמר is also a Palm-Tree. *M.* "A Palm Tree, which grows the highest and straitest of all Trees, and never

but

but where there are sweet, fresh Water-Springs: It is always green, and of a long Duration; its Wood cannot be pressed, or broke by any Weight." Hence all those Claims from God, that the Supporters of the Earth were in his Hands, or subject to him, &c. and hence the Palm Trees, the Emblems, were brought into God's Temple, made Supporters, and hung upon the Walls like Trophies; and in their Feasts appointed, *Levit.* xxiii. 40. they were to take כפת Boughs of the Palm Trees, and of a Tree called ערב, and others, which were Representatives of the Attributes, to ridicule them. Indeed כפת has a further Signification than Boughs, applied to some Condition of some Part of the Heavens, *Job* xxxvi. 32. R. cites *Jun.*—*Jer.* xxxi. 21. תמרורים " Obelisks, Pyramids, pointed and sharp, like the Top of the Palm." However you observe, as aforesaid, tho' this Support of the Cloud, and of Fire, was as much miraculous as that at first, and was perform'd without other Matter to support it, he uses the Word for the natural Action of Fire, and indeed, as you will see hereafter, שמש *Shemosh* is the Light receding; so the Spirit was made an Instrument of Motion, *and let there be Light* included that Motion, and implied some

Action like Fire, and produced that Motion of Light, which issued against a Side of the Sphere, directed the Force of the Spirit, and so determined the Rotation of the Sphere, and formed Night and Day; the Spirit was in Motion, and the Light was put into Motion; there was no other Agent, nor no other Sphere or Orb.

As those who espouse the modern Schemes to serve a Turn, take in the divine Writers, I shall take the Liberty to bring in a few human Writers; and tho' when they cite the Words of inspired Men, they make them but equal with the Heathens, Antients, but only Thinkers, I must make as much Difference as there is between God and Man, Scripture as infallible, human Writings, as Thoughts; and though it is not easy to determine the Meaning of these Words in any other Language, or to know what any *Greek* or *Latin* Author meant: For Example; by the Word *Aer*, whether in the State of Light, or how, except his own Words explain it; because tho' many used it in one Sense, or for the Matter of the Heavens in one Condition, some may use it in another, and so with respect to its Situation; because some took the Earth for the Center: There are always some who are singular

gular, and because there is no Standard but Revelation, I shall take them where they explain themselves. Whether the Authors thought or understood what they writ, or did as Authors do now, publish'd what they neither understood nor believ'd; whether we are to believe the same Heathen Author most, when he writ with the Bent of the People, or when he ventur'd to write against them; whether the Authors had seen or took Hints from the Scriptures, or only observ'd, or thought or judg'd from the Appearance of Things; whether the Antients were as able to make Observations and Experiments, and judge of them, as the Moderns, are Points which I shall not now spend much Time about; but only shew, by a few Scraps, that others have writ, what the inspir'd Authors say, that Atoms of the Heavens adhere in Grains, and are dissolv'd or separated, &c.

Pauli Merulæ Cosmog. Part I. Lib. III. Cap. II. p. 99. There are only three Elements: Fire is not properly an Element, cites *Cardanus, Alex. Aphrodisiensis,* and others.

Christ. Sceiner Rosa Ursina, p. 641. Fire itself, that is, Flame, is nothing else but kindled Air.

Pymander Merc. Trif. Lib. IV. *Com.* VI. *Cap.* I. p. 49. Air is fired by Motion.

Cardani Lib. X. *de rerum varietate*, p. 206. Air ſtruck, or ground between harder Bodies, ſtraitways paſſes into Fire.

Cardani de Subtilitate Liber ſecundus, p. 381. *Alexander* thinks right in this, that Fire is not ſtruck out of the Subſtance of Stones, but the Air that is contain'd within them, is by the ſudden Attrition turn'd into Fire.

Cardani de Subtilitate Actio prima, p. 680. He ſaith, that our Fire is elementary Fire condenſed, and upon that Account hotter, as Ice is Water condenſed, and upon that Account colder.

Platonis Timæus, p. 1059. Air while it is burning, is Fire; Fire extinguiſhed and concreted, becomes Air; and again, Air coming together, and condenſing, conſtitutes Clouds and Darkneſs.

Ibid. p. 1064. Again, when Fire is on all Sides taken hold of by Air, Water, or any kind of Earth, and it being little, has much to act in, and ſtruggling and overpower'd in the Action, is divided and broke, the two Bodies of Fire concrete into one Species of Air.

Ibid.

Ibid. p. 1067. Air compressed by Force is loosed by nothing but by Element, adhering without Force, Fire alone dissolves it.—*Speaking of Bodies mixed of Earth and Water,*—but the Fire penetrating the Pores of the Water, as the Water the Interstices of the Earth, and so affecting the Water, as the Fire the Air, is the Cause of Liquifaction to the common Body.

Platonis Op. Omn. In like Manner all the Parts of Fire freely cohere among themselves.

Cælii Calcag. p. 237. Others making Use of a more solid Principle, and more accommodated to Philosophy, imitate the *Greeks*, asserting that *Chronus*, that is, *Saturn*, is, *Chronos* Time, *Juno* the Air, and the Birth of *Vulcan* to be nothing else but the Change of Air into Fire.

Vossius de orig. & prog. Idol. Lib. I. *Plutarch.*—the *Greeks* by *Juno* allegorically understand the Air, by the Birth of *Vulcan* the Conversion of the Air into Fire.

Gyrald. &c. Hesiod records *Vulcan* to be born of *Juno* alone, in this Verse:

   Juno *brought* Vulcan *forth, without her*
      Jove's
   Embraces, or the Joys of stolen Loves.

There

There are many *Vulcans.*—*M. Cicero* in his 8th Book of the Nature of the Gods says, the first was Heaven born, &c.

Vossius, &c. Diodorus Siculus—*Vulcan*, which by Interpretation is Fire, they, (the *Egyptians*) think a Great God, which conduces much to the Generation and Perfection of all Things.

Ibid. &c. Isidorus made the Heavens either to be purer Air, or igneous, or igneous Air.

Compend. &c. Nor do any deny the Heavens to be hot, but rather they deny they are burning. Neither do they say the Light of the Sun warms by Repercussion solely, so that it solely burns by Repercussion.

Vossius, &c. Plutarch and *Stobæus, Thales* thought the Stars were of an earthy Substance, but *fired*; then they both add that *Empedocles*'s Opinion was that they were of that Fire which the Air first contained, but cast forth at its first Separation, — *Basilius* in his six Books — Who now doubts but that the *Æther* itself is igneous and burning.—*Hippocrates* thought these celestial Fires could no more be kept in without being fed by the Spirit or Air than our Fires here. His Words in his Book of *Blasts* are these; the Spirit is the
Food

Food of Fire, and Fire deprived of Spirit or Air cannot live.

Ibid. — The Sun draws Exhalations from the Æther and Stars.

Toſtat. Vol. II. p. 29.—We might make Fire from Air, if we knew but how to heat Air ſo as to reduce it to the Subtility of Fire: It would then put on the Form of Fire: In like Manner as when Lightening inflames the adjoining Air, ſo as to produce a Flaſh.

Sebaſt. Fox. Morzilli's Comment on the 3d Part of *Timæus* — *Timæus Locrus* alſo in his Book of the World, means the ſame Thing in theſe Words: — "In like Manner one Species of the Air is moſt pure, agile, and eaſily gives Way, which is called *Æther*, another is very groſs. For the Nature of the Air, altho' it is the ſame as to Subſtance, yet it alters its Conditions, and puts on different Forms."

Plotinus Ennead. II. *Lib.* I. p. 101. Since ſuch Fire affords the moſt pure Light, and reſides on high, where it naturally inhabits, it is not to be thought that this our Flame is mixed with thoſe above, but is rather extinguiſhed when it comes to a certain Height, by Means of too great a Quantity of Air ruſhing into it.

Iſidorus,

Morus, *Etymolog.* p. 68. Collision of all Sorts creates Fire—In like Manner Lightning or Fire is formed in Clouds; whence it appears they are first Clouds, and then become Fire.

Lud. Cœlij Lect. Antiq. p. 1348. That the Heaven is Fire, may be easily collected from *Plato*. For where the *Mosaick Mysteries* have it thus: *In the Beginning God created the Heaven and the Earth*, *Plato* saith, that God first made Fire, and then the Earth; by Fire undoubtedly meaning Heaven in particular.

Th. Bartholine, p. 26. of the Light of Animals — For אור *Ur*, is Fire, אור *OR* Light, from whence perhaps comes the *Aurum*, Gold, of the *Latins*, since *AV*, and *O* were frequently changed one for the other by the *Romans* after the Manner of the *Gauls*. Upon Account of which Affinity of the Names, the divine Writer in his sacred Narrative of the *Genesis* of the World perhaps omitted the Creation of Fire, designing to express both the Light and Fire by one Word.

Garcæus's Doctrine of Metereology, of the Triple Region of the Air, p. 3.—The highest is that next the celestial Spheres, and has the Appellation of Fire, not that Fire actually exists there, but because by the

the Motion of the heavenly Bodies carried round by continual Rotation, and the Vicinity of the Rays, that Part being chafed grows hot and inflamed, approaches near to the Nature and Condition of Fire: Whence *Aristotle* in his first Book of *Meteorologics*, or Doctrine of Meteors, Vapours, &c. teaches that Fire is nothing else but the purest and most subtle Air, heated by the Motion and Nearness of the Stars.

Lud. *Cælii*, p. 1348. But *Vitruvius*, a Person not unskill'd in Mathematicks writes, that there are some of the Stars of the temperate Kind, others Hot, and others Cold: From this Cause, because Fire goes upwards; whence it comes to pass, that the Sun burning the upper Æther with his Rays, makes it red or glowing hot; of which *Mars* is a Proof. But the Star of *Saturn*, which is next to the Extremity of the World, and touches the congealed Regions of the Heavens, is thought to contract thence a most intense Coldness. But let him look to these Matters.

Ibid. p. 14. That throwing of the celestial Rays into one Point, and, as it were, collecting the scatter'd ones, not only excites the most bright and clear Light, but thence

thence acquires a Virtue: Tho' I am not ignorant, that *Plotinus* writes, that such a mixing cannot happen to the Rays, so as they should, by that Coalition and Collection, obtain any new Virtue, or that any extraordinary Form should thence accrue to them.

Ibid. p. 1347. Add to this, that Fire which by its own Tendency is always in a Condition of Motion, is necessarily moved in an Orb or Circle, for this hath neither Beginning nor End, which cannot hold in a right Line. The Substance of the Heavens (saith *Phurnutius* in his Book of the Nature of the Gods) is fiery, as the Sun and the other Stars; whence the highest Parts of the Mundane System is call'd Æther, from the Greek *Aisthesthai* to to burn, or *&c.* altho' some derive it from the Signification of the Verb *ano Thein*, which is *Roiso pheresthai*, to be carried round violently, or with a Noise: The same Author saith elsewhere, as we contain a Soul, so doth the World, and that is *Jupiter*.

Plato op. om. Theætetus. For Heat and Fire, that generates and nourisheth other Things, is itself generated by Action and Friction, this is Motion, is not this the Genesis, or Source of Fire?

Tho.

Tho. Bartholinus, p. 141. of the Light of Animals.——*Aristotle*——says, that Fire is the efficient Cause of all Things.

But, to return to the Text, the Word אור is a Name for Part of the Matter of the Heavens in that Condition, which is different, or opposite to the Condition of that Part which is call'd רוח the Spirit. As the Spirit was made the Instrument of Weight, Pressure, or Impulse, and so of Motion, the Light was the Matter made opposite, or in the Condition of Levity; so that it should give Way to the Force of the Spirit, and so produce and direct the Course of that Force, and so of Motion. The Condition of the Spirit makes it the Instrument of Force or Weight; and the Condition of Light makes it recede, emerge, or do as the lighter Scale does, mount up: Tho' we use the Word for a Thing, which is comparatively of less Weight than another Thing, or which is less liable to be press'd; and also for that which is the Medium, and conveys Perception by the Resistance of Objects to our Eyes; yet we are first to consider its material Condition, which is the Smallness of its Parts, and consequently its Incapacity of being press'd as much as larger, or Levity; and after that we are to consider

the

the Effects it has upon other Things, as they are differently modified, placed, or &c. which are expreſs'd, in *Hebrew*, by different Verbs, as well thoſe Effects it wrought, for which it was approv'd for Good before there was any Eyes, as thoſe it has upon them. However the Light was made then, that Action is to be conſider'd as the Fire is now, but a Part of the Machine, the Mill where the Light is ground; the Light was not only the Thing wanted, but the Thing which was to act, or be of Uſe upon the Earth. We can ſay nothing, that is, we have no Words which can raiſe any Ideas; and tho' we uſe Words, if thoſe Words do not raiſe Ideas, tho' we ſpeak, we convey nothing about the immediate Actions of God. *Moſes* ſpeaks not of intermediate Means, how Matter was created, how the Spirit was formed into, and kept in Grains, or how the Light was formed, but that the Matter of the Heavens and the Earth was created, that there was the Spirit and the Light, and that there was a Firmament, and that this Matter, by being put into theſe Conditions, had ſuch and ſuch Effects, or produced ſuch Actions; and afterwards gives us a full Account, when the Machine of the Universe was compleated,

pleated. Before I go further, I am to prepare you, by extending your Ideas of this Matter, in this Condition, or to what this Word fignifies, by fhewing its Actions; for tho' we know little of it, how it was formed, or its Motion kept up in that State, becaufe it was put into the Manner 'tis now, by and by it will be endow'd with Dominion and Power, and be conftituted a Vice-God, a Ruler here: Firft, your Ideas will be enlarg'd, if you obferve, that the firft and chiefeft Ufes of Light was not for the Effect it has upon the Eyes for feeing; but was fet forward when there were no living Creatures, continued and directed the Motion of the Spirit, and fo gave Motion to the Matter of which this Earth was formed; when its Parts were loofe in a Sphere, turn'd it round, and formed a Night and a Day; when there were no compound Solids, or any Thing larger than Atoms, except the Grains of Air or Spirit, much lefs any Globes formed: And further, though the Atoms or Parts of Grains of the Heavens are in Light, equal to the whole, and take up no more Space than when they were in Grains; yet as Motion is one of the Conditions of Light, wherever there is Light, from the Plenitude and Motion of the Atoms, or Light one way, and of the Grains or Spirit the oppofite way, there muft be an Expanfion; and there cannot be Light, either in fmall or great Degree, without all thefe, and efpecially an Expanfion; and in the Eftate it was then, it was to raife an Expanfion, by Compreffure to form the Earth; carry down the Waters; and afterwards to make the Vegetables grow, &c. And it does not yet appear what it was to do, till it have its Powers expreffed, be put into a fettled Oeconomy, and have its new Commiffion with a new Name; but 'tis very likely, that the Degree of the Motion of the Light, and fo the Degree of Expanfion which put the Earth together, and formed its Surface in fo very fhort a Time, was much greater than it was after the Flood; by comparing that with the much longer Time, it was in reforming it then, when there were Creatures to preferve; and whether the Trees, Plants, Herbs, &c. were each formed, planted in a proper Condition in each Climate, to ftand the fucceffive Seafons; or if only the Seeds were formed, and it raifed the Vegetables in that fhort Time, compar'd with the Time fome Vegetables are in raifing from Seeds now, they were neceffarily greater than they are now; and

if

If the Seed was raised on all the Surface of the Earth at once, perhaps it acted, though not proportionably, nor in Form of Light, yet in its Effect of Warmth, in all Parts upon this Surface at once, to stock the Earth with Vegetables; that as the Light from the Lamp of the Sun was to begin to act in, or upon some Part of the Ecliptick, and as they were either planted, or the Light was to raise them from Seed then, or the successive Seasons were to raise the Seed in each Part; this Light was to raise all Sorts of Vegetables to such a Degree of Perfection, or enable them to endure the Seasons, grow on, where Spring began, and to stand rooted, or form Seed where Winter began, so as to recover next Spring; and this Light might be greater than was necessary to move the Sphere, which is now this Orb, and those it was to form; and keep them going alternately, in the Course of alternate, periodical Seasons; though by being differently applied, its Effects, in that respect, might be even slower than they are now; and it might raise an Expansion, too great for the Bodies of Mortals to endure; and the Light might be greater than the Eyes of Creatures were able to see

see with, or endure: Tho' the Effects seem to carry Evidence, that this Action was stronger, and perhaps different from what it was the fourth Day, and is now; we shall not dwell upon the Degree any more than we did upon the Manner: But we are sure, that the different Sorts of Atoms were each framed and proportioned to the settled Degree of Expansion, whereby each Mass of each Sort of them has its due Degree of Consistency, or Adhesion, and what they call Gravity, to answer their respective Ends; (of which in its Place) and that the Eyes, and all other Parts of Animals were contrived and formed to the Degree of Light, Expansion, &c. since established; that each Member might act with such a Degree of Strength or Force, without Sense of Compressure; their Eyes to feel Objects at Distances in some Proportion to the Degrees of Light, without being offended or hurt by it, in any of those Degrees: so אור Light is not a Thing new created, but a Condition which the Atoms of the Heavens were put into, with respect to Motion, Adhesion, and Division; and אור is not the Name of the Heavens, as they were, when they were first called Heavens, but

of

of that Matter as it was next kept, succeffively divided in all Places, except a little in and behind the Globes, and at the Extremities of the Heavens; and though the Atoms of the Heavens be the Matter of which Light is formed, yet when its Grains are divided to Atoms by Fire, or any other Agent, and in Motion you call them Light; though the fame Sort of Matter, nay, the fame Matter formed into Grains, and returning to the Fire, or any Part where that Fluid is in Atoms, or fmaller Grains be the Spirit; and the fame Sort of Matter, nay, the fame Matter put into Motion by the Spirit, and the Fire, the אור in attempting to expand, and fo comprefs itfelf, and every Thing in it, is called the Firmament: But the Word is no Ways appropriated to the Action, of feeing, or reprefenting Objects, otherwife than it is to the doing of any of its other Actions: Though they have lately robb'd it of all its Significations, except that of conveying Ideas of Objects, and their Colours, and of ferving for ************ to play with; and as it will, in its Place, be confider'd in its then next and prefent State, though under the Name of שמש, I muft refer thither: But fince we fuppofe the Scriptures have affirmed, that Light was and is formed of the Matter of the Fluid of the Heavens, and not created *de novo*, nor sent from any Repository, and without any Addition of the Parts of Fuel; to avoid Quibbles, we suppose, that after the Machine was compleat in general, 'tis formed in the Pores of, or between the Atoms of the Orb of the Sun on every Side, without difperfing the Atoms of that Orb; and that 'tis formed here between the Atoms of what is called Fuel, whofe Parts, fome few Sorts excepted, diffolve, and fome are diffipated: 'Tis formed or augmented, by obftructing, and reflecting, or collecting the Streams coming from the Sun, or from Fire, and obftructing the Returns of the Spirit to the Sun or Fire, in that Line, by denfe Bodies; after 'tis thus made, or collected, or mix'd and obfcur'd, or at Reft, 'tis feparated, and fo made by extracting the Grains; for Example, out of a Glafs Veffel, and moved by moving the Parts of Light, next without, through between the Atoms of the Glafs; and fo thofe within moving others alfo, through between the Atoms of the Glafs, and without the Glafs, each other fucceffively to your Eyes, at a confiderable Diftance: 'Tis formed abfolutely, where 'tis not on-

ly

ly obscur'd, but (if that were possible) where there is only Grains and no Mixture of those Atoms, by Collision of the Grains of Air, between the Surfaces of, or in the Pores of hard Bodies; 'tis form'd from the Grains of Air, in Fermentation among the Matter in Vessels, or in the Pores of Animals, in the Pores of Bodies, in Corruption, in the Pores of the Mixtures of the Parts of Solids and Fluids, in the Pores of the Mixtures of different Fluids, &c. And as soon as the Grains of Air, are each respectively divided into Atoms, they without Resistance give Way to other Grains pressing in, and retreat or recede from the Center, or upward, and each behind pushes that preceeding forwards. But as our Pretenders to more Knowledge than the inspir'd Writers, have imagin'd and publish'd, that they have found Falsities in the Scripture, which say the Light of the Moon, when it appears 'tis, as they call it, a Dark Orb, or the Light of, &c. I must observe to them that it is, according to their Sense, the Light of no Orb, and that the Matter of any Orb is nothing akin to Light; and this Fluid in Scripture is not in that Sense ascribed to any of them, but to the Heavens, the Fluid,

Jer. iv. 23. *To the Airs, and their Light was not.* Nor is it only afcribed or appropriated to the Action of Fire, in one of them, where that Action divides it out of Grains, or the Spirit, and fo by the Affiftance of the Firmament, new Grains are prefs'd in, and it prefs'd out, but alfo to any Thing which interrupts, and turns its Current to this or other Orbs, our Eyes, or *&c.* and there it is always appropriated to the Thing from whence it comes in a ftreight Line to the Orb, Eye, or *&c.* not only from the Place of Fire, or *&c.* where 'tis formed or made, or, *&c.* above; but when reflected from the Moon, and Stars, from polifh'd Armour, or, *&c.* nay, is always attributed to the Place it comes laft from; be it of Formation, Reflection, Pervafion, Separation, or *&c.* But as we muft come to confider only the great Light or Lights, after it was, and as it it now form'd, 'tis properly the Offspring of, or is form'd by that Part of the Machine, which is called Fire; and implies all thofe Atoms in their Motion from the *Focus* of the Fire, and all they fuccefsively pufh forward, and that fucceffively pufh them forward to their utmoft Progrefs; and its Effects near the *Focus* of the Fire is fo near to that of Fire, that the

Tran-

Translators, tho' improperly, have render'd it Fire, such as to singe Hair, warm a Person, or, &c. As Light has its several Degrees in its Nearness to the Fire, its Proportion to the Mixture of the Spirit, the Velocity it is mov'd with, &c. so it has its several Services; and either the Description or Use shews the Degree: In each of the three next cited, it has two; which those who sit or walk by a House-fire enjoy, *viz.* Warmth and Light; Isa. xliv. 16. *Ah! I am warm, I have seen* אור *the Light.* Ibid. xlvii. 14. *Not a Coal to warm them at; nor Light to sit before it.* l. 11. *Walk* באור אשכם *in the Light of your Fire; and in the Sparks ye have kindled.* Ezek. v. 2. *A third Part* באור *in the Light* תבעור *shalt thou dissolve and separate.* This was to be done without the Confines of the Fire, and in the Confines of Light; and any one may see that Hair will be dissolved, and the Parts separated at some Distance from the Fire; and it is scarce possible to put a small Quantity of Hair alone, into any considerable Fire; another Part was to be dispersed in the Wind; and the Part which was to be dissolved and dispers'd in the Light, is clearly distinguished by Opposition; ver. 3. *Thou shalt also take there-*

of a small Quantity and bind them on thy Skirts. Then take of them again, and cast them into the midst of the Fire, and burn them in the Fire. But as this *Precept was given at a Time when there was no Matter for Fire to act in, and is, as the rest is, a standing Precept, we must prosecute what came to pass under the Administration of God, or of this Spirit, and this Light, whilst they were supported by him without natural Means, and defer the Explanation of Expressions, about the Conditions of Fire, till we come to the Formation of the Place, where this Matter of Light was appointed to be successively and mechanically melted: First under the Word אחת, and after חמה; for though the Condition of the Fluid there, differs from that of Fire here, in Degree greater vastly, which makes it necessary that the Atoms of that Orb should be suited to that Degree, and in Situation one here on one Point, that on every Point of the Surface; so that the Atoms, the Parts of that Orb, cannot be dissipated, to the End that this Action may be, as it was design'd to be, equal and perpetual: Whereas Fire in Fuel prepared by Man, who by his Fall is doom-

---

* Let there be Light.

ed

ed not only to acquire his Food, but this fort of Heat and Light by his Labour, gradually diffipates the Parts of it, raifes and diffufes fome into the Air, which foon after lets them fall, and lets others fall immediately, without altering or hurting an Atom; that thofe for Vegetables may again be reform'd into Vegetables, for more Fuel, or other Ufes, to fupply Man's Neceffity by his Labour, in cultivating, gathering, or preparing them; yet as we can have no Idea but by Senfation, and that Action of *Chamah* being out of our Reach, after this Explanation, by Example in the Wildernefs, without Fuel, the divine Writers ufe the Word אש which they ufed for Fire in Fuel alfo, for illuftrating the Action of *Chamah*; the Matter and Manner of the Fire being the fame, though its Effects upon that it acts in, or its Situation is different; and as the Spirit and Light had not all the Sorts of Objects to operate upon in the four firft Days they have had fince, we muft fufpend the Confideration of the Effects they have upon thofe Objects fince formed, till we come to confider thofe Objects.

Though it no Way alters the Senfe, I think the firft Part of *ver.* 4. *And God faw the Light that it* was *good*, belongs to

the

the last Verse, finishes the Relation of forming Light, expresses that it continued going or in Motion, and was good. I shall not enlarge upon these here, because the chief End of this Part will be to shew how it moves, how, and in what it is good.

As it was not within the Design of the first Part, to meddle with the Motions of the Heavens, further than as they were concerned in the forming of the Earth, and carrying down the Water; nor with the Motion of the Earth at all, I hope I shall be excused for passing over some Points in the latter Part of the fourth, and in the fifth Verse, as unconsider'd, or not understood; because it was proper to keep off those who can publish a Book for their own, out of a stolen Paragraph, till those Points came to be considered in Course. Now I must attempt to discover their Signification, not only in their first Acts, but also in their Consequences; and I am to consider the said latter Part of the fourth and fifth Verse, though the Action be but a Consequence, as one entire Relation of another Action.

Ver. 4.—*And God divided the Light from the Darkness* (*Heb.* between the Light, and between the Darkness) *ver.* 5. *And God called the Light Day, and the Darkness he called Night: and the Evening* (was) *and the Morning were* (was) *the first Day.*

This is an Abridgment; 'tis saying that God (for the Machine was not yet form'd) did that one Day, which, as he afterwards at large describes, the Machine does every Day. This is the same Manner of Representation and Claim, as in the seventh Verse; *And God made the Firmament:* This was his Manner of making the Light, *Moses* gives us Accounts here of the Acts, but can give us none of the Means, much less of their Manner of being operated upon, or operating upon other Things; the first is a double Expression, God divided between the Light, and between the Darkness; if it had been to stop there, it would have been no more than saying, he made, or continued to make or form Light out of Darkness; but when he adds
God

God called that Light, which was succeſſively made (for there was no other) Day, and that Darkneſs Night, then it runs in, he divided between that Light alſo, which he call'd the Day, and between the Night; and made the firſt Evening, and the firſt Morning, as 'tis accepted, compoſe the firſt Day. But left for the preſent this ſhould ſeem uſhering a Caſe, for which there are few Precedents in our Manner of ſpeaking, I am ready to ſhew that it is the ſame Action, the one an Effect or Conſequence of the other; and as *Moſes* ſhews, a little farther at large, the Machine was all made to divide between the Day and between the Night, and ſo make Days, &c. and the Inſtrument of doing it was the Machine which divides the Light from the Darkneſs; and the firſt Motion produces the ſecond; and while the Light is divided or made out of Darkneſs, the Earth, without a Miracle, can no more avoid proceeding and turning about, and dividing between the Day and between the Night, than, in a ſufficient Wind, a Ship at Sea, with Sails ſpread, can avoid being driven before the Wind, and turning as it turns. We, to make it intelligible, muſt take along with us the then preſent Condition of Things:

There

There were Grains, doubtlefs, form'd of Air wherever, and from Time to Time, as far as there was Occafion for them to act: Thofe which were near this Sphere began to move, and then were called Spirit; and the Light which was firft form'd, was near this Sphere; and the Expanfion which was form'd next Day, began to operate, firft upon the Atoms or Matter of this Sphere, and they did not reach (for they went and go together) the Matter of which fome of the other Orbs were formed, till the fourth Day. But before we go farther, we muft take the Liberty to fet afide fome idle Stories, which have been raifed to difparage this Part of the Revelation, as well as that of the Formation of the Orb of the Sun. They are pleafed to tell us, that the Body of the Sun is a luminous Body, has a Property of yielding and fending out Light, that is, of making Light: This is fpoken of what God had done, or continued to do for three or four Days; but afterwards this Action was to be continued by Agents: If it was Matter that was to be divided, either the Parts muft adhere again, or be in fpeaking, infinite. If this Action was to be

perform'd

perform'd in one Place, or from a Point, either fix'd or moving, either the Matter to be divided must come, and that divided go, or else, in that Place, the Agent must divide the same, as they say, *ad infinitum*, which is a direct Contradiction to all our Ideas of Matter. But on the other Hand, it agrees with all our Ideas, as splitting or melting the Grains is, as you will see the Word expresses, taking from the one, and giving to the other, or putting the one in the Place of the other; taking from the Darkness, and giving to the Light; so if the Matter or Atoms divided, can, at the other End, adhere again into Grains, return and come about again, then that Action of making the Atoms adhere in Grains, is also taking from the one, and giving to the other; taking from the Light, and giving to the Darkness; and so is also dividing between the Light, and between the Darkness, *viz.* as it is now, between the Center of the whole Orb of Light, and the whole Sphere of Darkness including it. After they, to serve other Ends, have placed the Orb of the Sun at an infinite Distance, they have pretended to demonstrate how long the Light would be at first, or is now coming from the Sun hither, and how many Ages the Orb of the Sun would be in cooling again, while they are perfectly ignorant of the Expansion, by which the Motion of Fire and Light, at the Orb of the Sun, moves the Light in all the Way hither, and that here instantaneously. Though we cannot tell what Proportion of Atoms there was to Spirit, nor what Force this supernatural Power employ'd; if you go into a Cavern, where the most Part of the Air is in Grains and few Atoms, and light a Candle, it cannot if it burn, move Light to give that Sensation to your Eyes above a Yard or two, till by melting more, its Orb extend: Light one in a dark Room, or in a dark Night, where there is a sufficient Mixture of Atoms, which have been lately divided and rest there, and those Atoms pressed out from the Candle, move those which are next, and so succeffively to a vast Distance instantaneously, or in the same Moment of Time, that the first Atom moves the Distance of its own Dimension from the Candle. It is not necessary that the Parts of Light which touch our Eyes, and those which are between them and the Object, and those which touch it, should immediately have passed through the Sun, Fire, or Candle; no, they only want to be excited, or put into the Motion, Stress, or Expansion, which the Motion of the Parts of Spirit to, and those of Light from the Sun, Fire, or Candle give. If the Condition of the Matter of the Heavens were at first the same, in respect of Proportion of Grains to Atoms, as it or they are now, or the Fire at the Sun were now extinct, and the Motion stopt, the whole would be dark and cold in a Moment; and if the Fire in the Sun, or this Motion, were set forward again in an Instant, at that Instant it would be light, as far as 'tis light now.

Vossius de Orig. & Prog. Idol. Lib, II. p. 255.— "Nay it was the Opinion of many, that what we call Æther was nothing but a great Void or Vacuum in which the Stars performed their Revolutions, which is altogether void of Reason. For it was necessary for the Heavens to be of a corporeal Substance to answer the double Use: The one to carry the Stars, because as the Peripateticks know there can be no Motion without something immovable to move upon. The other that the Stars may act upon Things below, which could not be done without Contact, whither this be immediate without the Intervention of any other Body,

or

or intermediately by Means of some Medium. So that there is a Necessity for every Thing being continuous, or at least contiguous, that the upper Regions may impart their Light and Heat to those below." The Atoms do not receive, much less retain any Properties by being dissolved in the Fire, or any other Way; they produce the Sensation of Seeing, Heat, and all their Effects upon other Things, by their Motion; and as the Motion abates, they as we say, grow dark, cool, or &c. but when they rest, all the Effects cease; all they receive from the Fire is a Separation from those they had been joined with in Grains; so that they are each liable to be press'd outward, single or independent, and go off from the Fire with the greater Velocity, and nearer together than they do afterwards; and if they could have the same Degree of Motion, and the same Degree of Nearness to each other, 10,000 Miles from the Fire, as they had at first Starting, they would have all the Effects, and in the same Degree as they would have had nearer the Fire.

Kircher of Light and Shade, p. 10. —
" *Aristotle* when he could not deny Light to the Sun, denied it Heat; instead of
that

that substituting Motion, and said, that the Sun acted by Light and Motion upon Things below." As the whole Heaven is full, and the Spirit is press'd in, and Light out on every Side of the Orb of the Sun, each Grain of the Spirit has its Share by Contact of the Pressure or Impulse on the foremost Side, and of the Support on the hindmost Side, and what they call lateral Pressure on every equidistant Side, more and more, as they come nearer the Orb of the Sun; and they move faster and faster, as the Angle straitens, and the Atoms or Light slower and slower, as the Angle widens; as unalterably as Water in two erect Tubes, each of whose Widths should increase from little more than a Point, as a Degree of the Heavens widens from the Sun to the Circumference, united at their small Ends would move, if it were possible to press the Water in one of them with Quicksilver, or something instead of a Pistil to fit one of them at each Width; as the Pistil should be press'd down in one Tube or Line, the Water being most press'd in that would sink, and being less press'd in the other, would rise up or the contrary Way; and every Atom of Water would be employ'd to push on another; and the Spirit and Light move with the same Degrees of Velocity, in each

each Part of the Semi-diameter of the Heavens, in Proportion as the Water would do in each Part of each of the Tubes; at what Rate each Atom moves from the Sun, or here, or how long an Atom going from any Candle is in going a Mile; I say any, because they go in Proportion to the Quantity of Grains of Air melted in the Time, except it could be Earmarked, will be hard to prove; so as the Sun, the one Extream, is, by its being melted there, the Source of Light, and the Circumference, the other Extream, by their re-adhering, the Source of Darkness; and dividing between the Light and between the Darkness, is distributing them opposite Ways, making them Opponents, carrying the one the one Way, and the other the opposite Way, on each Side of the Sun, in the same Line; and as the other Orbs are all in their Way, and each must interrupt the Light on one Side, and the Darkness on the other, making Day and Night upon this Orb, which it also turns about, is a Consequence. But to return to the first Light. In whatever Part of the Heavens this Operation of dividing the Parts, which would be Light, out of the Masses, which would have continued Darkness, was produced, one Moiety of the Matter which composes this Globe, would oppose Part of its Course, and so be the Object of its Rays, Beams, Columns, Streams, or, &c. and of the returning Grains on the opposite Side; and as the Light and Darkness are distinguished by the Names of Day and Night, the Word they render divide, has also either immediately or consequentially, as a farther Effect of the same Action, a farther Signification; is to divide between the Day and between the Night; and tho' as we have hinted in the first Part, we have not, nor ever can expect to have, any Evidence how this Light was form'd, or whether it was issued from one fixed Point, or moved during the three or four first Days, we shall be able to prove how every Thing acts in the settled Estate; and we shall suppose that the Point from whence the Light issued, was fixed then, though not in an Orb of other Matter as 'tis now; this latter Operation is express'd distinctly in the Commission given to Light, by the Words to divide between the Day and between the Night, which is to take from the Morning, and give to the Evening, and take from the Evening and give to the Morning successively, or continually, so as to make a continued Rotation. If its Effects

upon

upon this Globe was to take Light from one Part, and give it to the other, that will be done upon this Orb, either by moving the Agent, which divides and sends the Light against the Orb, or by turning the Orb: If we prove by Scripture, that this Orb turns and moves, that will do without any Motion of the other: If we prove that the Point from whence the Light is issued, is fixed, even that proves, that this Orb turns and moves; and though this Action of dividing is for the Reasons mentioned, absolutely attributed to God; yet if we find that the Spirit and the Light when established, do the same Things, we may be allowed to suppose, that God by supporting those Actions, divided between the Day, and between the Night; and for Proof, we refer to the Signification of the Word.

M. בדל III. Its Signification is Separation.—בדל *Niph.* נבדל separated, divided, distinct, discriminated. *Hiphil.* הבדיל, to divide, to separate. *Chald.* To change.

Arabic, Badal. To change, to change between, to change with, or exchange, to barter, traffic, &c.

C. ibid. *Chald.* to separate.—שפע נבדל a mediating Influence.

בדולקי

בדולקי in *Medr. Schem. fol.* 58. 4. The Word תרפים, *Teraphim*, is explained by ביקורים של בדולקי, in *Jalkut*, Part II. *F.* 18. *Col.* 4. instead of this, read בדולקי, that is, Images that prophesy or foretel, *i.e.* Separate Truth from Falsehood.

Arabic. Erpennius. To take in Place of another, or one Thing for another, as a *Succedaneum*,——instead of this or that,——in his stead, by turns, alternately——

B. C. הבדל. A Difference, Discrimination.——Rabbi *Simeon*, in his Logic, says, בדל is that which distinguisheth one Thing from another.

הבדלה, Distinction, Separation: נר ההבדלה. The Light of Separation, or Division: The Lamp, or Light, bears this Name, which the *Jews* light up upon the Evening of the going out of the Sabbath, to separate and divide the Day from the Night, and the unhallowed Days of the Week from the holy Sabbath, &c. *Polyglot. fol.* 6. *Heb.* and *Samar.* Various Readings in the Book of *Genesis*——and to separate; the *Arabic* the same.

This is a Word of Office, implies several Persons or Things divided or divisible, and which are moveable, and that there is some Distance or Thing between them, to act among, signifies to separate some
Thing

Thing or Part, from one Thing to another, to take from one, and give to another, as 1 *Chron.* xii. 7. *And of the Gadites there divided unto David:* where 'tis double, as 'tis here, or to be a repeated Action, as 'tis hereafter, when the Machine is establish'd; 'tis also to take from the other, and give back to that one, to exchange between the Parties, and by such Exchange to change the Condition of the Things exchanged; something like that of Officers, exchanging Captives, or Prisoners; or of Princes, or Governors, whose Office *inter al.* was to judge and distribute; or of a King then, and of his Viceroy soon after; as, *Luke* xii. 14. *Who made me a Judge, or a Divider over you?* This it does between all the People on the Earth; but if Persons be excluded, and it be spoke of Things, 'tis changing Part of the one Thing, into Part of the other, alternately. This, in the two Cases before us, was attributed to God; afterwards one Part of the Act of dividing the Light from the Darkness, was to be the Task of Fire, which signifies to divide the Parts adherring one from another, and render them soft and smooth, *Job* xxxviii. 24. *Which Way is Light* יחלק *divided?* And the other Part is distributing it, from the one

Extreme

Extream to the other, which the Firmament does; and the other Act of dividing between the Day, and between the Night, was to be the Task of the Lights: These the *Jews* were to keep in Memory with great Solemnity, as you may see in many Places; and as I am forced to repeat, as the Heathens worshipped their God under various Names, which were, at first, no more than Attributes, so the Prophets claim those Attributes for their God, sometimes by a Name, sometimes by an Assertion, as the Heathens attributed these Actions to Fire, of which their חרפים were Representatives, by the Name of the Divider or Distributer. So *Job* xii. 22. *He turneth the under Parts up out of the Darkness, and bringeth forth the Shadow of Death to the Light.* Amos v. 8. *turneth the Shadow of Death into the Morning, and darkeneth the Day into Night.* And *Moses* here shews them, that God divided and distributed before their God was substituted. The latter *Jews* often used several of their *Chaldee* Words for one *Hebrew* Word, and *vice versa*, and the *Latins* have done the same, and they must either be set right by the Original, or remain Nonsense.

B. C.

B. C. פרש *Peres*—to separate, disjoin, discern, distinguish materially and mentally, &c. Gen. i. 4. *And the Lord distinguished between the Light, and between the Darkness.* Ibid. and 14. *To make Lights, to distinguish between the Light and between the Darkness*, can scarce, with any Allowance, be intelligible.

הפריש, to separate, to lay by, or put a Difference between, to take away, carry away, to remove, והפריש אחרת תחת. And he separated another for this, *i. e.* he separated and substituted, or placed another in the Room or Place of it.

פלג, to divide, distribute, share, &c. But to return to the Text, To divide, or be dividing, between the Light, or Day, or Hemisphere, that interrupts the Rays, and between Darkness, or Night, or the Hemisphere, which is hid from the Rays of Light, is causing that Motion, which is perpetually giving the Light, or Day, or light Hemisphere, Part of the Darkness, or Night, or dark Hemisphere, and giving the Darkness, or Night, or dark Hemisphere, Part of the Light, or Day, or light Hemisphere; and is giving the progressive Rotation, to the Earth: So now dividing between the Light, and between the Darkness, in speaking of the whole System, is

driving

driving the Grains to the Sun, diffolving them there, and fending their Parts out in Light; in fpeaking of the Earth, dividing between the Light, and between the Darknefs, is, as afterwards expreffed, dividing between the Day, and between the Night, exchanging equal Parts continually, and the latter is a Confequence of the former.

Ver. 5. *And God called the Light Day, and the Darknefs he called Night :* ----

We muft go back from the Difcovery of who was the Agent, to the Defcription of the Time, or Order of Action; we fuppofe that he is fpeaking of the Time when, or as foon as there was Light iffued on one Side of the Orb, and Darknefs on the other, God diftinguifhed them by the proper Names of Day and Night; for fo they were the firft Moment, and fo they muft have continued, if either the Point whence the Light iffued, or this Orb had not moved; but there would have been no Morning nor Evening, nor no Succeffion of Days: It would have been lighteft in the Middle, and equally darker near each Verge; fo that though, as foon as there had been a proper

per Proportion of Light, the Spirit would have rush'd in, and have mov'd the Orb; yet I cannot see how it could choose one Side rather than another, so as to turn it that Way, and move it in that Circle, which should answer those of the Planets and Stars unformed, without God's immediate Direction; for the Regulators were not then formed; but when that was once determined, and the Earth in Motion, supposing the Spirit, Light, and what supplied the Expansion supported in Action, as they are in this Machine; as I have hinted above, the Spirit would press in on the hinder Edge of the Light, turn the Earth gradually, and so successively present Part of a new Face to the Stream of Light; and the Spirit pursuing the Light, would successively impress its Force upon a new Edge; so a Day, if taken generally with respect to the whole Orb, and not to a particular Part, is a Hemisphere of the Earth, interrupting a Column of the Rays of Light, or now of the Light from the Sun, shifting or turning the Light on to another Part which was dark, and as much of the dark Part on to part which was Light, as the Earth proceeds, and turns till it make one Round; or an Interruption of the Rays of the Sun,

upon

upon a Hemisphere of this Globe, perpetually incroaching upon the other Hemisphere in the Morning, and leaving in the Evening till it has got it all, or till every Part of the Circle of the Earth has equally interrupted it, or them; so produced by a gradual Revolution of a shifting Hemisphere of the Earth, opposite to the Flux, or Stream of Light, now variable by Seasons. And a Night is a Hemisphere of the Earth, interrupting the Returns of the Spirit, now, with some feint Rays of Light from the Orbs of the Stars, and sometimes from the Rays of the Moon, shifting or turning the Darkness on to another Part, which was light, and as much which was light, on to part which was dark, as the Earth proceeds, and turns till it make one Round; or an Interruption of the Column of Darkness, or the Spirit upon one Hemisphere of this Globe, continually incroaching upon the other Hemisphere in the Evening, and leaving as much in the Morning, till every Part of the Circle of the Earth has equally interrupted it; so produced by a gradual Revolution of a shifting Hemisphere of the Earth, opposite to the nearest Extremities of the Heavens, variable now by Seasons; With respect to any particular

Part

MOSES's *Principia.* 239

Part of this Globe, without confidering the Declinations, or Seafons fince eftablifhed, from the Time that Part is turn'd into the foremoft Edge of Light, or Morning, till tis turn'd out of the hindmoft Edge of Light or Evening, 'tis Day, and from the Time that Part is turned into the hindmoft Edge of Darknefs, or Evening, till 'tis turned out of the foremoft Edge of Darknefs, or Morning, 'tis Night.

Ver. 5. ---- And the Evening and the Morning were the firft Day, Heb. *and the Evening was, and the Morning was the firft Day.*

We are firft to confider the Situation of Things at firft ftarting; in the Center of that Hemifphere of Light, it was, as we may term it, like our Mid-day or Noon, and at whatever Edge the Spirit made the Pufh, and gave the Earth Motion by Impulfe, whereby it became the hindmoft Edge, there was Evening, and at the foremoft Edge was Morning; but as the whole Surface of the Earth began to turn at once, the Queftion is? Where we muft begin to count: If we begin to count from Mid-day, and call it Evening, till
Mid-

Mid-night, and Morning from thence, till Noon, that suits our Language beſt, but ſeems ſtrange to end a Day in the Middle: If we begin in the Verge or Twilight, where the Spirit began to act, then it means at firſt Sight, as if we were to make all the Night Evening, and all the Day Morning, though that be not ſo, it ſeems that as a Memorial of this Beginning, many of their Ordinances were to be obſerv'd then, and thoſe who were polluted in many Caſes became clean then. Theſe Inſtitutions were in Oppoſition to the Rites their Predeceſſors the Heathens uſed at their Temple, dedicated to their God, the Heavens under the Name of this Condition or Power, or Attribute mentioned, *Joſ.* xv. 6. בית הערבה. *The Temple of the Mixer.* M. ערב ſignifies a Mixing, Mixture, and alſo Evening, &c.—mixed, mixed with, to have Commerce with, to contend—to mix together, and make Exchange — to adapt, direct, make congruous or fit together — *the Evening*, from the Light and Darkneſs being at that Time mixed together—It is the higheſt Sphere—the Heavens, or *Primum Mobile*, the higheſt Heavens—Rabbi *David* writes, that it is the upper Sphere that

cloſes

encloses all, and by its Motion moves all the other Spheres; and *Lev.* xiii. The Woofs or Threads shot one this Way, and the other that Way.

Syr. To sift, ventilate. It fits the whole Matter of the Heavens, because the whole is a Mixture in that Motion, and *the highest Part of the Heavens,* because there is a Mixture and Exchange, and the *Evening,* because the mixing and exchanging of the Spirit and Light there, is the Cause of the Motion of the Earth. This is a general Name of successive Condition and Action, implies the Mixture of Grains and Atoms, which are in every Part of the Heavens, one Sort being carried forward, and another backward, and each being exchanged at each End, the large for the small, and the small for large, as Merchants do Goods; or in the Manner of Woof, one Thread one Way, and the next the other Way, whence arises the Order, and all the Operations and Motions in this System; but it may be properly applied to the Circumference of the Heavens; and 'tis here to the Operation that Mixture has in the Evening, in the Motion, or the impelling of the Earth. The *Arabians* took their Name from this Attribute, as most other Nations did, each from an Attribute of the Heavens. The *Egyptians* and *Arabians* with them seem to have been punished with the Mixture of Insects, upon this Account; the *Jews* were forbid Mixtures almost of any Sort; *Levit.* xix. *Deut.* xxii. What Actions, or Representaions the Heathens had in their Worship of this Condition and Motion, is not before me now. But ערב is some Sort of Bird, which was a Representative of this Power, which they render *Corvus*. And some Sort of a Tree, which they render *Salix*.

Vossius of the Rise and Progress of Idolatry, Lib. IV. p. 121. *Erasmus Stella* in the Beginning of his Book of the Antiquities of *Prussia*, says, that for some Time they had no religious Rites among them; at the last they arrived to that Degree of Madness as to pay religious Worship to Serpents, wild Beasts, and Trees.

Ibid. Vossius of the Christian Physiology, *Lib.* V. p. 88. Some of the *Indians* likewise are reported to worship Trees. -St. *Oderic* in his Travels into the East, the second Book, and 5th Section writes —
" These People are guilty of Idolatry, for they worship Fire, Serpents, and Trees."
What he reports of the *East-Indies* is true of the *West*: *Jos. Acosta* tells us, that the

In-

Inhabitants of *Peru* at this Day pay divine Honour to a Tree, Book V. Chap. 2. &c.

Ibid. p. 90. *Pliny* in his 12th Book, Chap. 1. of Trees. These Species of Trees dedicated to their respective Deities, are constantly preserved and taken Care of, as the *Beech* to *Jupiter*, the *Laurel* to *Apollo*, the *Olive* to *Minerva*, the *Mirtle* to *Venus*, the *Poplar* to *Hercules*—and then adds—We believe them to be as it were Attributes of the Heavens.

Clem. Alex. Strom. Lib. V. p. 414. *Dionysius* the *Thracian*, a *Grammarian*, in his Book explaining the Symbols of the Wheels, says expresly, that some signified Actions not only by Words, but by Symbols—by Symbols, as for Instance, the Wheels that is turned round in the Temples of their Gods, taken from the *Egyptians*: And the Boughs of Trees given to those who worship. For so sings *Orpheus* the *Thracian*.

Boughs represent our mortal State below,
Like them we perish, and like them we grow:
Fate stands not still, nor lets Things keep
  their Ground,
But runs one constant, circulating Round.

Gyrald.

Gyrald. p. 72. The *Indians* took to worshipping every Thing, but chiefly the largest Trees, thought them Gods, and had them in Veneration above all others, being a Capital Crime to prophane them.

Voſſius, Rabbi M. *Maimonides* of Idolatry, p. 61. XX. How is a Grove prophaned? by pulling a Leaf or breaking off a Branch, *&c.* Notes, Whence among the antient *Romans* none cut down a Grove within his own Ground, until he had offered up in Sacrifice a Swine to appeaſe the Gods, *&c.*

Ibid. p. 50. XVI. If but a Tree be worſhiped, *&c.* p. 56. V. It is unlawful to make uſe of a Tree planted upon Account of religious Worſhip: And of this Nature is the Grove of which the Law ſpeaks.

And for that Reaſon at the Feaſt of the *Jews* appointed, *Levit.* xxiii. 40. they were to cut Boughs of this and other repreſentative Trees; and build Tabernacles of them, *&c.* Several great Men, and *Spencer*, have ſhewed their Skill to prove, that there could be no natural Reaſon why, God forbad the *Iſraelites*, the mixing of Seeds, different Sorts of Stuff, *&c.* and it is true, but as they knew not the Reaſon they ought not to have drawn ſuch
Con-

Conclusions as they have done. And I think they shew'd little Skill in pretending to find Reasons, for the Laws of God in the Rubbish they gave most Credit to.

And though this Text has been misconstrued, and that has misled many to think, that the Evening preceding, belonged to the next Day; because it appears otherwise, before I shew what this Text means, I must shew that 'tis quite contrary; for Instance in the Institution of the Passover; Exod. xii. 6. *And ye shall keep it* (the Lamb) *up until the fourteenth Day of the same Month; and the whole Assembly of the Congregation of* Israel *shall kill it in the Evening,* (*Heb.* between the two Evenings) between the Mixtures, between that Mixture of Light with so little Darkness in it, that it might be called Day, and that Mixture of Darkness with so little Light in it, that it might be called Night, in common; but in these Cases, in Reference to the Memorial of this, 'tis the Mixture of Spirit pushing in, and the Mixture of Light receding; V. 18. *In the first Month, on the fourteenth Day of the Month, at Even, ye shall eat unleavened Bread until the one and twentieth Day of the Month at Even*; Levit. xxiii. 5. *In the fourteenth Day of the first Month at*

at Even, (between the two Evenings,) is the LORD's Paſſover: V. 6. *And on the fifteenth Day of the ſame Month, is the Feaſt of unleavened Bread unto the* LORD — Numb. xxviii. 16. *And in the fourteenth Day of the firſt Month is the Paſſover of the* LORD. *And in the fifteenth Day of this Month is the Feaſt*—'Tis plain here the Day was counted before the Evening, for the Lamb was to be kept till the fourteenth Day, and that Day was to be kept holy. *Exod.* xii. 14. And the Lamb was to be killed in the Evening, and the Feaſt of unleavened Bread began with the Time of Eating the Paſſover, becauſe it appears, *Exod.* xii. 8, it was to be eaten with the Paſſover, Neither did the Evening include the Night; Deut. xvi. 4. *Neither ſhall there any Thing, of the Fleſh which thou ſacrificedſt the firſt Day at Even, remain all Night until the Morning.* The Evening and the Morning having no Relation to Duration, ſo as to include the other Parts of the Day or Night; each of them is but a Point in Time, or a Line on the Surface of the Earth; the Evening is the Edge, going out of the Light into the Darkneſs, *Prov.* vii. 9, *In the Twilight, where the Day mixes,* Deut. xvi. 6. *Thou ſhalt ſacrifice the Paſſover, when it mixeth,*
תשמש

בבוא השמש *at the going down of the Sun,* (which I shall shew is at the turning of the Earth, till the Light was under the Horizon) *at the Season thou cometh forth out of* Egypt. And in a Prophecy of a Change, Zach. xiv. 7. *At the Time of its Mixing shall there be Light.* There were also some Appointments for the Morning, which is the Edge going out of the Darkness into the Light, as Judg. xix. 25. *All Night until the Morning.* Ibid. xvi. 2, *Were quiet all the Night, saying in the Morning.* Ibid. ix. 33. *It shall be in the Morning as soon as the Sun is up,* which I shall shew is the turning into the Light. So Exod. xviii. 13, 14. *From the Morning until the Evening,* Which was the whole Day in that Place. The Words stand, thus ויהי ערב ויהי בקר In our Translation they have left out the Word for the one ויהי, which they translate, *was,* and put the Word *were* for the other, or both, after the Word Morning: In the Margin they have transposed the *was* from before the Word Evening, to behind it, and the *was* before Morning, to behind it; if such Practice be allow'd, it would render the Scripture as uncertain as the Works of any idle Author; and though Mankind have in Contradiction

tradiction to common Sense, conform'd to it in speaking; I must let the Words stand in the Order I find them in the Original — יהי which they render, *Ver.* 3. *Let there be*, might be rendered, *Be it*, or *Let it be*, for it has not only Relation to Place, but to Matter and Motion, and other Accidents, and must imply or conform to the Place, and the Manner in which the Thing, the Actions, or Accidents of the Thing were to be; as Creation gives Existence to Matter, this expresses Existence of Condition, Motion, Action, or as they say of Accidents; it might have been by Creation, and after by being put together of created Matter; or formed, by that together being dissolved; or of Motion or Action, nay, if it was to have been a complex Action, and twenty Agents concerned in it, each to act a particular Share, or some to act, and some to suffer; nay, if it were such an Action, whether of a single Agent, or sundry, so that the first Action should produce another by Consequence, and that another, and so a Train, as *inter al.* let there be, as a Consequence, an Inclination of the Earth to the Light, let it roll or turn, let there be such a complex Action, that every Agent may act his Part, and the Patients suffer in such

Manner

Manner as jointly to make up that complex Action, or let there be such an Action, and such Consequences. And tho' it is pretended, that the *Hebrew* Language is barren or poor, and other imaginary Languages rich; yet this expresses as much, and more certainly than Variety of Words can do. As this short Writing was enough for those who perfectly understood the Things, and as God foresaw what other Books of Scripture should be writ and preserv'd, and as they were all by the same Author, though publish'd by divers Hands, they are all to be accounted as one; and in treating of the several Parts of his Works, there are proper Words to distinguish each Branch, which would have been superfluous here; and there is one Beauty in these Speeches, which cannot be in the Speeches of any other Being; let it be, and it was; let there be, and there was; let it be made, and it was made; let it move, and it moved, or &c. are each expressed in the same Word, as יהי אור ויהי אור, which we are forced to render, *Let there be Light, and there was Light*; though his Will is the immediate Cause of Existence, for Motion, Action, &c. there was no Distinction in Time, so here *there was*, or *it was there*

Evening,

Evening, and it was there Morning; God had just made, and declar'd Night, the opposite or counterpart to Day; and *Moses* could never intend to confound that Distinction, God had so made, in the very next Words; that was impossible; he is only speaking of the Divisions which were neither Day nor Night, of the hindmost and foremost Edges of Day and Night, and of their Motions and Places in a turning or changing Hemisphere; there was Darkness before, and Night then, and after; and saying, there was a first Day, is sufficiently implying, there was also, at the same Time, a first Night; and if he had intended to put the Night before the Day, that might have been done without changing their Names; he is speaking here of shifting those Divisions or Boundaries of Day and Night, by turning the Earth, which till then had stood still, to that great End, that the whole Surface might alternately have the Benefit of that Light, which one half had; but then, as the first Motion determined which was Evening, and which was Morning, he tells you how far they shifted to make a Day; he need say nothing of Night: If he spoke of the Hemisphere, which was Light, before it moved, saying, there was

a second Day, is implying sufficiently, that it was Night between; he says there was between Light and Darkness, shifting Lines, or Lines shifted: If with regard to the Earth, that Part of it which was Evening, was Morning: If with regard to the Line of Evening, as it was shifted upon the Earth, that also, which was at the first Motion, Evening, would be shifted to the Place where, at the first Motion, there was Morning, and the Reverse exactly, for there was no Cause of Declination appointed then. It may perhaps be hard to dispossess People of the Notion of a natural Day, as they construed it. *Polyglot, various Readings. Arabic. And when Night and Day had passed, it was one (or the First) Day.* But if he had spoke of a Revolution of this Line in either Sense, then it should have been, the Evening was, and the Evening was, &c. But as People who are for losing nothing, are sometimes willing to exchange, if we can shew them, that in Life, or &c. the Days are only counted, and not the Nights, and that the Darkness, or Night, is counted as a Time of Sleep, or Inaction, a Shadow of Death, then *Moses* only speaks here of real Days. He speaks here of the Hemisphere, which was Day, and in order to
de-

describe how it went off, and was formed into a Day, *viz.* the first Day, he tells you that it turned off, and which Way it turned the Part, or Edge, or Line, which was by the Course the Earth took at its first beginning to turn Evening, by turning off a Line out of the Light, began to cut off a Segment, in order to make it a Day, and the Part, or Edge, or Line, that by the said Course, at its first beginning to turn, was Morning, was the Part which, by its being turned out of the Light, compleated the making of it a Day; and there is no new Precept for this, because this is a direct Consequence of, *Let there be Light*; and this Precept, with only the Description between, is also of the singular Number, and connected with a *Vau*; *And God said, Let there be Light, and there was Light*—for tho' I have hitherto taken the *Vau* in the Texts, where there are seeming Repetitions, only as signifying (and) because that expresses the Design of the Caution most strongly; yet in *Hebrew*, and all the neighbouring Languages, it signifies, in each Place, such Conjunction as the Sense directs, as, *so, therefore, thereby*;— so there was Evening; so there was Morning. The Spirit was ready, and as soon as there was Light,

un-

MOSES's *Principia*.

unavoidably, as I have hinted before, there would be a Rotation; and the Progression of a Day which was then, and the Declination which was added, are also fully expressed in the Description of the Uses of the Machine, when perfected.

They pretend to shew, that the sacred Writers not only affirmed, that the Earth stood fixed upon Foundations, but that its Surface was flat. *Job* says, (xxxvii. 12.) *Upon the Face* תבל *of the Sphere* ארצה *of the Earth. Prov.* viii. 31. *Rejoycing on the Sphere of his Earth.* Job xxvi. 7. תלה *hanging the Earth on* בלימה. *M.* בלם signifies a Stoppage, an Obstruction—*Kal.* to shut, shut fast, to stop, to constrain בלימה Constriction, a Curb.

B. C. " The Cabalists take this Word בלימה for a simple uncompounded one, and make it the same as Constriction from בלם. *Job* xxvi. 7. He hangeth the Earth upon the Constriction, that is, upon the Dominion of the superior Rulers, by whose Power the Earth is restrained as it were with a Bridle, that it may stand fast, and obey their Command, as the Mouth of an Horse restrained by a Bridle, is subject to the Management of the Rider. There is a triple Constriction of the Earth, or a triple Dominion by which it is governed: בלימה

MOSES's *Principia.*

בלימה ראשונה the first Conftriction is, the Dominion of the Ruler of the Univerfe: בלימה שנית the fecond Conftriction is, the Dominion of the heavenly Intelligences that move the Spheres: בלימה שלישית the third Conftriction is, the Dominion of the Spheres by their Motion. Thefe three Dominions are called, in the plural Number, בלימות." See the Cabaliftical Book גנת אגוז, the *Nut-Garden,* Fol. 53. 1. (which is an Attribute of the Airs, and, I think, is the Heathen Name of the Airs). " But it is a compound Word of בל the Spirit and ימח the Light, whence comes יום the Day: So a Name of the Mixture of Light and Spirit the Airs which fupport and impel the Earth." Thefe fhew that they knew that the Earth was of a fit Figure to turn, and fix'd to nothing, fo at Liberty to be turn'd; and they ufe Words which exprefs that Action in general, as מחר (one Thing had in Exchange for another, which of Days is the next) or *to morrow* (of Goods, or *&c.* is the Price) and the Manner of the Action explain'd, פנה as *Deut.* xxiii. 11. *But it fhall be when Evening cometh on,* (*Heb.* turneth toward) here they have tranfpofed the Words, 'tis לפנות ערב; he fays not, that the Evening turn'd, but when fomething underftood, stood, when the Land with the People of any Part of *Judea* were turn'd to the Evening, *Exod.* xiv. 27. *The Sea returned to its Strength,* לפנות בקר *when it was turned to the Morning.* Here is the same Word used with the Morning; so of Days, *Pſ.* xc. 9. *For all our Days are turned away.* Jer. vi. 4. *Wo unto us! for the Day is turned away: for the Shadows of the Evening* ינטו *are stretched out.* And very beautifully, *Judg.* xix. 9. רפה יום לערוב, *the Day yields to the Evening,* (gives way.) Further, they tell you expreſly what it is that is turned, *Job* xii. 22. *Turning round the Parts that are undermost up out of the Darkneſs: and brings forth to the Light the Shadow of Death;* the Place to the Light, not the Light to the Place: so *Amos* v. 8. *Who made the Light and the Spirit, and turns round the Shadow of Death to the Morning; and darkneth the Day into Night.* You are to obſerve, that not one of theſe Words hath any relation to deſcribing a Circle, ſuch as the Sun muſt make, if it were carried about the Earth, to make a Day, but turning upon a Center; nor to the Earth's deſcribing that Circle, which it is doing continually to make a Year; but when any conſiderable Number of Days are ſpoke of, they uſe Words

which

which express Part, or all of that Circle which makes the Year, 1 *Sam.* i. 20. *It came to pass when the Days* לתקפות *were gone round.* Job i. 4. *When the Days of the Feasting* הקיפו *were gone round.* Nay, they express the Agents which produce this Rotation, and so Day and Night by proper Words. R. פוח *is* נבה, *to blow, puff, breathe,* &c. *Cant.* ii. 17. iv. 6. *till* שיפוח *it blow Day, and the Shadows fly away.* This Word is used for the Impulse of the Spirit upon Fire, Fluids and Solids, and 'tis so here; and *M.* נשא I. signifies Impulse, or blowing in, as when you blow up a Fire with Bellows, &c.—To blow, to blow forth, or upon, to impell, drive about.

II. Twilight—which I have shew'd is the Twilight of the Evening, as *Prov.* vii. 9. *In the Twilight, where the Day mixeth,* which is a Name for the Part where the Impulse is successively given; so of the very Agent, *Gen.* iii. 8. *At the Spirit of the Day:* And of the other Agent, *Prov.* iv. 18. as, *the Light, shining, proceeding, and flowing unto* נכון *perfect Day,* (to machining, to regulating the Day) of which more hereafter. *David* speaking of these Turnings, says, *Psal.* lxv. 9. *Thou makest the* מוצאי *outgoings of* [as the *English* says,

and

MOSES's *Principia.*

and so it would have been without the מ; but with it, 'tis the *Instruments,* the *Causes of carrying;* or, at least, its *Actions,* the *Carryings from the Evening and Morning;* for it does not express the going of the Morning, or Evening, but implies, that they, the People, were carried by some Agent, upon some Carriage, out of] *the Evening and Morning to praise thee.* And as Years are compounded of the Progressions of Days, *Exod.* xxxiv. 22. *The Feast of Ingathering* תקופת *at the coming round of the Year.* 2 *Chron.* xxiv. 23. *It came to pass at the Revolution of the Year.* So, 2 *Sam.* xi. 1. 1 *Kings* xii. 22. 1 *Chron.* xx. 1. 2 *Chron.* xxvi. 10. *It came to pass at* תשובת, *the Return of the Year.* The Christians, by following the Translations of the *Jews,* and shunning the Knowledge of the Heathens, are become more ignorant in these Things, than the savage *Indians.* The *Canaanites* had a Temple to their God, the Heavens, by the Attribute mention'd *Josh.* xv. 6. and xviii. 19. ביתחגלה. *Beth Hgle, the Temple of the Circulator.* " *M.* The House of Festivity, from בית and גול; or the House of its Revolution, from בית and גלל. *Ibid. Pol.* As they have omitted the first half of the Word, I must insert it; הוג or חגג

Vol. II.   X   M.

M. To be in Motion, Commotion, Circumgyration, to be carried round, circulated.—*C.* To dance in Circles, go round, be turned round. *Coc.* חגג, seems particularly to signify Motion, and that in a Circle, that it may agree with חוג, which denotes a Circle: Such is generally the Motion of those who dance, or lead up Dances, 1 *Sam.* xxx. 16. *M.* גויל, to express the inward Joy of the Mind by the outward Gesture or Motion of the Body—they all agree with גלל, to roll:—גלל, a Sphere or Circle, *&c.*— *C.* גיל, to exult, leap up, it denotes the outward Expression of Joy, when any one shews himself joyful by Dancing and Jumpings. *Isa.* lxv. 19. *R. Coc.* It signifies rather the external Expression of Joy, than the internal Gladness of the Mind, when with Caperings and Jumpings and Turnings, any one declares his Joy. To leap for Joy, as we say. *C. Arab.* חגן—The Celebration of the *Mecha* Festival—A Bracelet of precious Stones, and a Pearl that hangs at the Ears—the Year, *&c.*— *C.* חגל *Syriac*, to go about,— Circuit. *Arab. Fut. O. & I.* to hop like a Crow, or with the Feet fettered or tied together; to hop or jump upon one Foot. *Avicenna* I. 359, 30, *&c.* —a certain Play or Sport: a Play in which

Boys hop upon one Foot. *Giggæus.* A dancing or hopping upon one Foot, called *Ascoliasmos:* Fox, to thy Hole, or *Scotch* Hoppers. *Avic.* I. 80. 9. C. חגג *Syriac.* An Eclipse, to throw, project, turn round, &c." This Attribute, in a God, is to make something go round, or in a Circle; and to make it turn round in its going, though there may be other Bodies which move in that Manner, if the Point were not clear'd by Scripture, 'tis applicable to nothing so evidently as to the Earth. One of the Services the Heathens paid to this Attribute, was to dance or move in Circles, and each turn round in their circular or progressive Motion: Hence the *Arabians* call'd their Bracelets, Ear-rings, &c. which were Representatives of this Power in the annual Circle, by that Part of the Word which expresses it; and so used the same Word חג for the Year itself. This was a Service requir'd by the Law of God, to be perform'd at stated Times or Feasts, under these and other Words, *Exod.* v. 1. The Reason urg'd for carrying the People of *Israel* from the *Ægyptians,* was to perform this Service to the Lord; this is the first Part of the Law was appointed; *Ibid.* xii. 14. and xiii. 6. and xxiii. 4. *& seq.* to be perform'd three Times every Year.

The *Lamb*, which was the Reprefentative of this Power, and was to be eat at the Paffover, *ver.* 18. is call'd חג, and 'tis fo call'd when 'tis made a Sacrifice in this Service, *Pfal.* cxviii. 27. This Service was an Acknowledgment, that he was Mafter of thofe Powers. This fettled, the Antients are clear'd of their Ignorance, and the facred Writers, and Texts, where thefe Words are join'd to the Earth, of the Nonfenfe in the Tranflation, or where the *Hebrew* Word גל is join'd, which expreffes both Motions, or to roll in a Circle or Sphere, as 1 *Chron.* xvi. 31. *Let the Airs* ישמחו *irradiate, and the Earth* תגל *revolve.* Pfa. xcvi. 11. xcvii. 1. יהוה מלך תגל הארץ *Jehovah is King, let the Earth revolve.* Ifa. xliii. 13. רנו שמים וגילי ארץ. *Let the Airs fhout* (jump backwards and forwards) *and the Earth revolve.* Thefe are pofitive Expreffions, fome, that the Heavens move, and all, that the Earth moves in a Circle, and turns round in that Motion, and it will appear, doing the firft does the fecond. The Heathens, in other Countries, attributed this to the Heavens, both by Words and Reprefentations; and many of their Words, which are mifconftructed, and Symbols which have had lately no Meaning, not only among the Heathens,

thens, but in the Tabernacle and Temple, will now explain themselves.

Voſſius de Phiſ. Chriſtiana, &c. *Lib.* IX. p. 269. *Phylarchus Gr.* Thoſe among the *Greeks* who ſacrifice to the Sun, make their Libation of Honey: They bring no Wine to the Altars, becauſe they ſay, that the Deity who contains and governs all Things, and conſtantly rolls round the World, ſhould be altogether free from Drunkenneſs.

Voſſius de Orig. & Prog. Idol. Lib. II. p. 177.—*Urania*; whom *Aſia* and all *Africa* ſo much worſhip. Nor is *Uranus* any other than the Sun; for he is the Ruler of the celeſtial Fires, as ſhall hereafter be more fully explain'd.

Ibid. Voſſ. Maimonides of Idolatry, p. 47. 8. Thoſe Images that are found placed upon the Gates of Cities; if they have in their Hand the Figure of a Rod, a Bird, a Ball, or Globe, or Sword, or Crown, or Ring; this ſhews them to be made for Worſhip, &c.

Ibid. p. 50. 15. If an idolatrous Ring, &c.

Voſſ. de Phiſ. Chriſtiana, &c. *Lib.* VII. p. 161. *Cicero* of the Nature of the Gods. By *Saturn* they mean, that which comprehends the Courſe and Revolutions of

Times and Seasons. This Revolution, or alternate Change of Seasons is, from the Revolution or Circumgyration of the Heavens alone round the Earth, or of the Heaven and the Earth, For that the Earth had a Rotation in the Space of 24 Hours, was the Opinion of many: as *Pythagoras, Aristarchus* the *Samian, Philolaus, Hicetas, Seleuchus, Cleanthes* the *Samian, Leucippus, Heraclides, Ecphantus, Plato*, even when Old, and, at least, half an Age before *Pythagoras*, of *Numa Pompilius*, who, according to *Plutarch*, made the Temple of *Vesta* a Rotund, order'd a perpetual Fire to be kept up in it, that by the Rotundity of the Temple, he might represent the Spheroidity of the World; and by preserving the Fire always burning in the midst, shew the Sun to be placed in the Center of the World, whose Symbol the sacred Fire was.

Ver. 6. And God said, Let there be a Firmament (Heb. *Expanſion*) in the midſt *(between the Atoms or Parts)* of the Waters, and let it divide *(be dividing)* the Waters from the Waters. *(between the Waters to the Waters.)*

Ver. 7. And God made the Firmament, and divided the Waters which *were* under the Firmament, from the Waters which were above the Firmament: and it was ſo.

Ver. 8. And God called the Firmament Heaven.

In my firſt Part, which was ſhort, and only to ſhew the Effect, or one of the Conſequences of this Expanſion, I was forced to leave ſome Difficulties in the Roads I had pointed out, till I ſhould have Time to draw a true Delineation of them, becauſe the Adverſaries watch all

Opportunities, and notwithstanding I used the same Caution in the Essay writ since, our Primitive——has introduced his sham *Sanchoniathon*, giving an Account of their worshiping Fire, &c. that his Antiquity and Authority might not be behind that of the History of *Moses*; I fancy it has not told him why, so well as *Moses* has done. My Design in this, has led me to explain some of the preceding Words, and so remove some Part of the Difficulties which were in the Way.

M. רקע signifies an opening, or dividing asunder, a drawing, or stretching out, according as where it is found, and what it is understood of—to expand, extend, distend, stretch.

Kircher's Concordance of the O. T. רקיע *Rakio*, an Extension, Expansion, compact, and firm : It is rightly render'd Firmament. For what is softer and more fluid than Air and Water? And yet God hath made that Extension so firm, that it shall be more durable than any Brass or Adamant, nor liable to be wore by the Friction of swift Motion." This is also a Word of Condition, and consequently of Office. We can have no Word in modern Language for it, because we have had no Idea of it. It expresses Motion of different Parts,

MOSES's *Principia.* 265

Parts, of the same Thing, at the same Time, one Part the one Way, and the other the other Way with Force; so of a Plate of ductile Metal hammer'd, of Wings expanded, or such Things, is extending one Edge one Way, and the other the other Way; and is of the Matter of the Heavens, what had been supported by Degrees, and was now brought to Perfection; the Motion of the Spirit one Way, and of Light the opposite Way in every Line, from a supposed Centre to the Circumference of a Sphere, which environed the Earth, and was shortly to extend beyond, and make and environ all the other Orbs; and when so establish'd, is strengthen'd and explain'd by what is express'd by the Word שחקים next explain'd. *Job* xxxvii. 14. to 18. *Hearken unto this, O Job; stand still and consider the wondrous Works of God: Dost thou know* how He on whom is the Curse, gave them Power that the Light of his Cloud should shine? Dost thou *understand* מפלשי עב (the rolling in and covering with the Ashes, or Dust, or Atoms of the Heavens, and so) *the growing of dense Grains, the wondrous Work of him who is perfect in Knowledge? How thy Garments are warm, when he quieteth the Earth from the South?* Hast thou with

it

it (*viz*, with the Grains) *given the expansive Power to the Æthers* (the Conflicters) *which are strong as a Molten Glass*. This Action, if it could be considered apart from its Consequences, is indeed itself but a Consequence of the Action in the Fire; when the Grains are divided, the Parts fly out to the Surface, and other Grains fly in from the Surface, or Circumference thither; which makes the Expansion each of those Ways, and every Way, and so the Conflict or Struggle between the two contending Parties.

Gen. i. 7. ויעש אלהים את הרקיע this is the first Time the Word עשה is used, 'tis used for making, framing, giving a Power of Motion opposite Ways, and so Circulation, Expansion, and Strength; and of renewing and continuing it to the Matter of the Heavens, and they to every Thing in them; from this great Work all other Works have their Names, so 'tis made the Root for making material Things; because making this has given a Power to that Matter, in part then, and wholly after God rested, to make; and it has made, does, and will make all Things, Motions, and Powers in this System.

As the Word שחק and the Plural שחקים have been rendered Clouds, in the Clouds,

from

from the Clouds, Clouds of Air, Heaven of Heavens, the Difpofition of the Heavens, of the Firmament, the flying of the Clouds, the Stars, Antiquities, Æthers, Clouds of the Heigth of Heaven, higheft Clouds, fuperior or upper Clouds, in the higher Heavens," And as the Thing or Things, it, or they fignify, have the higheft Attributes of Motion, Strength, Power, and Action, beftowed upon it, or them, that Words can exprefs, or which ever was, or can be given to inanimate Matter; and as it can have but one Signification, when applied to the Condition or Actions of the Matter of the Heavens, and as other fuch Words comparatively, when applied to the Actions of living Creatures, or &c. I muft endeavour to find one Signification, which will hold throughout. I need not make any Apology for myfelf, or tell you that we have not a Word of any of the later Languages, which expreffes or gives any Idea of this Action, or thefe Motions, I have done that in general; 'tis enough to difcover the Manner of the Action here, or under other Words which treat of it, and ufe the moft likely Word I can think of, and let thofe who come next find one fitter, or one that pleafes them better.

M.

M. שחק. I. signifies Contusion, or breaking into Pieces — to tread to Pieces, to beat, wear, tear, or rub to Pieces. — Dust beat very small: II. It is the Heaven or Air, a Cloud, the Æther, *Plural*, the Heavens, the Clouds, the Æthers.

Chaldee, Syriac, and *Arabic,* to bray to Pieces, to break or beat small, to tread or trample to Pieces. שקיפא *Baldness:* שחקן Things worn.. שחיקית Attrition, Age.

Syriac, Contrition, a Struggling, Interruption, a troublesome or unseasonable Debate, or Dispute, *Verb.* to disturb, or confound, to interrupt or hinder, to be troublesome.

Rabbi. a Grinding.

They all agree in one Signification; but because the modern Translators did not understand the Actions of the Heavens, they have confounded their Actions with the Conditions the Agents were reduced to by the Effects of the Actions.

The Verb used in the Singular, signifies to move to, and so strike one Thing against another, or others, and thereby beat that, or those passive, to Powder. The Verb Plural, signifies to move, and so strike two, or more Things, each on each Side; and so those of each Side, to beat the

other

other to Powder. The Action, a Contest, a Conflict, a Strife between two Parties in Motion, of Courfe, towards each other, and fo oppofite Ways. The Agent, the Matter of the Heavens, and from their Action, and the Manner of it, the Contefters the Conflicters. The Parties, as you will fee, are on one Side the denfe Parts of the Heavens, forcing their Way to the Center, and on the other Side the fmall Parts or Atoms, forcing, or rather being forced towards the Circumference; at which faid oppofite Extremities, the Center and the Circumference, each Party fucceffively change Conditions, and fo change Sides of Neceffity. This Conflict, which is fo very ftrong, muft be very clofe, no Space to fly into, but what is won from each other, each Mafs or Atom pufh'd on behind, and refifted before, and on every Side fucceffively, and fo continually. By this Conflict, and confequently Contufion in thofe Bodies, meeting, ftriking, and rubbing againft each other in their Journeys, where this Strife is moderate, the Parts of the Heavens are kept in Atoms and fmall Dufts, or Grains fit for this Motion; at the Center where the Action is exceeding violent, as you will fee, the Grains are melted; and near

the

the Circumference, where the Motion is slow, and so the Contest not so great, the Atoms are reformed into Grains, as *Job* xxv. 2. *Who maketh Peace in* מרומיו *his Heights.* *Chald.* who maketh Peace in the High Heavens.

Deut. xxxiii. 26. *There is none like unto the God of* Jeshurun, *who drives the Heavens to thy Help; and in his Magnificence the Æthers*, (the Matter, the Parts of the Heavens conflicting, or the Conflicters) which he drives in Magnificence, State, Light, Glory.

Job xxxvii. 18. תרקיע *Didst thou make the Expansion* (of which above) *with it in the Æthers* (the Matter in Conflict) *which are strong as a Molten Glass.*

Prov. viii. 28. *When he gave Strength to* שחקים *the Æthers above.*

Psal. lxviii. 35. *Ascribe Strength to the* Aleim; *his Excellency is over* Israel; *and his Strength is in the Æthers*, (in the Actions of these Agents,) or as it, and all such are to be taken, the Highness and the Strength that is these Agents are his; but any Way these Texts sufficiently express the Motion, the Solidity, the Contiguity, and so the Strength and Power of this Matter.

2 Sam.

2 Sam. xxii. 12. Ibid. Pſal. xviii. 12. עבי שחקים *The Denſities* (or denſe Grains) *the Conflicters.*

Job xxxvii. 21. *And now they ſee not Light* בהיר *how it is conceived in the Æthers,* the ſmall Parts, the Atoms, the Conflicters. Theſe ſhew the two Parties.

Job xxxv. 5. *Look to the Heavens and ſee; and behold the Æthers* (the Matter in Conflict) *they are lifted up above thee.*

Jer. li. 9. *Her Judgment reacheth unto Heaven, and is lifted up to* שחקים *the Æthers;* as high as the Motion of theſe Parts in Conflict. Theſe with *his Heigth* ſhew they are very high.

Job xxxvi. 27. *For he trickles* down the Drops of Water: *They pour down the Rain of his Vapour, which the Conflicters pour down; they diſtil upon Man abundantly.*

Prov. iii. 20. *And the Æthers* (the Matter in this Conflict) *drop down the Dew.*

Pſal. lxxviii. 23. *And he commanded the Æthers* (theſe Agents) *above, and rained down Manna upon them for to eat.*

Ibid. lxxvii. 18. *The Æthers* (theſe Parties in Conflict) *ſent out a Sound, thine Arrows alſo went Abroad,* &c. Theſe ſhew that theſe Agents by this Conflict duce Rian, Dew, Manna, Thunder, *&c.*

Job xxxviii. 37. *Who* יספר *numbered*, (who has contriv'd, created, and form'd Numbers; and so Quantity or Extent, and succeffively preferved the Proportion in Number and Strength, שחקים, the *Æthers* (of the Parties conflicting of the *Nebulæ* Grains defcending (which are the next Words) and thofe fmall afcending) *in Wifdom*; fo that they fhould neither form nor reform too faft or too flow, in too great or too fmall Numbers; fo that the one fhould prevail upon the other, fo much as to accelerate or retard their Motions, fo much that the one fhould bind too much, and the other open too much; in fhort, that they fhould anfwer their Ends upon other Things.) *M. Arabe. Safar*, To go, walk, take a Journey, go away, depart, pafs by, or over, go Abroad into a far Country, to tranfport, transfer," to fail, this Senfe may be taken in as the Effect and Confequence of numbering them.

This Word שחק is ufed, *Pfal*. xxxvi. 6. and the following Verfes, and in other Places, where God claims the Offices of thefe Agents, which they have tranflated Truth, Faithful, Juftice, &c.—as *R*. of אמן Nam of Office, but taken from the Action; אומן is a Guardian, a Nurfe—the Action

tion whence it takes its Name, is carrying the Infant in the Arms or the Bosom; as *Numb.* ii. 12. carry them in thy Bosom as a nursing Father beareth the suckling Child. *Coc.* אמן, *in kal*, it is to educate, to nurse; *Pag.* from the Care and Trust that is required in nursing and educating אמן is called a Nurse, Tutor, or Governor; for the Child is committed to the Trust of the Nurse, as you may say, the faithful or trusty one." But these Offices are not taken from the Nurse, &c. and applied to שחקים, but from them to the Nurses, Guardians, Stewards, for they are appointed such in Chief, and are such to all the created Things, and Creatures, and so to the Children of God in this System. Some of those Actions of giving Dew, Rain, &c. are already mentioned: But as I have not shew'd what the Mountains, the fluid Parts, *viz.* Water, &c. in this Comparison and the ירח and שמש in others do, I cannot now go through with them. This Word is also used for God's Actions, under the Name or Attribute of Wisdom. *Prov.* viii. 30, 31. And for a Conflict between the Champions, who all fell, and render'd *Play.* 2 Sam. ii. 14. *Let the young Men now arise, and* ישחקו *play before us:* And for the opposite Mo-

Vol. II. Y tions

tions up and down in Dancing and in Laughing. There is another Word nearly of this Sound and Signification, which I take to be from the Difference in Pronunciation of the *Chaldeans*, or some of the neighbouring Countries, that is צחק, and I have good Authority to use it, because the one is used for the other in Scripture, as *Gen.* xvii. 17. *Abraham* laugh'd, and the Child was call'd *Gen.* xxi. 4. יצחק, and he is call'd *Amos* vii. 9. *&c.* ישחק, and the Word צחק was used for their Service to the Golden Calf. *Exod.* xxxii. 6. M. צחק To play, that is to worship Idols. B. C. יום צחוק is taken for an Holy or Festival Day, *&c.* — בית הצחוק A Play-house, a Place where Plays and Sports are carried on. *Chaldee* and *Arabic* צחק To laugh—to lighten—Clouds Light—Splendor.

Though I meet not in Scripture with a Temple to the Heavens, under the Attribute of the Expansion, or the Conflicters, which there may not have been Occasion to name, or may have been out of those Confines, or may be comprehended under another *Hebrew* Word; as I have not the Authority of Scripture, I shall not insist upon it, whether this they name was a

par-

particular Temple, or this was a general Service at every Temple.

Kircher of Light and Shadow, in the Preface, p. 1. cites from *Plato, the Laughter of the Heavens.*

Voſſius, Martianus, Capella — ſpeaking of the Statue of *Apollo* with four little Urns or Pitchers placed by him to repreſent the four Seaſons and Elements, ſays Another (Urn) which was of Silver, ſent forth ſerene and bright Coruſcations, and ſhone with the Temperament of the vernal Air. This they called the Laugh or Smile of *Jupiter.*

But it was an Attribute, and there was a Service paid in this Manner to the Heavens, becauſe it, as all the reſt of the natural Services, were paid to God, as *Jer.* xxxi. 4. *Thou ſhalt again be adorned with thy Tabrets, and ſhalt go forth in the Dances of them that* שחקים *make merry.* And I find a Challenge, *Pſal.* lxxxix. 7. who in the Æther (in the Conflict, or of the Conflicters) *can be compared to* Jehovah ? *which among the Sons of* אלים *can be likened to* Jehovah ? Theſe ſtrongly imply that they performed ſome great Actions, and that ſome aſcribed thoſe Actions to them, and made them God's Rivals ; or elſe the Challenge, the Compariſon, rifon, would have been low, or to no Purpofe: Indeed they perform'd all Things, and all the *Gentile* World worfhipped them, and therefore the Challenge was noble, and to the Purpofe.

I hope my Readers of this Generation will not pretend to be furprized, or frightened at the great Attributes the Heathens gave to the Powers in this Machine, which they took for a God; becaufe if they reflect, they will find that the prefent Imaginers, and others after them, have given full as many, and as great, nay far greater Attributes to their imaginary Powers, which they call Projection, Attraction, Elafticity, &c. without fhewing us that ever any fuch had any Exiftence, or Appointment from God, or any Mechanifm; fuch as the Bringers together and Fixers of the Parts of Solids, the Movers of the Orbs, of Fluids, of the Tides, of Things dejected or projected, and all the reft which I fhall mention.

The firft Mention we have of a Temple, after the Tower of *Babel*, is hiftorically; *Abraham* came, *Gen.* xii. 8. in the Country of *Canaan*, near *Hai*, befides בית אל *Bethel*; which as appears *Jof.* xii. 16. was alfo the Metropolis of a Kingdom.

dom. This Temple was to the Matter of the Heavens in this Condition, Motion, or Conflict, which entitles it to this Attribute of Power and Strength, which is the Title which *Jacob*, *Gen.* xxviii. 19. gave to God, when he call'd another City, which had been call'd *Luz*, *Bethel*, and the Name which *Jacob*, *Ibid.* xxxv. 2. gave to the Images, Representatives of the strange Gods; and Ver. 7. *He built an Altar there, and called the Place El-beth-el.* The Word signifies Strength, &c. when applied to a Person, the strong Person, when to an Agent, the strong Agent. These Temples are frequently mentioned, and this Aribute is apply'd to *Baal.* *Jud.* x. 4 6. ברית אל בית. *Ibid.* ix. 4. בית בעל ברית; and 'tis applied to the false Gods, and to their Representatives, as well as to the true God, quite through the Scripture; whether they continu'd the Worship to this Power or only renewed it by the Golden Calves, God threatens, *Jer.* xlviii. 13. *And* Moab *shall be ashamed* מכמוש *of* Chemosh, *as the House of* Israel *was ashamed of* Bethel *their Confidence.* So he reproaches the *Israelites*, *Amos* xiv. 4. and ver. 5. Hence all the Claims and Attributes of Strength and Power to God, as *Exod.* xv. 11. *Who is like unto thee* Jehovah

vah, *amongst the Gods?* Hence these Distinctions. Psal. xlii. 3. לְאלֹהִים לְאֵל חָי *to the Aleim the living God;* so the Prayers of the Prophets, as Psal. lvii. *Be thou exalted, O Aleim, above the Heavens;* which the *Targum* renders, Be exalted above the Angels of the Heavens, O God. The LXX. where they durst, *viz. Isa.* xiv. 13. have rendered אל Ουρανὸς; hence the Descriptions, how the Machine of the Heavens under this Denomination in the Expansion, &c. had its Strength from God: And this Power had for one of its Representatives a Ram, which is therefore called by the same Name; hence the Skins of Rams were made Coverings for the Tabernacles; hence Rams were ordered to be sacrificed to God, and some Part of the Ram which they call by the same Name rendered the *Tail;* and hence the Claims of Lambs, as *Psal.* xxix. 1. *Give unto* Jehovah בני אלים *young Rams; Give unto* Jehovah *Glory and Strength.* This Word is used for some other Beast which they render a *Stag,* and in *Chaldee,* for *Scarabæus,* the *flying Stag,* sacred by being a Representative of the *Shemosh* in *Egypt.* And *M.* III. "It is the Name of a Star. אלית. Some construe it a Star, the Morning Star, or the rising of *Aurora,*

or

or Day-break, some Strength, *Psal.* xxii. 1." which is the same: *Coc.* makes it in *Cant.* a Representative of Christ, the Light, *Sun of Righteousness.* And this Power had for another of its Representatives a Species of Trees called by the same Name. *Polyglot, Vol.* I. *Chro. Sacra.* p. 45. *Sect.* XIV. אלה, so the *Hebrews* call every glandiferous Tree, or that which produces any Fruits of the Acorn Kind. This Word St. *Jerome* and the *Septuagint* translate sometimes an *Oak*, sometimes an *Holm*, sometimes the *Turpentine Tree*, sometimes the *Chesnut*, &c.

Vossius de Physiol. Christiana, &c. *Lib.* IX. p. 248. Of the Plants dedicated to *Jupiter*, is the *Oak*, the *Mast Tree*, or the *Beech*, and all glandiferous Trees, as appears from *Varro, Pliny,* and *Festus.*

And I think the Boughs of this Kind, or of that they render the Oak, was one of the Sorts they were to cut off and use for Tabernacles in their Feast appointed, *Levit.* xxiii. 40. call'd עץ עבת, *the thick Tree*, because I find that *Epithet* given to this Word. *Ezek.* vi. 13,—*under every thick Oak, the Place where they did offer tween Savour to all their Idols.* Hence Wood was burnt with the Sacrifices, and עצב was a common Name for Images,

though

though, 'tis likely, they made the Image of each of the Wood of its Reprefentative Tree; hence this Tree, which is alfo writ אלן, or this Sort of Trees, under other Names, mention'd by this, 1 *Kings* vi. 31. and many Times, in *Ezekiel*, were, with the *Willow*, *Palm*, &c. brought into the Temple, which they render *Pofts*, and thereby the Powers thefe reprefented were attributed to God; the Word אליל was ufed for the Images or Idols of this Power, and fo became a Word for Vanity.

The Inhabitants of *Canaan* had another Temple, by a Name which expreffes nearly the fame Attribute, mention'd *Jofh*. vii. 2. בית און *Bethaven*, which was near to that *Bethel* which had been *Luz*; the Word fignifies Strength, Power, Labour; and *Tromeus* makes it from the Root אנן, and to fignify *Refpiration*, *Glory*, &c. with the Difference as above, when expreffing a Perfon, an Agent, &c. And as the laft the Worfhip; Vanity, Falfity, &c. 'tis mention'd thus, 1 *Sam*. xv. 23. with *Teraphim*, and *Prov*. vi. 12. *Beliahal*, a Man *of* Aven: and Hof. x. 4. *Calves of* Bethaven, ver. 8. *High Places of* Aven. There was another Temple of this Name, or at leaft in *Hebrew*, mention'd *Gen*. xli. 50. and

Ezek.

Ezek. xxx. 17. in *Ægypt.* M. In *Greek, Heliopolis* is interpreted the City of the Sun.

Kircher Obel. Pamph. p. 48. *Heliopolis*, according to *Pliny*, was antiently called און *On*, and בית־שמש *Bethshemos*. The LXX render the Heavens, *Chamah*, the Light, the *Shemosh*, all by this Word Ἥλιος, and I may say as the next Author of the Translation of another Book.

Vossius de Orig. & Prog. Idol. Lib. I. p. 85. These Words—and the like, are not *Sanchoniathon's*, but his Interpreter's, who expressed the *Phenician* Names by *Greek* Words.—After that—he mentions also a God, whose Name was *Elioun*, or *Hypsistos*, that is, the Most High, who lived near *Biblus*, and begot *Ouranos*, from whom the Æthereal Region receiv'd the Name of *Ouranus*, or *Cælum*, Heaven.

Ibid. p. 188. *Zeus Eliopolites*, is nothing else but the Sun, or the Power and Virtue of the Sun and the Air, or Heaven.

The Translators of the Sacred Writings into differing, or other Languages, whether *Chaldean, Samaritan,* or *Heathen,* made no new Names, for the *Hebrew* Names of the Gods of the *Canaanites,* or *&c.* — Nor such as expressed the Sense of each of those *Hebrew* Words or Names, which they knew were reclaimed by, and applied

to

to God; they who translated into each different or heathen Language, each took the Liberty to put in such Names as the apostate *Jews*, who spoke the *Chaldee* or *Samaritan*, or the respective Heathens had each for their Gods; or what they thought fit, any Thing or nothing.

To this Expansion the Heathens attributed the Support and Carriage of the Orbs, Bodies, &c. which they represented by Wings, or Images with Wings, and with the Heads, Feet, &c. of their other Representatives with Chariots, after called Chariots of the *Shemosh*, (which is Light) Machines, &c. This was reclaimed in the Tabernacle first, and after in the Temple, which was a Figure of this World, and the Veil of Blue, &c. represented the azure Sky, and the S. S. God's Residence, or the Place of his Presidence, beyond the Verge of the material Heavens, by making such attend the Place of his Presence, in an obsequious Posture, as flying with a Chariot, the Emblem of Carriage; and, if one might say so, in his Absence guarding his Law, which prohibited any Respect to be paid to them, or to the Powers they represented; and by making two such stand in the Temple with their Wings extended, each with one to the Middle, and

and each with one to each Outside, as those they represent do from the Center to the Circumference. These Figures of the Cherubims were placed in the S. S. represented as the Heathens had represented them, flying, and carrying their God, the Presider, as 1 *Chron.* xxviii. 18. *Gold for the Pattern of the Chariot of the Cherubim, that spread out, and covered over the Ark of the Covenant of* Jehovah: which perhaps, like the Chariot in *Ezekiel*'s Vision, represented the Motion of the Spheres by Wheels, &c. as it seems to be hinted, 2 *Chron.* iii. 10. צעצע M. מעשה צעצעים *opere circuitus rotunditatis*, al. *Opere variorum ductuum*. Engl. Translat. *of Image Work* (or, as some think, *of moveable Work*) and at *Exod.* xxvi. 1. חשב M. מעשה חשב, fine Work, or Embroidery, חשבון *Philosophy*. Plur. חשבונות *Machines*. And because we find them carved upon the Walls of the Temple, and in Company, 1 *Kings* vi. 35. and vii. 29. with Oxes, Lyons, Palms, Flowers, and before with Colours, and because the Heathens used such.

Spencer de Leg. Heb. p. 750. cites *Clem. Alexand. in Calvit. encom.* p. m. speaking of *Ægyptian* Figures and Spheres.—They have *Comasteria*, which are Arks or Chests,

that,

that, they say, conceal certain Spheres, which if the People saw, would chagrine them, &c. and becaufe they dedicated them to the Powers in the Air, which move the Orbs in their Spheres, to reprefent their refpective Courfes; as, perhaps, the *Orrery* now is, to that of Gravity or Attraction. Hence, in Scripture, thefe Powers are call'd the Wings of the Spirit, &c. This is explain'd in the Vifion of *Ezekiel*, which was fhew'd, and, when writ, was to ferve to the fame End, as thofe counter Reprefentations in the Temple, then deftroy'd, had done: Where the Spirit, the Fire, and the Light firft appear'd, each in its refpective Action, then out of the midft of the Fire, the Likenefs of four living Creatures, Cherubims, with the Faces of all their Reprefentatives, and with Wings; then the Machine, or Wheel-work, and its Motion by the Spirit; then they ftanding under, and fo feeming to carry the complex Work of the three Agents, or of thofe two which went out of Fire, the Expanfion; and above that, God-man; and to prove more ftrongly to us, that the Action of thefe Figures was a Reprefentation of the Expanfion of the Air, the ftretching out of their Wings is expreffed by the fame Word, as this Action of the

Spirit

MOSES's *Principia.* 285

Spirit and Light is, as they always do to the immediate Representatives of Things; whereas they used the Word פרש, where the Cherubims in the Temple are said to have their Wings stretch'd out; or, perhaps, that Writing might, as near as possible, raise the same Idea as Sight.

B. C. 187. In the *Talmudists*, upon that Prohibition, *Thou shalt not make any strange Gods before me.* Exod. xx. 23.—לא תעשון כדמות שמשיי המשמשין לפני במרום כגון אופנים ושרפים וחיות הקודש ומלאכי השרת, that is, *Thou shalt not make to thy self after the Likeness of my Ministers, ministring to my Faces on high, such as are, the Wheels, the Seraphim, the sacred Animals, and ministring Angels.*

Kircher Ob. Pamph. p. 243. In the second Order are comprehended the *Ophanim* אופנים Representations or Wheels, to which answers the Letter *Beth*—after them the שרפים Seraphim —— last of all the כרובים bring up the Rear; all which Angels have their particular Offices in the Government of the World. For the World is completed by the Symbol, of the allfruitful Nature of God. Then follows *Caph*, the Letter that denotes the *Primum Mobile*, the first, moved from אל שרי himself, as it were immediately from the first

Cause,

Cause, &c." And I hope our Divines will no longer make us believe, that this Vision was of spiritual Angels, under the Figure of four faced Creatures; for between *Chap.* i. 10. and x. 14. it appears as the four Faces are enumerated and compar'd in the first, and a Cherub's Face, and three others, in the latter; that the common Face of a Cherub, was the Face of an Ox, the *Egyptian* Representative, which the *Jews* worshipped; and the Face of a Man, as appears elsewhere, with Rays of Light about his Head; and the Face of a Lyon, and the Face of an Eagle, were either all before, or, at least, then Representatives of these Powers, worshipped by their Neighbours, or themselves, of which three were ridiculed, 1 *Kings* vii. 29. Lyons, Oxen, and Cherubims; and the Eagle came in play afterwards.

B. C. נשר — *Baal Aruch* writes, that in *Arabia* there is an idolatrous Temple, and in it the Figure of an Eagle graven in Stone, which the Inhabitants worship." I need say nothing to prove mixing the Parts of Brutes and Man in one Figure, to the Meaning.

Clem. Alex. Strom. Lib. V. p. 413. — The *Sphinx* is the Symbol of Strength, joined with Cunning, which hath the whole

whole Body of a Lyon, but the Face of a Man. The Man likewife among them (the *Egyptians*) reprefented Underftanding, Senfe, Strength, and Ingenuity, and is engraved for fuch among their Hieroglyphicks.

Kircher Oedip. v. 3. p. 103. There was at *Alexandria* a Temple of *Serapis*, built Archwife, and of moft exquifite Workmanfhip, in which was an Image of the God fo large, that it touched with its Right-hand one Side of the Wall, and with its Left, the other, *&c.*" Nor muft they make us believe that the Wheels reprefented any more than the Celeftial Spheres or Motion of the Orbs, by the living, moving Creature, called Spirit, Fire, Light, or that the Reprefentation of the Son of Man, fitting upon a Throne, mov'd by Machinery, as fome Kings had then, or drawn upon a Chariot, as the Slaves ufed to do their Conquerors, was other than an Emblem of his fucceeding Conqueft over thofe Rivals, or prefiding over the Powers which rule this World. As thefe were Reprefentatives of the Hofts of Heaven, and as the Difpute was between God and them, and his greateft Attribute the Lord of Hofts, all the Reprefentations, nay Vifions, were to the fame same End, as 1 *Kings* xxii. 19. and 2 *Chron.* xviii. 18. *I saw the Lord sitting on his Throne, and all the Host of Heaven* עמדים *standing* (supported) *by him on his Right Hand, and on his Left.* And all the Expressions of being supported, of being on his Right and Left, before his Face, under his Feet, are Terms intended to convey Ideas of their Dependance, Attendance, and Subjection; and I believe the Prophecies must be explained, and the Countries be understood by the Emblems of Beasts each Country worshipped, the Mark of the Beast &c.

If we would consider who was the Maker of these Representations or Speeches, when they were made, who they were made to, what Condition they and the rest of the World were then in; what Effect he intended they should have upon them, or After-Ages; what Effect it could have upon them, or others who understood his Meaning; what it could have if they did not; whether he knew what those, to whom they were represented, understood; whether he did not intend to instruct them; and if so, whether we may not reasonably think, that these Emblems were the Means to make fuller and
stronger

stronger Impressions upon them, than others, or Words could have done.

The Heathens ascribed these Motions of Expansion, Compression, &c. to the Powers in the Matter of the Heavens; and pretended they were either independent of, or left to themselves by God. The Prophets, by proper Expressions, in Opposition to their Claim, sometimes by Scripture Words, and sometimes by the very Names or Words, the Heathens ascribed these Powers to Matter, ascribe them to God, as *Psal.* cl. 1. *Praise him for the Expansion of his Strength.*

Glass. Phil. Sacr. p. 560. that is, the Expanse, the Strength, which is expanded and diffused throughout all created Beings; in and by which, *they exist, live, and are moved, or live, move, and have their Being.* Psal. xix 2. *The Airs declare the Glory of God, and the Expansion sheweth his handy Work.* And in the *Revelations* writ among the Heathens, Chap. iv. at ver. 8. *And the four Beasts* (in the same Figures) *had each of them six Wings about him, and they were full of Eyes within; and they rest not Day and Night, saying, Holy, Holy, Holy Lord God Almighty, which was, and is, and is to come.* Ver. 10. *The four and* twenty Elders *fall down before him that sat on the Throne, and worship him that liveth for ever and ever, and cast their Crowns before his Throne*; renouncing the Sovereignty which had been conferred upon them. If we can be brought to believe, that the Scripture is a History of Beings, Things, and Actions, with which Man has Concerns, so as to make it necessary for him to know of, or understand them in this State, they may be understood: If these Representations were of Things in another World, we cannot understand them till we come there. In short, all these, and all the Expressions to the same Purpose, are levelled against the Rites of Worship and Attributes, which the Natives of *Judea* had given to the Heavens, in carrying the Orbs, &c. under these Representations.

The *Canaanites*, and perhaps the *Philistines* serv'd their God, the Heavens, I suppose, under the Attribute or Power of Mover of the Orbs in Circles, and of turning the Earth round, mentioned, 1 *Sam.* vii. 11. בית כר; as there is little Use made of this Word in Scripture, as it stands here single, and because there is an odd Piece of History about it, we must enquire

enquire of the Neighbours what it means. C. כרכר Q. כרר To dance, leap up—*de Dieu* Gal. *Tourtour*, a Whirl. *Æthiopic*, a Wheel, an Orbit, Circumvolution, Circumrotation—*Arabic*, a little Sphere or hollow Vessel, or such like Thing which the *Arabian* Women use as a Philtre; when the Inchantress says, *Arabick* א כראר כריה *Ja. Kerári Curribi*—spherical, round—a Globe, a Ball, *&c. Arab.* כור, future O, to wreathe a Turban round the Head in a spiral Form, *cca.* 2. To be round, to circuit or go round, *Giggæus*.

M. כרכר, Its Exposition is jumping, leaping—*Targhum*, Praises, (which will be explained in its Place.) B. C. the same as *Hebrew*, and a Weaver's Shuttle. This Word כר in *Hebrew*, Gen. xxxi. 34. is used for *Clitella*; in what Figures their Saddles, or *&c.* might be made, I pretend not to know; but I find *Judg.* viii. 26. that they had some Things of Gold about the Necks of their Camels, which they render Chains, which are reckoned amongst their Ear-rings or Collars, and were Representatives of this Power, and which *Gideon* converted to the same Use, and *Jacob* long before, Gen. xxxv. 4. buried such Trumperies; and so late as *Zech.* xiv. 20. *In that Day there shall be*

upon

upon the Bells (or Bridles) *of the Horses*, Holiness unto the Lord. The Word כור is used for several round Things, as a Furnace, a Vessel to melt in, a Measure, &c. and thrice in *Ezek.* they render כר Mansions, or Residence, which is a proper and common Way of speaking, by other Words in Scripture; 'tis thy going out, going about, or coming in, thy Circuits; and once *Isaiah* xxx. 23. which they render Pasture, which is the same, Tracts, Circuits to feed upon; 'tis used 2 *Kings* xi. 4. and xi. 19. for Captains, for Officers which either led or drove the Forces in their going out and coming in upon their Circuits, extreamly to the Purpose; and so Rams, the common Representative of Power, the battering Rams, &c. once *Isa.* lxvi. 20. כרכרות *Swift Beasts,* (*V.* in *Carrucis,* in Chariots) in Machines, which by turning round, go forward; *C.* Plural, Wheel, Carriages, and lastly, 2 *Sam.* vi. 14, *And* David *danced with all his Might,* Ver. 16. *leaping and dancing* (like a Goat) *before* Jehovah. This Evidence is enough to prove, that *David* and the People danced in Circles; and to prove, that serving this Power, was not confined to *Canaan*; and there is Evidence beyond Contradiction, that the

Services

Services the Heathens gave to thefe feveral Powers were to be paid to God; the Occafion was great and proper, though perhaps not a Day appointed: *David* was newly come to the Crown, and had conquered the *Philiftines*, who had formerly conquered the *Ifraelites*, and carried away the Ark, 'tis likely, with the Cherubims, &c. and he was now bringing back the Ark, &c. and as no doubt the *Philiftines* had praifed by this Attribute, he was now praifing his God with the Service the *Philiftines* had rendered to theirs; and the Words which *Michal*, *Saul*'s Daughter, and *David*'s Wife, fpoke to him upon this Occafion, would not have required fuch an Anfwer as he gave her; and have been an Occafion of her having been made barren, or perhaps of his not cohabiting with her afterwards, if fhe had not been offended at that Service.

As you will fee below, that there were Parts of the Heavens which were fucceffively made Leaders to go before, and direct the Way of the Earth, and other Orbs and Parts fucceffively made to go behind and impel them; fo there was of the fame Matter, inclofing each of them, and in which they were each fituated, as a Man, r &c. is in a Chariot; only, with the

Difference aforesaid, that these Chariots are not drawn, but push'd forward. The Heathens had a Temple to each Power, and among the rest, to this in which the Orbs were carried, mention'd *Josh.* xix. 4. and 1 *Chron.* iv. 31. בית מרכבת the Temple of the Chariot, indeed of the flying Chariot; Gold was order'd, for a Representation of this, to be made, and to be set in the S. S. of God's Temple, 1 *Chron.* xxviii. 18.—*for the Pattern (which David had by the Spirit) of the Chariot of the Cherubims, that spread out their Wings, and cover'd the Ark of the Covenant of the Lord*, and so to carry the Mercy-Seat, the Earth; but this Figure was lost at the Destruction of the first Temple, and no Foot-steps, that I know of, remain of it. The perverted *Jews* had something which (2 *Kings* xxiii. 11.) they call'd the Chariots of the *Shemosh*; but they were also destroy'd, and if they had any Resemblance to that in the Temple, their Figures perish'd with them; indeed there are some Footsteps of such Things remaining elsewhere: But to the Meaning of the Word, R. רכב is to Ride: *Pagninus*, to be carried, to be carried upon, to be bore upon, to ride upon.—Some observe, that this Word also sometimes includes

cludes the Government, Prefidency, and Adminiſtration of Affairs; either upon account that thoſe who held the Reins of Government rode in a Chariot, upon a Mule, or ſome other Beaſt; or that as the Brute Creation is govern'd by Bit and Bridle, ſo Subjects are, by Laws, Counſel, and Prudence. Hence the Scripture, in *Eze-kiel*, ſhadows out God's Adminiſtration of the Univerſe by a Chariot: To which, and the Driver, the Author of the Epiſtle to the *Hebrews* is thought to allude, when, in the Beginning, he uſes the Word Φέρων (render'd in our *Engliſh* Bibles, *Heb.* i. *v.* 3. Upholding) which ſeems to anſwer to רוכב, as it were acting, moving, and governing; as alſo, 2 *Pet.* i. 21. Φερόμενοι agitated, impelled by the Holy Spirit, *&c.*" *Pſal.* lxviii. 17. רכב *the Drivers of the Aleim are many Millions. The Lord is on them in* Sinai, *in the holy Place.* Ver. 4. *Extol him that rules over the Mixtures,* (Mixers, the Mixture of Light and Grains) civ. 3. *Who makes* עבים *the Denſities his Drivers; who walks upon the Wings of the Spirit; who maketh the Spirits his* מלאכי *Agents; his Miniſters the flaming Fire.* The מ join'd as aforeſaid, makes this an Inſtrument to be driven, and to carry Things upon or in. This has been, from

the

the Time of this Temple downward, an emblematical Attribute, to what they call *Sol*, the Celestial Light, the *Shemosh*, the Heavens in Circulation; and notwithstanding the Misconstructions of the Authors who cite Instances, I shall give you a few, as I find them. Notes upon *Maimonides* in *Vossius*, p. 48. But as *Maimonides* himself explains it in *Misnaiot*; If this be done after the Rites of the *Gentiles*, (it becomes prohibited) as, if, the *Sun* or *Apollo* be expressed sitting in a Chariot, or having his Head crowned with Rays: Many such Rings being to be seen in the Cabinet of *Abraham Gorlæus*.

Vossius de Orig. & Prog. Idol. Lib. III. p. 634. But what we have said of Griffons with *Ulysses Aldrovandus*, he contents himself with calling a winged Monster. *Jac. Biaus* hath, in his Coins, Fol. 60. given us the Figure of this Monster. They were put to the Chariot of *Apollo*, or the *Sun*; whence *Claudian*,

Revisiting his Tripods, *radiant* Sol
Turns his yok'd Griffons *from the Northern Pole.*

The Poet in this follows the Opinion of the *Indians*; as *Philostratus* informs us, in the

the 3d Book of the Life of *Apollonius* Chap. XIV. speaking of this Bird, saith, That these Creatures are in the *Indies*, and accounted sacred to the Sun : That the *Indians*, when they paint the Sun, join these to the four Horses of his Chariot.

Vossius de Physiolog. Christiana, Lib. VIII. p. 181. It is the Opinion of *Fulgentius*, in his *Mythology*, that the Sun had four Horses to his Chariot, in respect of the Number of the Seasons. *Isiodorus* also, in his 18th Book of *Origines*, Chap. 36. says, that a Chariot and four Horses were dedicated to the Sun, because the Earth revolves thro' four Seasons; Spring, Summer, Autumn, and Winter, and agreeable to these four Seasons were the Colours of the Charioteers in the *Circus*; which will be treated of in the Symbolical Theology. *Horas* is a Word derived from אור Light; namely, from the same Original as *Horus*, that is, *Chronos* (Time) as *Erotian* interprets it; likewise *Horus* stands for the Sun, among the *Egyptians*, according to *Macrobius*.——

Ibid. Lib. IX. p. 220. *Pliny* relates, from *Varro*, Book XXXV. Chap. 12. that the Statue of *Jupiter*, in the Capitol, was made of Earth, and therefore used to be vermilioned over; and that the Chariots

or

or Carry upon the Top of his Temple, were also of Earth, &c.

Ibid. p. 285. *Ovid* makes the *Horæ* (Seasons) Attendants of the Sun, in his second Book of *Metamorphoses*, where he describes the Chariot of the Sun.——— Moreover, because the four Seasons clothe the Earth with different Colours, the Charioteers in the Games at the *Circus*, wore four several Colours. Therefore *Tertullian*, in his Book of *Shows*, Chap. IX. after saying, that a Chariot of four Horses was dedicated to the Sun, whether this was done by *Erichthonius*, or *Trochilus* the *Argive*, or *Romulus*; saith, such being the Instituters of the Chariots, they, agreeable to their Idolatry, array'd the Drivers in Colours, which at the Beginning were only two, (*viz.* White and Russet) &c.

Ibid. p. 269. Of inanimate Things, the *Rhodians* hold Chariots sacred to the Sun. The whole Isle is sacred to the Sun. The *Colossus* is well known, one of the seven Wonders of the World, which they dedicated to the Sun. The Sun is also said to be carried in a Chariot drawn by four Horses; wherefore they thought this Symbol well adapted to the Sun. *Festus* reports, that the *Rhodians* every Year cast Chariots consecrated to the Sun into the Sea,

Sea, because he is said to be carried round the World in such a Curricle.

Ibid. p. 245. This is plain from the Coin of *Julia Augusta*, before mentioned: on the Reverse of which is this Inscription: *The* MOTHER *of the* GODS. Also, in the Coin of M. *Volteius:* She sits in a Chariot, driving two Lyons. As *Virgil, Æneid.* III.

And Coupled Lyons drew Great Mother's Carr.

Upon which *Servius:* "The Mother of the Gods is said, to be carried in a Chariot, because she is the Earth that hangs pendulous in the Air." Of this I have treated, Book II. Chap. 52. it follows: "Therefore it is sustained by Wheels, because the World is whirled round, and is voluble." Which I think is to be taken as spoke of the Æthereal World. For I cannot believe those *Phrygian* Priests had embraced the Opinion of the Diurnal Rotation of the Earth: of which I have elsewhere spoke. The Antients themselves vary as to the Number of the Lyons: of a Chariot drawn by a Pair we have made mention, from the Coin of *Volteius.* Others assign her a Chariot and four, &c.

Spencer

Spencer de Leg. Heb. Edit. II. p. 873, and 874. cites many to the same Purpose, as *Scheffer Lucian* of Vehicles from *Plato*'s *Phædrus*—*Jupiter* the Great Emperor of Heaven carried in a winged Chariot.

The Effects or Consequences of this Expansion are expressed by several other Words.

M. נטה Its Exposition is Expansion and Extension—to stretch out, extend, incline, decline, to nod, totter, turn aside, deflect, recede, to be extended, stretched out, to reach along. *Niphal,* Inclined, extended. *Hiphil,* To cause to incline, decline from a right Line, or the right Way, pervert, distort, extend. *R.*—To tend, decline, incline, divert, recede, extend, expand. *Pagninus,* " It signifies Motion every Way." Tho' this Word be also translated among other Things to expand, extend, it is put in Distinction to רקע, or as a Consequence of that Motion, and the Force exerted in it. This expresses all other Sorts of Motion, but that in the common Way, 'tis to decline, to go any Way, or every Way, aside, or out of the Way, and expand, or extend itself every Way it goes; this is more than is express'd in that Text they misapply to God.

Jer.

Jer. xxiii. 24. *Do not I fill Heaven and Earth?* (Have I not filled, or made full, the Airs and the Earth?) Every Atom of it is so infinitely press'd, that if less press'd or less resisted on one Side, than on another, 'tis driving in the weakest Line; this also exerts its Power over all other Fluids and Bodies contain'd in it; this comprehends all our modern Terms, and all their Imaginations of Gravity, Attraction, centripetal, centrifugal, lateral Pressure, Elasticity, &c.

Isa. xlii. 5. *Concreting the Airs, and* נוטיהם *extending them* (every Way.)

Jer. x. 12. li. 15. *By his Understanding extended the Heavens.*

Job ix. 8. *Extended the Heavens alone,* without any Assistance; by any Property or Tendency in them, or any other Matter.

Is. xl. 22. *Extending the Heavens as* רק (as a Man would do) *a frothy light Substance,* which requir'd a small Share of his Strength.

Psal. civ. 2. *Extending the Heavens, as it were a Curtain.* As a Man would spread a Curtain or Tent to cover him.

Isa. li. 13. *Extending the Heavens, and founding the Earth;* doing the first, did the second.

Zech.

Zech. xii. 1. נטה *Extending the Heavens*, and יסד *founding the Earth.*

As the Interpreters have been confounded with this Word, as expressing this Motion of the Parts of the Heavens, and that fixing the Parts of the Earth to each other; because the next Text ascribes to God, in Opposition to the deputed Rules he had given to these Powers, and to what the Heathens ascribed to them, the same Motion to the Parts of the Earth; and have endeavoured to give the same Letters another Meaning; and as both are exactly true, and this Text is confirmed by several other Words; and as the *Hebrew* Scriptures were intended to come into the Hands of the Heathens, and convert them: to answer that End it was necessary sometimes to use such Names, as the Heathens gave to these Powers they worshipped; that they as well as the perverted *Jews*, might understand the Formation and Uses of that Matter, and its Powers as derived from him: This Dispute is soon ended, as the Parts of the Heavens at first were press'd this Way, and that Way, they fixed the Parts of the Shell of the Earth. And at the Flood, as 'tis express'd, in Despight of those Powers, he made the Parts of the Shell of
Earth

Earth separate from the Middle this Way, and that Way, as *Psal.* xcix. 1. Jehovah reigneth, let the People tremble: *He sitteth on the Cherubim,* let the Earth נוט, and after that, they (*the Parts of the Earth*) were compressed together again, and are kept so; and as there are several other Words which in different Manners express this compressing and fixing the Parts of the Earth, which have occasioned that foul Mistake of fixing the Earth, so that the Whole could not move, and of dissolving and displacing its Parts at the Flood, which have been mistaken for Earthquakes, and I know not what; as these were the Points in Dispute with the Heathen, they are many Ways express'd; and as the Motion of the Earth was not then disputed by the Heathens, we are not to expect so many, or so differently express'd about it, though there are enow; and as misconstruing those Texts to make them fix the Earth, has beat out the Knowledge of its Motion as heretical, and so by Consequence the Knowledge of the Causes of its Motion; I shall insert a few of the rest to clear those Points.

Job xxxviii. 3. *Where wast thou when I founded the Earth? Declare if thou hast any Understanding; who set the Mea-*
sures

sures of it, if thou knowest? or who stretched the Line upon it? whereupon are its Hinges fastened? or who laid the Key Stone thereof? This expresses that it was founded upon a Line.

Prov. viii. 27. *When* חכינו *he machined the Heavens I was there; when he described a Circle upon the Surface* תהום *of the Deep* (of the loose Atoms) that Line is express'd to be a Circle among the loose Atoms.

Psal. xxiv. 1, 2. *The Earth is* Jehovah's, *and its Fulness: The Orb and all those that dwell on it; for he founded it upon the Waters; and* יכוננה *machined it upon Floods.* He ascribes to the Lord the Earth, and that which fills it, because he compress'd it from within, and from without, upon the Matter of the Seas, and machined it upon the Fluids.

Isa. xl. 20. *Chooseth a Tree that will not rot: He seeketh unto him a cunning Workman to prepare a graven Image that will not* ימוט *decay. Will ye not know! have you not heard! hath it not been told you* מראש *from the Beginning* (from Genesis) *will ye not understand the Foundations of the Earth?* הישב *He sitteth upon the Sphere of the Earth;* he reproaches them with being forc'd to chuse a Piece of hard Timber for an Idol, which would not rot, whose Parts would not separate, and be carried away; and queries if they did not know how the Atoms of the Earth were laid and rested upon one another, in a Sphere without separating, and being carried away from the Line in a Spherical Shell, (where the Atoms the Materials of the Building from above, and from below, began first to adhere, and from thence each Way, as Stones in a Building are laid one upon another) either into the Waters, which are their Ground-work beneath, or into the Sphere of Air, in and by which it is moved, which is its Ground-work above, which the Rabbies *inter al.* apply to *M. Linea Ecliptica.* So Jer. xxxi. 37. *If the Heavens above can be measured, and the Foundations of the Earth be searched out beneath.*

Psal. cxix. 89, 90. *For ever, Jehovah, thy Word is settled in Heaven, thy Faithfulness unto all Generations: Thou hast machinated the Earth, and* עמד *it will endure* (it is supported as a Part of the Machine) expressly in the Airs.

Psal. lxxv. 4. תכונתי *I have machined* עמדיה *the Supporters of it: viz.* the Earth; with another Verb.

Vol. II.　　　A 2　　　　M.

M. מוט Its Signification is Declination, or Nutation—to be moved from its Place, to nod, totter, stagger, &c. 2dly, It is a Bolt or Bar of Wood, &c." The Substantive is a Bearer or Pole, to carry Things upon between two Mens Shoulders, by Force to remove Things contrary to the Force of this Pressure. The Verb implies to overcome or weaken the Cause or Means of Support or Adhesion, and the Effects of such Overcoming or Weakning; when 'tis spoken of the Parts of Solids, or of a Solid composed of Parts, it implies a Diminution of Strength or Adhesion; so that the Parts may slip from, or be dissolved, and consequently by another Force be carried against the Law of Compressure, from one another.

Psal. lxv. 6. מכין *Machining the Mountains by his Power, being girded with Strength;* xciii. 1. Jehovah *reigneth: He is cloathed with Majesty:* Jehovah *hath girded himself with Strength. The Globe also* תכן *is machined, it will not* תמוט *decay.* 1 Par. xvi. 30. *Fear before him all the Earth: The Globe also* תכון *it will not* תמוט. *Let the Heavens rejoice, and let the Earth roll round, and let them say among the Nations, Jehovah is King.* Psa. civ. 4, 5. *Who hath made his Agents the Spirits;*

Spirits; *his Ministers the flaming Fire. He hath founded the Earth upon* מכוניה *its Bases; that it should not* חמוט *for ever.* Ibid. xlvi. 2. *We will not fear though the Earth be removed; and though the Mountains* מוט *be dissolved in the Middle of the Seas.* lxxxii. 5. *All the Foundations of the Earth* ימוטו *yield, give Way.* Isa. xxiv. 19. *For the Windows from on High shall be opened, and the Foundations of the Earth shall tremble: The Earth shall be utterly broken; the Earth shall be clean dissolved; the Earth* מוט *yielding* התמוטטה *shall be moved. The Earth* נוע חנוע *shall reel to and fro like a drunken Man, and* התנודדה *shall be removed like a Cottage.* Ibid. liv. 10. *For the Mountains shall* ימשו *depart, and the Hills* חמוטינה *fail* (ro:) *but my Mercy shall not* ימוש *depart from thee; neither shall the Covenant of my Peace* ימוט *fail.* xli. 6, 7. *They help one another, and say to each other, Courage. So the Engraver encourages the Founder: He that smootheth with the Hammer; him that smites the Anvil, saying, it is ready for sodering; and he fasteneth it with Nails, that it should not* ימוט *fall to Pieces.* Job xli. 23. *The Flakes* (V. Members, Z. P. Pieces) *of his Flesh are joined together: They are firm in themselves, they will not* ימוט *be*

A a 2 *move*

moved (*V*. carried to another Place, *S*. not move.) Does it follow that because the Wood of an Idol was hard, that it would not rot; or because the Parts of one of Metal were soddered or rivetted together, to make them adhere strongly, that either of them could not be moved from its Place? A great Part of their Use was, to be carried before their Worshippers: Or does it follow, that a Whale could not move or swim, because the Parts of its Scales or Flesh stuck so close and strongly together, that they could not be easily separated, and so be liable to change Situations, with respect to one another? Or because the Atoms or Parts of the Earth have been twice fluid, the latter Time the Mountains diffused in the Heart of the Sea, and twice put together by the Firmament, and is supported in it, and by it, and is to be no more dissolved till the End of the Creation of Men, does it follow, that all its Parts, either loose or adhering, may not be shifted locally? This Word is only used for dissolving, breaking, tearing, or separating one Part from another, as of Wood, Metal, or *&c.* from the Body of an Idol; as Hills from the Sphere of the Earth, either by gentle Dissolution of their Surfaces, for the Use of Vegetables,

bles, or of the Parts which constituted the whole Sphere at the Flood; or of the Parts of the Flesh from the Body of a Fish: besides, the Tendency of the Speeches hath no Relation to that Motion of the Earth, which they make this opposite to: It shews the Power of God more, in moving as it does, than if it were fix'd, so as it could not stir; and Man is no ways endanger'd, and so need not be afraid of that Motion; but a Dissolution of the Parts once shew'd the Anger of God, and destroy'd all Men, except one Family; and his Mercy in putting it together, and supporting the Parts, is here express'd, as well as his Power, and the Deputies, the Legates, the Ministers which do it, are named.

As the modern *Jews* did not know what this Expansion was, so they did not know where it was; and when they met with any Expression about it in any antient Book, as the next, which expresses, that it was in the Air on the Surface of the Water, it puzzled them as ill as the Top of the Tower of *Babel.* B. C. 2149. " Upon a certain Time we went in a Ship, and saw a certain Bird that stood up to its Thighs in the Waters, and its Head was in רקיע the *Firmament. Bara Bathra,* &c.

—and a Wood or wild Cock, whose Feet were upon the Earth, and his Head reached even up to the Sky.—A certain prodigious Bird, who stands upon the Earth, and hides his Head in the Clouds." And many more such upon this Mistake.—*Ibid.* 2287. " The *Hebrews* reckon seven רקיעין Firmaments, concerning which see *Rabbi Solomon*, Psal. xix. 7." The *Greeks* and *Romans* were puzzled to know what the Scripture and Ancients meant by the Strength of the Heavens; and some conjectur'd it was a solid Sphere at the Verge: I shew'd, in the first Part, it was every where in the Heavens, and that it pervaded the Mixture of Fluids; I must now shew, that the Parts of it pass between, and operate not only upon the Atoms of all Solids, but upon the Atoms of all Fluids they inclose, as *Psal.* xix. 4. *Their Line* (their Substances) *is gone out thro' all the Earth*. Athan. Kircher, &c. p. 274. *Æther* intimately penetrates all the Bodies in the World, that there may be no where a Vacuum. *Plato op. omn.* p. 1063. The Boundary of the Universe being Spherical, and embracing every Sort of Matter, and endeavouring to mix it equally, lays a Stress upon all, and suffers no Place to be void of Matter: Wherefore Fire principally

MOSES's *Principia.*

pally penetrates or pervades all Things, next Air, as being next to it in Fineness of Parts, and so other Things in Proportion." I may add as freely, and with no more Difficulty than the Atoms of Water can pass through or between a Heap of the Grains of Corn; and much more, because they are framed not to stick, or cleave much to Things they touch, or amongst which they pass.

One of the Effects of this Action of the Heavens is express'd by the Word צוק already explain'd, *compress*, which is a Force, next to infinite, upon what it encloses; but in this, where Force is oppos'd to Force, we only see the Difference; the whole Force is first upon every Atom of itself, which is loose, and upon the Outsides of those adhering in Grains, before it can be upon every other Thing within it, and therefore if not in a greater, at least in the same Degree: so it is a stupid Story, or an impudent Banter of the Imaginers, to talk of compressing any Part more, and so into less Space; or to put more of it into a Vessel with an Engine turn'd by one of their Hands, or with any other Power. They can indeed force out of a Vessel those Parts which will pass the Pores, and force larger in, till the Vessel be full of such

such as will not pass; or draw the larger out, and let those which will pass the Pores come in, that is all they can do. As this Fluid takes hold of each Atom or Mass, of itself in some Proportion to their Sizes, and is continually striving to mix them equally, to push the Spirit into the Parts, where there is the greatest Proportion of Light, and into the Pores of all other Fluids and Bodies; if there were not a Succession of Parts divided, and sent out to support the Motion, as soon as they should obtain such an Equality, all would stand still, as *Plato Op. omn.* p. 1063. For very Thing by changing its Size, changes its Situation or Place: Upon which Account an Inequality being always preserved, a perpetual Motion is kept up, and will for ever be continued." But the successive Change and Motion of its Parts keeping up the Compressure, it weighs, sorts, and places each Species of Atoms of all other Sorts of Fluids, and all Sorts of Solids, in them, in some such Proportion, drives those of proper Sizes and Figures for Solids together, and keeps them together, (though that is express'd by another Word, and is another Attribute) each Sort of Atoms, partly by their Figures, and partly by Degrees of Force, in said Proportion; and

impels

impels Bodies, form'd of each Sort of them, in the same Proportion: And tho' every Part of the Heavens be not, at the same Instant, in the Sense of the first, some Parts going from the Center, and some returning; nor every Part in the Sense of the second, going aside, or out of those first Lines; yet every Part open, or enclos'd, has this Force upon it, and by Contact, and no otherwise, upon every Atom of either Solid, or Fluid, which interrupts the opposite Pressure, communicates it to, or impresses it upon every Side of every Atom of other Matter; not only in Mass in the open Air, where there are Grains larger than the Pores of the Body they compress, or among such small Grains as they call a *Vacuum*, where the Atoms of amass'd Bodies adhere, Springs act, and altogether weigh the same; but even among the Atoms of Fire, where there are not Grains enow to keep the Atoms of Matter together, which elsewhere adher'd; and the Difference appears the same by weighing an Engine, when the gross Air is extracted, and other Matter in it together, and apart, or by weighing a Vessel in which Fire is acting, and other Matter in it, together and apart: In this Case, if either the Compressure be less, or
which

which is Part of the same Thing, if the Resistance be less on one Side than on the other Sides, Motion of the Body ensues; whether it be by the Difference of the Sizes, or Proportion of the Grains and Atoms, which compose the Fluid; that is, by the Vicinity of Light, or smaller Grains on one Side, which Motion among the Orbs will be steer'd by the Spirit and Light, as aforesaid; which they make a Composition of Projection and Attraction: Or when the Parts of this fluid Mixture of Air, which compresses a small Body, is made grosser on one Side than on the other Sides, by moving the Body, with a considerable Velocity, for some Distance, by Hand, or &c. and thereby moving the Grains before it forward, and forcing the Atoms to recede, and thereby giving Opportunity to the Spirit behind, to pursue, push in, make the Atoms give way, push the Body out of your Hand, and drive it till that Impulse be, by Degrees, wasted; which they also call Projection: But if it be (as we cannot prove it elsewhere) near an Orb, till the Impulse be partly wasted, and partly overcome, and describes a Curve between the two Impulses, which they call Projection and Gravity: Or when the grosser Parts of this fluid Mixture of Air, which

which compreſſes a ſmall Body, or the Spirit, is interrupted on one Side, and only the ſmaller Parts ſuffer'd to paſs, by the Interpoſition and Vicinity of ſome denſe Matter or Orb, the Body is preſs'd ſtreight to the denſe Matter or Orb; which Line to an Orb they call the Perpendicular; and this Difference of Compreſſure towards an Orb, they call Gravity; towards a ſmall denſe Body, Attraction.

The *Canaanites* had a Temple dedicated to their God, the Heavens, under the Attribute of the Projector or Mover of Things projected, mention'd *Joſ.* xiii. 27. בית הרם. Becauſe we have notable Remains of the Worſhip of this famous God in this Nation, and may have ſome Diſputes about the Extent and Manner of this Power, I muſt trace him downward. *C.* רמם to be lifted up, to be elevated. רום—to be ſet on high, to exalt one's ſelf." He ſhews the Word is writ twenty two ſeveral ways, and 'tis apply'd to theſe Powers, *Ezek.* x. 15. *The Cherubims were lifted up.*—*Ver.* 17. *When they were lifted up, theſe lifted up themſelves.* Or רמה to throw or caſt, to throw down, to project, to dart. הרם *Chald.* הורמין *Hormin*, the Name of a *Demon. Sanhed.* 39. 1. *Bava Bathra* 73. 1. הרמיני—*Armenia,* הרמין God, ſ. Lord. *B. C.*

B. C. Ibid. and in *Bava Bathra*, Fol. 73. —*Hormin*, the Son of Night, a Female Demon. *C.* חרם *Syriac.*— *Greek.* Ἑρμῆς *Hermes*, Acts xiv. 11. *Alchym.* Glaſs, and Quick-ſilver. *B. B. Mar.* 181. 511.— *Hermodachylus*, or Finger of *Hermes. Æthiopic.*—*Hermen.*—*Hermas. Arabic.*— *Pec. Du.* Two large Pyramids, ſtanding yet on the Weſtern Bank of the *Nile*, &c. *Kircher Obel.* p. 292. They acknowledge *Oſiris* in a Bull or Ox, *Ammon* in a Ram, *Mendes* in a Goat, *Mophta* in a Lyon, and *Mercury* in a Dog, *P.* 293. But above all is the Hieroglyphical Scheme that occurs in the Hieroglyphical Theatre, *Fig.* 38: where you will ſee *Mercury* with a Dog's Head, holding in his right Hand a Sphere, in his left a *Caduceus*, otherwiſe naked, ſtanding upon a Crocodile, with two Stars over his Head; on his right is *Ammon* conſpicuous with a Ram's Head, on his left *Serapis* with a Bull's. — 295. Theſe three Deities are called *Adelphi*, that is, the Brothers, becauſe, with joint Affection, as Brothers, they ſeem to conſult for the public Good of *Egypt*, committed to their Care and Patronage. *B. C.* מרקלים *Markolis*, *Mercury* ל and ר as uſual, changed one for the other; a Statue of *Mercury*, an Idol of *Mercury*, to which a certain

Worſhip

Worship was paid.———There was placed two great Stones, the one here, the other there, upon which was laid a third, covering both the others with its middle Part. The Antients call'd these בית־קולים, the Temple of *Kolis*, or *Mercury*, of which among the *Talmudists*.——To these aforesaid three Stones were projected other Stones, with certain Rites and Ceremonies: *Sanh.* c. 7. *fol.* 60. He that casts a Stone at *Markolis*, (that is, commits Idolatry) because this is his Worship." Sundry Authors construe *Prov.* xxvi. 8. רגם (to throw Stones;) so *Selden de Diis Syriis*, p. 260. and others of this Service: So *M. Maim. de Idol.* at the End of *Vossius de Orig. & Prog. Idol.* &c. p. 20, and 52. *Ibid. de Phil. Christiana*, Lib. IX. p. 255. perhaps from this Service to this Power, of taking up Stones, and carrying (as they have done in this Nation a vast Way) and casting, or projecting them into Heaps, God appointed Idolatry to be punish'd by the People, being all obliged to throw at the Offender, and so not only stone him to Death, but from such Numbers to raise a Heap, a Monument. The Attributes always express the Action, and imply Presence, Power, &c. Hence all the Expressions in Scripture under

der this Word. They comprehended the Motion of all Things, even to the Atoms of Vegetables, &c. under this Attribute, which is not under Consideration here. The latest Images of the Matter, with this Power, shew that they supposed, that it had Wings, means to fly upwards, descend, or any Way; and as an Attribute of what they took for a God, could by going with, communicate that Power to, and make other Things fly. Their idle Stories make it but a secondary God, as one always descending or ascending upon the Errands, or executing the Precepts of their chief God: each distinct Power in the Host was accounted so. Thus from the Prevarications of the *Jews*, and the Ignorance of the later Heathens, from a Power in the Air, form'd for the Support and Service of Man, what the ancient Heathens made a God, became to the *Jews* (as *Beelzebub*, another) a Demon, a God of the Air; to us a Devil, and to the latter Heathens a Person, not only a flying, but a talking God.

There were several Places in *Canaan*, and Parts adjacent, named from this Word, some with the ה prefixed, and some without, terminating with a ן, or changing the latter מ into ן, as the Rabbies write it,

some

some alone, and some with Epithets, as *Numb.* xxxiii. 19. רמון פרץ. *Josh.* xv. 32. רמון. *Ibid.* xix. 7. and *Neh.* xi. 29. עין רמון. *Jos.* xix. 13. ורמון המתאר הנעה *Judg.* xx. 45. אל סלע חרמון to the Fortress or Tower of *Rimmon.* 1 *Par.* vi. 77. את רמונו *Rimmon with her Suburbs.* And the King of *Syria* had a Temple to the Deity, mentioned 2 *Reg.* v. 18. בית רמון. God claims this Attribute in these Words. There were several Places to which this was joined, and the high Places where they sacrificed to these Powers, were called by this Name: There were Sacrifices appointed to be brought to the Temple of God, called by this Name, rendered the Heave-Offerings of their Hand. This Power had for their Representative, the *Pomegranate* called by the same Name. Hence *Exod.* xxvii. 33. & *seq.* The *Jews* were ordered to make Resemblances in Blue, and Purple, and Scarlet, of the *Pomegranate*, and hang them upon the Skirts of *Aaron*'s Garment; and 1 *Reg.* vii. 18. they were ordered to be placed upon the Columns, which were Representatives of their Supporters, and which supported the Spheres, or Representations of the Courses of the Orbs; and for its Representative some Stone,
which

which they render Coral; whether that be right render'd, or it was the Stone out of which *Mercury* was extracted, or what other, is not easy to determine.

It will be expected that I should give some Account how the Heathens suffered the Heavens, the Air, their God; and the Christians this Power in them, constituted by their God, and so the Power of their God, to be dispossessed of this Office, and who has set up these Pretenders.

Sextus Empireus, p. 401. Besides, all Motion implies three Things, Bodies, Places, and Times.

Alstedii Encyclopædiæ, Index, p. 606. Local Space is an imaginary Being.

Thomæ Comptoni Carlton Philos. Universa, p. 461.—The first Opinion denies that Motion can be caused by Impulse alone, but by some Medium in which the Thing is moved—by Air for Instance or Water: For say the Authors of this Opinion, the Hand of him that projects a Stone upwards, moves the Parts of the Air next them, which being put into Motion, move the next to them, and they others, which constantly rush in behind to hinder a Vacuum, so they propel or drive the Stone, and carry it so far, till being remote from the Parts of the Air first put
in

in Motion, they by little and little languish, and so being unequal to the Weight of the Stone, and not able to carry it any farther, give Way and let it fall. So of the Antients thought *Averroes, Simplicius, Themistius,* and others, which Opinion also *Pererius* defends, Book XIV. Chap. 5.

But the second and true Opinion affirms this Motion of the Stone not to be caused by Air, or any Medium, but by a certain Quality or Virtue impressed upon it by the Projector, namely, by the Impulse or Power of Motion communicated to the Stone by him that throws it. So *Albertus* the Great, *Capreol, Sotus, Conimb, Rubins, Murcia, Oviedo,* and others. The Opinion of *Aristotle* in this Affair is doubtful.*

Cardan of Subtilty, p. 391.—The second Opinion of *Plato* was, that *A.* for Example, put into Motion, was transferred by the Mover as far as *B.* then when it was left by that which moved or put it into Motion, the Air in the mean while, which was in the Place of the moving Body that is in *A*, fills the Place between *A* and *B*, and so by its Impulse commu-

---

* Is not this to an Hair the *Vis Impressa*, and the Projection of the modern Philosophy?

nicates Motion to the moving Body A, and in this Manner it always fills the Place that A, in Motion leaves, and that with the same Force or Impetus with which A, is at that Time moved: For this is necessary from the Motion of a Fluid (*raritatis*) or to avoid a Vacuum. This then is *Plato*'s Manner of Reasoning, with whatever Force or Impetus the Body is moved, the Air follows after, or rushes in, filling the Place and toucheth A, in Motion; therefore the Air will move A with the same Force as before by keeping up a perpetual Motion: And this Method he calls *Antiperistasis*, that is, a Change of Places, by continual Succession. *Aristotle* saith, that Motion cannot be produced in this Manner; because, although there be an *Antiperistasis*, yet the moving Body cannot be impelled by it. He reasons in this Manner: Whatever moves by *Antiperistasis*, is also itself moved; therefore while it is not moved, it cannot move. But when the Air in A, shall be in B, then it is moved by nothing, for it hath possessed the Place it was to occupy; therefore it cannot move A while it is in B out of its Place. This is evident, because a Body doth not move another Body, unless the Mover is itself moved. And this Demonſtrtiona hath not been underſtood by Expoſitors, and yet it clearly ſhews *Plato*'s Opinion to be falſe.

S. מדחפות *Chaldee* Impulſes. Ibid. C.

B. C. דחה to impel, expel, propel, in the *Targum*—אידחה אבן A Stone is projected *Erchin*, fol. 30. 2.

דיחוי דחיה a removing, Depulſion, driving away, a Propulſion forward, Impulſion.

דחית האויר Impulſe, or burſting in of Air.

Dionyſius, *Richelius* in *Gen.* cap. 1. art. X. *Plato* in *Timæus*, ſays, that the Stars are not fixed in the Firmament, but wander and dance in Chorus in it; and in this *Ptolomy* follows *Plato*. Whence they ſay it is not the Heaven, but the Stars of Heaven that are moved and carried about.

Plato in *Phædrus*—Some place a Vortex around the Earth, and make it remain fixed under the Heaven. Others underprop it with a Baſe of Air like a Broad Kneading Trough.

Paul Merula, *Coſmog.* p. 100. cap. 3. Of the Diſtribution of the Elements, of Air, which is derived, as *Iſiodorus* will have it, from *Plato*'s *Timæus*, in his Book of Etymologies 13, Chap. 7. from τοῦ αιρειν, becauſe

because it supports and carries the Earth, or because it is itself carried, as *Plato* derives it from τοῦ α'ὲὶ ῥεῖν, because it is always fluid or flowing.

Isiodorus's Etymologies, *I. B.* Air from τοῦ ἄιρειν, its carrying the Earth, or from its being carried.

Gravio of the Philosophy of the antient Philosophers, p. 84. *Anaximander* was of Opinion, that the Earth hung upon Airs and moved round the Centre of the World."

I cannot compleat this till after I have shewed, that they mistook the Light for the Orb of the Sun, and what it is that is said to draw; so must adjourn it thither.

Though these Differences of the Compressure shew but an infinitely small Proportion of that Power, which continually rests upon every Atom of Matter; there are other Instances, where the Difference may be shewed in any Degree, till it arrive almost to infinite; when any of the small Grains or Atoms of the Heavens, smaller than those without, are enclosed by any Shell or hollow Body, which is the Case of what they call a *Vacuum*, by an Engine drawing out the larger, or by issuing in the Atoms melted by Fire, through the Pores of the Shell, or by melting

ting suddenly by Fire the Grains of Air to Atoms, which were included in the Shell or hollow Body, whose Pores cannot instantaneously admit larger, and so for the Moment interrupts Part of each opposite Pressure, in Proportion to the Difference between those without, and those within; in a small Degree of the Difference of the Sizes, that without will not only crush in a strong Shell, or force down a Pistil into one, and expel the Atoms through the Sides with such Force as to extend the Barrel, and over-ballance, or lift with the opposite End of a Beam an incredible Weight or Quantity of solid Matter; but in a great Degree of Difference, where the Grains of Air are reduced to Atoms by a sudden Fire, the Pressure or Force of the Thickness, or Diameter of a small Thread of those without, which lies upon the Surface of every Thing, in every Place, or when in Motion of the Spirit, being admitted, will blow out any Body of any Weight properly plac'd; and if there be no Vent, will burst Rocks, and blow up Mountains. What the Remainder of the Force beyond this Difference is, has not yet been shew'd.

And though the Body not only interrupted, but in Motion, carries the Compressure on every Atom, varying as the Fluid without it varies; yet as in the open Mixture of Air, the Spirit, which can only act upon the Surface of the Body, has a Hand in accelerating the Motion; so where there are many small Grains, or mostly Atoms in a Vessel, which they call a *Vacuum*, where there is so small Difference in the Sizes of the Grains, that they can scarcely be distinguished with the Titles of Spirit and Light, Motion cannot be in equal Degree as without; and the little Degree of Velocity produced, will be little encreased in falling; and though perhaps the Grains, which can pervade the Pores of the Earth, may be as large as those which pervade the Pores of Metal, and those which pervade the Botom of the Vessel, are as large as those which pervade the Top: yet they pervade not the Earth in so full Quantity, as in the open Firmament, which makes that small Difference in Pressure, which gives the small Degree of Motion in their *Vacuo*; and we shall at some Time shew how fairly they deduct, and shew by this, that if there could possibly be a *Vacuum*, and a Body projected in it, the Body would

would move no farther than the Projector's Hand.

This Part of this great Action is express'd as above, and in many other Places; *Job*. xxviii. 2. *Melted Stone* (the Parts driven together, and adhering by Compression) *Ibid*. xli. 24. *His Heart as firm as a Stone, yea, as hard close pressed as a Piece of the nether Mill-stone.*

Isa. xxx. 6. *The Land of Trouble and* ציקה *of Compressure.* Iibid. viii. 22. מעוף *The Motion of Compressure, and* עפלה *by Grains of Air,* מנדח *Impulse.*

Zeph. i. 15. *A Day of Binding and Compressure,*

Job xxxviii. 37. *Who can cause to come down the Defluxions of the Air, to* יקף *come press the Dust into* מוצק *a Concrete that* רגבים *Lumps adhere.*

1 Sam. ii. 8. *For the Instruments of Compression* (the Compressors or Compressions) *of the Earth are* Jehovah's.

The *Canaanites* had a Temple to their God, the Heavens, under this Attribute, mention'd 2 *Sam*. xx. 14. בית מעכה. Hence all the Expressions of compressing Things; and besides his Claim of making the Heavens, 'tis show'd how they do it to quit all Pretence of Properties in them. Indeed it appears, that, lower down, they

included

included other Things within this Attribute, which are not under Consideration here.

There is another Word צור already explain'd, which tho' they, as above, construe to signify the same as the last, if יצר be the same Verb, it expresses compressing the Parts of Things together into their respective Figures, or Forms, and binding, or, by the continued Action of Compressure, keeping them together; and is, as we express Things, that powerful Agent, which not only forms, but preserves Bodies, or prevents their Dissolution.

Zeph. i. 15. *A Day of Binding* (of Things bound) Isa. xxx. 6. *The Land of bound Parts*, of Stone, or Rock, *(a rocky stony Country)* Job xxvi. 8. *Binding the Water in his Densities.* Hos. iv. 19. *The Spirit has bound her in its Wings.* Ps. xcv. 5. *His Hands formed* (and bound fast) *the dry Land.* Isa. v. 30. צר ואור *that bound, or the Grains, and that loose,* or the Atoms, *are storkned;* the Mixture compos'd of Grains and Atoms, is darkned. Isa. xxvi. 11. *The Fire* צריך *of thy Grains*, of the Parts form'd and bound by Compressure *(which support Fire) shall devour them.*

M.

MOSES's *Principia.* 329

M. צור, according to their Way of explaining Words, fignifies an Idol; but it was an Attribute, or a Name of their Deity, the Heavens, *Deut.* xxxii. 31, 37; 1 *Sam.* ii. 2. And the Natives had one, or more Temples, call'd, *Jof.* xv. 58. 2 *Chron.* xi. 7. *Neh.* iii. 16. and 1 *Maccab.* iv. 61. בית צור. and צור is a Legate; fo they were his Legates, as well as Plafmators, Binders; not the Things form'd or bound, but the Formers and Binders; and they, as Legates, were bound to obferve Orders, as all the other Legates or Attributes were; fo God is not the Light, but the Giver of Lights, fo the Father of Lights. There was a People call'd after this, as there was after each of the other Attributes; and, in Oppofition to this, there are, in Scripture, abundance of Expreffions of Claim by this very Word, in Behalf of the true God. But as none of the Tranflators in the Heathen Countries, durft make any Reflections againft, or take any Attributes from the Gods of their Country, or fhew the Oppofition of the Expreffions in Scripture to them; and as the *Jews* have told us any Thing but the Truth, fee what our Tranflators have done for us by following them. The Heathens made their God an Agent, they never had any paffive ones, the Plaf-

mator

mator and Binder of the Atoms, and so the Former and Preserver of all Bodies, Forms, Textures, and the Powers in them; this Word is also used for a Cord, or what binds Things, and so an Emblem made sacred; and therefore one of those *Spencer* and others mention, found in an Ark of the Heathens, with Rods of their sacred Trees, Wool of their sacred Rams, &c. They make ours in those Claims a Patient, a Stone, a Rock, which, with what is attributed to him under those Names, makes them not only as pure Nonsense, but, what is worse, as direct Contradictions to common Sense as ever were writ. *Deut.* xxxii. 18. *Of the Rock that begat thee thou art unmindful, and hast forgotten God that formed thee.* And 30.—*Except their Rock had sold them.* Psal. xviii. 31. *Who is a Rock save our God?* Ibid. xxviii. 1. *Unto thee will I cry, Jehovah, my Rock, be not silent.*

Thus far upon the Compressure towards the Center, or Inside of Things; next with respect to the forming the Shell of this Orb. Before I shew'd, in the first Part, how Things were situated: nothing but the Original *Hebrew* from *Moses*, &c. shew'd any Account of that; or, which is the same, that Account had never been made

made intelligible, since that People were in the *Chaldean* Captivity, that I know of. Indeed, our Undertaker durst not meddle with that Part, he, nor no other of his Creditors were able to shew what the Firmament was, or how it could form a Shell, nor make any Conjecture; instead of it only talk'd of Gravity; but in treating of it after it was made, he had pick'd up a frightful Story, and tells it more frightfully, of a Fire, which made an Explosion, and broke that Shell all into Pieces, and which, he supposes, has been burning among the Waters ever since, to send up Vapours, and so is his Counterpart to Gravity. Another, who only pick'd up a few of the Imaginations of others, and judges, as he says of them, according to Appearances, and so never pretended to take any Information from better Authority, has, in his way, by Appearances, prov'd more incredible Propositions than either of the other; and though no Bodies, (except by Projection) nor nothing but the Atoms of Light, Grains of Air, or Vapours, move from the Center, that there is some unknown Inclination in Matter, notwithstanding his Law of Attraction, or this Compressure, which enables it to fly off from the Center; and that there is, I cannot

not tell how, a Property in the Atoms of of this Fluid or Firmament, to take up more or less Space, or, which is the same Thing, to be present or absent, as he is pleas'd to appoint, whereby they can, at Discretion, press outward. But, waving these, the only Difficulty remaining is, to shew how the same Power, for there is no more than one, can move Things opposite ways, or, which is the same Thing, how this Agent, which compresses every Thing inward, or towards a Center, can also move Things outward, or from the Center: That Motion is what produces every Thing, and is, except as above, entirely a Secret: Indeed, I must not attempt to go through with it here, because this Effect belongs not to this Part, but is explain'd at large in other Parts, which shew the Formation of the inner *Strata* of the Shell, or the Manner of sorting Things that way, and all the Operations in the Abyss, and in all the other natural or artificial Imprisonments of the Spirit, or of any Grains, or Parts of the Heavens, grosser than those which are without, or of the Parts of other Fluids or Mixtures, which are enclos'd by a Sphere, or Case, or Shell of Solids, or Fluids, through whose Pores the Atoms or small Grains can only pass; this was

was the Case of that in the Abyss, when the Expansion operated, and the Compressure of those without, upon those in the Pores pervading, press'd in the small ones among the Grains within, and made the Grains within thrust or press against the inner Face of the Sphere outward: This is the Case of Grains press'd into a Receiver; if the Shell be less press'd, or weaker on one Side, than on another, and give way, the Grains when in Motion or Spirit, move that way, explode the Side; or if any Body be properly plac'd, and Vent given upon it, push and impel it, and give it what they call Projection; and so in a thousand other Cases, which if I do but name, nay, this lays them so open, that tho' I do not name them, they will, every one, be stole and mixt with Whims, to rob the great Author of the Glory of contriving and revealing his Works, before I have Time to print the Cases; some father'd by our Primitive—upon his sham *Sanchoniathon,* and some by our Undertaker upon the sham Name of his great Work, which as it never was, so now never will be begun.

I have treated at large of this secondary Action, or Effect of such a Motion, of such a vast Quantity of small Masses and

Atoms

Atoms close adjoining, of no less, if not then, soon after, and now, than of every Atom of the Heavens from the Sun, to or near the Outbounds, or Extremities of the Heavens, by which the Stress or Motion of the whole is communicated to every Part, in the first Part, so far as concern'd the separating those Atoms of the Earth, which it could make adhere, from those it was to keep fluid. I have now consider'd this Effect, as it concerns the Matter in the Heavens, and the Matter of the Heavens; and though these Precepts must succeed one another in the Manner of conveying them to us, and the Extent of Expansion, and so Degree of Compression, which was sufficient to operate and perform the Effects intended, is what is here order'd to be, or be effected, no Doubt a Degree of Compression commenced as soon as the Spirit began to move towards, and the Action, which did the Part of Fire or Light commenced, and increased, as it increased, and extended, as the Expansion extended: and that Recedence of Light from a Fire on every Side, which might properly be call'd an Expansion, is jointly further'd by its own Effects, as a perpetual Motion, of Necessity must be, by the Compressure re-uniting

ing the Atoms into Grains, and driving them towards the Fire, melting them there, and so circulating them, or circulating themselves, making the Atoms adhere where they are out of the Reach of Fire, and melting them in the Fire, pressing the Masses into the Fire, and pressing the Atoms from the Fire; and with these acting upon other Matter, according to each of their Species and Situations. The Archbishop of *York*, in the Margin of his Translation of the *Pentateuch*, printed 1574, against the Word *Expansion*, says, *Heb. a stretching forth, or sending out*. The first Act that was mention'd, that the Expansion did, was to make the Parts of the Earth, then fluid, separate, and those for Solids, adhere; when there was an Obstruction, and afterwards, when there was a Division between the Heads of the Columns, or Supporters of the Matter of the Heavens, on each Side, by a Shell of Atoms adhering, filled with Fluids, *&c.* and they and the Fluids grosser than that of Air, found their Places; (supposing Things in respect of the Operation of the Expansion, before the Celestial Candlesticks were form'd, was in Manner, as it was afterwards, when they were form'd in the progressive Revolution of the Earth, (some of the

the smaller Parts of the Heavens, or Light, would successively, and always be driven against one Side; and some of the grosser Parts would always be compress'd against the opposite Side; the Force or Resistance would be weaker in the thin Fluid, on the foremost Side of the Earth, and part of the gross Fluid would continually be press'd into the thin Fluid, on the hindmost Side of the Earth, whence its Motion and Direction would follow. I have preponed, and now repeat this, because though the Expansion be concern'd in the principal Actions, as settled; yet after it has fix'd the Parts of this, and of each of the other Orbs, and the Operations and Nature of that Power, and its Effects, up- the Bodies in it, are expressly explain'd, as it is but in Order of Revelation secondary; or an Effect of the giving of Light; that Action, after the Machine is perfected, is little further spoken of, under the Name of Expansion, but express'd by other Words, which describe its Effects, or are comprehended within the first or prime Motions. The Spirit was made an Instrument of Motion; or let there be Light; or giving Light; and though the Operation of the Spirit be concern'd in forming the Expansion, and in the principal Actions; nay,

even

even in giving Light, as it brings Matter to form it of, and helps to force it outward when made; that Agent is seldom mentioned by that Name, but expressed by other Words, which describe its Effects; and as giving Light is the prime Effect, and the most visible, these are seldom after mentioned by their Names, but included with, or part of that Action, or expressed by other Words which express their Effects; and whenever that Action of giving Light is mentioned, or the Operation of the Heavens, or other synonimous Words, nay, even the Actions of Words, which express further Consequences, we are to remember, that each of the other Parts of that Action, and each of the Effects of it, are to be distinctly considered, as previous to the Matter, though of the same Sort, and prior to, though at the same Instant with the Motion of the Matter called Light, Day, &c. and Expansion, Compression, &c. in the Fluid or Heavens, and upon Solids or Fluids inclosed in it, or them, and upon Fluids inclosed in Solids, &c. as much as the Power, and every distinct Wheel in a Machine acts its Part, when the Machine performs any one Operation; consequently when a greater Pressure against one Side of a Body, than against the other, Motion; and besides that at the Sun, when any Part of this Fluid is thinner than the rest adjoining, whether it be a small Part of the Hemisphere, or the great Space near the Line, which is most filled with Light, the gross Grains or Spirit will push in thither, and those of Light recede, &c. And though all Pores be full, the Parts of this Fluid are still at Strife, to take Place of one another; and those which can take Place, will be pressed into the Pores or Interstices between the Atoms of Bodies, the largest first, and the smallest after; and those which cannot enter, press upon the Surfaces of the Atoms, adhering in Solids or Bodies, and upon the Surfaces of its own Atoms, or of the same Species in the Pores of the Solids, or Bodies, and keep the Parts solid or adhering; and the Parts of this Fluid, which can enter into the Pores or Interstices between the Atoms of other Fluids, will be pressed in, the largest first, and the smaller after; and those which cannot enter, press upon the Surfaces of the Atoms in the Fluids, and upon the Surfaces of its own Atoms in the Pores, or Interstices of the Atoms of the Fluids, and keep them in a Degree of Fluidity; and so keep a Pressure in every Line, upon every Atom of Matter; and which Way soever you move,

move, or shift, or turn the Body, though the Degree of Pressure may be varied in this, or that, or perhaps in every Line, yet it cannot be taken off in any Line; and though differing Degrees of the Sizes, and Motions of this Fluid, will unite or dissolve the Parts of almost any Body, or Fluid, yet nothing can take the Compressure off any one of the Atoms; its particular Effects must be considered each in its proper Place.

I have hinted in the first Part, that there had been several seeming Repetitions; and there are some such to come, I mean of God's directing these Powers to form or do this, or that; and an Affirmation to each that they did it; and a Repetition, or seeming Contradiction to each of several, that God did those very Actions, or made those very Things; and I have since elsewhere, as well as in this, shewed sufficient Reason for those seeming Contradictions, which were for Cautions: But if, as I have since mentioned, the *Vau* instead of *and*, be construed *so*, it lessens the Appearance of the Contradiction, and answers the End of the Caution. And we are to understand for the future, that whatever is attributed to Fire, Light or the Spirit, though it should be done where this Fluid acts as Fire, or where it acts as Light, or where it acts as Spirit, yet strictly speaking, 'tis one joint Action, and they each act their respective Parts; or where any Thing is attributed to an Effect of this joint Action, as an Expansion, Compression, &c. 'tis in like Manner to the three Names, or to some one or more of the Names of the Hosts, Powers, or Effects they jointly produce; nay, when 'tis attributed to the Heavens, the general Name for the Matter in these three different Conditions, and in different Motions, thus put into one joint Motion, and operating in this, or that Manner, though divided into three Names, is still the same; and whatever in Scripture, or by Believers of Scripture, is attributed to any of these Names, is attributed to God; and whatever in speaking of the Oeconomy, or Operation of this material inanimate System, and to the material Microcosms in it, is primarily as aforesaid attributed to God, is secondarily attributed to these Powers, or Operations; and this will not be surprising, when we have considered his Commission, which will presently follow: For what is done by a Vice-roy, Governor, General or Judge, has always been said to be done

by

by the Prince who employs them; much more here, where the Prince made the Matter and Things which act, and gave it the mechanicial Powers of Action, and the Governor from nothing, who is to rule and divide, govern, and judge; and it was never accounted derogatory to a Prince, to fay fuch a Governor, or fuch a Judge did this, or that, fo it was within the Compafs of his Commiffion who did it; and it is the higheft Honour to a Prince to have it faid of him, he chofe or employ'd Governors, Generals, Judges, or, *&c.* who executed great Actions. But farther, befides the Manner of forming the *Hebrew* Words from their Ufes as hinted already; I am now able, by fufficient Authority, to diveft our Philofophers of the Liberty of making bad Ufes of fome Expreffions in the Scripture, which feemed to relate to God, but are too grofs to be applied to himfelf; but fuit very well with his faid material Agents, or Governors; and I muft defire once for all, that it may be remember'd, that after thofe Governors are fubftituted, all the local Motions, or material Actions, or Powers attributed to the Perfon of God, or to himfelf, are really and properly the Motions, Actions, and Powers of his material Agents, or Governors; and what is render'd *his*, is, and ought often to be rendred *its*, as, *thy Strength is in the Clouds*; or, *thy Strength which is in the Clouds*: The Strength of thy Governors, or Forces which thou madeſt, and ſo are thine, is in the *Nebulæ*, little Grains or Clouds.; *he maketh the Clouds his Drivers, his Darters*; *and walketh*, or make Things move, *upon the Wings of the Wind*; and infinite Numbers of ſuch, which have been, or will be, explained in their Places: For the inſpired Writers could not, as the Caſe ſtood, expreſs them otherwiſe; becauſe the Heathens attributed thoſe Powers to the material Agents, as you have ſufficiently ſeen, and will ſee more; and the divine Writers were to attribute every Thing, and Action and Power to God, which if that had not been the Caſe, would have been otherwiſe worded; and for the ſame Reaſon, where-ever any Thing is aſcribed to any of theſe material Powers in his Agents, or Governors, which is but in a few Places, 'tis, I think, I may ſay generally, if not always, guarded with an immediate Reſerve to God; though their Commiſſion ſubſiſts, and they execute in as full a Manner as they did at their Inſtitution. When we Men are ſpeaking of Gods, or God is ſpeaking againſt the falſe one, 'tis not he

is

is this or that Matter or Condition, or Action, but 'tis to Him, 'tis His, He is Poffeffor and Diftributer of it. When *David,* 2 *Sam.* xxii. attempts to praife God for his Deliverances, and to demonftrate his fpiritual Power, he could not defcribe the Manner, but by Comparifons, all taken from thefe Motions and Powers; wherein he alfo elegantly interweaves a Defcription of God's Power over them; and in Effect fays, God help'd me as quickly as one who had the Command of thofe Inftruments of fwift Motion, and had been brought by them; and help'd me, and deftroy'd my Enemies as ftrongly as one who had all thofe immenfe Powers at Command, and had made ufe of them; nay, defcribes the Manner as they, when God interpofes, act upon Matter. And when the Prophets pray, they borrow thefe Terms, nay the very Words; and of Choice apply thofe to God, which the Heathens had applied to the feveral Powers in the Heavens; as, *Lord, lift thou up the Light of thy Countenance upon us,* &c.

In the firft Part I have fhew'd, that by the Operation of the Expanfion the Shell of the Earth was form'd; I have one Step more to go, with regard to myfelf, in the Dark; with refpect to my Guide, who has

has recorded a Description of them in the fourteenth and three next Verses, in the Light, to explain the Operations of this Agent, in forming many more Bodies or Orbs, and a Figure of Light from each of them, which remain visible; the next Precept, which was, that it should form new Bodies or Orbs out of created loose Atoms, which should be Vessels, or passive Instruments to assist in carrying on, or regulating that Operation of Light, with all its Actions, Effects, and Consequences, which had already made Days and Nights, by turning this Globe, &c. which he by his immediate Power had till then supported, and its Consequences, Expansion, Compression, &c. to perform its Ministration upon this Globe, its Products, and intended Inhabitants, all mechanically, some in respect of Time and Place periodically, and the Series, as we say perpetually, to put Matter in the Heavens into such a Condition, that they should always keep going, and regulate all the Motions of the Earth, &c. so that when God had put them thus in Order, form'd Creatures, &c. he might, as they are pleased to express it, rest from his Work, make a Cession to his Legates, rest from working with his Legates. But why such vast

vaſt Numbers of Bodies, ſo diſpoſed and plac'd, ſuch vaſt Quantities of Fluids to be ſo circulated? Why ſo many Checks to the Light? Why ſo many Bodies in Motion to ſerve the Inhabitants of the Earth? Could not a Law have been impoſed upon this Orb, or any other Part of inanimate Matter to act alone, and turn and move according to preſcribed Rules? or could not a Law be given to one Body of inanimate Matter, to act upon other ſuch Bodies at Diſtance, and lead them according to that Law? or could not the Parts of the Fluid of Light have had Laws impoſed upon them, to iſſue and return from ſuch Diſtances, and in ſuch Quantities, and ſuch Lines, at ſuch Times and Seaſons upon the Earth, without creating, forming, and placing all thoſe Bodies to return it? Whether ſuch Powers be incommunicable, I ſhall not preſume to ſhew, but how ſuch a Power is communicable, I dare ſay no motal will ever ſhew; and if any one believes ſuch Powers exiſt, he never will believe that they were communicated; but perhaps God was in Mercy pleas'd, if ſuch Power were communicable, to prevent the Devil from having ſuch a Bait for Man; left he ſhould reaſon and conclude, that where he ſaw

there

there were occult Powers, unnatural and without Mechanism, he should conclude it was a God; as they afterwards, as plainly appears, took this very Machine to be; perhaps God might judge, that making a Machine of such an infinite Number of Parts, in such Positions, liable to such Alterations; so as to shew that all the Powers in it, or that it had upon other Things, were mechanical and natural, according to the Order he has established in making and framing them, might be reasonable Evidence that it was not a God; and that it could not be so contrived without a God.

After the Light was made, and that Light, by directing the Force of the Spirit, and circulating this Globe, had divided itself into Days: It was by its Effects, as aforesaid, to make some Things in such Manner, of such Forms, Sizes, &c. and they were to be plac'd in the Expansion in such Order, and at such Distances, that they were to interpose in this Operation, that they were to be for Lights, for making it into more Lights, or Streams or Currents than one; suppose for Furnaces, *Focus's*, Sconces, or for Instruments to hold Lamps, or Candles, &c. to the Ends and Purposes aforesaid. Here appears

pears something which this Agent might do, and some Things which it could not do; and which nothing but a God could do: And the first was, it could compress the Atoms of Matter, which would adhere, which it found, where it extended Step by Step, into Orbs, or &c. But God must, prior to that, create proper Species, proper Quantities, each placed in proper Places, at proper Distances, so as to be form'd into such Globes, liable to be moved in proper Spheres, or fixed at proper Distances by this Operation; for otherwise it would seem very strange, to give Dominion and Judgment to an inanimate Machine; that it should have Power and Dominion, and Judgment, over this new Empire; which if it had been divided in, and issued from one Orb, before these Bodies were form'd, could have done nothing but dissolve the Spirit into Light, storken the Light into Spirit, circulate them, and thereby the Earth, and make Days and Nights; and that this Dominion should be absolute, no Superiors, no Projection, nor Attraction; nor no joint Powers which had any Share in the Administration; and to appoint it Subjects that have neither Will nor Power to obey or disobey. Here can be

no

no rational Inducement to perfuade to any voluntary Obedience; the Rulers cannot go before and purfuade, or command them to follow; nor if they could were the Subjects able, either out of Love or Fear to obey; here are no fuch Faculties. As there was nothing on either Part, but inanimate Matter, it muft be a material Government; the Governors and the Governed were each fo ftupid, thefe muft govern, and thofe be governed by Force; and as one Atom of our Governors cannot move, except another by Touch and Preffure pufh it forward, and fo in Succeffion, I am afraid it will appear our Governors, and their Troops, their Hofts, their Forces, fo often mentioned, muft fome go before, and make Way for his Subjects, and fome go behind, and pufh them on; fome help to vary the March, &c. and that they will not move a Foot out of the Reach of the Touch, or forcible Impulfe of their Governors, or their Forces; infomuch that though thefe Governors and their Forces have but two Kingdoms named, two Hemifpheres periodically varied, yet they have more Subjects in them than ever any other Governors had; and they, the Governors, employ more Soldiers to govern them

than

than ever any Emperor paid; and every one of them is always ready upon Duty, some in moving, some in, or almost in, fixed Stations, and never fails to do his Duty. It may seem still stranger, how this Machine can execute the Office of a Judge, of a Distributer; we might suppose it possible, that Light might issue all at one Rate, Pace, and in one Quantity, and be proportioned so as to move the Earth, &c. each at one, and such a Degree of Velocity as they were intended; perhaps in some Proportion to their respective Distances from the Center; but there are many other Things to be done by this Machine, both in the Heavens, on and in the Earth; and when we have recover'd the Orbs of the Planets, Moons, and Stars from Being, or being employ'd for other Worlds, which Whims they borrow'd from *Aratus*, and other Worshipers of their God *Jove*; and after we have brought the Orb of the Sun, and them, a vast way nearer Home, and reduced them to their proper Sizes, perhaps we may find Uses for them all.

But further, the Agent which was in Action, which he spoke to now, as he had to the Spirit at first, next to the Light, next to the Firmament, and now the joint
Ope-

Operation, obey'd the three Precepts given to it: First, made the Organs or Instruments for the Light to act in, or against, or among, for all the Uses mentioned. Secondly, set forward the distinct Operations in, or on each of them, for all the Uses mentioned. Thirdly, by the Operation of the Firmament, supply'd their Expence with new Matter, and issued it, when fitted for the said Uses; but could not be said to contrive any Thing, and so give or take Dominion: So God, in the first Repetition, or in the Manner aforesaid, on his Part, asserts he made them, and gave the Dominion of the light Hemisphere, called Day, to the Light issuing directly from that great Furnace; and the Dominion of that dark Hemisphere, called Night, to the Light, be it reflex, or &c. which comes directly from the Orbs of the Moon and Stars: And in the second Repetition he tells you, that he did it by placing those Organs in the Expansion of Heaven, where it operates; so saying *in* it, as it is a continued Operation, is saying also *by it*, or subject to its Operation; that they might each form, or return Fluxes, and so give, or be Streams of Light upon the Earth; or that that Operation or Effect might so make each of them give

Light

Light upon the Earth; and that he did it also by contriving and ranging them as aforesaid, or the Matter of which each of them was to be formed, of proper Sorts, in proper Quantities, at proper Distances, and in proper Positions; so that this Operation did form and place them in such Order, that many should be fixed out of the Power of the Agent to move them; or if we should allow, what the Observers pretend to shew, at least, all together, and very slowly, some few Strollers excepted; and the rest, that it should move them in such Circles, and at such Distances as should answer the Design. We will suppose, that the Furnace, or *Focus*, should melt such a Quantity of Spirit into Light, that should raise such a Tension, that it should send it out with such a Degree of Velocity in all Directions, where not interrupted by those Bodies, or the Earth, to near the Extremities of the Heavens; and so in Consequence in such a Degree of Mixture, of the Spirit and Light in the Circle, at the Distance of the Earth, and of each, that the Moon, the Planets, and Stars, should each have a constant Share, in Proportion to Sizes and Distances; that the Streams from each might be turned upon each other, and upon the Earth; so as by the Direction of its Courfe, by the Pofitions, or Motions, and Diftances; and fo Direction, Quantity, and Degree of each of the various Lights, from each of the various Bodies, the whole, and each of thofe in Motion might be governed, each in their Rotation or Progreffion, in Point of Time ; in the different Degrees of Light, or Darknefs, or Mixture, in the feveral Parts of each ; in their Difference in, or by the different Parts of the Year ; in the different Pofitions of thofe which move, and fo together of Seafons, Days, and Years ; and of all the intermediate Means, the Things they were to work with, or work upon.

Firft, the Agent was to form thefe Organs, and divide the Light among them ; fo that there fhould be a Light with each in the Expanfion of the Heavens : Next, thefe feveral Lights were to divide between the Day, and between the Night; thefe were to do what the Light had done already: Then he explains further, let thefe Operations or Accidents of this Matter be vifible, for making and diftinguifhing of Seafons, Days, and Years : This was what a fingle Light could not do: after the Organs were made, and the Operation, be it be by bringing the Spirit

which

which had been formed, or made adhere near the Surface to the Center, dividing it into Light, and sending it out; be it by Reflection upon the rest, each stopping and diverting the Stream of Light, continually issuing from the Center upon each, and turning the Flux of Light, which comes to each, from each in another Line; there is still something more said: Let these Lights be, exist, and in Condition flow; let the Operation, or Accidents of this Matter, be continually supply'd; suppose, by bringing Spirit to the Center, by melting and sending it forth, or by returning it, to give Light upon the Earth: Tho' at present they make no other Use of Light, but for the Eyes; yet they were to do in gross, what the Light, which was given upon the Earth, before had done, and express the whole Manner in which the former Acts were done; and It, the Agent, formed them all, according to Directions: He could not say the different Lights acted according to Order, they had not yet had Time to perform any of their Rotations.

And more particularly he says, as it is now translated, God made two great Lights, which issued from the two great Bodies; and the Streams, which issued from the other or smaller Orbs, which he calls Stars: This, so far as concerns Formation, is what the Operation did; the great Light to rule that light Hemisphere he called Day, and the lesser Light, and the Stars to rule that Hemisphere of Darkness he called Night. The Operation had put the several Orbs of Matter together, and set forward the Action of a *Focus* in one, and, perhaps, the Action of Reflections on the rest; that it would vary the Hemispheres of Days from Days, and Nights from Nights, form Seasons, *&c.* and so distribute or rule, that every Part of the Earth might have its Proportion of Light or Day, Seasons, *&c.* But it was God that created the several Sorts and Quantities, *&c.* so that they were fit, when the Operation had put those of each together, and set forward the *Focus's, &c.* in them, to rule. And God set them in the Expansion of Heaven, to give Light upon the Earth, and to rule the Day and the Night, and to divide the Light from the Darkness; the Firmament could operate upon Things where it found them, or could remove them according to the Power it then had; and it could carry out the Light, bring Matter for Supply of more Light, and turn this Globe; but it could

neither

neither place the Matter within its Reach, which if that, of any of them, had not been, there would have been no Light brought to, nor iffued from thofe; nor could it range them in proper Places, and in Order, fo that each Light fhould contribute its Share in the Operation, fo as to rule Day and Night, by varying them as aforefaid; and tho' it continually divided between the Darknefs, and between the Light, which God had claimed before, it could not produce or place the Matter at firft, nor ufe any Skill or Power upon that Account, any more than it did to fet forward the firft Motion, and divide between the Light, and between the Darknefs; fo God now claims that.

356 MOSES's *Principia*.

Ver. 14. And God said, let there be מארת Lights *(a Candlestick)* in the Firmament of the Heaven, to divide the Day from the Night : (Heb. *between the Day and between the Night)* and let them be לאתת for Signs, ולמועדים and for Seasons, ולימים and for Days, ושנים and Years.

As every Word, nay, every Letter here, is of the utmost Importance, nothing deficient, nor nothing superfluous, we shall consider the Meaning of these Words, which have not been settled, Word by Word. יהי *Let there be,* consider'd already, here spoken as God all along had spoke to the Agent, or Operation, or Branch, or Effect of the Operation; and here he says, let this Operation, now working, form the Atoms of Matter, which are liable to be formed, and which it shall find loose, within the Compass of its Operation, into מארת an Instrument to hold Lights; for tho' all Light be the same, and, suppose, all Light pass thro'

one

one Fountain; yet when it is split into divers Instruments of Reflection, and so Streams, they are commonly call'd Lights; and tho' this Set of Words are, as I shall shew, all singular, I shall, to avoid the Repetition of Branches, Knops, Flowers, Parts of the Marth, or of the Athth, and the Trouble of explaining the Meaning of each of those Words, conform, at other Times, to common Usage, and put them Plural. Whether the *Mem* be a Part of the Word, and so the Word be a Root of itself, and signify a Frame of Bodies for the Use of Light; or the *Mem* be a Particle, or, as the *Hebrew* Manner is, to denote a Substantive, an Instrument for that Use, and the Word be אר, or ארה, or ארת, something Light was to perform some Offices in, does not vary the Matter much. Many have writ about this Word. *Marinus*'s Questions and Comment. on *Genesis*, &c. "The lesser *Massora* observes, that this Name [מארת] *Meorot* is twice defective, because ו is wanting in two Places: The Root is אור, and they differ from each other just as the Cause and the Effect, for the Luminaries, as the Candlesticks, in which the Primæval Light was placed, give their Light." And *Waltoni Pol. Proleg.* XI. *Sect.* 20. in Favour

vour of his Idols, the *Samaritan* Letter and *Pentateuch*, which infert the *Vau*'s in this Word, and so makes it Inftruments to give Light and plural, has made himself very merry with the Rabbies, for their Myfteries, as he calls them, in this Word, and the Candleftick which was a Figure of this, *viz.* that the Candleftick, Branches, Knops, *&c.* was to be all of a Piece, and that the Moon, *&c.* had their Lights from the Sun; I hope he will lofe moft of his Jefts. We will fuppofe, that when feveral Words are ufed for the fame Thing, each of them expreffes a different Condition or Action, or *&c.* of the Thing; there are feveral ufed here for this Inftrument; Firft מארת for a Candleftick with Branches, Sockets for Lamps, Knops, Flowers, *&c.* as after defcribed, reprefenting the Ufes the Orbs are of, to the End of dividing between Day, and between Night. Second אתה which has alfo a *Vau* in the *Samaritan Pentateuch* to make it plural; but 'tis fingular, and the Verb plural refers back to the Orbs, the Parts of the Candleftick, or to the Light, and the Candleftick which were to be joined; this was to be likewife one joint Inftrument, or rather Agent; that Matter of the Heavens, melted in the Action

of

of Fire at the Sun, made Atoms, Light ready to recede, sent forth, pushing that Light still before it, and putting that interrupted against each Knop, into the Action of Reflection, &c. there, so that the Light, though seemingly divided upon the Orbs, by the Streams between, is all one, as the Receptacle, though in many Bodies, is all spoke of as one, and by the Figure of the Candlestick represented as one. Third מאורת which has also another *Vau* in the *Samaritan*, but 'tis singular, and the Verb plural refers to the Parts of the Candlesticks, and the Parts of Light at each of them, and they each, and both, were to be one Instrument, one Machine, all placed in the Expansion, and all to give Light upon the Earth, by the Strength of the Expansion, driving the intermediate Light between each Orb and the Earth, in Streams against the Earth. The respective Uses of these Streams are described in the next Verse. The first is once used for the Candlestick, and there is another Word also often taken from the Word נהר to flow, the Condition of Light first, and so apply'd to Water, &c. and so from נור Fire or Light, whence with the *Mem* joined מנור an Instrument for Light to flow from, or to

make

make Light flow. In the Language of the later *Jews*, which we call *Chaldee*, they fometimes varied their Letters, as *B. C.* p.248. "אנתתא the fame as אתתא and נ is in the room of *Dagefh*, as is often the Cafe," but we muft not depend upon that here. " They underftood the Word thus, *B. C.* פרח " a Flower, and metaphorically the top Part of the facred Candleftick containing the Light, *ibid.* מנרתא מנרא the Candleftick yielding Light from the Light placed in it, which is called the Candleftick of the Light, *Lucibulum*, that which fends out the Light, *Exod.* xxv. 32. *Numb.* iv. 9." It feems that Things which held Candles here, were firft made of Wood, and fo whatever the Matter be, what holds the Candle is called a Candleftick; but there they burnt Oil, and fo it was an Inftrument to hold Lamps; fo when fpoke of the Orb of the Sun, *Eccleſ.*xliii. 2. The Sun a marvellous Inftrument or Veffel, the Work of the moft High. So firft *Exod.* xxv. 7. שמן למאר Oil for the Light (to act in.) fecond and third, *Exod.* xxv. 32, to 35, and xxvii. 17, *&c.* and *Numb.* iv. 9. מנרת המאור *the Candleſtick of the Light,* (now acting and illuminating) and ונרתיה *its Lamps,* xvii. 16. שמן המאור *Oil of the Light,*

(acting

(acting and illuminating.) There was but one Candlestick with Branches for sundry Lamps, and the Reflections in the Tabernacle described in the Texts above; and one would think by *Zech.* iv. that there were Conduits in the Branches to convey the Oil from the Center to Lamps in the Branches. The *Sam. Pent.* would not make it Grammar, it does not agree with the Verb, nor would it agree with the Representations of the Things, nor with the Things themselves, and their Actions; we must, how difficult soever, make it Grammar, as used in other such Cases, and construe it, to make the Description true. The Verb יהי, and the Name מארת is singular, whether the Verb refer to the Agent, which was to make, or the Matter of which it was made, or to the Thing-made; the Thing is a Frame, an Order of the Matter of the Orbs in the Heavens; a Part of the Machine with one great Receptacle for Light at the Center; and the smaller on the Sides, with Branches or Pipes, or Streams between, as the Instrument for the Lamps, or Lamps and Balls to reflect, represented. If ממארת used for the Action, or burning Heat of the Leprosy, rendered *corrodens, perseverans, &c.* as כוה also is, which is also used for the

Action

Action of Fire, be the fame Word, then 'tis there alſo expreſſive, that this was to be a Place, where the Fire or Light was to burn, a Place of burning, iſſued out into ſeveral Spots; perhaps on one Orb on each Side, and each of the reſt on one Side; the ſame as the *Chaldees* expreſſed by נרח *Theca Solis*, and in their Way, as *B. C.* אתיך by *Aphel*; ſo ארת, and if it were of the Root ארה it might be a Station; nay if of אר or ארר, 'tis not the only Inſtance, by many, where the Prophets have uſed a Word, which was, or related to, an Object of falſe Worſhip, for curſed, or wicked, or, &c. but by the late *Jews*, making this Word of the Root אור, they have loſt the Knowledge of the Root, and have made little or no Uſe of it. *Munſter*, &c. *Chaldee* "מאר a Veſſel, an Inſtrument. *C.* ארת *Chaldee* a Mill," a Houſe where a Mill to grind ſtands; a Mill, whither Corn is ſent to grind, and whence 'tis ſent out in Flour. *C.* ארת *Arabic*, "Fuel, with and in which Fire is kindled. If one were to admit the firſt ו, and make מאורת, it would not be true; and if one admit the ſecond ו, and make מארות, it would be inconſiſtent with what follows; becauſe the Orbs were not yet an Inſtrument which could

give

MOSES's *Principia.* 363

give Light; when these Orbs, and the Light were joined, that Word מאורת, in the fifteenth Verse, is properly and truly used; and because the second or secondary Candlestick, and its Course, is described in the sixteenth Verse, this cannot be מארות here. The Orb, or whatever Figure the Body of the Sun, Moon, Planets, or Stars, or each, or any one of them is of, had no more Fire in its constituent Parts than a Piece of Iron, or a burning Glass, or a Piece of Wood has; nor no more than there is of Water in the Atoms, or constituent Parts of the *Strata* of Stone, where Vapours rise for Rain, or into a Spring; nor no more than there was in the Golden Candlestick, before the Lamps were placed in it, and lighted: Nor does any Change ensue any more, when some of the Atoms of the Bodies are separated, and born off by either of these Actions, than when they adhere. Making these Bodies was the first Step, the next was placing the Fire in one, and issuing Light; so *Psal.* cxlvii. 4. He *appointed the Number* לכוכבים *of the Fluxes or Streams of Light*: For though these Bodies had nothing of Light in them till the next Precept, yet this constituted their Number, and though it is one Act to make Light, and issue it, and another

only

only to ſtop and return it; and though there be but one that makes it, and each of the reſt only return it; yet making theſe Bodies conſtituted the Number of the Stars, or Fluxes, or Streams of Light. So *Marinus*'s Queſtions and Comment. on *Geneſis, &c.* p. 952. *Anaxagoras* died for aſſerting this Truth, that the Sun, which the Vulgar looked upon as a God, was red-hot or ignited Stone.

Chriſ. Sceiner Roſa urſina, p. 632. 2. *Damaſcenus*, Book II. Chap. 7. A Luminary is not the Light, but that which holds the Light.

Juſt. Lipſ. p. 585. *Cicero* ſays, the Stars are totally igneous—in the Opinion of others he ſaith they are ſolid and earthy Bodies, which came from *Thales*—who ſaid the Stars indeed were earthy Bodies, but ignited. And alſo *Anaximines*—that the Nature of the Stars was igneous, but there were earthy Bodies mixed with them.

Voſſius de Orig. & Prog. Idol. Book II. p. 262. For upon this Account (the making Years, Months, and Seaſons) it was neceſſary for (*viz.* the Primæval) Light to be divided and diſtinguiſhed as to Magnitude and Places; and *Moſes* gives the ſame Reaſon, *Gen.* i. 14. The Antients very elegantly expreſſed this Change of the firſt Light, as *Apolinaris*, which he ſaith—The pureſt of the Primæval Light He, God, places in the Sun: the reſt he diſtributed to the Moon and Stars. So *Baſilius* in his ſix Days Works, *Homily* the 6th, calls the Stars the Vehicles of Light, as *Damaſcenus* the Receptacles— Alſo *Maximus* upon *Dionyſius* in the *Scholia* —— The firſt created Light was the fourth Day transferred into the Sun." with many more. It ſeems this was was repreſented by the Heathens. *Voſſius de Phyſiol. Chriſtana, &c.* Book VI. p. 153. "Alſo many Veſſels belonging to their Temples were of Braſs, as at *Rome*, the Candleſticks in the Temple of *Bacchus*, which from thence were tranſlated into the Church of St. *Agnes*." As theſe Orbs are abſolutely paſſive and ſubſervient to the Operation of the Air, which was before, and only for the Lights, this Word expreſſes the Orbs, and they are ſeldom ſpoken of in Scripture, and little Notice is taken of them either by this, or any other Name, except *the Heads of the Stars*. The Light of each being chiefly conſider'd, the Situation of theſe Orbs, in reſpect of Place, tho' not of Diſtance, is viſible, not only with their Light, but ſome of them are ſo in

Eclipſes

Eclipses without their Light ; and it would have been of no Service to have said, they were set in the Heavens ; 'tis not for nothing that they are order'd to be in the Firmament of Heaven, 'twill now be of Use that 'tis revealed ; we could not have known this; but by Inferences ; we now know they are plac'd in that Fulness;and under that Stress, and Tension; occasion'd by that Motion ; and thereby; that the Stress of that Strength or Force; which is sufficient to move the whole שמש from the Sun outward, to the Extremities of the Heavens, and return the Spirit to the Sun, is impress'd upon them, and upon the Streams of Light, from each of them, and upon every Atom of Matter. Tho' our Imaginers neither knew what the Firmament was, nor where it was, they have by other Words denied; that the Matter which constituted it was continued to any great Distance from the Earth, or that it etach'd thither ; and this is to disprove them and those who have made a *Vacuum* the Cause of Motion, and to prove as every Experiment will do, that 'tis that Effect which does the Work continually.

Ver.

Ver. 14.----- להבדיל to divide the Day from the Night (Heb. *Between the Day and between the Night*) and היו let them be לאתת for Signs ולמועדים and for Seasons, ולימים and for Days, ושנים and Years.

Ver. 15. And let them be לאומרת for Lights in the Firmament of the Heaven to give Light upon the Earth, and it was so.

This is partly Preceptive, and partly Descriptive, the ל all along is *to*, to the Use. He tells us to what Uses, to the Use of what other Things, and to what Ends the Light and this Candlestick of Orbs were made; and afterward, when God had made the את, he tells you what Uses it was designed for, and directs the Manner, to be to the Use of מאורת an Instrument, an Agent to make and give Light; to make Light run, flow outwards against all other Orbs, and against this Earth; to enlighten, warm, or enflame

Things

Things here; to become thin upon its Surface, that the Spirit may push in, and the Parts of Light recede, and so produce Motion, Rotation, and Progression: And afterwards the Commission was given to these Parts of Things, so joined and placed, *viz.* to the Instruments of Light. *Cajetan*, Vol. I. in *Gen.* Cap. I. ver. 14. p. 9. "And upon this Account it is said very significantly in the Text, without a Note of Conjunction: *Let there be Lights in the Extension of the Heavens, to divide between the Day, and between the Night,* &c. and not, *Let there be Lights in the Extension of the Heavens, and let them divide,* as the Vulgate Edition hath it: For it is clear from this Text, that God meant, *Let the Light, placed in the Luminaries, perform the Office of dividing,* and the other subordinate Offices. Under the Appellation of Luminaries, you are to comprehend all the Orbs; namely, the Sun, and Moon, and Stars."

Though the Word יהי before was writ both for the Command, and for the Report of the Fact, and is so for the Report here, to shew that the Agent or Patient was spoke to, and spoke of in the singular Number, and that the Time of speaking and coming to pass, was the same, "for the Word

Word of God is his Act"; yet here supposing the Candlestick of the Orbs formed,
and the Light then to be placed in, or divided, or distributed into Parts, a Part to
each Orb, and from one on each Side,
and from each of the rest on one Side outward; he says, היו let them, the Spirit
and the Light in such Motion or Action
as they are now in, whereby they have
hitherto made Light, comprehended within the Word Expansion, be so set to work
in the Candlestick, as to be ל *to*, to the
Use, or that they may make אתה an Action of Fire at the Center; and so of Light
between, and upon every Branch of the
Candlestick. If this Word be taken to
be singular, that it signify a single Action,
or Action continued from one Place, as,
suppose, in and from the Sun, and that
the other Actions at the other Bodies are
form'd out of that, or that the lesser Athths
are from, and subject to the great one, then
it must not be plural, but singular, as the
Candlestick is, and as the Instrument of
Light next after is; and 'tis, as he speaks
of Man, *in the Image of God created he
him, Male and Female created he them.* If
the Action of Fire be only in the Sun,
there could but be one Athth, till there
were Streams of Light between the Orb

of the Sun and the rest of the Orbs; but as the whole Heavens had a Mixture of Light in each Part, that would be, as I have said, instantaneous; and then it refers to the Action at every Branch of the Athth, upon every Branch of the Candlestick, as well the small ones as the great one, those in Motion as that fixed. The next Enquiry is, what is meant by the Word which they have translated *Signs*, or if it signify Signs, in what Sense are Signs here to be taken, and what is signified; the Word in Scripture is primarily apply'd to the Forerunner of some Action or Thing to be performed or produced by the immediate Power of God, as these were to be of Streams of Light, the most glorious of inanimate Matter. The antient Heathen Philosophers had imagined, that they had found out, that the Heavens not only govern'd the Fortunes and Lives of Men, but that the Stars, like the since formed Letters in a Book of some Dream they call'd Fate, might be read and understood by them; and that not only the Fortunes or Revolutions of Empires, *&c.* but of particular People, were indicated; and that when some Situations or Appearances happen'd in their, or the Earth's Revolutions, they were Signs of some great

great Good, or great Evil, and they were Signs that those Lights were to be worshipped; and they had Days of Sacrifice, &c. *Lucret.* Book V. L. 1204.

When to the World's great Frame we lift our Eye,
And view the heavenly Domes and starry Sky:
And then reflect how regular the Sun
And Moon, their annual Revolutions run:
That Doubt which lay by other Ills opprest,
Begins to raise its Head, and plague our Breast:
That Power supreme may o'er the Whole preside,
Which in their Spheres these radiant Orbs may guide.

The *Canaanites* had a Temple to their God, the Heavens, under the Attribute of the Intelligencer of Signs, mentioned *Josh.* xix. 6. בית לבאות compounded of לב and אות. *M.* "לבב Mind, Soul, Will, Thought, Genius, Wisdom, Intellect, Motion of the Mind — Strength of the Mind — Council. *C.* לבה *Chald.* Metaphorically, to blow, blow up, kindle Fire by Blasts. *Kama* 59. 2. לבוי a Blast, a blowing out, *Kama* 60. *Gemara,* לבוי *Æthiop.*

To underſtand, perceive in the Heart—to make to underſtand; to inſtruct—Intelligence, &c. לוּב Chald. Lub. Libia, &c. לאב Arab. Labon, a certain Perſon, from whom the *Aſtrolabe* had its Name, according to the *Arabians*, &c." This laſt may be true, but they have omitted, that the Man had his Name of Office from the Attribute. *M.* אתה, its Signification is, Acceſs, Congreſs. This Word is uſed to expreſs Force, Strength, Agility, the Power of Action in the Perſon or Thing, of moving itſelf, or other Things, or in employing what is under its Command or Power, to move ſome Thing to it, or to ſome other Perſon or Thing, which we ſhall ſhew in material Things, is moſtly or chiefly by the Action, or Power of Fire; the Subſt. is alſo uſed (*Job* xii. 19.) for mighty Men, and elſewhere for an Aſs, whoſe Employment was to bring or carry Things (in *Chald.* for a Wife or Woman who brought forth) and thence apply'd to that Power which can bring to paſs future Events. אות its Signification is a Sign. *Plural.* אותות Signs——Things future, to come, Signs of future Events, Prodigies, Portents, from the Root אתה to come. *Rabbinical* אותות Meteors. ספר אותות Book of of Meteors." They conſtrue this in *M.* "The Houſe or Temple of Lyons, from בית and לביא, and 'tis evident the Lyon was a Repreſentative of this; and alſo the Houſe or Temple of the Heart, from בית and לבב," the Athth was called the Heart of the World, "and the Houſe or Temple of the Letter or Sign, from בית and אות, or the Houſe or Temple of Events, from בית and בוא." This Attribute implies, that they had neglected Tradition, and ſought for the Knowledge of the Will of their God here; thought the Heavens, by the Lights in the Orbs of the Stars, &c. order'd the Events of Things, or Actions or Accidents upon the Earth, by the Courſe of their Motions and Influences; and that they were to be obſerv'd and foreſeen by Men. Theſe and ſuchlike Obſervers were the Men who robbed God of his chief Attribute, and were order'd then, and ought ſtill to be puniſh'd with Death. Hence roſe the Calculations of Nativities, and afterward the Devil took Advantage of this Folly, and conſtituted Oracles; and in Oppoſition to this the Anſwers by God, and the revealing of his Will, and recording it by Writing, was inſtituted; hence all the Claims of this Attribute, and here God ſettles that Point, tells you they were

were to be, not Signs of Events, but for Seasons, and for Days, and Years. But these Things had so possessed their Heads, that they, when they began to translate the Bible, would have what they translate *Signs*, to indicate that Knowledge, or predictive Astrology; and we, out of Regard to the first Paraphrasers or Interpreters, follow them, and use their Words; whereas these general Precepts to those Agents, or the Descriptions of their Offices or Uses, had no Regard to the Opinions or Customs of the Heathens, but were directly in Opposition to them; and to shew, that the Office of these Agents was to supply Life, produce Food, and all intermediate Steps of moving the Globes, producing Days, and Nights, and Variety of Seasons, which were in order to these necessary Ends. As the first Paraphrasers had put, or rather, kept up this Signification upon the Word, and imagin'd, that they could both bring, or make come to pass, and were predictive, or, by the Help of the Astrologers, could dictate what was to come; the *Jews*, who were infected with this Distemper, were caution'd by *Jer.* x. 2. *Thus saith the* Lord, *learn not the Way of the Heathen, and be not dismay'd at the Signs of Heaven, for the Heathen are dismay'd at them.*

them. Ver. 3. *For the Customs* (Heb. Statutes or Ordinances) *of the People are* הבל הוא *Vanity itself* (which, if I was to construe, should be of *Bel* itself, which the Prophets call Vanity, *&c.*) And this continued down to the Times of the Apostles; and to which their Questions often refer, What Signs shall there be before these Things come to pass? But as our present Philosophers now, I think, give up the Sense of Signs as the first Heathens took them, and employ them to a much worse Purpose, so I shall give them up in that Sense, and seek for another Sense. But in the mean Time the *Jews*, who at first had no other Times of solemn Worship, but the Sabbath, or seventh Day, by the Wickedness of their Neighbours, and of some among themselves, were forced to have Feasts, and fixed Times of Worship, of Days, of Months, of Years; several of them to be determined by the Appearances and Situations of these Stars, or Lights, or when some Revolutions were performed; and some of the later *Jews* were so zealous for them, that they fancied these Athths were set there, and had their Motions, *&c.* chiefly to determine those Times which by Appointment became Sacred, as you may see in *Targ. Jon.* upon this Text.

And our Interpreters or Philosophers have since made nothing of them, at first only a Parcel of Link-boys, now of other Worlds; whereas two Lights might have done as well as the infinite Number, if to give Light had been their only Use, and if that Action could have been without such a Number. But the Meaning of this Word does not depend upon my Construction, there is Evidence beyond Contradiction, that besides this Construction of Signs, which the Translators put upon it, the Word was well known to signify, the celestial Fire, *Chamah*, &c. and it was worshipped under that Name, *and* Temples, Altars, &c. were dedicated *to it.*

Vossius de Physol. Christian. Book IX. p. 233. The Sun is called the Producer of Fruits, whence in an old Epigram, *Attis,* who is nothing else but the Sun, is said, Θεμετερωτα πάντα Φυών.

H. Stephen's Greek Thesaurus, Ate in *Homer,* is a Goddess that inflicts Punishment and Misfortunes upon Men — *Hesiod* makes her the Daughter of Night, others make her benificent.

Gyrald. de Diis Syr. p. 60, *Ate* a Goddess, or rather looked upon as a Demon by many from these Verses of *Homer,* 19th *Illiad,* which translated, run thus:

From

*From his all radiant Head, where perch'd
　　she sate,*
Jove snatch'd the Fury-Goddess of Debate;
The Dread, th' irrevocable Oath he swore,
*Th' immortal Seats shou'd ne'er behold her
　　more;*
*And whirl'd her head-long down, for e-
　　ver driv'n*
From bright Olympus, *and the starry
　　Heav'n:*
Thence on the nether World the Fury fell,
*Ordain'd with Man's contentious Race to
　　dwell.*　　　　　　　　　　Pope.

Christian Authors interpret *Ate* by *Lucifer*, that is, the Light-bearing Goddess, as *Justin* a Philosopher and Martyr, *Suidas* and others.

Vossius de Orig. & Prog. Idol. Book I. p. 78. In *Phrygia, Cybele,* and along with her *Attis,* was worshipped; whence *Servius* upon the seventh Book of the Æneid—Attis *was a Deity joined with the Mother of the Gods.*

Book II. There is an Altar at *Rome*—The Inscription is M. D. M. I. & AT-TINIS; where the single Letters stand for *Magnæ Deum Matri Ideæ* (viz.) the great *Idean* Mother of the Gods — On another, on the left Side, you have *Attis*

tis mitred" with all their Symbols, Bull, Ram, Pine, &c. The Goddess *Cybele* is frequently joined with *Attis*, 'tis taken from the *Hebrew C.* שביל שבל " *M.* a beaten Path (in general it denotes a Duct, Course, or Flux of any Thing.) Hence *Cybele*, a Flux, a Flowing, a Running River, or Runner, *Psal.* lxix. 16 a Water, Flood. *Chaldee*, the same, &c." I take it to be a Compound of שב. *M.* A Spark, a Flame, a Fragment, or Splinter of Fire, and שול Defluxions, as Fire and Light are.

Ibid. *Vossius* 300, &c. variously terminated *Attes*, *Atte*, *Atten*, *Attis*, *Attin*, *Attios*, *Atteos*, whence also in an old Altar that is at *Rome*—*Attei* construed

—*To the High one* Attis, *which nothing in the World is hid from, or escapes.*

Several other Inscriptions, ATTIDI ATTHIN, &c. and from several antient Authors, some *Masc.* some *Fem.*

Vossius, Book II. p. 182. " The *Phrygian Attis* was the same with *Osiris* and *Adonis*, which *Martin Capella* reports in his second Philology concerning Marriages (in that Verse which begins The High Power of the unknown) where he saith,
the

the Sun, *Serapis, Mithras, Dis,* or *Pluto, Typho Attis, Ammon, Adonis, &c.* are all the fame. *Macrobius,* Book II. p. 319. *Attis* is confidered in two Views, either as it is the Sun, or as it is the active Power implanted in the Earth. The fame, p. 376. *Petronius.*

—— *Struck* Athos *flamed.*

Macrob. p. 259. In like Manner the *Phrygians,* by the Change of their Fables and facred Rites of the Mother of the Gods and *Attis,* fhew the fame Thing to be meant. For can we doubt the Mother of the Gods is the Earth? This Goddefs is carried by Lions, Animals that abound in Impetuofity and Fire, of which Nature is the Heavens, within whofe Circumference is contained the Air that carries the Earth. They adorn the Sun, under the Name of *Attis* with a Pipe or Rod. The Fife or Pipe fhews the Condition of the Spirit to be unequal; becaufe the Winds in which there is no Conftancy, derive their proper Subftance from the Sun. The Rod afferts the Power of the Sun, who governs all Things.

Ibid. *Voffius* Book II. p. 366. *Macrobius* in the Place above-mentioned, has very well

well explained the Reason of *Attis* being adorned with the Pipe or Fife, and the Rod. For the Rod is the Symbol of the regal Power which he hath as the supreme Governor. By the Fife is signified the Wind or Air that surrounds the Earth, nay, that also carries and sustains it; as *Lucan* not only speaks, who is reprehended by *Julius Scaliger* (in his 6th of Poeticks, which is inscribed Hypercritics) for this Verse:

— *While Earth the Seas, and Air the Earth sustains,*

But also *Claudian*, who has it thus;

The Earth is carried by the ambient Air,
At equal Distance round the Solar Sphere,
Nor drove too distant, nor press'd in too near.

Nay, *Pliny* himself, who in his 2d Book, Chap. 5. writes thus concerning the Air: The Earth with the 4th Element of the Waters, is suspended in the Middle Space by the Pressure of the Air on all Sides. And of this Air that surrounds the Earth, and carries this Terraqueous Globe, the Lions carrying the Chariot of the *Pessinuntian* Mother *Cybele*, were the Symbol; whence

whence *Lucretius*, Book II. Lib. 559.

*The Poets sing, that thro' the Heavens above
The Chariots drawn by fierce yok'd Lions,
   drove,
And riding to and fro she wanders there;
Teaching by this, that in the spacious Air
Hangs the vast Mass of Earth, and needs no
   Prop,
Of any lower Earth to keep it up.*
CREECH.

And *Macrobius* in the Place above cited: This Goddess is carried by Lions, impetuous and fiery Animals, of which Nature is the Heaven, within whose Circumference is contained the Air, that carries the Earth."

The inspired Author is not speaking here of Consequences, but of the Cause of Motion in Matter, which was for Days, &c. and with which these, and infinite Numbers of Evidence from the Heathens, under such Expressions of circulating the Heavens, carrying the Earth, &c. accord. No, these primary Descriptions, or Precepts, had no Regard to particular Notions, nor to other Worlds, and we must give them an original general Sense; the Thing this Word expresses must be, and be perceptible,
before

fore the Parts can be Signs; and muſt, in this Senſe, be placed in proper Places, and be of a proper Sort, or in a proper Condition to be ſeen; though the Fire, the Athth, or Fire in a Light-houſe, be as much Fire as that in an Oven, yet ſo placed, beſides being Fire, it may be a Sign to direct Sailors, &c. Hence the Uſe of theſe Orbs appear, as well that fixed, as thoſe moving. The Action of Fire could not be ſuſtained in the open Air, without the immediate Power of God, ſo *is* ſuſtain'd in the Orb of the Sun. If the Light had been iſſued thence, and there had not been Bodies to intercept Parts of it, all would have gone to the Extremities, none could have been Signs; if any of the Orbs could have been ſo ſituated, with Reſpect to us and the Sun, as to have been dark, they might have ſerv'd for Signs; but then they would not have anſwer'd their other Ends. But to purſue the farther Meaning of the Word, with reſpect to themſelves, from the Verb אתה explained above, *Dan.* vi. 27. אתין Signs; and *ibid.* iii. 17. the Furnace, (vulg. *Caminus*, Chimney) which indeed is not that which environs the Fire, nor the Fuel in which the Fire ſubſiſts, but the Fire itſelf.

C.

C. אתה to come, to come to, איתון Entrance, Ingress. *Coccæus* איתן איש "somewhat rough, difficult, uneven, sharp, &c. a Course of Water, a Flux of Water," and *Ezek.* xl. 15. something in the Temple, perhaps the Sun Gate.

S. איתן strong, vehement, middle. A. אתא to hang over the Head, to fly, to be carried with Impetuosity. *Forster*, the same.

1 *Kin.* viii. 2. The seventh Month was honour'd with this Name plural האתנים, render'd *Fortium*, or *strong*. If apply'd to Signs, it would be *strong* Nonsense; but apply'd to those Powers, to which so many other Attributes of Strength are apply'd, it will be Sense and Truth. And the *Israelites* were, in this Month, to observe חג, which they translate Feast, but was the Dance mention'd above; and they choos'd this Time to bring the Ark into the Temple.

C. *Chald.* אתא אתה and אתי, to come. איתי to bring to. באיתיותי in bringing me, —היתית and a Stone was brought—*Dan.* vi. 18. איתאה a bringing, אתתא a Wife, a Woman. *Syr.*—to bring, bring to—to be brought—bringing, carrying to—a Sign &c. Leaders, or Bringers to—*Arab.* אתן —an erect Thing, a great Personage, which seen afar off, seems to come towards us,

and

and meet us, and hence, perhaps, Uprightness in Walking or Gait, and, as it were, conspicuous in coming; Velocity, a quicker Gait, which makes towards coming on.

אות a Sign, as well natural, as miraculous.

Chald. אותנטיאה, Αὐθεντία, Authentia, Authority, Denomination, Power over another. *Breſh. R. ſ.* 25. 40. and 64. אותנטין Αὐθέντης, Authentes, a Lord, a Governor, who acts and governs freely according to his Authority. *It.* Chief, Principal. *Breſh. R. S.* 16. *C.* אתן an Aſs. איתן ſtrong. *Chald.* אתנא an Aſs. אתונא אתון a Furnace.

Syr. An Aſs, a Furnace. *Samaritan*, a Furnace. *Æthiopic,* a Furnace.

Arabic, a Furnace, *Matth.* xiii. 42, 50. A *Balneum,* a Calcinatory, or Glaſs Furnace, &c. 2d. Synecdoche, the Fire itſelf lighted and burning in the Furnace. 3d. The Place of Generation, where any Thing is generated and formed; as the Womb upon Account of ſome Likeneſs to a Furnace." This Root has ſeveral Branches, as well as the celeſtial Fire has many and various Effects; this expreſſes moſt evidently the Power of directing Motion, and Production; hence this is a deſcriptive Name

Name of that Fire, where it is in Action, or in a great Proportion of interrupted Light. *Joh. de la Hay* in *Exod.* p. 116. treating of this Fire, says, "It is always in Motion, and by that same Motion compressing or raising a Compressure, moves other Things." This Motion as I have shewed, produced by the Condition, the Matter is put into by the Action of Fire in melting the Spirit or Grains of Air to Atoms, *is* expressed by the Word יקד which is the same in *Chaldee, Syriac,* and *Arabic. M.* יקד "to kindle, light, to burn, fire, consume by Fire, &c." For as the Grains become melted to Atoms, and as they are within the Compression, it makes them give Way, or Room, to more Spirit, or any Thing grosser, as if the Place was void; hence comes the Word *Vacuum*; and our Philosophers will never find any other, but where this Action of Fire is; or where the small Parts are interrupted by the other Orbs, or by other Means separated from the Spirit. The chief Aththꓼ or that at the Orb of the Sun, is call'd חמה. *B. C.* "ככב with the *Rabbins.*—The Names of the seven Planets are חמה the Sun—*Synecdoche* לבנה the Moon. *M.* חמם, its Signification is Fire, Heat. The Noun חמה signifies the

Star of the Sun. The Sun, so call'd from Fire—Fury.—*Arab.* to warm, to cherish. *Heb.* חמם to warm, make hot or warm, to be heated, or warmed, to use Coition, to conceive. חמנים wooden Images; chiefly so called, because the Worshippers of the Sun made them in the Likeness of the solar Orb. *Chald.* Rabbinical, *Arab.* the same, and *Arab.* a Pigeon, a Stock-Dove. *C.* The same, and those who heat, or warm, or inflame themselves (*coite*) with their Gods, *Isa.* lvii. 5. *Chald.* The same, and a Stock-Dove. *Arab.* Whatever is burnt by Fire—a Ring-Dove, a Pigeon, a Stock-Dove, a Turtle, a Wood-Pigeon.——a Garden Herb with broad Leaves, *al. Nebathæa, Calamith.* חמר. *Arab.* God commanded the Sun to kindle to a vehement Degree. *Cam. Giggæus.* *C.* חמץ to ferment, it is spoke of Dough and Wine, which grow acid or sour, the one turning to Leaven, the other into Vinegar. *Seb.*" This appears to be compounded of חם and מץ. *M.* " Unleavened Bread. מץ, from which is formed מצה, unleavened, unfermented; an unleavened Cake of Meal and Water alone. חמץ *Chald.* the same. *C.* חמץ *Arab.* to be acid, to grow sharp.—a bitter and saltish Plant.— a square Garment of a black Colour, and

having

having two Fringes, or some such Ornaments, *S.* adorned with a double Ornament, *al.* a kind of Checquer, or Mosaic-work Garment. *Gol. App. Gram.* p. 223. 2. by Similitude, black Hair. R. חמם, *Avenarius* gives a new and peculiar Root to this Noun, as חמן a Sun-Dial: also an Image of *Ammon, Hammon,* or *Jupiter,* set up in an open Place that receives the Heat of the Sun: also the Temple of *Hammon,* which others call the Furnace of the Sun, the Sun-Chimney, *Helio-Caminus,* &c." I must repeat, as the Heavens, *Moloch, Gad,* &c. were general Names; so *Chamah, Baal,* and *Shemosh,* were Names descriptive of the three Parts, in different Motions, and the Hosts of Heaven were the particular Powers, the Matter in these Motions produce; whether they worshipped this Power, sometimes at their Altars, or Images, on the high Places, or without a Temple, is doubtful; we find several Places which were named from this Power, as *Jos.* xix. 28. and 1 *Chron.* vi. 76. חמון; and *Jos.* xxi. 32. חמות דור; and 2 *Kings* xiv. 25. *&c.* חמת. The addition of דור to חמות is a high Epithet; there was a Town of that Name in *Canaan,* and one in *Babylon;* the Thing the Word expresses, is a " Pile of Fire, a Combustion;

bustion; *Focus*, where Fire is acting." The Condition, as apply'd to other Things, is to live, to procure, or generate. *Chald.* " a Circle. *Arab.* to circuit, to make a Tour or Circuit round any Thing, a Circuit, the Æquinoctial Circle, &c."

Kirch. Obel. p. 17. *Zurafter*, the Sun is a living Star, a living Fire, *p.* 208. which *Zoroaster* handling mystically, saith, that all Things are generated by Fire alone, *p.* 157. *Heraclitus* calls it, the Heart of Heaven, *p.* 197. *Archemachus* the *Eubæan*—saith, that as among the *Grecians* —*Juno* signified the Air, so the Birth of *Vulcan* was the Change of Air into Fire.

Gravio, &c. of the Philosophy of the antient Philosophers, *p.* 99.—*Laertius*.— When the Air is attenuated or ground small by the Sun.

The same, *p.* 86.—*i. e. Anaximenes* is reported to be of Opinion, that the Air is the Cause of all Things, that it is infinite in its Nature, but definite in its Qualities; and that all Things were generated by its Condensation and Rarefaction" and sundry others.

Tho. Bartholinus de Luce Animal. p. 140. from *Hippocrates*, in his Book concerning the Heart,—who doth not see, that it is intirely owing to the Light from the Stars, that

that the Machine unconquer'd or unretarded by Cold, compleats its Courſe by a moſt ſwift and quick Motion in an Orb. And alſo thoſe Operations that are common to each, depend upon the Light of the Heavens, as well that conglobated, as that diſperſed through all. For Light is of the Eſſence of the Stars and Heaven, nor is the Element of the Stars any Thing but Light itſelf.

Raphaelis Volaterrani Comm. Urbanor. ſpeaking of *Ægypt*—They think Fire to be an Animal—which the *Perſians* take for a God.

Spencer de Leg. Hebræor. p. 820. *Lev.* xxvi. 30. את חמניכם your Solar Temples, Temples dedicated to the Sun. The famous *Bochart*, in *Phaleg.* Part II. Book II. c. 17. The Sun is called by the *Hebrews* חמה, whence חמן is the Temple of of the Sun, which the antient *Phenicians* looked upon as the ſole Lord of Heaven —*Numb.* xxxiii. 52. משכית (which the *Vulgate* renders, Title) the *Chaldee* interprets by בית־סנדרא, the Houſe or Temple of Adoration."— שכה is a Picture, ſomething to look at; but משך is, to draw, to carry; and they muſt be a Sort of Images, which denoted theſe Powers, in what they repreſented.

Voſſius

Voffius de Orig. & Prolog. Idol. p. 180. חום is Heat, whence חמה the Sun or Fire, from which comes חמנים *Chamanim*, which the *Greeks* call *Pyræthæa*, Fire-Hearths; hence, *Lev.* xxvi. 30. חמניכם *Chamanicem*; which is translated, your Images, but I would rather render it, your *Pyrea* or *Pyræthea*, that is, your Inclosures, in which, to the Fire kept perpetually burning, you sing your Verses or Song.

God literally claims this, and another, two of the three Attributes, *Nah.* i. 2. יהוה ובעל חמה, and predicts the Church, express'd by כרם, of Christ, express'd by שלמה, out of the Worshippers in the Temples of these Powers, *Cant.* viii. 11. כרם היה לשלמה בבעל חמון.

Bibl. Max. Patr. f. 2. p. 391. The Recognition of St. *Clement* to *James* the Brother of the Lord, Book I. In the 17th Generation, *Nimrod* first reigned at *Babylon*, and built the City, thence he went to the *Persians*, and taught them to worship Fire.

Kircher Odyp. V. III. p. 535. *Procopius*, Book II. *Strabo*, Book XV. at their sacrificing to Fire, they offer it Food, and say, *Lord-Fire, eat.*

B. C.

MOSES's *Principia.*

B. C. יונא a Dove, was the standing Symbol of the *Assyrians* and *Babylonians.*

Ibid. ציהוב.—the golden Brightness about the Neck of Turtles and Doves, is called by this Name: לתחלת הציהוב שבזה ושבזה, in the Beginning of the Brightness in these, and in those; that is, they are fit for Sacrifice or Oblation. *Cholin,* fol. 22. 2.

Vossius de Orig. & Prolog. Idol. Lib. II. p. 185. *Macrobius,* Book I. Sat. ch. 21. Therefore *Ammon,* which God, in the Opinion of the *Lybians,* is the Setting Sun, him they paint with the Horns of a Ram, because this Animal has its Strength in his Horns, as the Sun has in its Rays.

Kircher Oedyp. V. III. p. 113. The Image of the Sun holds a Goat by the Horns, because the Solar Force is express'd by Horns.

Kircher Obel. p. 279. *Herodotus* in *Euterpe.* Those who worship at the Temple of *Theban Jupiter,* all of them abstain from Sheep, and sacrifice Goats: Those who observe the Rites of *Mendes,* abstain from Goats, and sacrifice Sheep.

Tostat. on *Exodus,* Vol. I. p. 96. c. 1. They worshipped a Bull, because *Apis,* the God of the *Egyptians,* was worshipped in the Figure of a Bull.

Ff 4 *Tho.*

Tho. Bartholinus of the Light of Animals, *p.* 176.—the *Ægyptian* Ox *Apis* represents the Celestial Light.

Spencer de Leg. Hebr. p. 728. *Horace,* and *Selden,* of the Gods of the *Syrians.* But having affumed the Head of a Bull, imitated by its Front (the curled Hair and Horns) the bending Rays of Fire.

Kircher Oedyp. V. III. p. 509. An Ox with an human Face, vibrating Flames from his Head" (befides the Horns.) The *Canaanites* had a Temple to their God, the Heavens, under the fame Attribute of the Action of Fire, Giver of Heat, &c. mentioned *Jof.* xvi. 3. בית חרון from בית and חרר, or חרה. *M.* " חרר Combuftion and Summer, and whatever is thence derived. *Chaldee* and *Arabic, harrar,* the fame as the *Hebrew. C.* חרר *Heb.* the fame, & — illuftrious Perfons—fuch as were dreffed in White. *Chald.* the fame, and the Area of an Hearth. To make or bake Cakes, ftrictly, by fcorching them upon the Embers. Something produced from a Serpent and a Toad—a Species of Snake. *Fo. French, Orver. Tanhuma. Syriac. Æthiop.* the fame. *Arab.* the fame, and to be hot, rage, &c. The Sun, Heat, fcorching Heat, Fire, a Serpent twifted round in a Circle. *Camus,* a kind of Sparrow.

sow. *Giggæus.* חרה to burn, &c. חרון the Heat or Rage of Anger, hot, or burning with Anger." The hot Anger of God or Man, *Psal.* lviii. 10. lxxviii. 49, &c.—
" חרם the Sun. — *Judg.* viii. 13. *Deut.* xxviii. 27. עיר החרם the City of the Sun, *Isa.* xix. 78. *Heliopolis*, which is called בית שמש, *Bethshemosh. Jer.* xliii. 13. where there is a Temple of the Sun, and the *Egyptians* have yearly Meetings in Honour of the Sun, with Sacrifices; the Study of Astronomy flourishes, and there are Schools for all Arts and Sciences. *Jud.* ii. 8. תמנת חרם the Effigy, or Image of the Sun. *Arab.* Sulthan — a Species of Fish," (though they make this, and שמש the same, you will see they are mistaken) of this, *Job* ix. 7. *commanding* לחרם *the Solar Fire, and it* לא יזרח *springs not up;* it does not go forth in any Sense. B. C. חרה *to burn,* &c. חרח a kind of bitter Herb, formerly used in the Feast of the Passover, *Pesachim*, fol. 39. 1. חרם the Sun: hence the Sun is called by the *Persians* Κῦρος, *Cyrus;* according to *Plutarch,* in the Life of *Artaxerxes.*" Hence we know what fiery Serpents were, and why God sent them to punish the doubting *Israelites.*

The

The *Israelites* had seen what Services the *Egyptians* had paid to this Power, though perhaps under other Names; and what Representations they had made of it; and were to see, or hear, what Representations the *Canaanites* made of it; what they attributed to it, and what Services they paid to it: And as the whole Intent of the Miracles were to convince them that God was Master of these Powers, so the whole Intent of the ceremonial Law, the Types of Christ excepted, was to make them render the Attributes, and perform the Services, which they had attributed and performed, to these Powers, for the Benefit accruing to them by their Actions, directly to God. Hence the *Israelites* were commanded to destroy their Temples, break down their Altars, and Sun Images, offer Sacrifice by Fire, sacrifice Doves or Pigeons at certain Times, to forbear eating of leavened Bread, and then to eat bitter Herbs, to pour out fermented Wine, and use Salt in Sacrifices; to carve out some sort of Herbs and Flowers, which resembled the Orb and Rays of the Sun, on the Walls of the Temple; wear peculiar Sorts of Garments, of this, or that Form or Colour, &c. in executing the Office of Sacrificing, &c. *Athan. Kircher*

Kircher shews how the Antients represented this: *Ob. Pamp.* 230. "The Sun, says he, his august Head, adorned and set round with flaming Rays, resembles, as it were, the Golden Head of Hair,—*Fulgentius*— They give him a Bow and Arrows, because his Rays fly out in a Circle as Arrows from a Bow. Pag. 383. The *Persians*, as *Brisonicus* testifies, when they called *Jupiter* the Lord of Heaven, thought to offer Sacrifices to him, when they had ascended the most high Rocks or Cliff.—They adorned their Gods with a Circle of Rays— The Light round the Sun was divided into Rays"—After citing sundry Authors, Statutes, &c. The *Ethiopians* had also this Custom as *Heliodorus* attests, who in his 9th Book of his *Æthiopic* History elegantly describes it—surrounding his Head with a kind of Wreath, they stick it round with Arrows, the Head or feather'd Part they turn to the Head (of the Image) the Point in the Manner of Rays they project outward."

This agrees with *Job* xxii. 12. ראש כוכבים the Heads of the Stars, in other Terms, with that *Cælius Calcal.* p. 392. "And of all Kind of Motions that which is circular preceding from itself, and returning into itself—p. 393. For we read in *Plato*, that

a Mind inhabits the Center of the World, and thence extends itself to the Extremities, actuating all Things, and by turning itself into itself pervades to the utmost Parts or very Back of the System." I must observe that these not only represent the Action of Fire at the Orb of the Sun, but also include the *Shemosh*, or the *Ashteroth*; and also *Baal*, or those returning, and ought to be repeated, or remembered under those Heads; and that modern Writers have forgot one, or two Thirds of the Meaning of a Sun Image, and only speak of the bright or gilded Rays, or Arrows pointed outward, or from the Center of the Sun; and not of the dark Rays pointed inward, or towards the Center of the Sun, which on every Side pass between one another; and which they could not otherwise represent, except as above, with Darts and Arrows; for those Figures as those painted or gilded *in Plano*, represent the Fire at the Center, or in the Pores of the Orb, the Spirit coming in in the dark Rays, and the Light going out in the bright Rays; and for want of Understanding this, they imagined that the Orb had a Property of being turned into Light. These two Sorts of Rays represented *Baal* and *Ashteroth*,
which

which are the two chief Powers, with the Addition of the Hosts of Heaven, which the Natives of *Canaan*, and the seduced *Jews* are, in gross, said to have serv'd.

I have in the first Part shewed, that the Spirit and Light were the Parts of the Heavens, the Airs put into Motion; and that they fill'd, or possessed, or were all the Space, not possessed by other Sorts of Matter; and that Motion raised an Expansion, so that they compressed the other Sorts of Matter inclosed, or included in them. It was not my Business then, but 'tis now, to shew that the Matter which performs that Operation called Fire, is the same, that *Aer* divided into Atoms at the Centre, is called Fire; further dispers'd, perhaps, Flame; further, if not intrerrupted by the Way, or too far dispers'd, Light, and also Heat; if it pervade opake Bodies, and be not too far dispers'd, Heat; and the *Hebrew* Word, which is mostly used for Light, and still sounds *Aer*, is used for that just issuing from the Fire, and still acting in Imitation of Fire.——Fire is the Matter of the Heavens in such Action, which has its Effects in Dissolution; the very Word Fire implies a Circulation; Light is the same

same Matter, at farther Distance from that Action, and has the same Effects in lesser Degrees, divides those it can, and expands or thins those it cannot divide; sometimes by dividing, and detaching Parts of Fluids from among those of Solids, leaves the Solids more liable to be made more so; at further Distance, as the Motion weakens, these Atoms, by the Compressure in itself, adhere into Grains, which are continually pressed towards the Sun; and where there are enough of them too large to enter the Pores of the Body they include, they compress, and keep it solid; at this Distance from the Sun or Fire, the Atoms or small Masses interpose, or their Matter is pushed in between the Grains of Air and makes them expand; nearer the Fire, they will make the Parts of Water expand; nearer those of Metals; nearer those of Diamonds.

Though I cannot shew the Manner of the Operation of the Heavens, in the Action called Fire, in the Orb of the Sun, to Sense, otherwise than by shewing the Operations of Fire here, and making Allowances for its Situation, Degree, and Effects it has upon the Matter, whose Pores it acts in, which belong not to this Part, I can shew by the descriptive Words

the

the sacred Writers use, that it has all the Actions and Effects I attribute to it; and what the Light, which comes from it, does here, admits of Demonstration.

M. יקד (before mentioned) Its Exposition is Combustion—to be kindled, set on fire, burned, to burn or be on fire. Isa. x. 16. *He shall kindle a Burning like the burning of Fire.* *C.* the same, *Syriac* the same, and *Seraphim,* and Arrows— a *Sardonix,* an *Hyacinth. Samar,* the same, and a fiery Serpent.

M. דלק Its Signification is Combustion, a burning out. *C.* the same. *Chaldee* and *Syriac* the same. Dan. vii. 9. *His Wheels as burning Fire.*

M. קדח The Exposition is Combustion, a Fire kindled and burning. *C.* the same. *Chaldee* the same.

M. מסס—To loosen, separate, weaken the Adhesion, to dissolve, melt, make liquid, fluid, liquify, make thin, clarify. *C.* the same. *Chaldee, Syriac,* and *Arabic* the same. Isa. lxiv. 1. *Oh that thou wouldst rent the Heavens, that thou wouldst come down, that the Mountains might flow down at thy Presence, as when the melting Fire burneth, or the Fire of Meltings.* Isa. liv. 12. אקדה *a precious shining Stone, or a Carbuncle.*

C.

400 MOSES's *Principia:*

C. Syr. The chryſtaline Humour of the Eye. *Arab.* a Flint, a Stone that ſtrikes Fire. *C.* מסם *Chald.* The Stomach of Beaſts that liquifies, conſumes and concocts the Meat. *Col.* c. iii. 1. *&c.*

M. שאף Its Signification is the Attraction of the Spirit or Air— to draw in the Air, to breathe, to ſup, ſup up, *&c. C.* the ſame. *Eccl.* i. 5. *At its Station drawing in the Spirit,* ſo *Jer.* x. 13. li. 16. יצא *bringing the Spirit out of his Store-houſes.*

M. נגד Government, Sovereignty. *Chald. Syr.* to draw *C.* the ſame, and *Chald. Syr.* and *Sam.* the ſame. *Dan.* vii. 10. *a Stream of Fire drawing.*

M. נפח (of which before as an Attribute) ſignifies blowing in general; to blow, blow to, blow up, blow out, breathe, *&c.*— *Paul.* to be blown, ſufflated, or made fervent, boiling hot. *Hiphil.* To inſpire, or to cauſe to blow. *Chald.* The ſame. *Syr. Arab. Naſach*, the ſame. *C.* The ſame, to kindle the Fire by blowing; *Chald. Syr. Æthiop. Arab.* the ſame, *Ezek.* xxi. 31. *I will blow againſt thee in the Fire of my Wrath.* xxii. 20. *To blow the Fire upon it, to melt it: Job.* xx. 26. *A Fire not blown ſhall conſume him.*

M. רצץ Its Signification is Contrition (in the material Senſe,) to break, break to pieces,

pieces, to dash together, break by Collision. *Nab.* ii. 5. *They shall meet*, be dashed together, *like the Lightnings*.

M. נשא Signifies eighthly a total Consumption by breaking and burning—— So as a Noun a Flame, a Burning, a Fire, Combustion, because in Fire the flame is carried upwards; this is from its first Signification, to be lifted up. *Jud.* xx. 40. *And the Flame* or Combustion *began to rise. C. Chald.* משיאין They lighted Fires to celebrate the new Moon. *I. B. Sanh. C.* 3. 6. *&c. Arab.* A Female Diviner, a Soothsayer, a Prophetess.

M. בער Its signification is Combustion, and Fire. *C.* the same. *Isa.* xliii. 2. *The Flames shall not kindle upon thee.*

M. פוץ from נפץ Its Exposition is Dispersion, or Breaking, or Tearing to pieces. —— To scatter, disperse, to shake off, to strike or dash, or brake by Collision, to pour out or shed, to project; it signifies Dispersion with Fraction, *&c.* —— *Chald. Syr.* the same as the *Heb.* To scatter, disperse, break, break or pound to pieces, *&c. Arab. nafad* to shake, shake off, shatter, expel, cast out, project, pound, beat, or bray small, so diminish, lessen, impair and destroy the Adhesion of Parts, *&c. Job.* xxxvii. 11. *The Serenity* or pure Fire *viz.*

at the Orb of the Sun *shall break to pieces* or dissolve the Adhesion of *the Grains of Air, his Light shall disperse the Cloud.* — xxxviii. 24. *What way is the Light parted, which scattereth the East Wind upon the Earth.* Psa. cxliv. 6. *Cast forth thy Lightnings and scatter them.*

M. נפק Chald. Syr. to go out, proceed, go forth. Arab. to make go out, to bring out, &c. C. Æthiop. to cut in pieces, divide into Parts Dan. vii. 10. *Drawing, and going forth.*

M. נתך Its Signification is Fusion—to pour out, Distill, drop, &c.— to pour forth, drop, melt, liquify. Nah. i. 6. *his Anger is poured out as Fire.* "Hence Chald. Images formed of Metals melted by Fire and poured out.

M. עוף Its Signification is instantaneous Motion, vehement Motion, light and easy.*

M. גבה Altitude— to be lifted up, elevated. Job. v. 7. *The Sons of the burning Coal lift up to fly.* i. e. The sparks of Fire fly upwards.

M. יפע Its Signification is to shine— according to some it has a quite opposite Signification, to be darkened, to be obscured." This is a common Case, to have the Translators make a Word they did not understand, express things as opposite as

* Hence perhaps the English Word—*Huff, Huff* up as Froth, &c.

Light

Light and Darkneſs; and indeed it has equal Relation, or no Relation to either; and ſo will be eaſily reconcil'd by giving it its true Senſe: It ſignifies that Motion of Atoms or Grains, where each one ſucceſſively impels that before it in a Line; expreſs'd by the Word *irradiate*; and 'tis applicable to אל, Grains of Air, or Spirit, when moving towards the Fire, or *&c.* as well as to Atoms or Light moving from the Fire, or *&c.* as *Job.* x 22. תפע *Irradiates as* אל *Grains of Air*, or Spirit, as the Grains move inward in Lines from the Circumference to the Center or Orb of the Sun. ſo to *Job.* iii 4. *Nor let the Light irradiate upon it*, as Light moves outward in Rays from the Center to the Circumference. The Heathens apply'd this ſort of Motion to their Cherubims, *&c.* And *Moſes* and the *Pſalmiſt*, by way of Claim, apply it ſeveral times to God. Theſe oppoſite Motions were expreſs'd by the antient Heathens; by Arrows pointed, ſome to the Head, and ſome from the Head of the Repreſentation of that Diety, as has been; and will be ſhewed in their Places.

As the Motion of the Spirit, on each Side to the Fire, is in ſtreight Lines, each directed to the Center, and is Spirit till it
arrive

arrive there; and as the Parts in the Action of Fire are moved in all Directions, and those in the Flame to and from the Center, as soon as the Parts of the Fire rise above the Flame, they are properly Light, and make thence in streight Lines; so several of these Words used for the Action of Fire, express also the Motion of the Spirit, and of Light: For as the Spirit comes till it be converted into Light, so the Light goes in the same manner, till it be interrupted, or converted into Spirit. " *Cajetan*, Vol. I. *Gen.* ch. i. V. 14. p. 9. The first Day the Light it self is considered absolutely, without regard to its Division or Diffusion into the Sun, Moon and Stars. I say Division or Diffusion, because we are uncertain whether the Stars shine by their own, or receive their Light from the Sun: but upon the fourth Day the same Light may be considered as divided into distinct Luminaries and Stars." And if all the rest of those Athths be produced or issued from one, we cannot speak of them, without speaking of the Means, the Stream of Light between it, and each of them, tho' strictly speaking the chief Athth is extended no further than the Orb, which appears to us like Flame on each Side the Marth of the Sun; and each of the rest is extended no further than

than the Cap on one Side of its Marth, which is of a whiter Colour than Flame; and whether the grosser Parts of Light interrupted at each Orb, be further divided, or only collected there, each quantity of Light so collected, serves in Proportion to answer the End of that Athth; and besides the miraculous Act of their Formation, their several Capacities may be distinguish'd at Leisure, as productive, eductive, predictive, indictive, &c. And here need only be considered in gross; with respect of God, as they are his Workmanship, and his legated Ministers, both by Contrivance, Creation, Formation and Power of mechanical Action; with respect to its or their Operation upon its self, the Spirit was to be driven into a Furnace or *Focus*, and divided by the Action of the Atoms there, which we call Fire, and those Atoms, so divided, driven out in form of Light, Parts interrupted, reverted, or inverted by each of the rest of these Marths; and so the Force renewed, reflected and driven from several Athths, into several Streams of Light, to move those Streams to or against the Earth, &c. with respect to the Mind of Man, for 'tis not the Athths, (except that upon the Earth) but the Streams of Light from them which reach his Body. They must be Signs in the Sense spoken by Isa. vii. 11. *Ask thee a Sign of the* LORD *thy God, ask it either in the Depth, or in the Height above.* An Act, or something produced by Action, or Operation, that it may be a Demonstration of the Ability of God, with an intent to produce Faith, and Dependance in Man; and as the Word is used there, and in many other Places, may be said to be Signs extraordinary, and at first miraculous Operations, beyond the Power of any Concatinations of pretended second Causes to produce, if all that our greatest Imaginers can talk of were real. And the Athths not the Marths, for none of the Bodies, except that of the Moon when she is not full, and some few others in Eclipses are visible, were to continue to be Signs, to represent and bring to Mind these Actions, and evidence what was to be seen in seeing their Power; and by their continued Operations to shew the Wisdom and Power of the Agent, who set them forward; and Evidences, or Pledges, or Proofs, or Tokens, that they will, by their Operation, continue things in this order, produce in like manner, support Life, &c. till he change them: And Signs of what was, or is to come; so that one might, by observing their Motions, foretell their Situations, the

Effects

Effects of Times, Seasons, Days, Years, Oppositions, Changes, Eclipses, &c. And so that the place on this Globe being known, they are Signs of the time of the Day, Night, &c. of the Season or time of the Year, or *vice versa*: The time being known at a known Place, and at the Place of Observation, Signs of that Place, so to guide Men at Sea or Land; and not only with respect to the Earth's Years, but as some of the Marths, with their Athths, are longer times in revolving; so that by the annual Motion of the Earth, and Motion of the Planets, and their Situation, in Respect to the known fixed Stars, they may be Signs or Measures of their Motions, Rotation, &c. so with Respect to their Operation, as it affects the Earth, and Things on, or in it; though the Parts in Motion in the Athths do not reach the Earth, yet the Motion of the Parts of Light issuing out of them, move the next, and so the intermediate ones, each other successively till the foremost reach the Earth, and so enables them to produce Things to come, by their Operations upon Bodies and Fluids, in moving the Earth obliquely, make Seasons, and so all the Effects of Seasons; the Operations positive, performed by the Effect of those Atoms divided, and in Motion, which effect we call Heat, by thinning the Fluids of Water, Mixtures, Sap, Blood, and producing Motion in them; or alternately, or negatively, by the Effect of those Atoms, adhering in Grains, which we call Cold, upon Solids, Fluids, Vegetables, and the Bodies of, and Fluids in viviparous or oviparous Animals, in their Production and Growth, Perception by the Eyes, or other Senses, or Deprivation, Vigour, or Weakness, Life, or Death. By Rotation of the Earth for Days, and all the Effects of Days; by Progression of the Earth for Years of Days, and all the Effects of Years; by Circulation of the Moon, of which hereafter, for Months of Days, and the rest of the Planets and Moons for their Courses, and all the Effects of them; so as *Psa.* civ. 4. *his Ministers, the flaming Fire*; as Athth, Fire, in the singular, and Ministers in the plural. And under these annual varieties of Seasons in the several Parts of the Earth; tho' in some Parts varied by the Patients of clear Weather, Rain, Tempests, Thunder, Lightning, Winds, Cold, Heat, Dry, Moist, Frost, Clouds, and those Things which follow those Effects, as Plenty, Scarcity, and their Consequences,

Confequences, and no otherwife, Difeafes, Wars, &c. Tho' this Agent is the Caufe or Director of all Motion, and by the Declination of the Earth, of the regular periodical Seafons of Spring, Summer, Autumn, and Winter, and of all the Seafons of Rains, Winds, &c. near the Line, where they are nearly periodical, and of Froft, Thaw, &c. near the Poles, where they are nearly periodical; yet as there are many Things, and Situations of Things, which contribute to the Variation of thofe fecondary Seafons, of Wet or Dry, Windy or Calm, Froft or Thaw, &c. they are not folely for the Determination of thofe faid fecondary Seafons.

Ver. 14. --- ולמועדים, and for Seafons.

M. יעד --- מועד Time, or a certain and appointed Place; a proclaimed Meeting, a Convention, a Time appointed by one to the other: It is taken for Time in general, and any appointed Day: thence particularly for the Seafons of the Year, holy, and anniverfary Feftival Days, which are celebrated at a certain Time of the Year." This Word has been ufed for, and
inter

inter al. signifies the Seasons of the Year, occasion'd by the Earth's Declination; and the *Canaanites* had a Temple to their God, the Heavens, under the Attribute of *the Decliner*, mention'd *Judg.* vii. 22. בית־השטה, *the Temple of the Decliner*, or Causer of the Declination of the Earth. *M.* שטה its Signification is Inclination—to turn aside, divert, decline,—Decliners,—Declinations. *Chald.* The same;" and the Name of some Sort of Tree, which they render " the best Cedars, others, Rosen or Pitch-Wood," which was order'd to be used in the Tabernacle, and Temple, writ generally שִׁטִּים, once, *Isa.* xli. 19. שטה. "*C.* שטט the Cypress—the *Arabian* Thorn"—This Attribute expresses that Action of the Athths upon their respective Streams of Light, which vary the Motion of the Earth, and put the Parts of its Surface into those periodically different Positions or Inclinations to the Line of Light from the Sun, whereby they enjoy'd, and we enjoy the alternate Seasons of Spring, Summer, Autumn, and Winter, and all the Consequences or Effects of them; thence such Claims as this, *Psal.* lxxiv. 17. *Thou dost set all* גבולות *of the Earth, the Summer and Winter; thou* יצבתם *dost form them.* They render these the *Borders of the*

the Earth; these *Borders* are not the utmost Lines or Parts of the Surface of the Earth; they are those without the Earth, the Airs; as *Jer.* v. 22. *I have placed the Sand for a Bound to the Sea.* Psal. civ. 9. *Thou hast set a Bound that they may not pass over.* Ezek. xlv. 7. *From the Border of the Sea.* As the Sand is without the Sea, and the Sea without the Land of *Judea*; and 'tis the different Conditions and Motion of the Matter of the Heavens, next the Surface of the Earth; 'tis these Borders, as they call them, which he has framed into Summer and Winter.—This Word is also used for fixed or appointed Periods of the Revolutions of the Earth or Moon, which are now properly called *Times*; yet here it had a higher Signification, as all Vegetables and Animals were framed to be operated upon, with the intermediate Light by these Agents; and the very vegetable Matter, Water, &c. which supply them, was to be raised by this Agent; Here it must also refer to the proper and fixed Force of this Agent, by the Quantity of Spirit melted into Light, and emitted; and thence a proper Degree of Expansion to the proper Sizes and Distances of the Orbs concerned, &c. that the Declinations, Rotations and Progressions

ons should be thereby so proportioned in Point of the Velocity of their Motion, and so of Time, to the frame of the Parts of Vegetables, and those of the Bodies of Animals, that the several Sorts of Vegetables, proper for each Climate, might grow, the Annuals to Perfection, and the Standards make a Progress, bear Fruits, Seeds, or &c. so that the Herbs for Cattle, and the Fruit for Men may be gathered in sufficient Quantities for the time, till a new Supply; and be of such a Constitution, that the necessary ones might be preserved till a new Supply; and that the Roots, or Stems, or Seeds may be preserved the Length of the Winter from perishing; that the Days may be of due Length to thin, and raise their Sap, by turning up their Tops to the Sun, and giving the thin'd Sap an Opportunity to rise; and the Nights to cool, strengthen and refresh, by turning their Tops the opposite Way, and so giving the Spirit an Opportunity to condense, compress, thicken and fix the Parts, that the Summer may be hot enough or long enough to thin the Fluids in Animals, and the Sap in Vegetables, and to ripen the Fruit; and that the Winter may not be too keen, or too long, to thicken the Fluids in Animals, or the Sap in Vegetables,

MOSES's *Principia.*

tables, so that they may be kept from growing, and the Sap driven to the Roots, but not too hard or too long, to set the Sap, or destroy the Buds; that the Day may be of due Length for Animals to perform this Labour, gather daily Food or Stock; and the Nights of such a due Length as to refresh their Bodies, and not so long, that the Food in them should be spent, and their Bodies impaired; suitable to the Time that each Species of brute Creatures are inclined, or indeed forced to couple, and to the Time they go with Egg, or Young, or with Spawn, and Milt; that when they bring forth their Young, hatch their Eggs, or their Spawn comes to Life, there may be a proper Season, and also proper Provision made for them; so that as the fixed Degree of Expansion, regulates these, and a vast Number of other Things, (which have been long since considered and described) and the Expansion is to be in such a Manner, that *Job* says, xxxvii. 18. *Strong as a molten Speculum*; and is, in such a Time, to send forth so much Light against the Side of the Earth, and to give such a Degree of Force to the Spirit, or grosser Grains of Air, as to keep it in the same Circle, or at the

same

same Distances from the Sun, turn it so fast, and drive it so far in such a Time: Thus *Job* xxxviii. 12. *Didst thou make the Dawn to know its Place?* Psa. cxiv. 19. *The* שמש *Sun*, (which you will see is the Light irradiating directly from the Sun) ידע *knows its Departure*, (from each particular Country,) And I am to observe, this is not attributing Knowledge to the Light, but is used in Opposition to those who were called by this Name ידעוני "Gnostics, Augurs, Diviners, Southsayers who aim at knowing Futurity. *C. Syr.* the same and Magi, Sciolists." So *Job* xxxviii. 32. *Dost thou cause* מזרות *the Grains to come forth in their Season*, (of which in their Place.) The Knowledge of the Cause and Manner of this Motion was never lost; but only set aside, and over-ruled, to make way for their Whims, who pretend to understand things better than he who made them. *Gassend. Tom.* I. p. 647,—" It rather seems more likely to be effected by this Transmission of Corpuscles, which may find the innumerable little void Spaces through which they are trajected, than solely by a Pressure from one Extremity to the other without the Interception of a Vacuum, and in a Plenitude of Matter possessing all Space; and this is partly gathered from the

the Inconvenience, partly deduced more largely from other Confiderations." But as there are no ftated Times, or Times appointed of any comparative Confequence to this; and as this was the firft Occafion, upon which the Word was ufed in Speaking or Writing, all the reft, or other ftated Times, are but diminutive Comparifons to this. The whole Quantity of the Heavens or Airs, every Body and their Diftances, and every Vegetable, and Creature, to a Mite, are proportioned to this Operation. If the Sun could have fent out more Light or *Shemofh* at firft, than it does now, and the Earth could have been turned and moved fafter, and the Days and Years had been vaftly fhorter than they are now, no Creatures nor Vegetables, as they are framed, could have lived but near the Line; and if, as it muft have been in Confequence, the Compreffure had been much greater than 'tis now, no fuch Creatures could have lived any where; and thofe Creatures, who are now bufy fearching to find how much this Globe has gone fafter than it does now, would never have been, if any fuch Exceffes or Alterations had been made, in thefe Points, after the Creatures were made.

VER.

Ver. 14.ーーー And for יָמִים Days, and for שָׁנִים Years.

I have already, at its Place, shewed how the Scriptures describe the Cause and Motion of Day and Night; so that I need not add any thing here; save that these Marths, and Athths were to be Parts of the Machine, to keep the Spirit and Light in Rotation, and consequently, the Light in Streams against the Earth, to do what God had by his immediate Power done, in continuing the Motion of the Spirit and Light, for the first four Days; and also to vary and regulate the Days as aforesaid. As Days are Parts of Years, I have also shewed how they expressed the Progression, together with the Rotation. The first account we have of this is, that *Moses* required *Pharaoh* to let the Children of *Israel* go, in the *Egyptian* term, to hold חגג a Feast, as they call it, to the Lord, which was to attribute the Circulation and Progression of the Earth, &c. by such Services as the *Egyptians* had paid to the Heavens. Sometime after, when they were delivered, and in the Wilderness, they pulled off נזמי their
Golden

Golden Ear-rings, which were Reprefentatives of this Power. C. *Arab.* חוג *Fut. O.* "To Trip it as in Dancing, to lead Dances," and elfewhere called עגל, and caſt them into a Figure of that Name, which they render a Golden Calf. If it have any other Relation to the Word, befides being chofen a Reprefentative, 'tis a Yearling, one which had, with the Earth, made one Circle, one Tour. *M.* עגל Its Signification is round, rotundity, particularly, an Ear-ring, Circular, Orbicular— little Gold or Silver-rings with an an Union, or Pearl Pendent.

II. It is a Waggon for carriage of Burdens. עגלה a Waggon, or Cart, either becauſe it was round or becauſe it revolves upon round Wheels; a Charriot, &c.

III. A Calf.

IV. It fignifies a Path of any Kind. מעגל a Path, a way worn with a Waggon or Carriage, a Carriage Way, an Orbit, a Wheel-Rut, &c. *Chald. Arab. Rab.* the fame. *Syr.* to roll, roll round, roll to, *C.* the fame, &c. *Chald.* מעגל a Mountebank, or Fortuneteller *D. D.*" Inſtead of attributing this Power to God, they, I doubt, attributed it to the material Agent, the Power, which executes this, by eating

Vol. II. H h and

418 MOSES's *Principia*.

and drinking the Products of thefe Actions, and by rejoycing, finging, and dancing in Circles. By the Nature of the Service, I fufpect this to be a compound Word of עג, or עוג, and גל. C. *Arab.* עג " a violent Windy Day, a murmuring muttering Noife — a Clamour — any thing that makes a Sound, or Noife, the Sound of any Vocal Inftrument. C. *Heb.* ענב an Organ. *Chald.* עוג to draw a Circle. *Æthiop.* ענת to furround, incompafs. M. גלל Its general Interpretation is a Sphere or Circle — to draw, or lead a round, to make a Rotation or Gyration." The fame as the Revolution of the Year, by the Rotation and Progreffion of the Earth, already mention'd. They offered burnt Offerings, and peace Offerings; they fat down to eat, and to drink, and rofe up צחק to play. Whether this be a Word for a particular Action of laughing or playing, or it be a general Word, and thofe after expreffive, or nearly the fame, as שחק, for *Sarah* יצחק, and the Child was fo called; but is alfo feveral times as *Amos* vii. 9. &c. called ישחק does not appear clearly; but Walton. Pol. Vol. I. of the Idioms of the Hebrew Tongue, p. 45. f. 11. צחק — fometimes fignifies to worfhip Idols, or to inftitute Dances in honour of them," and as already explained at

MOSES's *Principia.* 419

קֹשׁ: and *Joshua* heard their רֵעַ Noise; so רעם is Thunder; and Moses distinguished it to be the Voice of עֲנוֹת Singing. *Æthiop.* ענן " an Organ—a Singer." And saw the Dancing מחלת. *M.* חלל Its Signification is a Drum, a Pipe, and a Quire of Singers— to lead up a Dance, to play on a Pipe, to Dance or Trip it to the sound of the Pipe; thence חליל an Organ, *&c.* and thence מחלה a Chorus, and חוללים Dancers, Pipers, or Dancers to the Pipe. *C. Chald.* חליל a Pipe, חלילה a Reciprocal Revolution— from its Signification of Dancing because Dancers used to turn them round, and reciprocally return— מחול a Circuit. *Sam.* Heaven. *Æthiop.* חלי a Song, a Singer, of either Sex, a Cowherd or Herdsman.

This was paying a double Service, or Acknowledgment, to the Agent, the Spirit which impels, by vocal or wind Musick, and to the Light which directs the Force, expressing the Manner by Dancing in Circles. This shews from whence these Services came, and why the *Israelites* were commanded to pay them to God. And tho' they had several Sorts of Dances, I have already shewed, that one was to acknowledge the Power, and express the Manner of the Earth's Rotation, and Pro-

H h 2   gression

greſſion in expreſs Words. 1. *Par*. xvi. 31. *Pſa*. xcvi. 11. &c.

Ver. 15. --- And היו let them be למארת for Lights in the Firmament of Heaven, להאיר to give Light upon the Earth, and it was ſo.

Tho' there was a Precept to make a Marth an Inſtrument, to hold an Athth for dividing between the Day, and between the Night; and another, that they ſhould be for an Athth for Seaſons, for Days, and Years, theſe were not expreſſive enough; he was pleaſed to ſhew how this Action was to ſubſiſt, and how it was to make Seaſons, Days and Years; and we are ſtill to obſerve, here are no Repetitions in theſe Precepts, every thing ſaid before is included in every Speech. The Spirit was made the Inſtrument of Motion, and Light was produced; and that Action produces Expanſion, that ſupplies the Fire, &c. Every one, but Philoſophers, knows the Athth could not continue without Supply, no more than a Fire here without Wind, or Spirit;

and

and they cannot be supplied, except the Light be sent out, because they, and all the Streams of Light, are situated in the Expansion, and all is full where they are; and every Body will know, that nothing can bring the Spirit to the first, and the Light to the Branches of the Athth, and thence to the Earth, but that Operation; so *let them be*, let the Candlestick, the Spirit, and Light circulating, and in the Action of Fire in the Athth, and so the Light moving to, striking upon, and reflected from the Knops, Flowers, &c. in the Branches, be one Instrument of Light, as it is in the Day, when the Athth in the Sun over-rules all the rest; as you will find when he divides the Dominion of Day and Night; so let them be for a Flux; and so much as concerns the Earth, for Streams of Light, by the Expansion, to put all the intermediate Parts of Light in Motion, between them and the Earth. This includes all the Conditions and Actions; so here is a third Branch or descriptive Precept; let them be, or make, or form Matter for Fluxes, Streams, Instruments of Light, in or by the Expansion, &c. what, or how? as I said before,

before, the whole Number of Atoms was created at firſt: This muſt be either by Formation, in uniting or dividing of Atoms, or in Motion of them adhering, or looſe; ſo if they are to be Things compoſed of Atoms, or divided from Grains into Atoms, let them be made; if they are to be Actions, let them operate; if they are to be Motions of Things, let them move; if they are to be a complex Operation, or Motion of ſeveral Parts at once, and that the Effects, or Conſequences of the whole, be to do the Act; if all the Operations, of all the Hoſt of Heaven, were neceſſary to ſupply the Athth, to give Light upon the Earth, his Word included all, all worked for him, all obeyed his *Let:* If it be a Command, all was in Order to go on; If it be a Permiſſion, if they were Things, or Actions, to be by Continuation, let them continue; If they were to be by Succeſſion, let them ſucceed; If they were to be by Circulation, let them circulate, and by the Operation of the Expanſion, let them be in, or to the Athth, to ſupply them; ſo to give, or to ſend, or to move the Atoms of the Heavens, in that Condition called Light, from them, thro' all the Parts of the Firmament of Heaven, and to, or aginſt, or upon the Earth;

let

let this Operation, now divided into Lights, conjointly move in the Lines these Athths shall direct, or let Part of the Atoms be united, or adhere, be moved to the chief Athth, be divided, and be sent out continually, and successively, every way; so part directly to the Earth, and other Parts, first to the other Athths at the Orbs, and thence to the Earth, all to be Lights upon the Earth; every Atom of Light, between the Center and the Circumference, is concerned, and acts its Part; each is pushed forward by that next behind, and pushes forward that next before; and though some of them miss the Earth, and all the other Orbs, 'tis all to that Purpose; so in the Stream from the Sun which hits the Earth, every Atom is in the same Manner acted upon, and acts upon others, 'till the foremost successively act upon, illustrate, inflame the Earth, expand the Fluids, &c. so in each Stream from the Sun, which hits each Athth, every Atom acts in the same Manner; so in the Streams which shine, or recede from each of the other Athths to the Earth, each Atom acts in the same Manner; thus they light, and thus every Atom in the Stream is Part of the Instrument which lighs, heats, &c. otherwise we must

must suppose, that the Matter acting in the Æthths, notwithstanding a *Vacuum* between, could affect our Eyes, the Earth, &c. or we must suppose, as they do, that a small Quantity of Matter can be infinitely divided, and infinitely extended; and that the Orb of the Sun, from its own Substance, gives Light which fills all enligtened Space, and so extends further and further; at the same Rate, they say, it would be in coming from the Sun hither, (and so slowlier, as the Angels widen) towards Infinity. For all their Cant about luminous Bodies, and I know not what *Rosicrucian* Metamorphoses, these are Fluxes of the smallest Parts of a Fluid, and not of Atoms formed for solid Bodies; there is not any thing which, in this Respect, can be changed; there is not an Atom of any other Sort of Matter, which can become an Atom of Light; to give without receiving, is the Attribute only of God; every Parcel of Matter, or formed Creature, has received all it has, and if it gives any thing, it is so much less; if it at once, or in Succession gives, without Supply, as many of its Parts as are equal to the whole, it ceases to be what it was made by Formation to be; if what the chief

Marth

Marth or Candlestick sends out, had been from its own Body, without Supply, that must long before this Time, nay in a very short Time, have wasted it, and filled other Parts fuller; and have made such Alterations, as would have overturned the Machine, and altered the Course of other Things, and soon put an End to Motion; nothing less than the whole Heavens, or Airs, can supply the Athth in it, because it moves the whole every Moment; nothing can move, except all be so full, that that Motion can raise a Compression; no Motion would commence, or continue, except there were small Bodies, of different Sizes, in every Place or Part of that Fluid, and those in some Places or Parts, smaller than those in others; and that State and Motion cannot continue, except they adhere towards the Extremities, and be divided at the Center. So here, what things soever were each at a Distance from the Earth, and whatever was between each of them and the Earth, were all to prosecute the End of Lightening, Warming, &c. of the Earth; and though the Lights were formed, or interrupted at the Orbs; and though the Athths in or upon, the Orbs were Light, yet they were not
Light

Light to the Earth; though the Streams between were Light, yet no Part, but those which touched the Earth, was Light to the Earth, and each Part has its proper Name. Those three Words, the מארת which expresses the Order of Orbs for Fire and Light; and the אתת which expresses the Fire at the Sun, and all the Streams of Light between that and each other Orb, and that in a Cap upon each Orb, and the מאורת which expresses the Instrument Light, which includes the whole, all the Flux and Refluxes of Light, most especially that to the Earth, can never be used again, nor any of them, without Distinction by other Words, or by Letters, so as to vary, gender, or *&c.* because it is described in a new Manner, and more distinctly in the next Verses.

Ver. 15. ------ ויהי כן and it was *(is)* so.

He spake the Word, and it was made; he commanded, and it came to pass; but the Word כן, as already explained, says much more *than it was so*, and is the going Machine called Nature.

Ver. 16. And God made את־שני המארת הגדלים two great Lights, את־המאור הגדל the greater Light to rule the Day, *(for the Rule of the Day, &c.)* ואת־המאור הקטן and the lesser Light to rule the Night, ואת הכוכבים he made the Stars also.

I must beg Leave to make this Grammar, Sense and Truth. He has already given a Relation of the making of the Candlestick, with Branches, Knops, Flowers, &c. and of the Fire, and ultimately of the Light, which forms Day; before this the Night was as it was called Darkness; he is now telling you how, and what Provision God made for a Share of this Light for the Night; here is no Repetition, שני is not two, but a second or secundary; and מארת though there be two *Vaus* in the *Samar. Pent.* is, as before, singular, the Distinction from the Candlestick, which had the Aththt, the Fire, this had it from the other, and so,

as

as we say, at second Hand; upon misconstruing this hangs that idle Story in *Targ. Jon.* of the two Luminaries being equal, and after 21 Years of the Moon's being made less; נדלים is not an Adjective plural depending upon מארת, but a Term in Astronomy descriptive of the Courses and Changes of the Moon, and so the great Attribute of the Heavens, for producing that Motion or Course of the Orb of the Moon, which with the Orbs of the Stars in the Night, is the secondary Candlestick. The Heathens called that Temple at *Babel*, we render Tower, and many more afterward, by this Name; one or two of several of the Representations which had been made of this by the Heathens, was ordered to be made by the Jews, *Deut.* xxii. 12. rendered *Fringes*, lat. *funiculos*, which were to be fixed by each upon the four Skirts of his Vesture; and 1 *Kings* vii. 17. *Wreaths of Chainwork for the Chapiters which were upon the Top of the Pillars.* Whether that mentioned, *Numb.* xv. 38, 39. by the Word ציצת, rendered *Fringe*, lat. *fimbria*, be as the Translators have taken it, the same, is not clear.

The Natives of *Canaan* had some Sort of a Chain or Collar, which the great Men wore about their Necks, call'd ענק, and they thence, *Anakims*. So Kings had in other Places; *Pharaoh* gave one to *Joseph*. C. *Æthiop*. To put a Chain, Neck-lace, or Collar about the Neck, *Gen.* xli. 42. and 1 *Kings* xii. 14.——a Turtle——a Ring-Dove, and ענד has much the same Signification; whether this represented the Course of the Earth, or Moon, or both, deserves to be consider'd.

B. C. סהרנין little Moons, a kind of Ornaments, so call'd from their resembling the Moon, סהרוניא בר מן, *besides the Moons*. *English* Bible, Ornaments, *Judg.* viii. 26. Although *Rabbi Solomon* puts for it עונקיא. In the *Jerusalem Talmud*, c. 6. of the Sabbath, ענקיא, Chains, a Collar, &c.

Ibid. ענק a Collar, Neck-lace,——*Judg.* viii. 26. *Isa.* iii. 19.

Was not the Translation of this Text, one of the false Constructions which the *Jews* had put upon the Law? Have we not this from their LXX. *Targums*, and all the rest? Has any one search'd the Scriptures, to alter the Faults in their Translations? Have we not taken their Traditions, Rules of Grammar, and Pointing, which,

perhaps,

perhaps, were all writ since Christ forewarn'd us? He only shew'd us a few of the moral Precepts which they had perverted; but can any Thing tend so much to make the Law of none Effect, as to make it pass for granted, that the Writer was not only fallible, but ignorant.

Now this common Jest of the Coffee-houses is lost, that *Moses* had made the Moon a great Light; and that they who knew better, had shew'd, that it had its Light from the Sun; and notwithstanding the Precedence they have given to the Opinion of these Men, as they thought, tho' of *Aratus*, and the idle Stories they have cited from him, and others collected in *Vossius de Orig. & Prog. Idol.* Lib. II. p. 200, and 201. of the Moon being habitable, and having Creatures in it, &c. we must trust *Moses*, that 'tis but a secondary Candlestick, a Sconce to reflect the Light from the Sun to the Earth.

After he has made the Distinction, described the making one, and then the making of a second Candlestick, he tells you the chief Instrument of Light was for the Rule of the Day; and the inferior for the Rule of the Night, with the Stars; and 'tis of great Importance to observe, that after this, as I hinted before, thro' all the Bible,

Bible, these three Words are changed in Gender, and in Termination; the first, which has no Plural, in the Singular, and the second and third each in the Singular, and consequently in the Plural; מארת which after this is found but once, is chang'd to מאר: And the Word אחת is found אותות and אות אתין אתן איתן איתין: אותיות איתנים אתונות: And the Word מאורת is found מאור, and in the Plural מאורי, and מאורים; this was, and is the Giver of Light, the God of the *Chaldeans*, mention'd *Gen.* xv. 7. from whom the Lord took *Abram*; and in the Tabernacle and Temple, where they use this Word, for that which represented it there, 'tis as generally, when a Word is not understood, render'd variously, as *Exod.* xxv. 6. שמן למאר *Oil for the Luminary* (*V.* to supply the Luminaries. *S.* to make a Light. *Ibid.* xxvii. 20.—*Pure Oil-Olive beaten* למאור *for the Luminary* להעלת *to cause Light to ascend always.* xxxv. 14. *and* מנרת *the Candlestick* המאור *of the Luminary* (*V.* to keep up the Luminaries, *S.* of the Light.)—*and the Oil* למאור *for the Luminary* (*V.* to feed the Fire. *S.* the Light.) *Lev.* xxiv. 2. למאור *for the Luminary.* (*S. V.* for the Light.) Applied to other Things, *Psal.* xc. 8. למאור פניך *in the*

the *Light of thy Countenance.* (*V. S.* האיר *the Illumination.*) Applied to the Things; *Ezek.* xxxii. 8. *All* מאורי אור *Enlightenings of Light* (*all the Instruments of Light*) *in the Airs. Eccl.* xii. 2. *and* האור *the Lights, and* הירח *the Moon, and* הככבים *the Stars.* 2 *Kings* xxiii. 5. לשמש *to the Sun, and* לירח *to the Moon, and* למזולות *to the Stars.* (*V.* the twelve Signs; *S.* the Planets) *Ps.* lxxiv. 16. הכינות מאור ושמש. *Thou didst machine the Instrument of Light and the Stream from the Sun. Ps.* cxxxvi. 7. who made the great אורים *Lights. Prov.* iv. 18. *like Light that shines, proceeds, and flows.* This describes the Manner of its Progress. The next shews what their God *Shemosh* was, *Jer.* xxxi. 35. *who gives the* שמש *for the Light of the Day;* (or, *who makes the Shemosh be the Day-Light.*) חקת *the appointed Courses* (&c.) ירח *of the Moon, and* בוכבים *of the Stars, to be Light by Night. Isa.* lx. 19. *The* שמש *shall be no more thy Light by Day; neither* הירח *the Moon* יאיר *shine* לנגה *a Light unto thee.* 2 *Sam.* xxiii. 4. *like the Morning-Light He shall arise;* (*like*) *the* שמש. *Isa.* lviii. 10. *Thy Light shall* זרח *arise in the Darkness.* Here אור and מאורי *includes* האור and מאור. The Flux and Stream of *Shemosh,* which flow from the Sun against the Earth, up-

on

on that Hemisphere where it is Day; and that Part of the Instrument of Light which is without, and issuing streight from the Sun, and the *Shemosh*, is the same; and ירח is the Flux, or Stream of Light, which flows from the Moon against the Earth, and enlightens it in the Night; and so הכבבים and מזלות, that which flows from the Planets or Stars, against the Earth, or helps to enlighten it on that Hemisphere, where 'tis Night, are the same.

The Historian, in a Series, gives us his revealed Relation of the Acts of God, of forming the Light and the Spirit, producing an Expansion, &c. and then what that Agent had done pursuant to his *Fiats*, in forming this Instrument with a Root, and the Branches for a Candlestick to hold the Fire in the Center, and a Cap of Light upon the Knop of each Branch, all in the Expansion; and next in placing the Matter in the Action of Fire, in the Chief; and the Action of Light between that, and upon each of the rest, in the said Expansion of Heaven, where there was Spirit to supply the Fire, send out the Light, &c. Then makes all concur to be one Instrument or Machine, to give Light in the Day; then appoints a fubordinary Candleftick which was but at the End of a Branch, and received its Light from the Athth in the Chief, to be itinerant, and from that given Light, and that upon the Stars, (which fome think were reprefented by polifhed Stones, or &c. fixed in the Ceiling of the Tabernacle) alfo given to give Light to the Hemifphere of the Earth, which fhould in Succeffion be Night; he firft defcribes and explains the Spring, and then the Wheels one by one in Succeffion, makes the Watch go firft in one Motion, defcribes the Ufe each Part was for, as he goes, divides between the Day and between the Night, for the Ufes then proper; after divides the Spring, and makes it into Variety of Springs, and makes an additional Set of Wheels for Regulators, to make it fhew Seafons, and Days, and Years; and immediately after, as fhewed in the firft Part, attributes all thofe Operations to his Mafter, which befides the Caution againft ferving them, is alfo explanatory; though he has told you, that the Agent had made the Orbs, and the Athths, as they fay, the Orb of the Sun, and the Fire there; the Orb of the Moon, and the Cap of Light upon half of the Orb; the Orbs of the Planets and Stars, and the

Cap

Cap of Light, or Aththt on each of them: He besides those made Fluxes or Streams of Light from each: He divides them here, and tells you their Uses. He says God made, and he might truly say, that he made, because he both created and formed them; but as since the Creation there has been no Atom or Thing created or annihilated, nor does any of the Atoms lose, or alter their Figure, or Space; to make the Instruments to hold Athths here mentioned, is to put the Atoms designed for each of them together. He created the Sorts of Matter, each in proper Places, gave its respective Atoms Existence there, and formed those Atoms into Orbs, by the Firmament, and then gave the Athths Existence there; and successively made Light, by dividing the Atoms adhering in Grains: For the Operation of the Fire is nothing more than dividing, or dissolving the Combination of the Parts, or Atoms; and so by the Force of the Firmament, made Circulations of Spirit to, and Light from the Athths, and thence Streams of Light thro' the Firmament of Heaven: For where a material Fluid is an Agent, is in Action, and has Power and Force, to be in the Fluid is to be in the Direction, or to be worked upon or moved by the Laws, Power and Force of that Agent, in that Action or Motion: And the Atoms of the Air, when so divided and made fit for Light, acquire no new Properties of Heat, or &c. but when separated by the Interposition of the Earth, or kept separate from the Grains, returning towards the Sun by the Interposition of the Earth, have that Effect upon other Things by their Sizes, Motion, Impulse, and Pervasion, which they call Heat; so God made two great Instruments to hold each an Athth, and it is presumed, nay visible, that each Athth is proportionate to the Size of the Instrument which was to hold it. And that the Power of each is in Proportion to the Action, or Emission of Light, be it from Fire, or from a Reflexion. The Stream of Light from the greater and more powerful to rule the Day, and the Stream from the lesser and less powerful, with the Streams from the small Orbs and Athths, to rule the Night; and afterwards in the Day, and in the Night, the great Stream, and all the lesser Streams, were to rule upon Earth, in two equal Divisions, exchanging continually, and exchanged in every Rotation of the Earth, variable and varied continually for, or by the Seasons; and they

they were to rule all Matter, in and upon the Earth, each in a different Manner in each Part, during each of their floating Possession, with those alternate and different Effects hinted at before, and many others. The Word לממשלת to rule, to have Dominion over, to have Power over, to dilate, extend, and by the Force of the Spirit to lead, to direct the March, or Root, not only of the Globes, but of every Part to the smallest Atom of Matter, as *Job* xxv. 1. *Who maketh Peace in his high Places. Is there any numbering of his Troops? And on what does not his Light arise?* implies, that the Ruler, Viceroy, gives something to the Subjects of his Master for Obedience, either Estates to live on, or Wages, or Food, or Protection, or Direction, so as his Government is to be for the Benefit of the whole; and he is supposed to have Directions from his Master, to set Laws, or Rules to their Actions, and to judge and divide between them; hence these Expostulations. *Jer.* xxxi. 37. *Thus saith Jehovah; if the Heavens above can be measured, or the Foundations of the Earth be fathomed beneath.* Ibid. xxxiii. 22. *The Host of the Airs cannot be numbered, nor the Sand of the Sea measured.* Isa. xl. 21. *Hath it not been told you from the*

Beginning? Will ye not understand the Foundations (the Materials) *of the Earth? He sitteth upon the Sphere of the Earth, and the Inhabitants thereof are as Grashoppers: He extendeth the Heavens as it were a light frothy Substance, and spreadeth them out as a Tent to dwell in: That bringeth Princes to nothing, that maketh the Judges of the Earth as* תהו *Vanity* (loose unformed Matter. And *Job* xxxviii. 33. *Knowest thou the Ordinances of Heaven? canst thou set the Dominion thereof in the Earth?* The chief Lord gives every Thing, and what he has put into the Hands of these Rulers, his Subjects, by him constituted Governors, he gives by their Hands, (which in Propriety of speaking, notwithstanding the learned Cavils, are his Hands) to the rest of his Subjects in this Empire. The Heathens, as aforesaid, thought they were to rule all Things, nay, the very Minds, Actions, and Fortunes of Men; that is still to God, not included in this Grant; so God was pleased here to shew how far their Dominion went, to put an end to their Mistakes, and that they were only to rule the Day and the Night, and the Matter in them; and as some since have got Notions of Bodies ruling at distance by Properties, sending forth *Effluvia*, and

I know

I know not what Whims; that thefe Governors were limited in their Dominion, that they neither governed nor affected any thing, but what they touched, and that even their Force was limited; that the Fluid acts, and not the Solid, and how it acts, tho' other Words before thefe have fettled this Point; We fhould alfo confider how the Cafe ftood between the two Governors, the Word גדל fignifies greateft, chiefeft, Majority, of Lights the moft glorious, more honourable in Quality or Power; and the Word קטן fignifies Minority, as well as lefs in Quantity; and a Minor is as a Servant, has nothing of his own, and is put under the Gouernment of a Major; and here, where fpeaking of Governors, or Officers, it fignifies Inferiority; the Chief has the Command of the Forces, and the inferior Officers have their Power from him, and are fubject to him, and they act by Direction of the Chief; and I fuppofe that is the Cafe here: The great Light gives Part of the Power to govern, by communicating Parts of the Light, which is the Authority; he puts Part of the Dominion into each of their Hands, and fo Part of the Forces under each of their Command.

Ver. 17. And God יִתֵּן set (*gave, placed, constituted, substituted*) them in the Firmament of Heaven, לְהָאִיר to give (*act the Part of*) Light upon the Earth.

Ver. 18. And to rule בְּיוֹם over (*in*) the Day and over (*in*) the Night, and to divide the Light from the Darkness, (*between the Light and between the Darkness*) and God saw that it was good.

God placed them, the Marths, the Orbs, each of proper Sizes, and at proper Distances, which was the chief Point to settle Proportion and Time; and the Athths in or upon them, each to issue proper Quantities, and each of the Fluxes, and so Streams to be of proper Force, one from every Side into the whole Firmament of Heaven, and each of the rest, except what comes by Reflections from one another, only from one Side; all the Orbs, Athths, Fluxes, and Streams in the Expansion in that Operation, in that

that immensly strong Motion, and so by that Operation to act the Part, perform the Offices of Light upon the Earth; as they are Matter, he placed the Orbs, some fixed or moving slowly, some in moving and circular Stations; he placed, ranged, disposed or applied the Athths as Agents, with Action to attend the Orbs in proper Places, at proper Distances from each other, and from the Earth, that the respective Operations might perform their respective Tasks. He put the Parts of Light in Fluxes, and so in Streams, Parts of them as Governors in Possession, appointed them their Range, and the Bounds of their Empire, placed their Rendezvous in the Heart of their Empire, in their Palace, on their Throne, (which I hope, without Offence, in the Sense aforesaid may be, as it is called, God's Throne,) from whence almost half of them are continually marching, and whither almost the other half of them, as Spirit, are continually countermarching; and placed several smaller Camps, some itinerant in Circuits, and many fixed, whither smaller Numbers are continually detached, so that all are always upon Duty to supply these Streams, which hit and act the Part of Light upon the Earth; and vested ed them with the operating Power of the Expanfion, by which they were to execute their Charge to flow, or circulate Light againft the Earth, to rule in the Day, and in the Night, and to divide the Light from the Darkneſs; tho' the Word Heaven mean the ſame Matter here, as it did at firſt, and all along, yet it does not mean, that the Matter is in the ſame Condition, it is not only Heaven, but a Firmament, and calling it a Firmament includes all the Conditions, Motions, and Actions of the Parts, which make it a Firmament, in every Part, where there is either Orb of Sun, Moon, or Star, or whither any of their Fluxes, or Streams of Light reach, and every Atom of the immenſe Space (as Space is determined above) is comprehended under the Name Heaven; and every Atom of it, which is kept fluid by this Operation, is Part of the Firmament of Heaven; and 'tis ſo full, that nothing elſe but its ſelf, and the Bodies and Fluids which are placed, and incloſed in it, can be there. I ſuppoſe the Atoms are each of the ſame Size and Figure, becauſe if they had differed in that, they would have differed in Names; but ſome Atoms adhering, or united in Grains, ſome of more Atoms, ſo larger; ſome of

fewer

fewer Atoms, so smaller; and some Atoms independent; and that here, near the Earth's Surface, there may be in the Day one sixtieth Part in Quantity which will not pass the Pores of Glass, and so several Degrees smaller; as '10'. 9'. 8'. &c. till those of single Atoms, of which Grains some will not pass the Pores of some sort, of Solids, some pass the Pores of one sort, others of other Solids, or Fluids, and the Units or single Atoms those of all others, but not those of their own Grains: Nearer the Sun, which makes Light by dividing the Grains, and issuing the Atoms, there are more and more single Atoms, farther from it more combined ones; here more single Atoms in Day than in Night, and more in Summer than in Winter; and near the rest of the Orbs, which we suppose only takes them from the *Shemosh*, and gives it, or sends it out in near the same Condition, as they had it given, the Proportions must differ as each is in distance from the Sun, the Size of the Orb, &c. And their Streams outward hither must be in said Proportion, and in Proportion to their Distances; and tho' they so divide it into many Streams, the Light is but all one; and being moved from one to another, it may still be put single, so the

Precept to all preceding, and laſtly to the Streams, to prepare, ſend, drive, give, be, or act the Part of Light, or Lights, upon the Earth, makes the Lght no way appropriated to any ſingle Meaning, otherwiſe than that it is the Sun, the Offſpring of Fire: 'Tis not only making the Heavens in ſuch a Condition, that Man and other Creatures might ſee; and tho' all the other Attributes and Actions, for which it was ſo univerſally, tho' unjuſtly ſerved and worſhiped, are impiouſly attributed to Words for imaginary Properties, ſuch as Attraction, &c. it was then called *Shemoſh*, and was, and is now the Atoms of the Heavens ſucceſſively diſſolved out of Grains, at the Sun, and moving in its Courſe from the Sun, the ſhorteſt Way in every Line, to the Extremities of the Heavens, or interrupted by the Earth, Planets, or Stars; and ſo making the Airs on the Side of the Earth next the Sun in ſmaller Grains than thoſe on the other Side of the Earth, making what our learned Men call a *Vacuum*; and ſo giving the Spirit, the groſs Grains, an Opportunity continually to puſh it about, and forward; and thereby the Parts of Light have an Opportunity, beſides what thoſe ſucceſſively left on the dark

dark Side of the Earth do alternately, to operate upon Vegetables, and Animals directly; 'tis doing every thing which is done by sending the Light, and by the Light when 'tis sent, or which it gives any thing an Opportunity to do; it has here on the Face of the Earth next the Sun, as much Strength left as that Light, at the same Distance, which misses the Earth, and other Orbs, and is pushed on to the Extremities of the Heavens. This is one of its Manners of ruling, which has determined the Meaning of the Word or Phrase, to Light upon the Earth. If we attempt to describe Heat, we may assert, that there must be small Bodies which can enter, and pervade Pores; put into Motion by some Agent, and continued and supplied by the same, or some other Agent, and perhaps there must be the thing acted upon, or heated; there is the Substances of those small Bodies, their Motion, and the Effect that Motion has upon the Thing acting, upon those small Bodies backward, and upon the Thing it, or they by it act upon forward. The Effects that behind has upon that which operates upon the small Bodies, and which the small Bodies in Action have upon themselves, is each always in some
Degree

Degree the same; the Effects they have upon other Things are differenced by the Difference of the Things; besides being the Cause and Director of the Motion of the great Bodies, this Action of these small Bodies raises Vapours for Springs, and makes them collect, issue, and form Currents to carry them down again, and those for Rains; makes them form Drops, and fall, raises Part of them again from the Surface, some Parts thro' the Tubes of Vegetables, and so carries on Water for Drink, and Vegetation for Food, for Life; are not these couch'd under that Speech? Is not this Part of their Dominion? Is all this a Property? Have not the different Sizes of the Grains, which constitute the including Fluid, their Effects upon each other Part of the Body, and upon all other Bodies and Fluids they inclose, as well as upon the Eyes from that Degree in which the Waters become solid, and no Vegetable or Animal can live through all the Degrees, till you come to the *Focus* of a Burning-glass, which dissolves the Adhesion of any Thing? Nay, lest Art should have any Share till it come to Lightening, which, for the Time, infinitely exceeds that of a Glass; nay, without such Accidents, nothing is
hid,

hid, or escapes being touch'd or acted upon by those small Bodies in Motion; tho' they do not, in some Places, produce Light, they produce some Degree of Heat, and many other Effects in all.

After the Precept or Declaration of the Manner of their Action, and of their Uses, to light, or give Light upon the Earth, which, in plain, is all they did or do, I mean, that Action by which they give Light upon the Earth, is all they do; and is the same Action as that which gives Light from the Center to the Circumference, to the Extremities of the Heavens on every Side: Though the Earth interrupts but a little of that at once, nor of that which is return'd in Streams from the other Athths; yet here is a Continuation of Precepts, or an historical Declaration that he set them for those Ends. He had divided their Employment, appointed one to rule the Day, and the others to rule the Night; here he tells you they were to rule in the Day, and in the Night; they were not only constantly to give, but to give it for such Lengths of Time, in such Places, and with such Variations, so as to produce proper Effects, alternately, upon every thing solid or fluid, upon or within in the Earth. If the Orb and Athth of the Sun could have been moved about the Earth, the Stream from it could have had no Dominion over the Day, nor that from the Moon, or &c. over the Night, to divide between Day and between Night, and so for Seasons, Days, or Years: For we can easily shew, that if the Sun had moved with that Velocity, necessary to go round the Earth, in the same Time as the Earth turns one round, it would scarce give us Light enough to see here, and none for any other Uses; and perhaps it would shew a Tail like a Comet. And 'tis as easy to shew, on the contrary, that the Orbs of those Stars which are fixed, or move infinitely slow, will receive and emit, or reflect greater Streams of Light, than those which are in swift Motion, Sizes and Distances considered. But if the Orb of the Sun do not move, as none of the Antiens ever dreamed, or any of the inspired Writers ever said it did, as we have seen, and shall see by and by; either this Alteration in the Fluid, on each Side of this Globe, must be the Cause of its Motion, and the Power which governs the Hemispheres alternately, and every Thing in them; for both these Actions are given in Charge to the same Agents: Or else

Pro-

Projection or Attraction, or Names for some Causes, which no body knows any thing of, must govern them, and every thing in them; and the Sun, &c. does but hold the Candles. Tho' it be not my Business now to measure the Strength of the Power, or the Weakness of each Part of this Fluid, which gives Opportunities to the Spirit to produce Motion, and by making several such weak Parts to direct or vary that Motion: Whether the Light proceed all from the Sun, and the other Orbs should be purely passive, placed or moved to return Streams in proper Directions, or the Light at each of those Athths receive some Increase or Strength; the Stream from the Sun to the Earth will still rule by Day; because the Motion of that Light is so much stronger than that from the Moon or Stars, that it, in a great Measure, diverts their reflected Streams; and the Streams from the Moon and Stars strike upon the Earth in the Night, because the Earth interposed, interrupts the Motion of the *Shemosh*, and hinders it from diverting the Streams from the Moon, Planets and Stars. And this Government consists in what is before called dividing, in taking from the Night. and giving to the Day, on one Side of the Horizon; and in taking from the Day, and giving to the Night, on the other Side of the Horizon, on the East and West Sides, or in the Rotation; and at the same Time, in taking from the Night and giving to the Day on one Side of the Horizon: and taking from the Day and giving to the Night on the other Side of the Horizon, on the North and South Sides, or in its Declination. And as בדל is a Segment, so in the Rotation on the East and West, and in the Declination on the North and South, there is successively a Segment divided, from the first and given to the second; and a Segment of the same Size, divided from the second and given to the first; and, as hinted before, to carry on their different Dominion in Fluids, Vapours, Vegetables, and Animals in the Day and in the Night. The other Expression, *between the Day and between the Night*, might have made one suppose that this Agent had nothing to do but to divide; and after it had divided, to have had nothing to do in the Ground, in the Premises on either Side; But this determines that they were to rule in, as well as between; and, I hope, I shall sometime have

have an Opportunity to shew, that fitting Things even from the Sizes and Figures of the Atoms, to the complicated Parts of Vegetables, Animals, &c. each Sort of them, and each Sort of the Fluids in them composed of proper Sorts of said Atoms, so as they might be governed by this Agent, was, what Chance, or the settled Operation of the Agent, could have no Hand in; all that was there, or were to be there, was contrived and framed by God to be subject to this Operation. The remaining Precept, or Reason why he set them in the Firmament, was to divide between the Light and between the Darkness. At first, when there was but one Light, and no Orbs but the Earth, there was only the Matter formed in Grains near the Extremities, and there, in that State of Darkness, to be returned to that Light or Fire; melted, and others successively, by being carried off, and uniting the small Parts formed into Grains, and making them Darkness, at the Circumference or Verge; so taking from the Darkness, and making it Light, and taking from the Light, and making it Darkness. This, except that small Quantity continually returning to the Backside of the Globe, which is Part of it, and proceeds as the Earth removes; and the Parts of Light which were passing outward, which for want of proper Motion seemed dark, and were driven forward by those interrupted on the Foreside, as the Earth removed, was then the only way of dividing between the Light and between the Darkness. After God at *Ver.* 5. had named the Air on the Hemisphere of the Globe, from which the Passage of the Light was succesfiely interrupted by the Interposition of the Earth, Night; and that Hemisphere which interrupted the Light, Day, in Distinction to other Light, and to other Darkness, which being a very small Proportion, in Quantity to the whole, and is really dark, he speaks no more of them under the old Names, but under the new, as at *Ver.* 14. and when in the Repetition he speaks of that Action, *Ver.* 17. he repeats the same Words to divide between the Day and between the Night, and the very next Words, between the Light and between the Darkness, which if it was meant of Day and Night, would be a needless Tautology here, when he speaks of the still remaining Darkness, the Air, at the Verge or Circumference of the Heavens beyond the fixed Stars; whither

the

the Light moves but in a small Degree, both in respect of its Distance, of its being diffused by the widening of every Degree, and by its becoming languid in Motion, and so by Degrees adhering or uniting into Grains, and becoming dark; as is evident by viewing the most distant Stars with the best Glasses: And the Units of Light adhere into Grains, in the Manner beautifully expressed by *Job* xxxvii. 16. and in the same Manner as Grains of all other Sorts of Matter are formed, and as already explained. But now this Operation is of several Kinds, in many Places, and to several Uses, by the Compression of the Firmament, to bring the Parts of Darkness from the Circumference to the Center, where there is Light and Fire, and less Resistance, to divide them by Fire, by squeezing to carry the Matter so divided from the Center to the Circumference, and reform them by Compression into Grains. To divide the Streams of Light which hit the Orbs, and are hindred from going directly to the Extremities of the Heavens, by Interposition in keeping back the Darkness behind, from returning into them, so that these Streams or Currents might be separated and continued, or reflected, or returned to the Earth; besides all its Actions in and upon the Earth, which belong not to this Part; so that without the Providence of God in the Contrivance and Operation of this Machine, not the least Pile of Grass is formed, nor a Hair of ones Head falls to the Ground.

Ver. 17. ---- And God saw that it was טוב good.

He had pronounced before that the Light was good; the Earth was good; the Vegetables were good; and that the Spirit, the Power, and Light, the Orbs, Athths, Fluxes, and Streams, as put together, and kept going by the Expansion, were pronounced well or rightly put together, and set agoing, so as to act mechanically; and when God has related what he did on his Part, then pronounced to be good. Where is the Difference? I have hinted at the Difference between the Contrivance, Preparation, and Placing of the Matter, and the Action of the Agent in putting each Parcel of Matter together, and the Effects of its Motion; so the Acts of the Agent were כי explained already, and the Acts of God in in this Affair were טוב good. But this is not all, God has made thefe, Governors, Judges, Dividers, and Diftributers, and the Relation is between them and his, and as far as their Commiffion went, their Subjects: And they are in an eminent Degree clothed with Beauty and Glory, vefted with vaft Power, poffeffed of vaft Riches, and mechanically framed to be beneficent to their Subjects, and to divide and diftribute all they in that Refspect want equally.

If this Hiftory, in the Senfe it is explained, agrees not with the Relations which *Mofes* in other Places, or other Prophets have given of thofe Things, it will ftill be fuggefted, that this is not truly explained, or that either this, or his other, or theirs, is not true; and there will be Grounds for fuch Suggeftions, till fome general Errors in the Tranflation of the Bible concerning the Names, Motions and Actions of the Orbs and Fluids, or Patients and Agents, be rectified: which Miftakes were introduced by taking foolifh Notions from the *Greek* Philofophers, and making them the Philofophy of the Times, of the Tranflations of the Bible, who when they by——— had loft their natural Religion, and with it their Philofophy, divided into Sects, and each fell to work to fupply their Ignorance of the Truth, which is fhort and intelligible, by ftudied Jingles of infignificant Words: That Bodies acted where they were not prefent by Sympathy and Antipathy, by innate Virtues, Miffion of *Effluvia*; and confounding all Diftinction, by calling Things, and imagined Properties, Virtues, Influences, and *Effluvia* by the fame Names; fo that the Body may be locally in one Place, potentially or vertually, or by its *Effluvia* in every Place, within what they imaginarily call the Sphere of its Activity: That a Body of certain Dimenfion can continually fend forth Parts of its own Matter, which can be infinitely divided and infinitely extended, and fo form unbounded Quantities of *Effluvia*, and infinite Virtues and Powers, without diminifhing the Body in Virtue, Dimenfion, Solidity, or Quantity; and all this geometrically: And thefe Notions of *Effluvia*, Properties, &c. have made Men tranflate, and write, and fpeak fo uncertainly, that they have taken what they accounted *Effluvia*, as Parts of the Body, and thereby miftaken a few Names in the Tranflation; and in Complaifance to the

then

then Philosophers, who were in the same Scrape, by those Mistakes in the Translations, led the World into a Notion, that the Orb of the Sun moved about the Earth: So later Languages following their Translations, and so mistaking the *Shemosh* for the Orb or *Athth* of the Sun, made this Confusion between Philosophy and Scripture. The Readers of Scripture observ'd, that the *Shemosh*, which they thus took for the Sun, was said to move in Circles, or go and return; and some Texts in Scripture speaking of the Earth's Firmness, they were desirous to reconcile them. The Orb of the Sun seeming to move, as Land does from a Ship under Sail, so translated the Sun to move, and the Earth to stand still; thence the Christians oppos'd those who retriev'd the Knowledge of the Sun's standing still, and the Earth's moving: But tho' they retriev'd the Knowledge of the Motion of the Earth, the whole Translation being suited to the contrary, they could not then retrieve the Knowledge of the Cause of the Earth's Motion; and were as much perplexed with occult Qualities as ever: And tho' this Mistake was made by Philosophers of the same Principles with the present, for this Piece of Complaisance to those,

these,

these, in the Way of their Gratitude, have destroy'd the Authority of the Bible. Some Time after they had recover'd the Knowledge that the Earth mov'd, they observ'd, that it was not the Sun, but the Matter of the Heavens which the Scripture said was circulated; this drew Mr. *Des Cartes* into forming of *Vortices*, and he thought to have stole it, and have made a System of it, and great Matters were expected for a while; and if he had declar'd what he aim'd at, perhaps he might have been helped out; but 'tis observable, that how capable soever any one is before he make such an Attempt, after that they lose their common Faculties, and so the *Circuens* or *Gyrans* turn'd his Head; when that could not be made intelligible, they relapsed into occult Qualities, and the Expressions about the *Shemosh*, Attracting, &c. which others took for the Sun, of which hereafter, drew them into the Mistake of Attraction; and the only Reason that ever was given for coming into it is, we cannot be without a Philosophy, and though we know no Cause but Words, we must keep them till we get a better.

There are now four Things translated so as to be taken for one; the Body of the Sun render'd great Light; the Athth of of the Sun render'd Sun; the Stream of Light from the Athth of the Sun to the Earth, which is render'd greater Light: The Flux (including that Stream) of Light from the Athth of the Sun on every Side, to the Extremities of the Heavens, and so half of the Matter of the whole Heaven, which is render'd Sun. The first, is the Philosopher's Sun, a round Mass of Matter, bounded and passive where it is, and cannot act where it is not present. The second the hot Athth, which is the Atoms of the Grains of Air, or Spirit, successively press'd in by the Firmament, melted by the Action of Fire, and that melted press'd outward; and this Matter, under this Name, only acts in the Pores of that Body, and at a small Distance about its Surface, where it is present, and while it is in Form of Fire, or Flame. Indeed, it may be said of this, as of a Wheel in a Machine, that by the intermediate Parts of the Heavens going to, and coming from, it acts upon the whole Creation; and that the Matter which composes it is continually changing, or changed; yet neither of these will hinder the Distinction. The third is that Part of the Matter of the Heavens which is put into Motion from the said Fire, in Form of Light, and successively hits the Earth, whose

whose End is called Light, to which the Government of and in the Day is given. The fourth is the Matter of the Heavens, thus put in Motion from this Fire in form of Light, to the Circumference on each Side, (the said Stream included) and with respect to itself, each Grain or Atom of it acts upon those next adjoining, for the Time being; and with respect to all other Matter included in it, the Parts which immediately, and so successively touch each, act upon it.

Tho' I have already touched upon this in a few Instances, I must take a little more time to clear these Points, and not only distinguish between the Names which God gave the several Things, but between the Names of Attribute which the Heathens, in their Sense, gave to each, and between the Names which God, when he claimed the Attributes the Heathens had given to each as his, theirs being his, or in that Sense. When there was a vast Number of Orbs and Athths, one great Flux, so Streams between, and smaller Fluxes of Light from each, with each of the Ends of their Streams reaching to the Earth to be made, each sort had a general Name, without any other Distinction than that of the greater and

less

less of two: When any one of the Prophets saw it necessary to speak of any one of them particularly, he must give it a Name; after the Formation of the Orbs which are perfectly passive, neither People nor Prophets had any thing to do with, or say of any of them, and so neither they, nor any of them, are named by the first, or any Word that I find, except in the Representation which was made of the chief of them, and the Reflections from a few of the rest in the Temple. When any of the Prophets had occasion to speak of any one of the Athths particularly, which was but seldom, and of a few of the Chiefs, he must use a particular Name, either such as God gave it, or such as the Heathens gave it, or such as God claimed the Attribute by: I shall at present chiefly confine my self to the two great ones, חמה and לבנה: When any of the Prophets had occasion to speak of any one of the Fluxes particularly, which happened only to be a few of the most eminent, or of the two Governors, or of the Chief, because they were most active, they had much to do with them, and particularly with the chief Minister, he must, as aforesaid, use a particular Name, as אור or שמש and ירח: Becaufe the Streams are included in in thofe Fluxes, they do not ufe any particular Name for either of them, but the general one מאורים, or thefe of the two great Fluxes שמש, and ירח, and with them moftly a general Name כוכבים for the reft. And becaufe the Parts of Light which reach and influence the Earth, and every thing there, from the two great Streams, are included in their Fluxes, they ufe the general Word of אורים for Lights from thefe two, and moftly the general Word of מזלות for the Influences from the reft, as the Word expreffes. *M.* נזל I. " Its Signification is a Flux. II. מזלות The Influence of the Stars. *Chald.* to flow, flow from, to run down, or ftream from on high, to defcend, &c."

Where there is any doubt about the Meanings of the Words, what each of them fignifies, as here, whether I have fet them right, and whether שמש be the Orb of the Sun, or the Athth in and near the Orb of the Sun, or the Flux of Light, the Moiety of the Matter of the Heavens kept in Motion by the Spirit, and that Athth, and reaching in Streams to the Earth, and all other Orbs, and the reft to the Extremities of Heaven, muft be determined

determined by the Descriptions we meet with of the others, and of its Situation or Course, of the Place of its Presence, of the Company it keeps, of its Actions or Effects upon things, whose Places are known, of the Order of Things, of the same sort the Scripture ranks it with, and the Usage of the Words among the eldest Writers.

Cant. vi. 9. *Fair as the* לבנה *white of the Moon;* ברה *clear* (Pura) *as* חמה *the Fire of the Sun.* Isai. xxiv. 23. *and* הלבנה *the White of the Moon shall be confounded and* החמה *the Solar Fire ashamed.* Ibid. xxx. 26. *and the Light of* הלבנת *shall be as the Light of* החמה; (not of מארת,) *and the Light of* החמה *shall be seven-fold as the Light of seven Days.* Here we have a Name affixed to each of the two great Athths, to distinguish them from each other, and from the rest of the Athths, and from the Orbs, and from the Fluxes and Streams of Light moved by them, or any of the other Athths.

Next you will have a Name affixed to the Light moved in Fluxes from each of them, to distinguish them from the rest of the Fluxes, and from their own and the rest of the Orbs and Athths. *Deut.* iv. 19. *And*
lest

lest thou lift thine Eyes to the Airs and see את השמש *the* Sun, (Solar Light) and את הירח *the* Moon (Lunar Light) *and the Stars, all the Host of the Airs; and be driven to worship them and serve them; which* Jehovah *thy Aleim hath imparted to all the Nations under the whole Air.* Ibid. xvii. 3. *and worshipped them, either* שמש *or* ירח, *or any of the Host of Heaven.* xxxiii. 13. *and of* Joseph *he said: Blessed of* Jehovah *be his Land, by the pretious Things of the Airs, by the Dew, and by the Deep* (the Fluids) *that lyes below, and by the pretious Things the Produce of* שמש *; and by the pretious things thrust forth by* ירחים *the Streams from the Moon.* Jos. x. 12, 13. *and he said in the sight of Israel,* שמש *Stream of Light from the Sun stay upon* Gibeon : *and* ירח *thou Lunar Stream upon the Valley of* Ajalon. *And* השמש *the Solar Stream* ידם *stayed; and* ירח *the Lunar Stream* עמד *was supported; until the People had avenged themselves of their Enemies. Is not this written in the Book of* Jasher, *so* השמש *the Solar Stream* עמד *was supported in the midst of the Air, and hastened not to depart about a whole Day.* 2 K. xxiii. 5. *Burning Incense to* בעל Baal, *to* שמש *and to* ירח, *and to* מזלות *the Streams from the Stars,*

and

MOSES's *Principia.* 465

and all the Host of the Airs. Pſa. lxxii. 5.
They ſhall fear thee as long as the שמש *and*
ירח *endure, throughout all Generations.* Ibid.
lxxxix. 38. *His Throne like that of* שמש
the Solar Light before me: as the ירח *ſhall
be be eſtabliſhed for ever: and the Appointment fixed in the Æther.* Ibid. civ. 19. *He
made* ירח *for appointed Seaſons: The* שמש
knows its Departure. cxxi. 6. *Jehovah is
thy Keeper, Jehovah is thy Shade upon thy
right Hand. The* שמש *ſhall not ſmite thee
by Day; nor* ירח *by Night.* Ibid. cxxxvi.
8. *Who made* את השמש *to rule by Day:
for his Mercy endures fer ever:* את הירח
and the Stars to rule by Night. Ibid. cxlviii.
2. *Praiſe him all ye his Hoſts: praiſe him*
שמש *and* ירח *: praiſe him all ye Stars of
Light*———— *He appointed Rules which ſhall
not be broke.* Iſa. xiii. 10. *For the Stars
of the Air, and the Conſtellations thereof
ſhall not give their Light. The* שמש *ſhall
be darkned when it goes forth; and* ירח *ſhall
not cauſe her Light to ſhine.* Ibid. lx. 19,
20. *The* שמש *ſhall no more be Light to thee
by Day: neither* ירח *ſhine a Light to thee——
Thy* שמש *ſhall no more depart: neither
ſhall thy* ירח *withdraw itſelf.* Jer. viii. 1,
2. *Shall bring forth the Bones*———— *out of
their Graves, and they ſhall ſpread them to*
שמש *and to* ירח *and to all the Host of*

Vol. II.　　　L l　　　*Heaven,*

Heaven, which they have loved, and which they have ferved. xxxi. 35. *Thus faith* Jehovah, *who gave* שמש *for Light by Day; the Appointments of* ירח *and of the Stars to be Light by Night.* Ezek. xxxii. 7. *When I shall put thee out, I will cover the Airs, and darken their Streams of Light: the* שמש *I will cover it with a Cloud; and the* ירח *shall not make its Light to flow. All* מאורי אור *the Streams of Light in the Airs, I will make them dark over thee: and set Darkness upon thy Land.* Joel ii. 10. *The Earth shall quake before them; the Heavens shall tremble, the* שמש *and* ירח *shall be darkned, and the Stars withdraw their Light.* Ibid. iii. 4. *The* שמש *shall be turned into Darkness, and* ירח *become inactive (Torpid, Silent, Quiet, or at Reft.) and* 20. *The* שמש *and* ירח *shall be darkned (ftorken'd) and the Stars withdraw their shining.* Hab. iii. 11. *The* שמש, *the* ירח *are fupported,* עמר, (as obferved p. 191. the fame Word as is appliedto the Earth, and which they conftrue to ftand ftill) *in their Habitation; at the Light of thine Arrows they go, at the shining of thy glittering Spear.* Pfa. lxxiv. 16. *Thou didft Machine* מאור *the Light (viz. that Part of the* שמש *which hits the Earth,) and* שמש. Ibid. cxxxvi. 6. *who made great Lights; for his Mercy endures*

for

for ever: את השמש *to rule in the Day.* cxlviii. 1. *Praise him Sun and Moon; praise him all ye Stars of Light.* Eccl. xi. 6. אור *Light is sweet ; and a pleasant Thing it is for the Eyes to behold* את שמש Job. xxxi. 26. *If I beheld* אור *the Light when it shined, and* ירח *marching in Brightness.* xxv. 5. *Behold even to* ירח *and it shineth not ; and the Stars are not pure (or clear) in his Sight.* Psa. viii. 3. *When I consider thy Heavens, the Work of thy Fingers the* ירח*, and the Stars which thou hast ordained.* xix. 5. *In them hath he set a Tabernacle for the* שמש *which is as a Bridegroom coming out of his Chamber, and rejoiceth as a strong Man to run a Race. From the Extremity of the Air is its coming out ; and its Circuit unto the Ends of it, and there is nothing hid from the Heat thereof.* Gen. xix. 23. — *The* שמש *Solar Light* יצא אל הארץ *was come out upon the Earth.* 2 Sam. xxiii. 4. *and like the Morning Light, the* שמש *shall* ירח *be arise.* Isa. lxix 10. שרב *the Heat nor the* שמש *shall smite them.* Cant. i. 6. *because the* שמש *hath looked upon me.* Isa. xxxviii. 8. *Behold I will return again the Shadow of the Degrees which is gone down in the Dial of Ahaz, by the* שמש *going back ten Degrees ; so the* שמש *returned ten Degrees, by which it had*

Ll 2 *gone*

gone down. Jonah iv. 8. *And it came to pass when* השמש *was* זרח *risen, that God prepared a vehement East Wind* ותך שמש אל ראש יונה, *and the Light beat upon the Head of* Jonah. Mich. iii. 6. *And the* השמש (*Solar*) *Light shall depart from the Prophets.* Exod. xvi. 21. וחם השמש ונמס *and when the Light warmed, it melted.* Dan. xii. 3. *And they that be wise shall shine as the* זהר הרקיע *Brightness of the Expansion; and they that turn many to Righteousness as the Stars for ever and ever.* Job. iii. 4. ואל תופע עליו נהרה, *nor let the Light irradiate upon it.* Pro. iv. 18. כאור נגה הולך ואור *like Light that shines, proceeds and flows, till the Day is formed.* Isa. v. 30. ואור חשך בעריפיה, *and the Light is storkned in its Defluxions (or, as it flowes along.)*

Let us see how the Antients used these Words.

B. C. p. 1694.——— " With the Talmudists. The Incision of לבנה the Moon, that is the Horns of לבנה the Moon in an Eclipse. Hence this Question was its Incision before חמה the Sun or behind it? that is, did the Horns of לבנה the Moon look towards חמה the Sun, or from it. *Rosch Hasch.* Fol. 23. The חמה Sun never saw

saw the Incision of לבנה the Moon, or the Incision of the Rain-bow, *Talm. Rosch. Haschana*, fol. 23. 2. The Heads of the Incision, that is the Horns of לבנה the Moon increasing or decreasing."

B. C. 1407. " At the Time חמה the Sun rose, the Rays were dispersing themselves from it. *i. e.* from חמה."

B. C. 1382.— " In the Hour חמה the Sun rises the Rays sparkling go out from it —The Splendor of חמה the Sun, the Solar Rays, unto the Splendor of חמה the Sun, while חמה the Sun goes forth and begins to shine and send forth Rays."

B. C. 2473. " The Year of חמה the Sun, or the Solar Year—the Year of לבנה the Moon or the Lunar Year."

B. C. 2023. " The Diameter of חמה the Sun.

B. C. 2608. The Column of חמה *Chamah* rising—namely the ascending Column of לבנה *Lebanah*."

B. C. 1600. " And it covered or hid the Eye of the *Shemosh*; (Flux of Light from the Athth of the Sun) upon the Earth, *Exod.* x. 15. that is the Rays, the Light, with which the Sun looks upon and enlightens the Earth."

B. C. 2081.— "Gyration, Circulation, *Guido in Zohar.* — Radiation, sparkling of the Rays of the *Shemosh.*"

B. C. 1845.— "The Atoms or small Dust, as Sun-motes which are seen in the Sun-shine, it is read in *Rabbi Saadias*, Dan. iv. 32. upon the Word כלה which he thus explains— *Kelo*, (as it were nothing) is the small Dust or Motes which are seen at the rising of the *Shemosh*, as if Atoms flew about like the minutest Particles of Dust; but is a thing of no Subsistence, but transient and ceasing with the *Shemosh*, in whose Substance there is nothing solid.

B. C. 822.— "It is called לא that is אין nothing, from that of *Daniel*, *and all the Inhabitants of the Earth are reputed* בלא *as nothing*; upon which the Gloss of *Rabbi Saadias*; לא that is— most minute Corpuscles like Dust which are seen at the rising of the *Shemosh* coming in at the Windows, which come with the *Shemosh* and vanish with it, and pass into nothing."

B. C. 267.— *Rab.*— "The Moon has neither Light nor Splendor, but from the *Shemosh.*"

B. C. 2140.— "In the sixth Hour the Day or *Shemosh* stands in Horns, that is between Horns, in the middle Point of two Horns that comprehend in the Meridian the rising and setting *Shemosh*, that is in the very meridional Point, *Pesachim*, fol. 12. 2."

B. C. 2320— " The Refractions or Fractures of the *Shemosh* are more grievous or fiercer than the *Shemosh* itself, *Joma*, fol. 28. 2. The Splendor or Light of the *Shemosh* refracted thro' Clouds is more fierce than the full Light."

Besides the Word for the Orbs, 'tis evident the Scripture uses two Words, one for the great Athth, and one for the secondary Light; and two others, one for each of the greatest Fluxes, besides the Words for Parts of them; and we render each Athth, and each Flux of Light passing from, or rather put into Motion by the Motion of each Athth, by the same Name; and in Acceptation we comprehend them both under the Name of Sun or Moon: The Distinction in Scripture is very evident; first, as those two great ones of the same sort, where both named, are always placed together, that is, the Athths together, and the Fluxes together; and those two which we have the most Occasion to understand, are by being very frequently mentioned most exactly described: These two Names for the two great

Athths, and the two Names for the two great Fluxes are kept up by their Attributes, by their Descriptions, by the Things they are compared with, by their Duties, their Actions, their Motions, the Places of their Actions or Motions; and tho' as I have said elsewhere of the Opinion of the Heathens, I intend not to offer the Opinion of the *Rabbies*, for supporting a System; I have a Right to shew the Usage of the Words, whereby it appears plainly and strongly, that they took שמש for the Flux of Light from חמה the Athth of the Sun; and that they took ירח for that Flux of Light from לבנה the Athth of the Moon; and more evidently, because they describe לבנה to be horned, as the Athth of Light upon that Orb is, and appears; which the Orb of the Moon, the only Orb that can be seen clearly, except some few at Eclipses, which way soever viewed, can never be, or appear to be; and the Scripture and the antient *Jew* called the Stream of Light from its first coming to their Sight, or upon their Land, till its going off, ירח ימים *Luna dierum*, or a Moon; and several such ירחים Moons, which could not be spoken of the Orb of the Moon; it was but one, and never became new;

nor

nor of the Athth, it was not upon the Earth, to rule that Part called Night. Juſt before the Formation of theſe Orbs, and the transferring the Actions of Fire or Light thither, there was no Word for the Matter of the Heavens or Airs, then including the Matter of the unformed Orbs, but thoſe Parts whoſe Names by Alteration of their Condition or Situation, were called Part חשך Darkneſs, Part רוח Spirit, Part אור Light, including לילה Night, and יום Day, which were not Things created, but Conditions, which Parts of the Heavens or Airs were put into with reſpect to Motion, Adheſion, Diviſion, &c. After theſe Orbs were made, and the Matter of the Heavens was put into Fluxes, to and from the Center, ſome Parts of thoſe Fluxes interrupted in their Courſe by the Orbs, and thoſe Parts of Light reflected from the Orbs, &c. and the reſt paſſing uninterrupted from the Center to the Circumference, there was no other Name, but שמש for that Part which is in Motion directly from the Sun, and forms Day here, and the reſt of the Athths upon the reſt of the Orbs; and ירח, for that which is in Motion directly from the Moon; and כוכבים for that which is in Motion direct-

ly

ly from the Orbs of the Planets and Stars, and forms the Lights by Night, and the Parts which are obscured or interrupted, by the Interposition of this Orb, which form the Parts of Darkness by Night, and the Parts which move obliquely, as Twilights, except that Part of the Heavens or Airs at so great a Distance from the Sun, where the Motion of the Light is so far abated, and its Parts so widely dispersed among the Grains, formed and forming, that they successively form Grains, which form Darkness, and those Grains, or the Spirit which is continually in a Reflux from thence, some interrupted or diverted by the Orbs, and the rest directly on every Side through the *Shemosh* or Light to the Sun, to be melted there, to supply these Fluxes of Light. But Things are of late come to that Uncertainty, I do not say in vulgar speaking, but philosophically, though we see the Hemisphere of a dark Orb this Moment, and call it the Moon, as soon as the smallest Edge of Light is issued upon it from the *Shemosh*, and reflected from one Side, we call the Edge of that Cap or Athth of Light the New Moon; and when that Motion puts the intermediate Light into Motion, and by that present strikes

strikes our Eyes, we call that the Moon; and when we endeavour to speak of the last, as something separate, we speak of it as an Effect, and call it Moon-shine. Though all is full between and by the continual Compressure of the returning Spirit, that which is divided at the Sun, only drives the intermediate Light in that Line against the Moon, and being resisted and reflected there, drives the foremost of the intermediate Parts of Light which are in a Line from that Part of the Moon opposite the Sun, and next us to our Eyes, &c. And when Light is so struck against polished Armour, or &c. and that reflected, puts the intermediate Light into Motion, or each Atom puts that preceding it into Motion, till those next our Eyes are moved against them; instead of calling it as we ought, the Line of that which reflected it, we only say, that which reflects the Light shines. We write and speak as uncertainly of the several Things, our Translators call the Sun; and as our Translation stands, though it does not say, that the Orb of the Sun, or חמה that Athth moves from their Place; yet translating the שמש the Sun, and making it be taken for the Orb, or the Athth of Fire while in the Orb,

Orb, and joining that to its circulating about the Earth, or going to the Extremities of the Heavens, and returning to the Extremities, being upon the Earth, staying in *Gibeon*, being upon *Ahaz*'s Dial, being dashed against the Head of *Jonah*, ruling the Day, and in the Day, bringing forth the precious Fruits, pervading all Things, are in our Language positive Lies. They, the Orb and the Athth, while acting in it, were not to come to the Earth, but to be instrumental to send Light, part of that from the Sun, called שמש, the vast Light in Succession of Time to the Earth, and, it seems, to all the rest of the Orbs, which will be explained next. But if *Shemosh* were translated what it really is, what is ascribed to *Shemosh* in the Scripture going upon the Earth, being blown against the Head of *Jonah*, going to the Extremities, or near the Verge, or Circumference, or Surface of the Heavens, or Airs, and returning, and the rest as above, or as the *Jews* express it, radiating, or being pressed from חמה in Streams of Light to the Earth, entering in through the Windows, are all, whether spoken of these Actions, or by Comparison, to illustrate higher Things,

Things, of which no Ideas can be otherwise conveyed, simply and literally true.

Having settled Names for each chief Thing, Agent, or Patient, and their Places, Actions, or Motions: As one of the Citations which expresses the Circulation of the *Shemosh* most clearly, is coupled with the Description of the Agents which move the Earth, and of its Motion by the Royal Prophet *David*; we may now venture to consider them together, and shew how exactly they tally with what *Moses* and the other Prophets have said. *Psal.* xix. 1. *The Airs declare the Glory of God; and* הרקיע *the Expansion shews his Handywork.* יום ליום *Day after Day indicates* אמר *the Command, and Night after Night shews Knowledge. There is no Speech, nor are there Words: Their Voice is not heard.* קום *Their Line is gone through all the Earth; and to the Extremity of* תבל *the Orb their Indications. In them hath he set a Tabernacle for the* שמש*, which is as a Bridegroom coming out of its Chamber, rejoiceth as a strong Man to run a Race; from the Extremity of the Airs is its going out, and* תקופתו *its Circuit (or coming round again) at the Ends of them; and there is nothing hid from the Heat of it.* This great Prophet endeavours

vours to represent a Glimpse of the Glory, Power, and Wisdom of God, through the Glass of his Works to Men; he pitches upon the Heavens, and the Expansion; the first, the Matter in the same Condition as we now see it; and the latter, the Expansion, the Action or Motion of the Parts of that Fluid, and the Effects of it. How, or wherein, or whereby does the Matter of the Heavens, and the Motion, or the Operation of the Expansion, demonstrate the Glory and Workmanship of God? Our Translators render it, *Day unto Day uttereth Speech, and Night unto Night sheweth Knowledge*. As it stands, one would be apt to take the Meaning to be, that Day spoke to Day, and Night shewed Knowledge to Night. Surely he meant, that the Matter of the Heavens, in this Condition, and by this Action and Motion, not only shew'd his Glory, &c. but brought to pass some other and useful Motions and Changes, which are couch'd under the Phrases, *Day unto Day, and Night unto Night*; which should declare and shew some Degree of the Glory, Power, and Foreknowledge of God to Men, by their Productions of Things or Actions, so circumstantiated and varied, as Days and Nights are; for tho' these Things or

Actions

Actions may, by their Actions upon other Things, shew that to Angels or Men, they, neither Agents nor Patients, can shew them to, or instruct one another. He uses an Expression something like this, *Psal.* xcvi. 2. which they render, *Shew forth his Salvation* ליום מיום *from Day to Day*. And the same is used in *Esther* iii. 7. which they render thus; *They cast Pur, that is, the Lot, before Haman, from Day to Day, and from Month to Month, to the twelfth Month*. In these Places we have it, *from Day to Day*; but that is not the *English* of those Words, for from or between one Day and another, is Night; and those are not used to the same Purpose as these Words are; it is here, Day after, or succeeding Day, and Night after Night, the alternate Intervention of Night between Days, and Day between Nights; the Succession of Day and Night, which is perform'd by their Operation upon the Earth, as already shew'd, not only by Rotation, but by Declination, and all their Effects by, or in them.

B. C. פנסים in Midrasch, *Psal.* xix. There are four principal Revolutions (תקופות) of the *Shemosh*, the two Solstices, and the two Equinoxes. From the Winter Solstice to the Vernal Equinox, the
Night

Night pays to the Day: From the Vernal Equinox to the Summer Solstice, the Day borrows of the Night: From the Summer Solstice to the Autumnal Equinox, the Days pay back to the Night: From the Autumnal Equinox to the Winter Solstice, the Night borrows of the Day. In the Vernal and Autumnal Equinox, Accounts are ballanced between them, neither owing the other, the Night the Day, or *è contra* any Thing, they receive the one from the other in an Instant or Point, neither do they call in any Witnesses, as Men are wont to do in their Payments. Hence *Guido* renders it punctually, that is, in a Point or Moment.

C. Calcag. of the perpetual Motion of the Earth, *p.* 394. We see *Empedocles* to have been of the same Opinion, where he writes, that these Demons are impelled by the Earth. We have thus translated his Verses:

The Æther's vehement Motion drives them round,
The Sea receives, and with an active Bound Retorts them to the Earth; nor rest they there:
The Earth returns them to the Solar Sphere:
Th' incessant Action of th' unweary'd Light Propels them upward to the Æther's Height.

These

These are the Things and Actions by which the Heavens and Expansion declare and shew the Glory, Power, and Wisdom of God, and indeed, his Goodness to Men. The Word render'd Speech, *M.* אמר, with Respect to God, is *Edict, Command,* (with Respect to the Heavens) *Arab. Authority, Power* ; and this sets the next Verse right. *There is no Speech nor Language*, where *their Voice is not heard.* If we leave out the *(where)* which they have inserted, 'tis Sense, and true ; 'tis as much as to say, tho' they make no Words, tho' you hear no Noise (and, pardon me for adding, though this is so wonderfully contriv'd, that it gives no Disturbance, does not interfere with, and scarce comes under the Cognizance of any of your Senses) *yet their Line is gone thro' all the Earth, and their Words to the Ends of the World.* What Things or Operations are meant by *their?* He is speaking of the Matter of the Heavens, and that Motion of the Parts of them call'd the Expansion. What can be the Line of the Matter of the Heavens in that Motion? Here has been Imagination! The Word קום has no Relation to Line ; they thought, I suppose, nothing but their imaginary Circles, Lines, &c.

VOL. II. M m could

could be, or act in, or go thro' all the Earth and Waters. The Word, as they divide it, has several Significations, and they are all applicable here: The Parts of the Heavens or Airs have their *M.* קוֹם Station.—Place, the Space in which one stands. Subsistence, (and as the Effect of the Expansion) Firmness, Stability, *&c.* through all the Earth, *&c. Athanaf. Kircher's* Itinerary, *p.* 274. (before cited) Æther thoroughly penetrates all the Bodies of the World, that there may be no where a Vacuum. *Plato's Timæus*, and others." Though the Rendering of מליהם *Eloquia* be tolerable in the Translation, a Word of that Signification could never be writ to express their mute Actions; if it were only a human Writer, as 'tis said, just before, they had no Speech, it would look very odd, that a Word with that Meaning should follow so close. *C.* מְלַל, to speak: but with the old *Hebrews*, to rub, wear. *Pabul.* Prov. vi. 13. See also *Chald.* and *Syr.* it intimates a short, mincing, jetting, harlottress Gait, *Tritutæ fimilis,* says *Buxtorf,* like Grinding or Thrashing, to indicate something.——*Piel.* מִלֵּל. *Chald.* and *Syr.* מַלֵּל, to talk, speak. *Prov.* vi. 13. Winking with his Eyes; מוֹלֵל, speaking with his Feet;
teaching

teaching with his Fingers. LXX it signifies to shew. *Targum* חכם, rubbing, fricating. In this Sense they, without Words, by their Substance, Motions, Actions, and Effects, point out and shew the Glory and Workmanship of God, to the Extremities of the World.

To the *Shemosh* he hath placed a Tabernacle in them, *viz.* in, or included within the Matter of the Heavens, and their Parts in that Motion, call'd the Expansion, so that they are co-extensive. The Word שמש has generally been taken for *Sol*, and *Sol* for the Sun; and either the *Latins* mistook, or we misunderstand *Sol*. I suppose, by the Sun, they mean the Fire at the Sun. B. C. 2461. שמש has no Plural, as *Elias* has remark'd "; and it seems to be a compound Word of שם Heaven, and אש Fire; but that will not agree with its Condition and Motions, so I think it must be compounded of שם Heaven, Name, Place, Substance, Matter, Power and מוש receding, issuing outward from חמה in Rays of Light, and circulating or returning thither; the same as *M.* במוש, as it were receding," mention'd *Numb.* xxi. 28. 1 *Kings* xi. 7. 2 *Kings* xxiii. 13. *Jer.* xlviii. 46. and with an Explanation, *Jer.* xlviii. 13. and *Moab* shall be asham'd of

Chemosh, as the House of *Israel* was a-sham'd of *Bethel*, their Confidence. He made that the Throne, as *Job* xxvi. 9. *He holdeth back the Face of his* כסה *Throne: He spreadeth his Cloud upon it.* And given him Possession, in Respect of Quantity, and so Space of an undivided Moiety of the rest, half to that receding or rising, and the other half to that acceding, going to the Center or falling, or as Governor of all between חמה and the Circumference, his Tabernacle to minister in, the Place where he started. *M.* חפף, a Bride-Chamber, from its being the secret Place of the Bride with the Bridegroom. *C.* מחפתו the Nuptial Chamber, or Room: (which, from *Cant.* iii. 9. must be either the Place of Marriage, the Place of Feast-ing, or the Bed-Chamber.) *Chald.* The Nuptial Room, a Veil. *S.* The Nuptial Canopy, which four *Jews* support with four Poles, under which, as under a Kind of Heaven, the Bridegroom and Bride are consecrated and betrothed. *Sota* 49. 2."
'Tis plain חמה is where he is consecrated, and made fit for his Ministry; made light and fit to run his Race, made beautiful or adorn'd, as the Bridegroom and Bride, were then; made strong as a Governor to march his Circuits, as, in like Words, *Jud.* v. 31.

As השמש *the Shemosh*, (the Flux of Light from the חמה) *when he goeth forth in his Might:* Vested with, and attended by the Power of the Expansion, to carry him on in every Part of his Dominion. Whether as the Center, you term it the Extream, or as the Matter against the Surface of that Orb, in which חמה acts, you call it the *terminus*, or extream Part of the Heaven; 'tis plain it sets out or springs, as *M.* מוצא, (the Substantive of the Word implies) " when spoken of the Sun, it is the Rising, the East: when of Waters, it is a Fountain, a Spring, a Place where Waters spring up, or flow from," rises out of חמה, and in rising runs, pushes against the Side of the Earth, and against the Side of every Orb in its Way, and that which misses all to the Circumference or Extremes of the Heavens; and thence makes its Return or Revolution, by changing its Condition as aforesaid; as, *B. C.* בימה, if it was not for the Heat of *Orion*, the World could not subsist, for the Cold of the *Pleiades*; and was it not for the Cold of the *Pleiades*, the World could not subsist, for the Heat of *Orion*.—*Berachoth*, fol. 58. 2." Or, in another Sense, as the Grains are split and mix'd in the Fire at the Center, some of the Parts of Light, which went to one

Side of the Circumference at one time, may, next time, go to another Side, and so, in time, from Side to Side, or to every Side of the Circumference. And, as he said before, that the Parts of the Heavens pervaded all the Earth, and pass'd through all this System, now he says, (without Exception) there is nothing hid from the Heat thereof, or the small Parts thereof in Motion; what *David* calls *Shemosh*, is by another called Light; *Baruc* iii. 33. *He that sendeth forth Light, and it goeth, calleth it again, and it obeyeth him with Fear:* so *Job* xxxvii. 11. "*The Solar Fire dissolves the Masses of storkened Air, his Light breaks in Pieces the Densities; and it is turned about by his Council that they may do whatsoever he commandeth them upon the Face of the World in the Earth.*" But מתהפך which they render *volvens*, is reverting, and בתחבולתו which they render *in consiliis suis*, is here spoken, I think, of the Matter; and if it be a single Word, signifies in Chorus's, as the Word is used 1 *Sam.* x. 5. &c. so *Prov.* xvi. 18. "*before* כשלון *the falling down there is a* גבה *rising up of the Spirit*, *Sebast. Fox. Morzill* upon the third Part of *Timæus's Comment.* p. 301.—" But *Plotinus* also affirms it in his Book of the Motion of

of the Heavens, in which (he says) that the Fire is constrained into an Orb, and turned round or circulated, because the Heavens hinder it from moving upward by the Force of the Celestial Motion, by Reason it cannot move upward for the Obstacle of the Heavens or Air." This is what *Macrobius* so often calls *conversio Cælorum*, (or Circulation of the Heavens.) And his Definition of the World is p. 145.—
" The Latin Word *Conversio*, signifies to be moved by itself. Nor let the Verb being passive confound you, *&c*," which all the Antients, even to *Lucretius per Tan. Fabr. Salmarii* Edit. 1662, p. 163. calls *Machina Mundi*, (or Machine of the World; and p. 42.

But this thin Vapour issued by the Sun,
And Light serene, does not resistless run,
Thro' a meer Void, but makes a Passage thro',"
Resisting Air, and therefore moves more slow."
Nor go the Atoms singly, but combined,
Among each other move in Conflict joined.
And therefore from without, resisting Force,
And adverse Motion must retard their Course."

What

What concerns the rifing and fetting of the שמש, upon any Part of the Earth, will come in under the Confideration of *Eccl.* i. 1. *&c.* This determines feveral Points of great Importance, fuch as that all the Orbs have their Light in the Manner aforefaid, from the Sun; that the Expanfion, the Motion, and Countermotion of the Parts of the Heavens, of which the Matter of the *Shemofh* is Part, goes, and all its Effects take place from the Center to the Circumference; and now when this Motion is fettled, to be from the Center to the Circumference on every Side in ftreight Lines, if it had not been revealed, 'tis evident to Senfe, that the Earth turns round to form Days and Nights; and if thofe we call fixed Stars, be fixed or move flowly, 'tis evident to Senfe, that the Earth makes a progreffive Circle about the Body of the Sun, which we call a Year.

Though many Citations from the Heavens, concerning their *Sol, Shemofh,* Rays of the Sun, the Heavens circulating, *&c.* are intermixed with, and have been inferted at thofe, for the Heavens or *Jupiter,* at *Chamah,* &c. I muft add a few here.

Kirchir's

Kircher's *Obelisk*, p. 547. *Trefmegestus* in *Pymander*——Fol. 42. " The Sun is the most excellent Deity of all the Celestial Gods; the other Celestials obey the Sun as their Prince and King, &c."

Kircher's *Oedipus*, Vol. II. Part ii. p. 157. *Hermes*.— " These sensible Powers consimilar to each of their own Origins, form all Things by a sensible Nature, the one by the other, every one illuminating his own Work. *Jupiter*, (whom the *Egyptians* also call *Hempta*) is the chief Essence, the Ousiarches of Heaven, or whatever it is that is comprehended under that Name. By Means of the Heaven or Air, *Hempta*, or *Jupiter*, gives Life to all Beings. The Substance of the Sun is Light: the Benefit of Light is diffused to us by the Orb of the Sun; thirty-six (which are called *Horoscopes*) are always in the same Place of the fixed Stars: The chief Essence or Prince of these, is what they call *Pantomorph*, *All-Form*, or *Uniform*, who gives diverse Forms to diverse Species."

Kircher Obel. Pamp. p. 287. *Plut.*— " That *Hercules* is the Sun, is proved both from his Club with the Addition of the Lion's Skin, the Ensign of *Hercules*, as also from

from the Etymology of his Name, concerning which *Macrobius*, Chap. xx. Book I. has these Words:" " And truly it is even apparent from his very Name, that *Hercules* is the Sun; for what else is *Hercules* but *Heras*, that is the Air, and *Cleos*, that is Glory? and what other Glory is there of the Air, but the Illumination of the Sun, at whose Departure Clouds and Darkness come on:" And this Explication so pleased (it seems) *Pontanus* in his Book of the Stars, that he made it the Subject of these Verses.

When Phœbus *going forth in all his Might,*
 The Clouds dispels and ministers the Light;
The Name of Hercules *delights his Ear,*
 Proclaims him God and Glory of the Air.

Vossius de Physiol. Christ. Lib. IX. p. 232. " *Asconius* upon *Tully's* second Oration against *Verres.* They thought no Temples should be built to the Gods, since the whole World was scarce sufficient for the Sun alone, whom they worshipped."

—*Statius Papinius Thebais,* Book I.

—*Beneath*

*—Beneath a Rocky Cavern's dark Abode,
The* Persians *worship* MITRAS *for their
God;
Wresting a strugling Bull's reluctant Horns.*

Upon which an old Interpreter of the Poet.

" The *Persians* worship the Sun in Dens or Caverns, and here the Sun's proper Name is *Mithras*; and because he suffers an Eclipse, he is worshipped within a Cave. He has also a Lion's Face with a *Persian* Tiara upon his Head, and is holding with both his Hands the Horns of a Bull."

Vossius de Phys. Christiana Lib. IX. p. 268. *Ovid's Fasti.* 1.

———Hyperion crowned with Rays.

" The Sun was figured in an human and juvenile Form, but his Head surrounded with Rays, as appears from the Words of *Ovid* above. Likewise from *Martian Capella*, Book I. p. 6. The august Head of the Sun decked and surrounded with flaming Rays resembleth a golden Head of Hair, *&c.*"

Selden de Dis Syris, p. 86. " The antient Writers mention the Effigies of both
Adad

Adad and *Moloch* as the same; and as formed to represent one and the same Thing, namely the Sun. *Macrobius* says ADAD was pictured with reclined Rays, by which is shewn, that the Power of the Heavens is in the Rays of the Sun darted down to the Earth."

Vossius de Orig. & Prog. Idol. Lib. II. p. 308. gives us this Passage more fully. *Macrobius* Lib. I. Sat. Cap. XXIII. before. " The *Assyrians* gave the Name of *Adad* to the Deity whom they worship as the chief and supreme: They join to him a Deity called *Adargatis*: and to these two do they attribute all Power over all Things; understanding by them the Sun and the Earth —— *after, Adargatis*'s Image is distinguished with Rays reclined upward; to shew that by the Force of the Rays sent from above, arise all the Products of the Earth. Under the same Image are a Species of Lions; which for the same Reason shew the Earth, as the *Phrygians* feigned the Mother of the Gods, that is the Earth, to be carried by Lions."

Christ. Sceiner Rosa Ursina, p. 759. in the Notes. " Hence again we learn that the Antient Mathematicians judged the seven Planets, not only to be Wanderers, but also to move freely in the Æther, and

that

that the Æther itself kindled by the solar Fire was hot, and that the other Planets kept at a proper Distance, propelled, or attracted in strait Lines by the solar Rays: and that their Nature was of a cold or a temperate Quality. The extreme Parts of the World beyond the *Saturnian* Region, were according to the same Doctrine, froze up and congealed."

In like Manner many of the Antients write about the attractive Force of the Sun by Means of his Rays; among whom *Isidorus* in his third Book of Originals, the second Chapter, from some of the old Poets.

The Sun divides the Seasons, and his Light Makes the Vicissitudes of Day and Night;
His powerful Rays, as tethered in a Chain, The Stars and Planets in their Orbs retain.

Kircher Obel. p. 202. " They interpret *Osiris* of the Sun, and *Isis* the Moon, because by the Rule and Influence of these Stars all Nature is sustained." I have set a clear Description of these Rays to *Chamah*, the Head, which ought also to stand here. " *Kirch. Obel.* p.383. *Heliordorus*, Lib. IX. elegantly describes these Circumpositions of Rays— furrounding his Head (fays he) with a kind of Wreath or Turban, and fixing in it Arrows in a Circle; they turn the feathered Part toward the Head, and project the Points in the manner of Rays outward. *Voſs*— and *Macrob*:— The Sun the Governour and Director of all Things, the Spirit of the World, the Power of the World, the Light of the World."—*Orpheus*—

*Oh thou who by the Airs converſive Force,
Rolls in perpetual circulating Courſe,
Th' Æthereal Vortex of the Heavens vaſt
 Sphere;*
Jove, Bacchus, *Earth and Seas great
 Parent bear!*
*Thou Sun all-generative radient Flame
Changing thro' all, and yet in all the ſame.*

Vetuſt. Tabul. p. 40.— " The People of *Delphos* formerly worſhiped a Wolf as the animated Emblem of the Sun, becauſe this Animal as *Macrobius* expounds it ſeizes every thing like the Sun, who by virtue of his Rays attracts or draws all things to himſelf."

Voſſius de Orig. & Prog. Idol. Lib. II. p. 325. אור " *Or* Light, Brightneſs, the Sun whence the *Egyptian* Horus and the

Aurion

Aurion that is the Morrow, the next Day of the *Greeks*."

Voſſius de Phyſiol. Chriſtian. Lib. IX. p. 236. " From *Philo Byblius*— The *Egyptians* delineating the World with the ſame Deſign, mark out a Circle with a Sky-coloured Circumference reſembling Flame or Fire, in the middle a Serpent extended, in the Form of an Hawk, *&c.*

Ibid. p. 254. "The Words of *Porphyry* about *Vulcan's* Effigy deſerve to be put down; as *Euſebius* has given them in the third of his Evangelical Preparation.— Cap. XI. p. 112. Edit. *Paris* an. 1628.— They called the Irradiation or Power of Fire *Vulcan*, and placed upon his Image, which was in an human Form, a Sky-blue *Hat or Cap* the Symbol of the celeſtial Periphery, or Circulation where the principal Action of the Fire is, and where it is the pureſt. For that Fire when brought down from Heaven to Earth, is much weakened, loſes its Tone, for want of the Prop and Support of its proper Aliment: wherefore it limps or halts, for Defect of Matter to ſuſtain it."

Clem. Alex. Strom. Lim. V. p. 415. Plectron— " Some will have it the Pole; ſome the Air which ſtrikes and puts in Motion every thing to its natural Support and Growth, or which fills all Things.
But

But these have not read *Cleanthes* the Philosopher who openly calls *Plectron* the Sun. For establishing his Beams in the East, by which striking the World, he drives out the Light in a regular disposed Course.

Kirch. Oed. Vol. III. p. 576. *Tresmegistus*—perpetually containing all things in his Mind, Light and Spirit."

Kircher Ob. Pamp. p. 246. *Minutius Felix* " very elegantly in *Octavius*. Look again upon the Sun who tho' he be fixed in the Heaven, yet is dispensed to all Parts of the Earth. In like Manner being present every where is intersperfed and intermingled with every thing."

Ibid. 247. " *Macrobius* indeed above all endeavours to prove by many Arguments that all the Gods refer to the Sun ; and that he was the one Deity which the *Gentiles* worshipped under various Appellations."

Sallust. &c. p. 83. " The Sentences of *Secundus* the Philosopher. What is the Sun ? the Eye of Heaven ; the Adversary of the Night, the Etherial Circuit, the Index of the World ; the inmixed Flame ; the Raiser and Clother of Fruits : the inextinguishable Ray ; the all supplying Lamp, the celestial Traveller, the indeficient
Light,

Light, the Ornament of the Day— *Ibid.* p. 97. the Distributor of the Hours."

Vossius de Physiol. Christian. Lib. VII. p. 162. *Virgil.* 4 *Georg.* p. 221.

———————— *A Deity*
Pervades the whole, the Heaven, the Earth, the Sea,
Hence Men and Brutes their Origin derive,
And by his powerful Radiation live.

Ibid. Vossius Lib. IX. p. 250. "The Sun grows not old, but always renews his Youth." With Evidence from Antient Authors, Inscriptions and Figures. "*Valerius* concerning his Quiver, adds whereas he is wont to be figured with this Instrument and Arrows: It signified that all Things were penetrated by the Solar Rays. *Servius* brings this Reason from *Porphyry, &c.*— He is also figured with a Lyre or Harp to denote that sweet Harmony or Concert which according to the *Platonic* and *Pythagorean* Doctrine arises from the Motion of the Heavens. *Ibid.* p. 252.— An Hawk was sacred to *Apollo,* — and the *Greek* Schohliast of *Aristophanes* adds as the Eagle was dedicated to *Jupiter*, the Hawk which was the lesser Eagle was agreeably enough dedicated to *Apollo* as the Minister of *Jupiter*: *Eustathius*

thius on the first *Iliad* pag. 87. *Edit. Rom.*—brings a double Reason why the Hawk was sacred to *Apollo*—the Hawk is consecrated to *Apollo*, the Sun upon account of the Swiftness of his Motion, for the flight of the Hawk is swift and rapid, and so is the Motion of the Sun (or Light.) Hence by Affinity of the Words from Etymology: as the Sun (or Light) *Ietai* runs swiftly; thence *Ierax* the Hawk was named? Whence he is called by the *Epithet Delius*, because he makes all things *Dela* manifest and conspicuous. Ibid. *Vossius* p. 251. *Homer* over and over again mentions Bulls sacrificed to *Apollo*, *Iliad* first, and likewise *Virgil* speaks of the Bull, *Æn.* III. p. 251.

— *A Bull to thee, O bright* Apollo.

Nor was the Victim always a Bull, but also a Ram, a She-Goat or He-Goat, as we learn from the same *Homer*, &c."

" *Raph. Volaterani Com. Urban.* p. 395. The *Bedvins*—(The People of *Arabia*) go cloathed in Goats Skins, and worship the Rising Sun."

Bochart. Geogr. sacra pars prior, p. 114. " Sabis is the Sun, *Myrrh*, and Frankincense are from every where amassed together into the Temple of the Sun, (or Light in Irradiation.)"

The

The *Canaanites* had three Temples to their God, the Heavens under the Attribute of *Shemosh*, one mentioned, 2 *Par.* xxviii. 18. בית שמש " named so according to *Jerom* in Queſt. Hebr. before *Abel*;" and another *Joſ.* xix. 22. and the third *Joſ.* xix. 38. and *Ver.* 41. *The City of* Shemoſh. And the *Egyptians* had one, and the Repreſentation of that Matter with that Power mentioned, *Jer.* xliii. 13. We need not enquire of the Heathens what they meant by this Attribute, or the Matter in this Condition and Motion, or Action, which is a deſcriptive Name of the Light. The Scripture ſhews it was appointed Governor of the Day, which has been conſidered; and in the Day, where they alſo aſcribe to it, *Deut.* xiii. 14. putting forth the precious Fruits, and the vaſt Number of Claims, which God makes of what is executed by the Matter veſted with this Power, ſufficiently expreſs them; but many of them come not within the Conſideration of this Part.

As the Heavens *Molock*, *Gad*, &c. are each general Names, ſo *Chamah*, *Baal*, and *Aſhteroth*, as it it taken for Fluxes of the Light or Stars, are each general Names of the three Parts, each deſcriptive of each of their reſpective Motions; the Scripture once

once comprehends the Powers, which the feduced *Jews* ſerved in the manner following. 2 *Reg.* xxiii 5. לבעל *that burnt Incenſe to* Baal, לשמש (which you ſee is the Flux of Light from the Orb of the Sun) and לירח (which you ſee is that Part of the Flux of Light from the Sun, which ſtrikes upon the Orb of the Moon, and ſo is turned to the Earth, &c.) *and* למזלות (which you will ſee is a general Word, for the Condition or Effect of the Streams of Light from the Stars, and is put in their Place) and all צבא חשמים (which you ſee are the particular Attributes or Efficient Powers of the Heavens, to which they had diſtinct Temples, of which ſeveral have been explained.)

M. נזל I. "Its Signification is a Flux—to flow, flow from, flow upon, ſtill, diſtill, inſtill, run down from on high—נוזלים Fluxes, Streams. II. It is the Name of a Star, or Sign of a Limit in a Sphere or celeſtial Orb. מזלות the Influxes, or influences of the Stars, or the Name of one Star, nay it is taken for all the Stars. The *Planets* upon Account of the Influence that they have on theſe inferior Things. *Chald.-Syr. Arab. Nazel,* to flow, flow from, run down from on high, deſcend, ſend down, depreſs." 'Tis plain, theſe are the Parts of
the

the Flux of Light from the Sun, which strike upon the Orbs of the Stars, and are returned, and so called their Lights, each in Lines from each of their Centers, thro' each Part of their enlightned Hemispheres; what Influences they have, has in part been hinted; what other Influences they have, and what Influences they imagined they had, belong not to this Place.

The Scripture frequently comprehends the Powers which the seduced *Jews* served, under the two descriptive Names of *Baalim* and *Ashteroth*. There was indeed a Place of the Name of the latter, but I meet with no Temple among the *Canaanites*, except that was a Place of Worship. 'Tis said to have been a Goddess of the *Sidonians*. We have an Account of a Temple to this Power, 2 *Sam*. xxxi. 10. — בית עשתרות among the *Philistines*. As making these Powers Persons, was long after introduced, so they made this a Goddess by Mistake, because most of the Powers as such are Feminine. We find the Place, *Gen*. xiv. 5. עשתרת קרנים, *Jos*. ix. 10. עשתרה 1 *Par*. vi. 71. עשתרות the Object of their Worship. *Judg*. ii. 13. עשתרות 1 *Reg*. xi. 5. עשתרת. This is singular or plural as the Light is considered as one, or divided in Lights; tho' the Languages were the same after the People were divided, and every one who believes the Hebrew Writers were inspired, may believe that they might infallibly use the original Words, the same Letters to the same Words, and know, the Meaning of Words infallibly; yet none will imagine that the Heathens of other Nations did so, but that they, even when *Moses* writ, made some Difference in Pronunciation; and afterwards when they writ, especially so low down as those, we have preserved, misunderstood some of the Hebrew Words and Letters, and used improper Words and Letters, gave different Sounds to Letters, &c. By Observations made upon such Alterations, and Rules drawn from them, others have been allowed to account for the Meaning of Hebrew Words; and according to such Allowances, it might seem enough to shew, that in the Usage of the Words from whence it came, or where it was first served, that they meant the same thing; as שוש the Part of the Heavens receding, or that from the Sun, Moon and Stars. We have been often told that the *Chaldeans*, &c. frequently used and writ their S, as St, and their א, for ע, as אשא for עשאת Fire. *Targ. Job.* xxxi.

xxxi. 26. " If I behold אשתחר the Sun, (Heb. אור the Light) when it shineth, and the Moon, &c. B. C. אתור Assyria, אתוראת an *Assyrian*." When הדסא was chosen Queen of the *Chaldeans*, they changed her Name to אסתר *as* אצ After, " a bright Star, the Planet *Venus*, in an unlimited Sense, the Sun. עסח *C. Venus.* B. B. the Name of a City and an Image. v. *Maf.* & עשתרות *Ibid.* אסתרק *Arab*— The Star *Venus* to which of old sixteen different Names were given by so many Nations. *Ibid.* אשיור many stringed Plantain. *Kircher's Oedipus* C. 2. p. 70. *Coc.* עשתרות *Aftarte*, many-breasted *Venus*, namely the Giver of Fecundity, B. C. איסטרוביל a *Vortex*," which is two Words, the first this Word the Flux of Light, the second the Spirit, as *C. Syr.* ביל *Jupiter* with ו *and* between, the descriptive Names of the Matter of both Powers in Motion, so a *Vortex* going and returning, circulating. These two Motions are described among Questions in natural Philosophy by Agur, *Prov.* xxx. 4. מי עלה שמים וירד *who hath lifted up the Heavens, and pressed them down?* And in truth the *Chaldeans*, &c. have not changed their Letters, as 'tis pretended in this Place, but changed Words for Words of

nearly

nearly the same Signification, and which were more adapted to their Religion and Philosophy; for שור is a Prince, and תור, a Leader, and אש Fire is applicable to תור, or שור, as well as עש; so to stick to the Text, Ashteroth is a compound Word of עש, or עשה, and תור, or תר. I find the Word עש but twice used for inanimate Things. *Job.* ix. 9. " *Which maketh* עש Has, Chesil, & Chima, *and the Chambers of the South*. Ch. xxxviii. 31. *Canst thou bind the sweet Influences of the* Chima *or loose the Bands of* Chesil. 23. *Canst thou bring forth* Mazaroth (the Grains) *in their Season, canst thou guide* עיש *with his Sons*. B. C. עש *Arcturus*, the Tail of the Ram, the Head of the Bull, &c." once with People, *Joel.* iii. 16. עושו *assemble yourselves, and come all ye* Heathen. B. C עשש A Candle, or Lamp,— a Candle fixed in the middle of a Lanthron— a Lamp burning from Year to Year *M.* a Moth-Worm."

But the Word עשת several times *Coc.* עשת " to shine, shining, Brightness, Splendor, התעשת to be serene, bright,"— which as you will see is the same as to be horned, and with respect to Operation may be from עשה to make.

M. תור

M. תור A searching out, a Scrutiny; To Explore, look about, wander and search about, to view all over, survey strictly. *C.* To explore, scrutinize, investigate, going round about and looking round and peeping into every Hole and Corner, *Coc.* a Series, a Circle, an Orb: Order and Place in a Series, *French* a Tour. *B. C.* תור a Spy, a Watchman, an Observer, a Leader, a Guide---- a Driver or Leader of Oxen, that is an Husband-Man, or Farmer or Tiller of the Ground, a Plow-Man, Plowing one Furrow here, and then going back, another there, from another Part of the Field.

M. עשתרות "Flocks. (*S.* Sheep-Coats)", you will see תור is a Sheep, and here by the Context in every Place, עש or עשת signifies their Flock or Coat, or Pen of Sheep, or of their issue Lambs, or in Distinction (as we now say black Cattle) to other Sorts, white Cattle for Sheep. It is not worth while to go out of my Way, and attempt to explain *Job*'s Words; for in which Sense of the two you take this, matters not much, whether עש be the one great Light; and so the Light, the Conductor, or the Matter which issues, a descriptive Name of Light the Conductors,

or

or the Flock or Coat of Conductors, which proceed all from one, and is the Office of of the Light or Lights; or the shining Conductors, the Representatives of this Power expressed by the same Word or Name, M. חור "a Sheep or Lambs. A Turtle, a Chain for the Neck, &c. *Chald.* and *Arab.* a Bull. *C.* Ornaments shaped like a Dove, whose Neck is wreathed or ringed. *Chald.* A Species of Turtles, an Ox, an Heifer, a Sea Ox, or Calf. *Æ- thiop.* an Animal most like an Ox, and *Arab.* a Bull, the same as the *Heb.* שור. *B. C.* חור a Turtle— an Ox, an Heifer; it answers to the Hebrew שור and פר."

We find a Word beginning with an א and without the ת inserted in the Place of עשתרות *Judg.* iii. 7. *And served Baalim and* את־האשרות: 2 *Kings* xxii. 4. *And the Instruments made for* Baal, האשרה, *and all the Host of Airs.* Ibid. xvii. 10. *Set them up Statues and* אשרים *Groves in every high Hill, and under every green Tree.* Ibid xxi. 7. *A Graven Image* האשרה xxiii. 6. *Brought forth,* את־האשרה *out of the House of* Jehovah. Isa. xxvii. 9, *The* אשרים *and Fire-Images shall not stand up.* Deut. xvi. 21. *Thou shalt not* חטע *set up for thyself an* אשרה *of any Wood near the Altar of* Jehovah,
thy

by Aleim. As any Pretence which would ſerve to miſlead us in theſe Points, has been made uſe of, I ſuppoſe becauſe they found נטש, to plant, fix, fix in, which is a Word for ſetting any thing in the Ground, and commonly uſed for Trees, but ſometimes for any other Thing, as a Pillar, or Statue, or &c. annexed to this Word, they have made it, ſignify a Grove; who could ever have imagined that a Grove ſhould be ranked with *Baal*, and the Powers of Heaven; or that there ſhould be a graven Image made of a Grove, or that a Grove ſhould be brought out of the Houſe of the Lord, aud carried to the Brook, and burnt, and ſtampt to Powder; or ſet under every ſpread Tree; or that the Images of a Grove ſhould be ranked with Images of the Light. I take this to be a compound Word as aforeſaid, of אש Fire, and *M.* שור a Prince, Ruler or Lord, an Inſpector, an Obſervator, שרה a Lady. *Coc.* a Prince having Power to ſubject and enforce. *C. Sam.* Glory, Dignity, Power in Chief. And *M.* אשר (beſides this Object) to look upon, regard, to go on, lead, direct." No doubt, as I have obſerved in my Eſſay, there were Sects at firſt among theſe ſen
ſible

sible or natural Atheists, as there is among the insensible or unnatural ones now; that some of them ascribed most to the Fire, others to the Light, and others to *Baal*, and so some more to one than another of the particular Powers or Hosts of the Heavens; and though they generally separated from *Babel*, into Bodies of each Sect; yet these Sects would intermix, or some of each would arise or be in each Country; and there seems to be nothing more in this, than that some of the perverted *Jews*, as the *Chaldeans* mostly did, made Fire the Prince or Captain, as others of the *Jews* more truly and generally made the Light. Indeed שור had also for its Representatives, or Things which they made Representatives to it, and so gave the same Name to them; (whence many different Names to the same Creature, or Thing.)

" *M.* An Ox, a Species of Cedar which sends out Rays like the Sun, (the Prince of Trees,) a Wall. *C.* שיר *Chald.* Bracelets, *Syr.* Ear-rings. שור a Wheel, a Chariot. *C. Syr.* סיר a Salamander, a fiery coloured Serpent, shining brightly, (or sending out Rays.) *B. C.* סור to recede —— Lustrate (which still keeps the Idea, for from a shining Body to recede, is to send out Rays to irradiate, and in seeing we send

MOSES's *Principia.* 507

send out Rays, or cause something to recede.) סוריא *Syria.* B. C. זיהור Light, Splendor, זיהרא the Moon, the ז *Zain* is put instead of ס *Samech;*" as each of the Nations had their Name from some great Attribute, so *Gen.* xvi. 7. and xx. 1. שור. And where a Person has been first named by an Attribute, it does not follow that the Country took its Name from the Person, but both from the Attribute. And for the Service, " *M.* a Song. *Chald. & Syr.* to dance. *C. Chald.* a Dance, a Dancing. *Syr.* a Dancing, a Dancing or Skipping of Animals. A Ball, or Dance where many dance together, a Dancing by Turns, alternately."

If *Ashteroth* were not sufficiently intelligible by the *Hebrew* Language, there is a descriptive Word, the same in all the Languages annexed to it, *viz.* the Rays the Horns, " *M.* קרן Howsoever it is found it is a Horn — an Horn metaphorically signifies Strength; as it is the higher or eminent Part of an Animal, and is his Strength, also Power, a Kingdom. *Abac.* iii. 4. קרנים is by some rendered *Splendors. Verb. Kal.* קרן to irradiate, shine, coruscate, glitter, vibrate, to shine out in the Manner of Horns, to diffuse Rays. *Exod.* xxxiv. 30. And behold

hold the Skin of his Face (namely of *Moses*) קרן shone (*V.* was horned) *Chald. Syr. Arab.* the same. *C.* the same, and *Arab.* the Rays of the Sun —— a certain horned Serpent, —— a Kind of a long-legged Insect like unto a Scarabæus, but a little larger. — A Clove-July-Flower. *Lat.* Cariophylum. *R.* the same. "It appears they called the Streams of Light between the Sun and the Earth, &c. and moved from *Chamah*, &c. Rays or Horns; and as the Power of horned Beasts is in their Horns, they made the Horns issuing out of the Heads of Beasts, the Representatives of the Powers of those Streams, which from these Athths reach the Earth, and exert their Powers there.

Athan. Kirch. Ob. Pamp. p. 221. "They put Horns to him (namely *Jupiter* or *Pan* as *Bocatius* testifies) to signify the Rays of the Sun, Moon and other Stars: His red and fiery Face denotes the Ethereal Fire."

Vossius de Orig. & Prog. Idol. Lib. II. p. 207. "*Eusebius* in his first Book of his Evangelical Preparation from *Sanchoniathon* where *Astarte* (*Heb* עשתרות) is called the Daughter of Heaven: — And in the same Place—*Astarte* placed the
He

Head of a Bull upon her Head as the Enſign of her Power or Kingdom."

Selden de diis Syris, p. 155. "Aſſuming a Bull's Head reſembled by the frized Hair on the Forehead, the Curlings of Fire."

Voſſius Lib. III. p. 533. *Dionyſius Halic.* in his ſecond Book, (ſays) "that certain Miniſters ſounding Bull's Horns, called the People together to their ſacred Aſſemblies."

B. C. in שׁוֹפָר, See an Account of their Laws and Traditions about the Sorts of Horns, the Manners of ſounding, &c. They did not call the Aththts, as it has been ſuppoſed they did, Stars, but the Streams, the Stars; and the Aththts, the Heads of the Stars, as *Job* when ſpeaking in their Language explains it, xxii. 12. ראש כוכבים *the Head of the Stars*; thence the Ridicule of ſerving thoſe Powers, by ſounding with the Horns to invoke to the Worſhip of, or to praiſe God: Thence the Heads of Cherubims, or Oxen with Horns, upon the Hangings of the Tabernacle, the Walls of the Temple, &c. And thence the Attribute of Horns, ſo often claimed and tendered. In Oppoſition to this *Moſes*'s Face iſſued or reflected Streams of Light, expreſſed by this

Word

Word; and hence almoſt all material Repreſentations of Divinity or Power, iſſuing from God or Chriſt, or his Apoſtles, have been, and are repreſented by Rays of Light, ſtreaming from the Head of the Repreſentative.

Now after I have ſhewed, that the Heathens univerſally meant, by that which we have tranſlated *Sun*, the Matter of the Heavens or *Aer* in its Circulation, or *Jupiter*, and that the Scripture and they in ſome Places expreſſed what we have tranſlated *Sun*, the Light, and ſometimes ſeemingly alſo that which returns; becauſe the Light has the Dominion over the Spirit, I am to ſhew you, that though they put Rays and Horns upon the ſame Head, and though the Rays from the Sun and from the Circumference in ſtreight Lines perform many, nay moſt of the Actions in Nature, yet there is another Sort to which they more immediately aſcribe Strength, that is the Columns of the Spirit which continually purſue the Light upon each Orb, and ſo impell the Orbs in bended Lines, which the *Jews* call *Spheres*. And as theſe Horns are perfectly obedient to and obſervant of the Light here, and of ſmall Parts after each projected Body, they are properly called Horns of the Light;

Light; and the Claims of these in the Old Testament run very high; and so in *Revel.* v. 6. where the Lamb had the seven Horns, and the seven Eyes; and the Heathens bestow'd the utmost Pains and Expence to represent these. *Kircher Obel. Pamph.* p. 64. " *Pliny* hands down to us—calling them Obelisks sacred to the Deity of the Sun: The Signification of its Rays is in the Figure, and so much is signified in the *Ægyptian* Name. P. 44, Obelisks, in the *Ægyptian* Tongue, are call'd the Fingers of the Sun. Hence some of them, as you may see at *Hermes*, which is the Power of moving Things in, or by these Horns, were so called."

There is yet another Figure, which they made a Representative of this Power, which is express'd by this, and several other Words, and was the highest Attribute, *viz.* a Crown, R. קרן—" also, *Latin Corono*, to crown, a Crown: for a Crown has its Plates like Horns." They represented the Athth of Light as it appears round about, or on every Side of the Sun; and that upon the Hemisphere of each other Orb, as the Cap of a Crown; and the Streams of Light from each, to each other Globe, by tapering Plates of Gold; and the Globe at the End of each by a bright

Stone. Thence all the Reprefentations of Crowns in the Tabernacle and Temple; the Claims and Tenders of that Attribute, and that Figure upon a Head, as the Emblem of Sovereign Power.

We find a Place call'd, *Numb.* xxxii. 2. העטרות, v. 34. עטרת *Jof.* xvi. 2. הארכי עטרות, v. 5. and xviii. 13. עטרות אדר xvi. 7. ינוחה עטרות which *Caftel.* takes for *Afhteroth. M.* עטר " its Signification is, a Crown, Circuit. *Chald.*—to crown. *Rabb.* The Fore-fkin of the Glans in a Man's Yard, refembling a Crown, the Prepuce being cut off: The Crown of the Glans. *Syr.* Smoke, Fume, Vapour, Breath. עטרן Pitch. *Arab.* —A T A R, to fmell, or yield a Scent. *Chald.* To go from, go away, recede, depart. *C.* עטר to furround. —a Crown.—a Tiara, or Turban. *Chald.* Under the fame Word, a Crown is the firft of all the Attributes of God. *Jefira* 8. The Glans or Nut of the Penis. *Schab.* 137. 2. *Jeram.* 74. 2.—to go from, recede, &c.— Pitch, Rofin, &c. *Syr.* Incenfe, Frankincenfe, a fweet Gum, Perfume, &c. *Arab.* in the fame Place. *B. C.* עטר to crown; עטרת, עטרה a Crown— the Glans or Head of the Penis, its Crown, and Inclofure :—the Flefh covering the Glans or Nut of the Penis. עטור

an

an Ambit, Ambient. Circuit. עטר to recede, go from." This gives a ſtrong Suſpicion, that they had made this Part of the Member a Repreſentative to this Attribute of Crown, Circle, &c. and that it occaſion'd the Law of Circumciſion; but proving thoſe Things, belongs not to this Part.

Tho' the three conditional Powers of the Heavens act jointly; yet the Matter of two of them do but reach us here; and though neither of them can ſtrictly be ſaid to do any Act without the other; yet ſome of their Actions are more immediately aſcrib'd to one, and ſome to the other; one of them is more adapted to perform this, and the other that, by the Difference of the Sizes of their Parts, the different Direction of their Motions, &c. And ſo under each of theſe Heads, the ſeveral Attributes are, in ſome Meaſure, ſorted; and as they had a Temple to the Power, which brought forth the Matter, or Atoms to augment, or from Seeds form Plants, or Creatures, Things whoſe Parts are liable to adhere, ſubſiſt for a Time, and afterwards be diſſolv'd; and as this Attribute is, in general, aſcrib'd to this Power of *Shemoſh*, tho' it belongs not to this Part, I cannot forbear mentioning it;

becauſe

because the Oppofition to that Abufe procur'd that noble Hiftory of the Creation and Formation, to fet us right in that Matter, which no Senfe could have reached. 'Tis mention'd, 1 *Chron.* iv. 31. בית־בראי the Temple of my Creator, or of the Creator *Jod*. This is writ and ufed ברא to create from nothing, which no Power but God can do; and בריא to augment or make Fat, by producing the Atoms out of, that is, from among thofe of Earth and Water, and applying them to Things or Creatures in Miniature, in Seeds, whilft growing, or when grown; and this the Heavens did, and do; thence God not only claims the Reprefentatives of thefe Powers to be facrificed to him, but the firft Fruits of every Thing, even of Men, to be redeem'd by other Creatures, and particularly of the Parts of Fat. To fuperfede all Abufes of Excefs afcribing more, or of making any Acknowledgment to the Heavens, God tells you, he created the Heavens and the Earth in Atoms; that they were fo far from acting upon other Things, that they were themfelves inactive: He tells you, Step by Step, how he begun and fupported Motion by his own Power, and by that Motion, enabled them to feparate the Earth

from

from the Waters, form the other Globes, &c. till he had framed and difposed the Parts, fo that they were fit to go by themfelves, and fupport Motion in other Things. That he formed the Vegetables of proper Matter, and in proper Manner, before they were put into the Earth, fo as each might renew and multiply their Species, and made the Fifhes and Fowls of the Matter out of the Waters, and the Beafts, and laftly, Man, of Matter out of the Earth, with proper Provifions, Powers of Multiplying, &c. without any Affiftance or Help from the Heavens: and after all, he made a Ceffion of the Government of his Works to them, his Legates.

There was one or more Places or Cities, where the *Canaanites* worfhip'd their God, the Heavens, under the Attribute of גלגל Revolution of Revolutions. *C. Chald.* בית גלגל " was a noted Place in the Land of *Ifrael*, whofe Afcent was very lofty and fteep, its Defcent fteep and winding, *Erab.* fol. 22. 2." The Scriptures, 1 *Sam.* x. 8. *Ibid.* xiii. 12, 15. feem to make one ftand low; there was an Altar, but whether a Temple, appears not; there were graven Images, mention'd *Jud.* iii. 19, 26. Its Reprefentatives are call'd גלולי, *Deut.* xxix. 17. render'd by the *Interlineary,* " Torna-
" tilia

"tilia Gods, turned, or made with the Turner's Wheel;" by the *English*, Idols; Margin, Dungy-Gods: There were Figures in the Temple in Opposition to this Power, mention'd 1 *Kings* vi. 34. *Ibid.* vii. 41, 42. and 2 *Chron.* iv. 12, 13. render'd *Volubiles*, Wreaths, and Orbs; in our *English* Bible, Pommels, &c. Whatever their Figures were, which is not the Business here, they are said to be, *Ezek.* xx. 7, 8:—Idols of *Ægypt*, v. 24. Idols of their Fathers, 2 *Kings* xvii. 12. in the *Chald.* Paraphrase בעליא: "*Syr*. Deities, *Ezek.* xxii. 4. *Arab.* the Devices which thou hast framed." A bad Translation, but a good Comment, for though no solid Figure could represent the Circulation of this Fluid, and its Powers; yet an Image is in the Imagination first, and afterwards framed of Matter, with an Intention to represent what the Person had imagin'd of the Power, or the God. The Word גל is often join'd with it, as *Ezek.* vi. 13. so either all Idols are comprehended under this Name, or 'tis call'd so, because it represents the universal Power which includes the *Fire*, and *Baal*, and *Shemosh* or *Ashteroth*: And as this is the Revolution which produces all others, the Word is used for all lesser of that Sort, and all other Sorts of Revolutions.

tions. The Signification is too long to be copied, when 'tis applied to a Solid, 'tis turning it round, one Part up, and the other down alternately, and so moving it forward. 1 *Sam.* xiv. 33. *Roll to me a great Stone:* when in the *Air,* in a Circle, as *Isa.* xvii. 13. *Like a rolling Thing before the Wind.* When of the Fluid of fresh Waters, 'tis going down, and returning up, as the Revolution of Water by Springs, as *Judg.* i. 15. *Give me also Springs of Water.* When of salt Water, the Flux, and Ebb or Reflux on the Surface of the Sea, or Flux into, or among the fresh Water in the Mouths of Rivers, and so Reflux, as *Job* xxxviii. 11. *Here shall thy Waves* (Tides) *when lifted up, be staid.* Jer. v. 22. *Though its Waves* (Tides) *toss themselves, yet can they not pass over it.* When of the Blood in Animals, where it cannot be understood otherwise than of this Sort of Motion, for mentioning whereof Dr. *Harvey* was so maul'd, *Eccles.* xii. 6. ונרץ הגלגל אל הבור, *and the Wheel* (Revolution) *be broken at the Cistern.* One would wonder how any could imagine there was a Wheel near the Heart of Man, but this was only in Conformity to cover something else. When of the Grains and Atoms of Air, of which all is full, one Sort accedes, and the other recedes in the same Lines. *Pfal.* lxxvii. 18, 19. *The* שחקים *Æthers gave* forth *a Voice; yea, thine Arrows went abroad: The Voice of thy Thunder* בגלגל *in the Revolution,* (the Matter of the Heavens circulating) *Lightnings enlighten'd the Globe.* Ifa. v. 28. *Their Wheels* (Revolutions) *like* (thofe of) *a Whirlwind.*

B. C. גלגל — " A Sphere — a Circle ---- Hence among Aftronomers, the feven Orbs of the Planets are called גלגלים *Galgalim.*"

" *Ibid.* ספירי *Saphirine, of Saphire: Lucid, pellucid. plural* שחקים סיפריים *the Sapphirine* Heavens הגלגל ספירי והכבים אונם ספירים *the Sphere is pellucid, but the Stars are not pellucid.* Mor. Par. 2. Cap. 19. &c."

Thefe Spheres in, and by which the Earth and Planets are moved, expreffed here by the Word *Gilgal*, and faid to be pellucid, and in the fame Condition as the Conflicters, which fo much Work has been about ever fince the firft Ages, are not *Vortices* of the whole Matter of the Heavens in each Circle at once ; but that Action of the Heavens at each Globe, occafioned by the Interruption of the Light, and driving in of the Spirit, which constantly

stantly attends and pushes each of those Globes, and so in the Progression of each Globe about the Sun, makes a *Vortex* in each Part of each Sphere, but only where the Globe is at the Time: Besides the Earth has its rotular Motion, represented by Wheels, which were Emblems of the Power which turns the Earth; and the Service to this Power, as has been shewed, was running, and so turning of Wheels, as the Earth is in its progressive Course: Thence Wheel-Work in the Temple, as Chariots were an Emblem of carrying it in the progressive Motion, and so brought into the Temple.

Clem. Alex. Strom. Lib. V. p. 114.———
" They signified also by Symbols, as the Wheel that is turned in the Temples of their Gods, which is derived from the *Egyptians*----- for *Orpheus* the *Thracian* saith----

Fate stands not still, a Mind turns all about,
To the same Place from whence they first set out."

When this Prophet had Occasion to use the Word for Wheels, where it cannot be mistaken, he uses another. *Isa.* xxviii. 27. וְאוֹפַן עֲגָלָה " *and the Cart-Wheel,* v. 28. עֲגָלָתוֹ

וחמם גלגל עגלתו *nor break it with the Wheel* (Revolution) *of his Cart, nor bruise it with its Teeth* (English Bible, *his Horsemen.*) Whereby 'tis plain עגלה was an Instrument which threshed Grain by revolving. The Prophet *Ezekiel*, in his two Visions which were directly levelled against the Service of this Power, and for that Reason had more Concern with this Word than all the other Prophets, in his first Vision, *Cap.* i. uses אופן frequently for Wheels, or what they represented; and expresses this Revolution by a Circumlocution, or Description, or proper Words for every Part and Manner of their Motion. In his second Vision, *Cap.* x. after he had been shewed by a Vision, what Service had been paid to these Powers at *Jerusalem*, he not only uses the Word אופן frequently, but also uses the Word גלגל several times, once in the second, once both in the same, the 6th *Ver.* and once both in the 13th. And they render אופן Wheel, and גלגל Wheel also. 'Tis very hard Usage to charge an inspired Writer with committing such a Blunder, in describing Things which had been shewed him in such a solemn, nay, terrible Manner; but as if that had not been sufficient to make him

understand

understand, or remember, by a supernatural Voice that Part of the Appearance was called in his own hearing *Gilgal*, which we render--- *and as for* אופן *the Wheel, it was cried unto them in my hearing* גלגל *O Wheel*--- And left he should not understand the Substance, as well as the Sort of Motion of the Matter, the same Voice had ordered the Man in white Linen to enter between the Revolution, and take out Coals of Fire, and he saw him take it: Let us enquire how these Blunders in the Translation came. *B. C.* מרכבה " A Chariot, a four-wheeled Machine---- Hence the *Hebrews* call the Beginning of *Ezechiel* מעשה המרכבה the Work of the Chariot. This Work is full of Mysteries, and therefore is not to be explained by every one, of which there is a Tradition in the *Talmud, Chaggia* Fol. 13. see also the Preface of R. *David* upon *Ezechiel*." Why was not this to be explained? There could be no Law of God against it; if it was difficult before it was compleated, it may not be so now. It indeed contained two Mysteries, the one shewed what it was that the Heathens, and their Fathers, and perhaps some of their Descendants served for God; the other, that Christ the Son of Man was to reign over the Subjects of these Powers, and

so

so be carried by them and their Representative Beasts in Triumph. If they had been so honest as to have told us, either that they did not understand them, or if they did, that neither the LXX. whether they were *Jews* or *Greeks*, nor the Authors of their *Targums*, nor those of their other Writings, when in the Country of, or subject to the *Greeks* or *Romans*, or those who worshiped those Powers, durst, for fear of their Laws, translate this or other Parts of the Bible, which shewed that the Powers which those who they were subject to serv'd as Gods, were only the Effects of created Matter and Mechanical; or that they, the *Jews*, had made Laws among themselves to hide those Parts, or not commit them to Writing, lest Christians should come to the Knowledge of them; or that, as before hinted, they endeavoured to cast a Veil over the Failings of their Fore-fathers, that had been dealing above board with us; but though they have not told us why, they have told us it is not explained; Is not that a sufficient Reason to induce us to use our Endeavours to do it? 'Tis only my Business in this Place, and in this Part to shew, that in the first Vision such Expressions at רצוא ושוב *ran, and returned*, and in the second גלגל

Revo-

Revolutions, and in *Daniel*'s Vision, vii. 9. whatever כרסיה signifies, which they render *his Throne was like the fiery Flame*; וגלגלוהי *and his Wheels* (Revolutions) *as burning Fire*; *a fiery Stream issued and came forth from him*, have the same Signification, are expressive of the Revolution of the Matter of the Heavens, and these Visions were to that End: There may be some who may take *from before him*, as they have done, literally; I shall only, as I have done before, hint that such Terms are borrowed, that from a Servant which attends his Master, receives his Orders from him, and goes out from his Presence, when he goes to execute his Commands, and returns thither successively for new Orders, so 1 *Kings* xxii. 19. *The Host of the Airs standing* (supported) *by him*, Ibid. 2 *Par.* xviii. 18. And it was these Beasts and Elders who praised and threw down their Crowns, the Ensigns of their Sovereignty when Christ prevailed.

There is another Word used several Times in the Description of the Circulation of this Matter in these Visions, which is expressive of the Revolution on every Side, as *Ezek.* i. 4. *I looked, and behold a Whirlwind came out of the North; a great Cloud* ואש מתלקחת ונגה לו סביב, *and a Fire*

Fire infolding itself, (exchanging) *and a Brightness was about it*. And in other Places, Pſa. l. 3. *a Fire ſhall devour before him: And it ſhall be very tempeſtuous round about him*. Ibid. lxxxix. 6. *The Airs ſhall confeſs thy wonderful Work*, Jehovah —— *and terrible in his Circuits* —— Jehovah *the Aleim of Hoſts, who is like thee, ſtrong*, Jah? *And thy Faithfulneſs* (conſtant, watchful Care) *is in thy Circuits* (or Agents that continually circulate) and in that glorious Deſcription, Job xxxvii. 12. already cited.

The *Jews* were required by the Law to pay ſeveral Acknowledgments to God in the ſame Manner that the Heathens had paid them to theſe Powers, and perhaps ſome others might be directed afterwards by Prophets upon ſpecial Occaſions; ſo that every *Hebrew* Word of Acknowledgment to God, ſuch as they have rendered Solemnizing, Feaſting, Rejoycing, Confeſſing, Praiſing, Singing, Playing, Sounding, Dancing, &c. not only deſcribe that, or the Actions of the Mind or Body, or upon the Inſtrument; but the Actions of the Heavens, for which God was thereby praiſed; ſo that Singing, or &c. as we ſay, ſuch a Tune, or upon

ſuch

MOSES's *Principia*. 525

such an Instrument, by the Sound, Motion, or *&c.* expressed the Attribute which the Heathens had ascribed to Matter, and which the *Jews* thereby ascribed to God. Such as 1 *Par.* xvi. 31. and *Psa.* xcvi. 11. ישמחו: *The Airs shall rejoice*; Ibid. c. 2. *Serve* Jehovah *with Rejoycing*. So *Isa.* xlix. 13. *Let the Airs* רנו *shout, and the Earth* גילי *exult*. Ibid. xliv. 23. *Let the Airs shout for* Jehovah *hath done it*. Psa. lxv. 9. *Thou makest the Agents that carry us out of Morning and Evening to shout.* (*a*) Ibid. xlii. 5. *With the Voice of shouting and* תודה *Confession*. Neh. xii. 27. *And with* תודות *Confessions*. This, though only thus expressed, was a high Attribute, and a Species of Bulls and Turtles were thus named, and both Representatives of it, and so ordered to be sacrificed; so *Psa.* lxix. 35. *Let the Airs* יהללוהו

(*a*) That is; the Airs which circulate the Earth and so make Morning and Evening, are by a regular and constant Mechanism supported in that vibrative Motion, or Vibration, visible through Telescopes, which is produced by the Irradiation of the Light outward from the Center, and the Irradiation of the Spirit inward towards the Center; and which produces that constant Gyration of the Earth and other Planets round their own Axes, and round the Sun.

יהללוהו *praise him.* (*b*) Ibid. cxlviii. apply‑ed to many Things. But *Job* xxxi. 26. *If I look on the Light when* יהל *it shined;* so *Jer.* xxxi. 4. *Thou shalt yet be adorned with thy Tabrets, and go forth in* מחול *the Dance* משחקים *of the Conflicters,* (the Parts of the Heavens moving oppositely). (i. e. *in such a Dance as was used to repre‑sent the Circulation of these Agents*); and *Par.* v. 13. with חצצרים Trumpets: C. *Chald.* חצוצרתא "a ſtrait Tube or Trumpet, that is, the Tube which was lawful, and permitted to be uſed at the Feaſt of the New-Year; as שופרא the crooked one. (*c*) — *v. Schab.* xxxvi. 1": And Numbers more, which I have no further Need of or Concern with here.

I ſhall but add, and endeavour to ex‑plain one Relation, that is, the Deſcrip‑tion which the wiſeſt of Men and the greateſt Naturaliſt completed by the Spi‑rit

---

(*b*) The one by its Irradiation and Circulation of the Earth, the other, the Earth by being circulated by that Irradiation.

(*c*) Perhaps the ſtrait Tubes repreſented the Rays or Columns of the Spirit, the crooked one thoſe of the Light as it comes from the Athth of the Sun; the ſame as in a Sun-Image, where the Spirit is the ſtrait Horns, the Light or Fire in bending or crooked ones.

rit of Prophecy, has left us of the Motion of the *Shemosh* of the Spirit, and thereby of the Earth: In *Eccl.* i. I must settle a few Points to remove some Notions, which Men are possessed with from the Translations. When the sacred Writers speak of the *Shemosh*, the Light, they use the Word זרח in the first Sense, for the going out of it from the opposite Hemisphere, into the Hemisphere, and so Country where the Writer lived, or which he spoke of, once *Gen.* xix. 23. *Moses* uses יצא, and they use בוא for the going in of it into the opposite Hemisphere. This way of expressing Motion stands a little opposite to our Manner of speaking, but that known, it makes no Difference. If these or any of the other Words of Motion be applied to an Agent which moves itself, it may be said to come or go, if to one that leads or drives other Things, it may be said to bring or carry them, but if to a Patient which is moved by another, to be brought or carried. The Word צאת—יצא *Jud.* v. 31. expresses the goings out of the *Shemosh* on every Side of the Sun. The Word זרח expresses the Manner. *M.* זרח " to diffuse itself, to scatter, or disperse Light. *A.* to rise, to shine out, and it is properly spoke of the rifing of the Sun and the Day, which at its Rife or Break fcatters and pours forth bright and fplendid Rays, and therefore hath fome Relation to זרח, to fcatter. C. זרח Arab. to move from place to place." 'Tis a complex Word, expreffes an Action where feveral Things, a Solid or Point fixed, and a Solid and Fluids continually, or fuceffively in Motion, each in their refpective Manners are concerned: The whole Root of the Word expreffes the Action of being preffed out, being forced to retire from a Point outward, or backward, and forcing what it can drive in thofe Lines, being pufhed forward by thofe in Succeffion behind, againft, and moftly ftop'd by fomething folid before. This Motion is firft, as has been defcribed, with respect to the Center of the Sun, 'tis by the defcending Spirit preffed outward, and fo upward; with refpect to the Earth in this Line towards its Center, or againft its Surface: But in Repetitions, or Succeffion of Parts of the *Shemosh*, ftriking againft the Hemifphere of the Earth, 'tis as we call it fhining or reflecting, each Atom by others in Succeffion being firft pufhed againft and then pufhed out or driven out by fucceeding Atoms, or by the Spirit, and each drives other againft, and from

from each Part of the Hemisphere, with respect to the Earth's Center, upward; and tho' the Word has no other Relation to Rising, no more than בא has to setting; yet Part of it, the Part we are speaking of, is always above that Side of the Earth opposite to the Sun, with respect to the Earth's Center: And tho' the Course of the *Shemosh* change not by the turning of the Earth, the *Shemosh* is alternately above and below any one Country, as a Man terms the Side he is upon uppermost: And the same Word זורח is used in this Description, where the *Shemosh* upon the hindmost Edge of Light on the Surface of the Earth, שואף (*M.* שאף "The Drawing in, or Admission of the Spirit,") yields, recedes, gives way for the Spirit to move and push in that Line, and so disperse the *Shemosh* there, or press it successively upward from the Center of the Earth, and so push against the Earth. If it had not been revealed expresly, that the Earth turns round, and goes in a Circle about the Sun, when it is shewed that the *Shemosh* does not turn or go about the Earth, the Revolution from Night to Day shews that the Earth turns, and so of Years; yet that is not all, this at once shews the Manner, and the Instruments by which

those

those are performed; the Light is the Ruler, the Leader; the Spirit, the Driver, the Impeller, and the Earth the Patient.

Eccl. i. 4. דור *A Generation* הלך *comes:* and דור *a Generation* בא *goes, but* הארץ *the Earth* לעולם *for ever* עמדת *endures, and* השמש *the Solar Light* זרח *shines forth, and* השמש *the Solar Light* בא *goes off.* ואל *and at (or into)* מקומו *its Station* שואף זורח הוא שם, *the rising Light is sucking in the Spirit;* הולך *going* אל *to* דרום *the South, and* וסובב *turning round to the North;* סבב *turning round in a Circle;* הולך הרוח *the Spirit coming on,* ועל *in* סבבתיו *its Circuits* שב הרוח *the Spirit returns.*

Surely those who translated this Book, did not, at first starting, intend that we should believe, that the Author was inspired by the same Spirit as *Moses* was, when they make him pronounce all God's Works, every thing which *Moses* declares God had pronounced, perfect and good, *Vanity*: our Author never intended any such thing; he is shewing, that every thing subject to the *Shemosh*, or as he expresses it in the next *Chapter* to the *Shemim*, is in a State of Fluxion, fleeting; he is not, as they have construed him, talking of Winds blowing, or such comparatively trifling

trifling Actions, but of the Motion of every thing which moves in this System of the whole Heavens, Earth, and afterwards of the Waters, &c. so that Man, when he has finished his Work, is himself carried off, and cannot keep or carry off any Surplus or Remains of his Acquisitions; because all these Things are supported in their respective Rotations, to supply the Race of Men in Possession, with Necessaries. He shews us their proper Business, what they were made for; and how vain soever the Works of Man may be, these are still perfect, and the Support of Man is produced by their Fluxions, and he expresses this Part of it thus.

Generations are brought forth, and Generations are carried in, and the Earth for the Use of all Generations is supported in all its Conditions, Motions, and Courses, (in its Rotations, Declinations, and circular Progressions,) therefore the bringing forth and pushing of the Light in streight Lines from the Sun, (against one Hemisphere of it, the Earth) and the carrying in, and pushing of the Light, (by Degrees against the opposite Hemisphere of it the Earth,) and therefore to the Place of it the Light upon the Faces of the Earth, or the Place of the Spirit's

Operation, upon its hindmost Edge, &c. (succeſſively turning) the drawing in of the Spirit, (the Inſtrument of Impulſe, and ſo of Motion) diſperſing it the Light there, and puſhing it the Earth there, carrying it the Earth to the South, and returning it the Earth in Circles to the North, being turned round, carried in a Circle, carried forward by the Spirit; and upon their Circuits, (the Circuits of the Spirits deſcending, and Circuits of the Earth proceeding,) the Spirit reverts, and ſucceſſively repeats —— beſides all Conſequences included—hence they make the Earth ארץ the Subſt. of רוץ to run.

Gravio (miſnamed *Caſmiro*, p. 322. and 385.) *de Philoſ. Vet. Philoſoph.* p. 224.

"And *Laertius*, in his 8th Book, in the Life of *Philolaus*, ſaith, that he was the firſt who aſſerted the Motion of the Earth in a *Circle*. Yet he adds, that others affirmed, *Nicetas* of *Syracuſe*, was the firſt Aſſertor of it. But *Plutarch*, beſides what he has ſaid in his 3d Book of the Opinions of the Philoſophers, Ch. 13. ſays expreſsly, that *Philolaus* the *Pythagorean*, was of Opinion, that the Earth was carried round the Fire in an Orbit obliquely, in the Manner of the Sun and Moon."

LEST

LEST it should be thought, that there ever was any Appearance of a Foundation for the Doctrine of infinite Space, Projection, Properties in the Matter projected to continue Motion; in all Matter to gravitate to, or attract each other, either from right Reasoning, or Evidence of Facts, tho' I am almost tired, I shall offer a few Hints, and reserve the Liberty of enlarging to another Opportunity, trace the present Philosophy upwards, and shew from what poor Conjectures and silly Stories it took Root, which by often telling, came almost to be believ'd.

Of infinite Space.
Gassend. Vol. I. p. 135. " The *Pythagoreans* were nearly of the same Opinion with the *Stoics*, contenting themselves with saying, as *Aristotle* does, that there was an infinite Void beyond the Heaven (or World); which *Themistius* saith, is not only Romantic, but like a sick Man's Dream, since it can neither be shewn what it is, nor to what Use it serveth: And yet *Plutarch* declares the *Pythagoreans* placed a Vacuum beyond the World, to this End, that there might be some where for the World to breathe in."

The Matter of the Heavens, and their Operations rejected as fictitious, useless, and troublesome.—

New——

The Cause of the Motion of the Orbs.

"*Magnetic Philosophy,* by *Nich. Cabeo Neap.* 1648, *p.* 72. Concerning the Great Magnet, the Earth.

Of the Magnet, and Magnetic Bodies, and the Great Magnet, the Earth, contained in six Books, by *William Gilbert,* in the Year 1633, a former Edition.

Athan. Kircher of the Magnetic Art, 1641-3. Whether there be a real Magnetic Virtue inherent in the Earth, the Sun, and the rest of the Stars, both the Wanderers and fixed ones, and whether they really attract one another, as a Magnet does."

Cited by *Kircher,* p. 477. out of *Gilbert,* "They are not carried, moved, or placed by the Firmament, much less are this confused Multitude of Stars circulated by the Primum Mobile, nor are they pulled about, or disturbed by any adverse and rapid Motion"—with high Insults upon the Scriptures.

Kepler's Com. of the Motions of the Star *Mars,* 1609. Introduction (after he

has

has roundly expos'd the Ignorance, as he thought of the Writers of the Bible.)

Wherefore, by Induction from all the Planets, it is demonstrated by Anticipation in the 3d Part; That since there are no solid Orbs, as *Brahe* has demonstrated from the Trajection of Comets, the Body of the Sun is therefore the Fountain of a Virtue which carries round all the Planets. I have proved also, by Arguments, the Manner, that the Sun remains in his Place, and turns round, nevertheless, as in a Turn, emitting from himself into the wide Space of the World, an immaterial Species of his Body, analogous to the immateriate Species of his Light: which Species, by the Rotation of the Solar Body, shall itself also have a Turn round, like a very rapid Vortex, thro' the whole Mundane Amplitude; and shall carry along with it, in a Gyration, the Bodies of the Planets, faster or slower, in Proportion as the Efflux is denser or rarer.

Chap. 33. *p.* 169. The Sun therefore being in the Center of the System, the Fountain and Spring of the Motive Virtue, from what has been just demonstrated, will center in the Sun, since it is but just now found to be in the Center of the World.

Truly,

Truly, if this which I have but now demonstrated *à Posteriori*, (from Observations) by a long Deduction; I say, if I had undertaken to have demonstrated it *à Priori*, (from the Dignity and Excellency of the Sun) that it should be the Fountain of Life to the World, (which Life is visible in the Motion of the Stars) which is of Light, by which the whole Machine is beautified, as it is also of Heat, by which all Things are vegetated; I think I should have deserved a favourable Hearing.

Let TYCHO BRAHE look to it himself, or whoever there is that chuses to follow his general Hypothesis of the second Inequality, and see with what Shew of Truth he can reject this physical Exactness (*Concinnitas*) in any one Part, after he has allowed of it in most Parts; for He himself places the Sun in the Center of the planetary System.

For, from what has been said, it appears that the Alternative must follow: Either that the Virtue resident in the Sun, which moves all the Planets, must also move the Earth; or, that the Sun, and the Planets, chained to him by his Motive Power, must, by some Virtue that resides in the Earth, be carried round the Earth,

" For

" For *Tycho* has himself destroyed the Reality of *the Orbs*: and I have, on my Part, beyond Dispute demonstrated in the third Part, that there is an Equant (æquans,) in the Theory of the Sun or of the Earth: From whence it follows that the Motion of the Sun, if it moves, is increased or decreased, as it is nearer or further from the Earth, and so it would follow that the Sun is moved by the Earth. But if the Earth is moved, it will also be moved by the Sun, and that swifter or slower as it shall be nearer or farther from it: a constant Virtue remaining perpetually in the Body of the Sun. Therefore between these two Propositions there is no Medium."

" P. 170. I acquiesce in the *Copernican* System, and suffer the Earth to be one of the Planets, and altho' with regard to the Moon the same thing may be objected to *Copernicus*, that I objected to *Tycho* with regard to the Five Planets; namely, that it seemed absurd for the Moon to be moved by the Earth, and beside to be chained and coupled to her, so that it shall be secondarily carried itself round the Sun, by the Sun: I had rather nevertheless let the Moon which has relation to the Earth alone, by the Disposition of its Body, (as I have demonstrated in my Optics) be moved by the

the Virtue refident in the Earth but extended towards the Sun, as fhall be mentioned by and by, in the 37th Chapter; than afcribe to the Earth, even the Motion of the Sun, and of all the Planets coupled with him.——

—— And altho' this Light of the Sun, cannot be the very moving Virtue; yet let others fee whether the Light may not be as an Inftrument, or fome Vehicle, perhaps which the Motive Virtue may make ufe of.

Thefe following Confiderations feem indeed to contradict this Notion. Firft, Light is impeded by opake Bodies; wherefore if the Motive Virtue had the Light for its Vehicle, Ceffation of Motion in moving Bodies, would be the Confequence of Darknefs. Again, Light flows in right Lines orbicularly, the Motive Virtue flows too in right Lines, but circularly; that is, it tends towards one Quarter of the World only; from the Weft to Eaft, and not contrariwife, not to the Poles, &c. But, perhaps we may be able to anfwer thefe Objections in the Chapters next following.

P. 171. Laftly, fince there is as much of this Virtue in a large and more remote Circle, as in a narrower and near one; therefore, there is nothing loft of this Virtue

in

in the Journey from its Fountain, nothing is difperfed, or diffipated between the Fountain-head and the thing to be moved. The Efflux therefore, as that of Light, is Immateriate; not fuch as that of Smells, where the Subftance is diminifhed; not fuch as that of Heat from a burning Furnace, or fuch like Things with which Mediums are filled. It remains therefore, that as the Light which fhines on all earthy Things, is an immateritae Species of that Fire that is in the Body of the Sun: So that this Virtue which embraces and carry the Bodies of the Planets, muft be an immateriate Species of that Virtue which refides in the Sun himfelf of ineftimable Vigour, and therefore the firft and chief Caufe of all Motion in the World.

Cap. 34. p. 172. We muft next, taking this *Species* which flows out, (or Archetype) for our Guide, examine into the more inward Nature of the Fountain; for there may feem to be hid in the Body of the Sun fomething divine, and what may be compared to our Soul, from which iffues that *Species* which carrys round the Planets, in like Manner as from the Soul of him that throws Stones, a Species of Motion adheres in the Stones, by which they are carried even after the Perfon who
threw

threw them, hath withdrawn his Hand from them. *

This Species therefore being moved in a Round, that by this Movement it may communicate Motion to the Planets, the Body of the Sun, or its Fountain must of Necessity move together with it; not from one Part of Space into another; for I have declared that I left the Body of the Sun with *Copernicus* fixt in the Center of the World: But upon its Center or Axis, they being immoveable, its Parts passing from Place to Place, his whole Body nevertheless remaining in the same Space.

P. 174. Furthermore, since we see that neither the several Planets at each of their Distances from the Sun, nor all of them at their different Distances are carried about with equal Velocity, but, that *Saturn* makes a lingring Journey of thirty Years, *Jupiter* of 12, *Mars* of 23 Months, the Earth of 12, *Venus* of 8, *Mercury* of 3, and yet the whole Orb of the Virtue which issues from the Sun, (as well from the lowermost Sphere

* Sir *Isaac Newton* attributes this Continuance in Motion to the *vis inertiæ*, a Force of Inactivity, as Mr. *Motte* translates it, so Bodies continue in Motion, that is Action, by a Force that is inactive. 'Tis hard to determine which Account is most philosophical.

of *Mercury*, as from the uppermost of *Saturn*, from what hath been said before, is turned round with an equable Whirl, with the Solar Body and in the same Time; in which Place nothing absurd is laid down; since the issuing Virtue is immaterial, and might be in its own Nature of infinite Swiftness, if it were possible to *give it* Motion from else where, for then it would not be impeded by Weight which it is void of, nor by the Resistance of any corporeal Medium:) From this, it therefore appears, that the Planets are not capable of attaining to the celerity of the Motive Virtue. For *Saturn* is more sluggish than *Jupiter*, because he is more slowly returned, or revolved; whereas the Orb of Virtue at the Revolution of *Saturn* is as swiftly revolved as the Orb of Virtue at the Revolution of *Jupiter*; and so consequently down to *Mercury*, who without doubt after the Example of his Superiors, will himself be slower than the Virtue which carries him. The Nature therefore of the Planetary Globes must needs be from the Property of Adhesion, materiate (Material) and thence from the Principle of Things must incline to Rest, or Cessation of Motion. From which Contrariety of Things, since there must arise a Strife and Struggle; that Planet will therefore have

the

the greater Advantage which is situated in the weaker Virtue, and be moved slower by it, and that less which is nearer to the Sun.

P. 176. If any one ask me, what I take the Body of the Sun to be from which this Motive Species issues! I desire him to proceed farther in this Matter with Analogy for his Guide, and to consider the Instance of the Loadstone before mentioned more accurately, whose Virtue resides in the whole Body of the Magnet, increases with its Bulk, and is lessened and divided when that is so. The Motive Virtue in the Sun, seems to be the stronger as his Body in all Probability is the densest of any in the whole World.---- I have indeed hit upon a pat Instance in the Loadstone, and come very near to the Matter. Nay, it is almost the very Thing itself. For what do I talk of the Loadstone as an Instance or Example? when, as *William Gilbert* an *Englishman* has demonstrated, the Earth is a large Loadstone or Magnet; and according to him who is an Assertor of *Copernicus*'s Doctrine, rolls round every Day, as I conjecture the Sun to turn round; and for this very Reason becaue it has magnetic Fibres, intersecting at right Angles the Line of its Motion. Therefore these Fibres are placed about

about the Poles of the Earth in various Circles parrallel to its Motion: so that I have the best Right to determine the Moon to be carried on by this rolling along of the Earth, and the transferring of the same magnetic Virtue to it, only thirty Times flower.

Cap. 57. p. 280. I have hitherto mentioned these Things upon Condition that the Libration which is avouched by Observations, cannot be performed by any magnetical Virtue innate or implanted in the Bodies of the Planets, and in Case it should be absolutely necessary for us to have Recourse to a Mind. But if we please to compare this natural and that mental Motion: that indeed stands by itself, wanting nothing; But this Mental, in what Manner soever you indue it with an Animal Faculty of moving a Body, seems to bear Witness to and call for the Help of the Magnetic. For first a Mind of itself can do nothing in a Body. We must therefore adjoin to the Mind a Faculty of executing its Offices in librating the Body of a Planet. That Faculty will be either animal, or natural, and magnetical. Animal it cannot be, for an animal Faculty cannot transport its Body from Place to Place (as is required in this Libration) without the

Vol. II.   Q q   Power

Power of another Body affifting it. It will be therefore a magnetic Faculty, that is a natural mutual Confent between the Bodies of the Planets and the Sun. *(a)* Therefore, a Mind calls in Nature and the Magnet to its Aid.

Chap. 39. *p.* 191. Thou feeft, confiderate and ingenious Reader, that this Opinion of a perfect eccentric Circle of the Planets in their Courfes, brings many incredibles into Phyfical Speculations, not indeed becaufe it puts the Diameter of the Sun for a Sign to the planetary Mind : for perhaps the trueft Opinion may do that likewife : but becaufe it afcribes incredible Things both to the Mind and to the motive Soul.

Chap. 57. 276. But if no mere material and *(b)* magnetic Faculty can perform thefe Offices feparately affigned to the Planets, from a Defect in the Mediums, namely, to keep the Diameter of a Body in its Circumvolution, always at an equal Diftance or Parallel to itfelf ; which Defect hath already appeared in the Globe, for inftance

---

(a) In modern Terms the reciprocal Attraction of the Planets and Sun.

(b) "Concerning this mutual Principle of Libration, I am afraid to fay *Rational*, left it be underftood of the difcurfive Faculty of Reafon."

of the Earth : Let a (*c*) Mind therefore be called in, which as is said in *Cap*. 39. from the Comtemplation of the increasing Diameter of the Sun, may bring us to the Knowledge of the Distances it describes; and let it preside over the Faculty whether animal or natural to keep his Globe in such a parallel Situation, that it may be impelled in a proper and just Manner by the Solar Virtue and be librated in respect to the Sun ; (for a bare Mind and destitute of a Faculty in any Degree, can do nothing in this Respect upon a Body,) and let it at the same Time use Judgment, to adjust the Times of Libration, not exactly to the periodical Revolution, and so to the transferring the Apses. The Probability of which is explained Chap. 39. above."

This mighty Discovery is only a Mistake, and he only took *Sol* for the Orb of the Sun, and so made it turn round upon its Axis, and turn all the rest round instead of the Motion, which you see is all along attributed to *Sol*, the Heaven in Circulation.

—*And for his Spirit.*

Voſſius de Phiſ. & Theol. Gent. Lib. VI. p. 100. " *Thales*, as *Laertius* says, was the

---

(*c*) Instead of this Mind Sir *Iſaac Newton* substituted his *Deus*.

first reported to attribute Souls to inanimate Beings, taking the Hint or Conjecture from the Loadstone and Amber. p. 119, 120." Hence our Philosophers had their Account, which they could not have by the common Way of Appearances, of that subtile Spirit already mentioned, to which they attribute so many Tricks.

Let us see if any Mistakes could put these Imaginations into Peoples Heads. *B. C.* p. 15. אבן שואבת "A Stone that draws or attracts, that is a Loadstone or Magnet, attracting Iron without Contact.--- *Sanhed.* Fol. 137. 2. *B. C.* p. 2297. שאב to draw Water, Air, or Wind. *Heb.* to Attract, Extract. *Rab.* Whence אבן שואבת an attractive Stone. Chap. 3664. שאב To draw Water as שאף is to draw Air. *Chald.* 1. q. *Heb.* אבן שואבת see אבן, א being cut off, שיוב מישב to draw out, or exhaust by Drawing. *Pesac* 74. 2. שיאוב Panting, drawing of the Breath. *R. S. Isai.* 34. 16. *Ar.*--- The Heat of the Sun, Tract of the Sun, namely the Way. *Chap.* 3665. שאף to draw, thro' the Ears, (Nostrils) or Mouth, to draw up Air, namely Wind, to aspire, or blow up, to be Intent, to Supp-- *Eccles.* i. 5. &c."

'Tis plain the antient human Writers gave the same Attribute to something at-
tending

tending this Stone, as they gave to the Light of the Sun interrupted by the Earth, a Capacity to admit any Thing, the Spirit, or what the Spirit should drive in, and no Power, either to the Earth or the Stone as you will see, but Solidity and so Obstruction.

Since our Philosophers have taken or mistaken most of their Maxims from *Lucretius*; we ought to look into his Design: He, in Edit. 1662. at p. 58, and 137. (as the perverted *Jews*, and all the *Heathens*) allows a God, but supposes him in another System, and that he concerned not himself with this. The Knowledge of the Operation of the Heavens was then almost lost, and the chief of his Design through the whole, was to ridicule Men for worshipping those Powers, p. 282. and to shew that they had no Knowledge in them, because as *inter al.* at p. 293. they destroyed their own Temples and Images. When he pretended to give us a Cause or Definition of the Eternity of, or of the Beginning of Motion, and neither pretended to be coeval with that Motion, nor to have any Communication with any Being which was, if it had been as Evidence in a Court, he must have been pilloryed or sent to *Bedlam:* Suppose we should allow what

is

is not proved, that any of the *Heathens*, or he intended to bestow the Epithets of eternal, or infinite in the Sense People do now, let us see how it would stand; let us compare him with himself.

V. 166.— *For every Part of empty Space,*
Or midst, or not, must equally allow,
To pondrous Movements easy Passage then.
Creech.

Since a void Infinite extends around,
Seeds without Number, thro' the vast Profound,
Struck with eternal Motion fly.

Book vi. V. 973. *Creech*'s Translation—

First from the Magnet numerous Parts
   arise
And swiftly move, the Stone gives vast
   Supplies;
Which, springing still in constant Streams,
   displace
The neighb'ring Air, and make an empty
   Space.
So when the Steel comes there, some Parts
   begin
To leap on thro' the Void, and enter in.
V. 992.

MOSES' *Principia*. 549

V. 992. *Besides; the* Air, *before the Steel, is rare,*
And emptier *than it was, and* weaker *far;*
And therefore all the Air, *that lies behind,*
Grown strong, and gathering like a sub- Wind,
May force it on."

It no ways suited *Lucretius*'s Scheme to talk of an infinite *Vacuum*; for Space, or a *Vacuum*, in their Way of talking, must exist before any Body, or else it was not Eternal and Infinite: He would have drop'd Space, rather than the Eternity of Matter, or its Seeds: And if Bodies, nay, any one Atom be coeval with Space, or a *Vacuum*, or Eternal; then either *Lucretius* did not mean what they make him say, or else he did not understand what he said: For they may as well say, an infinite Body with a *Vacuum* in it, as an infinite Space with Substance, Body, or Matter in it; and a Description of infinite Space, or of an infinite *Vacuum* with Bodies, always or eternally moving in it, will eternally be infinite Nonsense, because the one destroys the other; but if we let him construe

550 MOSES's *Principia.*

ſtrue himſelf, he means nothing by Space by *rarior Aer*, thinner Air, nor nothing by Infinity but *vorſus*, the circular Courſe of the Heavens. We will try him next about his infinite Motion:

Book II. Ver. 83.

For ſince they thro' the boundleſs Vacuum rove,
By their own Weight, or others Stroke, they move.

This is fairly left, he knew nothing of the Matter, what begun Motion, and in allowing it a Beginning; he has loſt his eternal Motion; but we find the Word Gravity, let us ſee what he ſays of that.

Gaſſendus, p. 389. *Lucretius*, in Imitation of *Epicurus*, Book I. v. 421. *Creech*'s Tranſlation:

Wherefore thoſe heavier Things of equal Size,
Do more of Matter, leſs of Void compriſe.

I muſt do one of them the Juſtice of having laid down this ſo perfectly, that there has not been a Tittle improv'd upon it.

it. Did he design this as a Power in Body to move itself? Why

"Or perhaps by the Stroke of another,"

Which is a good Hint for Projection, and so they have taken them both: This is but playing; enquire what any such say about Spirit, and the Truth comes out.

Book III. Ver. 165.

"*Nothing's done without Touch; and all that touch*
Are Bodies; therefore Mind *and* Soul *are such.*"

Upon this Law of Impulse by Touch, and consequently that, which Way soever the Impulse is strongest, Motion of Bodies, of Fluids among Fluids, through the Pores of Bodies, &c. he proceeds.

But because he has told us in his Preamble to the Loadstone, p. 309 & *seq.* that several Sorts of Fluids by Name, penetrate and pervade the Pores of several Sorts of Bodies by Name, in Proportion to the Sizes of the Pores between the Atoms of the Bodies; and the Sizes of the Grains of the Fluids, or the Sizes of the *Semina*, his Name for Atoms; and that the Pores in the Bodies of Loadstone and Iron are so small, that none larger than those of Fire, Light, or Heat pervade them; and that these Fluids in pervading some Bodies, partly solid, partly fluid, detach some of the fluid Atoms, which form Odours, &c. for this they have fathered a thousand of their Mistakes upon him, such as Bodies emitting *Effluvia*, Fire, Light, &c. from their own Substances: As the Body of the Sun emitting Light, and emitting an immaterial Power to draw or attract Bodies at any Distances, &c. whereas there is not the least Suspicion of any such Thought in his Writings. The Light or Atoms of *Aer* which pervade the Stone or Iron, do neither push nor resist with that Force in that Line, as the loose Spirit, or, as he calls it, *Aer*, does in the opposite Line; and so the *Aer* carries and pushes the Iron to the Stone, or the Ring to the Iron, as he says expresly, and supports it there: Nay, even the Word *Pellicio*, (entice) which is the only Word which was ever twined that Way, signifies only as a Woman allures by offering an Opportunity and resisting weakly, which is the very Case here.

I think they could not by Mistake draw their Elasticity, &c. of *Aer* from him, because at *p.* 14. he writes positively against it, and it signifies not a Farthing who was the Inventor.

Every one who has treated of these Powers of Attraction, or Gravity, has been attempting to make Tables to settle its Proportions, as every one was at Liberty, and did make their own Distances between each; the Magnitudes of every one, except the Earth, the Densities of every one, and the Force or Velocity supposed to be given, and continued from Projection; as they could not prove those were the Powers, so if those had been the Powers, none of them could give the least Appearance of Evidence about its Proportions; and I'll give my Consent, that their Patent for the sole doing it shall be perpetual.

Though all that is shewed out of the sacred Text about the Cause of Motion, is not only confirmed by the universal Consent of the Heathens, but is capable of being demonstrated to Sense; yet it cannot be amiss to shew the Sense of the Christians, when some of the Notions which have lately prevailed were aimed at.

Vossius

Voffius de Orig. & Prog. Idol. p. 231. "But in this Part *Origen* agrees with *Philo*, as with many others, in his Book of *Principles,* Chap. vii. as also in his Commentary on *John.* And for this, St. *Jerom* reprehends him in his Epistles to *Pammachius* and *Avitus*. And in the Epistle of *Vigilius* the Pope to *Cæsarius* of *Arles,* among other *Anathematisms* against *Origen,* there is this. *If any one say the Heaven, and Sun, and Moon, and Stars, and Waters that are above the Heavens are animated and are certain Material Virtues, let him be* Anathema. Which was approved and confirmed also in the second Council of *Constantinople,* or the fifth of the universal Synods, &c."

Thus far I forbear, but if this do not take Effect, I am ready from divine Authority to shew the Author, the Time when, and Reasons why he taught every Article of this Philosophy, which will make every Believer ashamed of it.

F I N I S.